nickelodeon

降击神通

AVATAR

THE LAST AIRBENDER

THE SEARCH

Created by
BRYAN KONIETZKO
MICHAEL DANTE DiMARTINO

script
GENE LUEN YANG

art and cover
GURIHIRU

lettering
MICHAEL HEISLER

DARK HORSE BOOKS

publisher
MIKE RICHARDSON

editor
RACHEL ROBERTS

assistant editor
JENNY BLENK

designer
SARAH TERRY

digital art technician
SAMANTHA HUMMER

Special thanks to Linda Lee, James Salerno, and Joan Hilty
at Nickelodeon, to Dave Marshall at Dark Horse, and to Bryan
Konietzko, Michael Dante DiMartino, and Tim Hedrick.

This book collects *Avatar: The Last Airbender—The Search* parts one through three.

Published by
Dark Horse Books
A division of
Dark Horse Comics LLC
10956 SE Main Street
Milwaukie, OR 97222

DarkHorse.com
Nick.com

To find a comics shop in your area,
visit ComicShopLocator.com

First edition: October 2020
eBOOK ISBN 978-1-50672-178-1
ISBN 978-1-50672-172-9

5 7 9 10 8 6 4
Printed in China

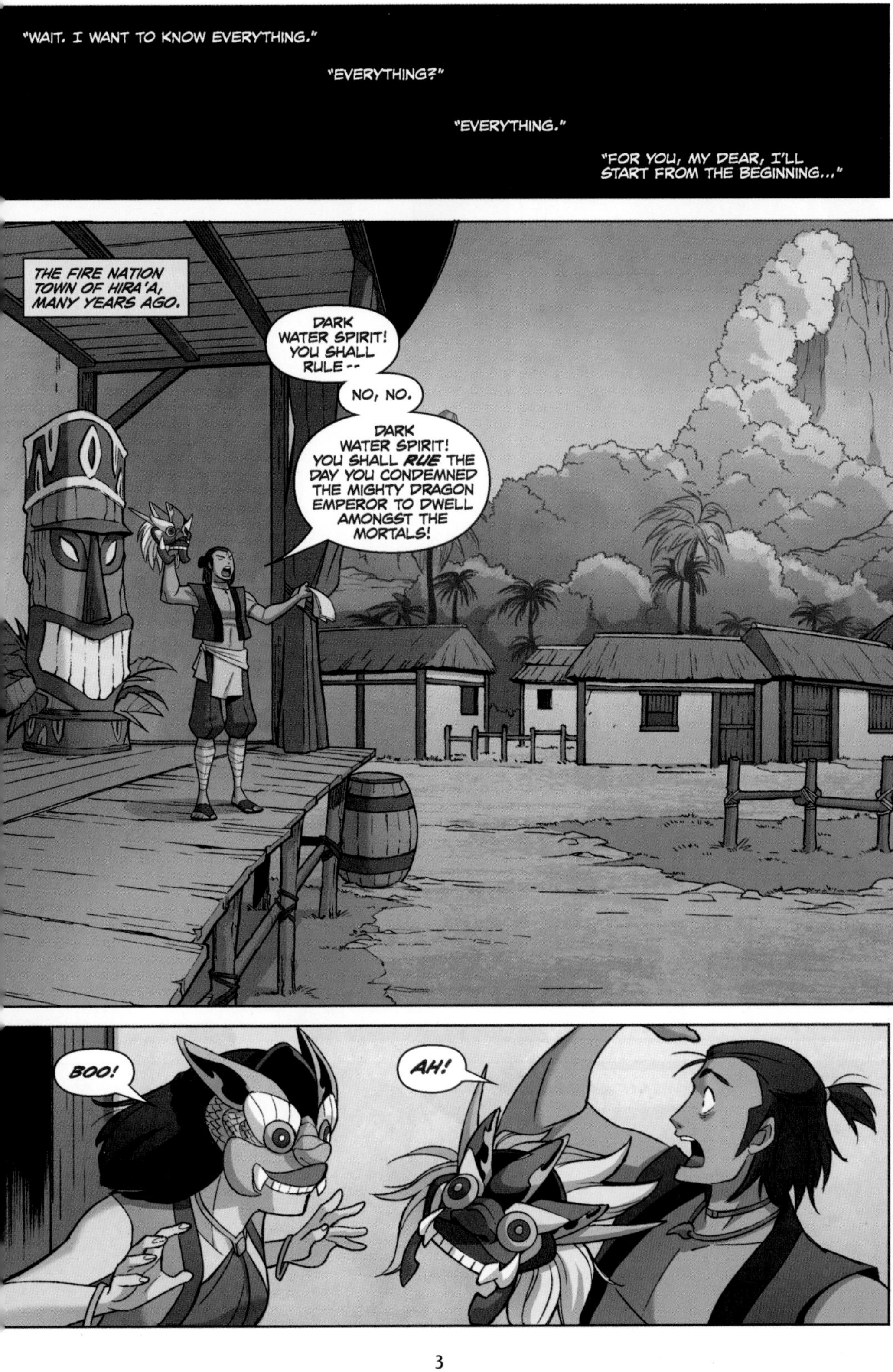
"WAIT. I WANT TO KNOW EVERYTHING."
"EVERYTHING?"
"EVERYTHING."
"FOR YOU, MY DEAR, I'LL START FROM THE BEGINNING..."
THE FIRE NATION TOWN OF HIRA'A, MANY YEARS AGO.
DARK WATER SPIRIT! YOU SHALL RULE --
NO, NO.
DARK WATER SPIRIT! YOU SHALL *RUE* THE DAY YOU CONDEMNED THE MIGHTY DRAGON EMPEROR TO DWELL AMONGST THE MORTALS!
BOO!
AH!

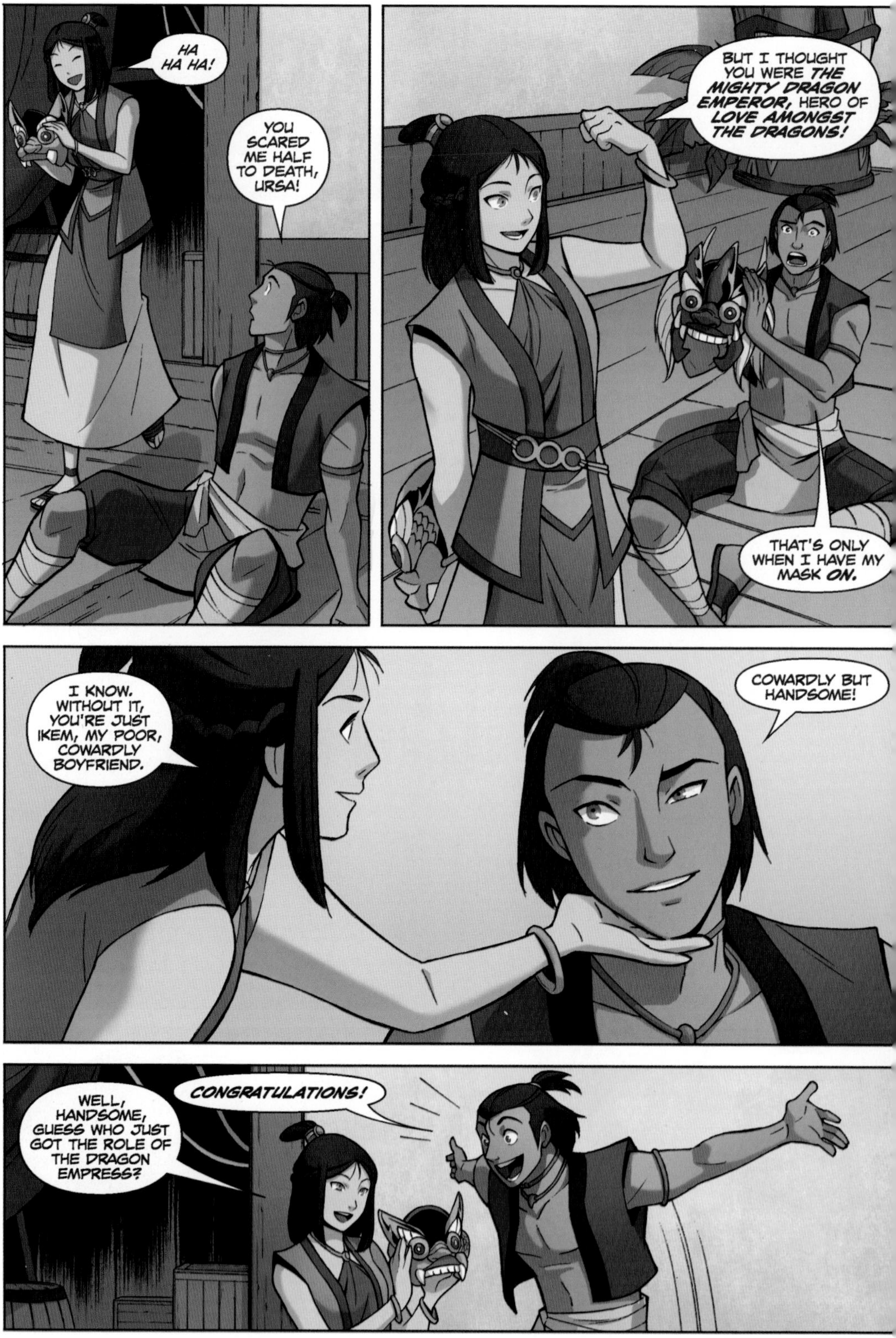
HA HA HA!
YOU SCARED ME HALF TO DEATH, URSA!
BUT I THOUGHT YOU WERE THE MIGHTY DRAGON EMPEROR, HERO OF LOVE AMONGST THE DRAGONS!
THAT'S ONLY WHEN I HAVE MY MASK ON.
I KNOW. WITHOUT IT, YOU'RE JUST IKEM, MY POOR, COWARDLY BOYFRIEND.
COWARDLY BUT HANDSOME!
WELL, HANDSOME, GUESS WHO JUST GOT THE ROLE OF THE DRAGON EMPRESS?
CONGRATULATIONS!

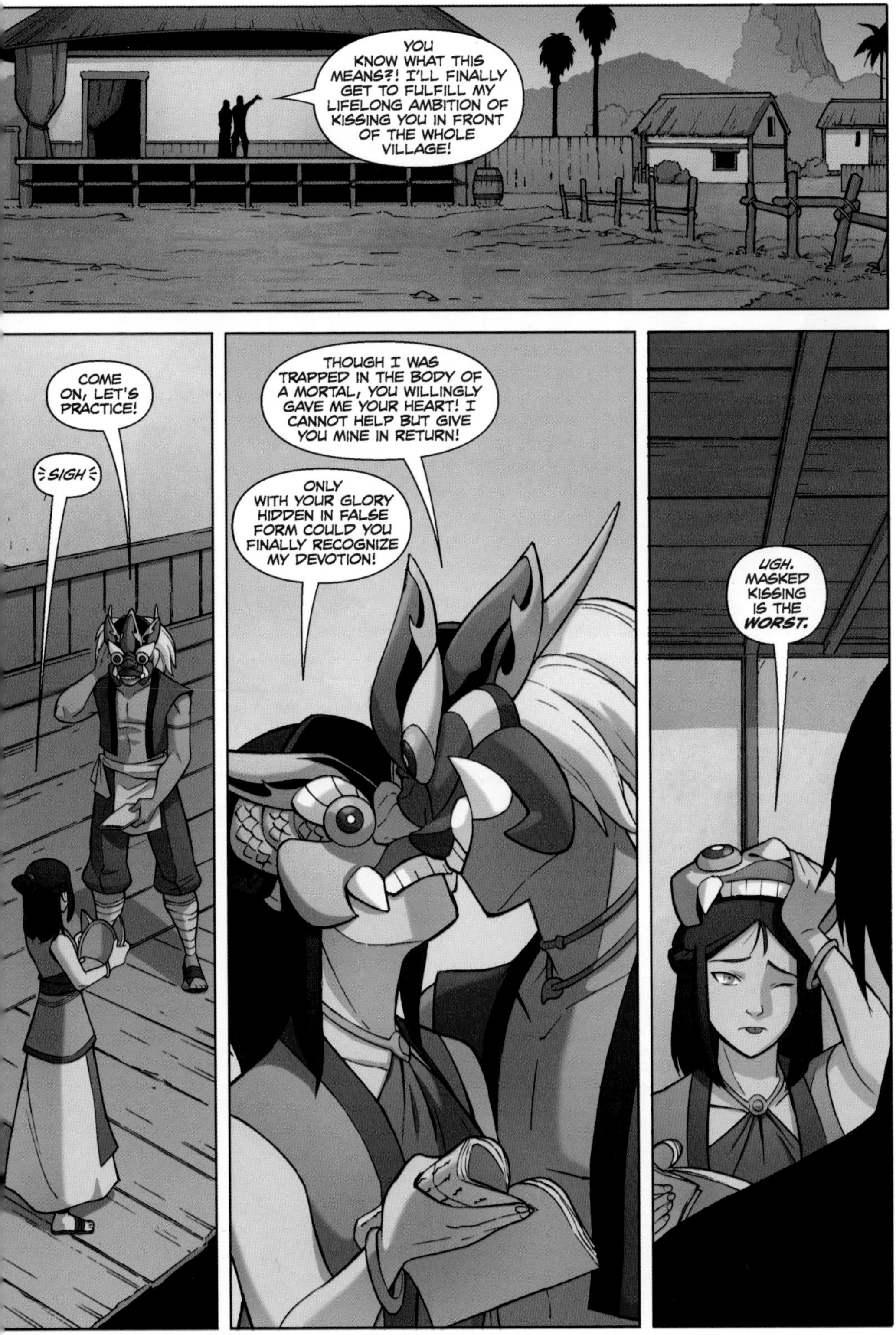
YOU KNOW WHAT THIS MEANS?! I'LL FINALLY GET TO FULFILL MY LIFELONG AMBITION OF KISSING YOU IN FRONT OF THE WHOLE VILLAGE!
COME ON, LET'S PRACTICE!
SIGH
THOUGH I WAS TRAPPED IN THE BODY OF A MORTAL, YOU WILLINGLY GAVE ME YOUR HEART! I CANNOT HELP BUT GIVE YOU MINE IN RETURN!
ONLY WITH YOUR GLORY HIDDEN IN FALSE FORM COULD YOU FINALLY RECOGNIZE MY DEVOTION!
UGH. MASKED KISSING IS THE WORST.

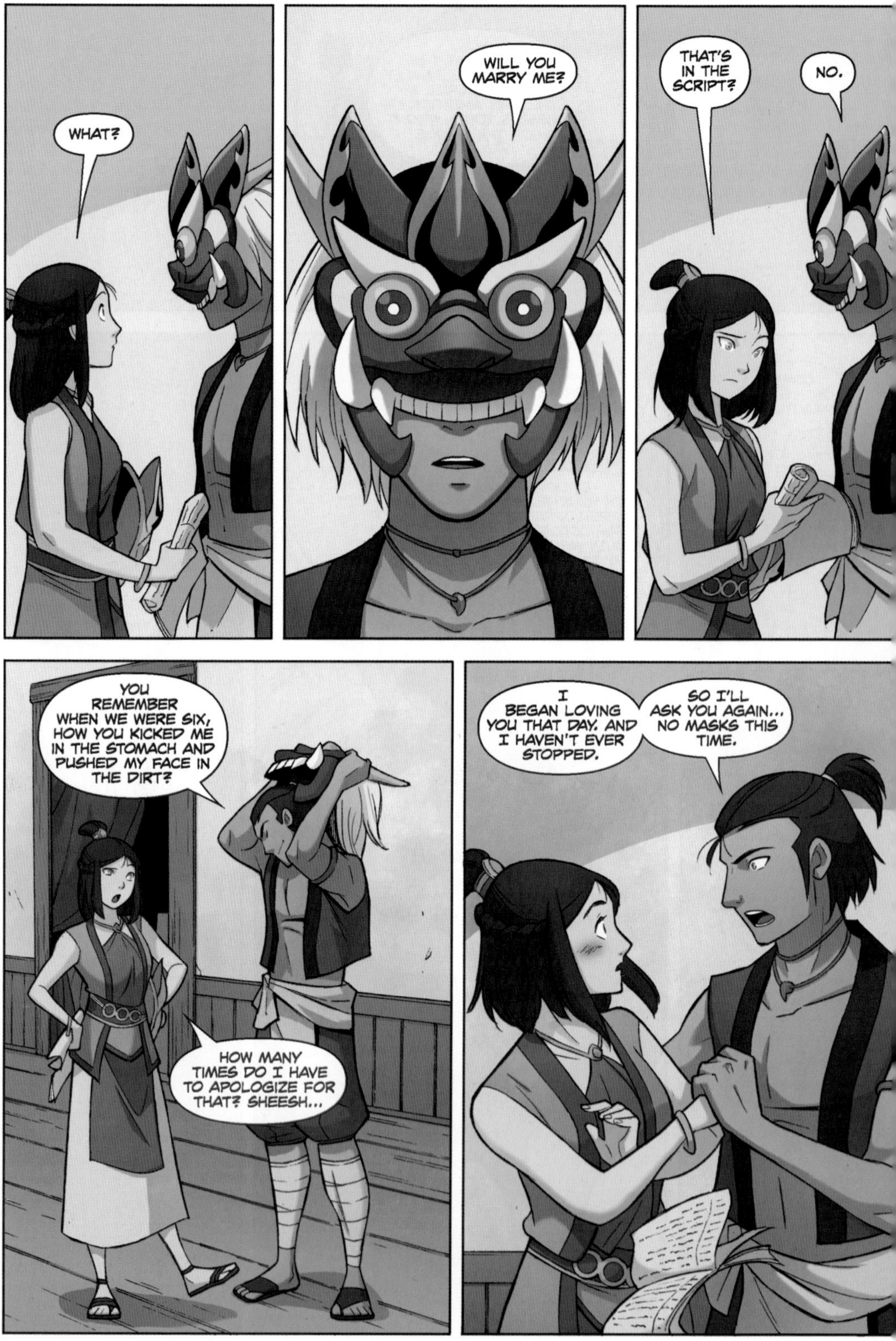
WHAT?
WILL YOU MARRY ME?
THAT'S IN THE SCRIPT?
NO.
YOU REMEMBER WHEN WE WERE SIX, HOW YOU KICKED ME IN THE STOMACH AND PUSHED MY FACE IN THE DIRT?
HOW MANY TIMES DO I HAVE TO APOLOGIZE FOR THAT? SHEESH...
I BEGAN LOVING YOU THAT DAY. AND I HAVEN'T EVER STOPPED.
SO I'LL ASK YOU AGAIN... NO MASKS THIS TIME.

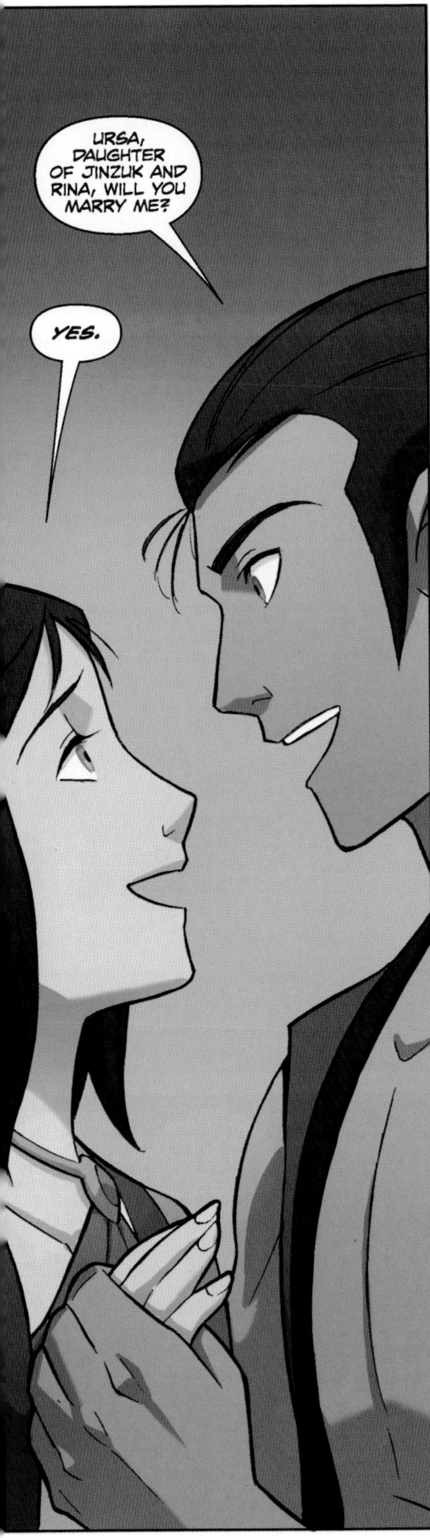
URSA, DAUGHTER OF JINZUK AND RINA, WILL YOU MARRY ME?
YES.

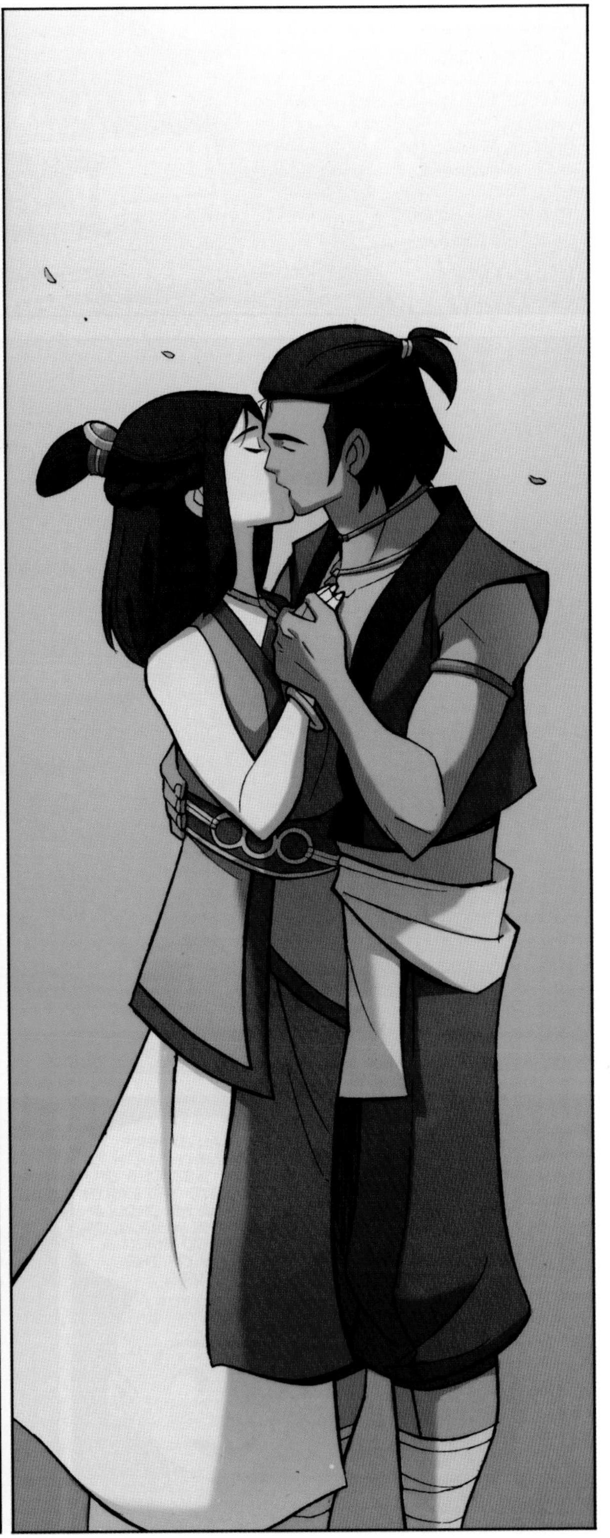

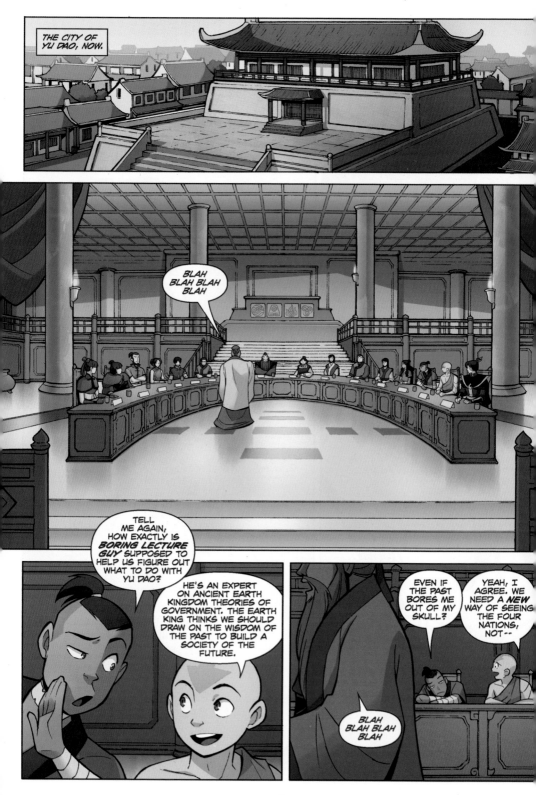

THE CITY OF YU DAO, NOW.

BLAH BLAH BLAH BLAH

TELL ME AGAIN, HOW EXACTLY IS *BORING LECTURE GUY* SUPPOSED TO HELP US FIGURE OUT WHAT TO DO WITH YU DAO?

HE'S AN EXPERT ON ANCIENT EARTH KINGDOM THEORIES OF GOVERNMENT. THE EARTH KING THINKS WE SHOULD DRAW ON THE WISDOM OF THE PAST TO BUILD A SOCIETY OF THE FUTURE.

EVEN IF THE PAST BORES ME OUT OF MY SKULL?

YEAH, I AGREE. WE NEED A *NEW* WAY OF SEEING THE FOUR NATIONS, NOT--

BLAH BLAH BLAH BLAH

8

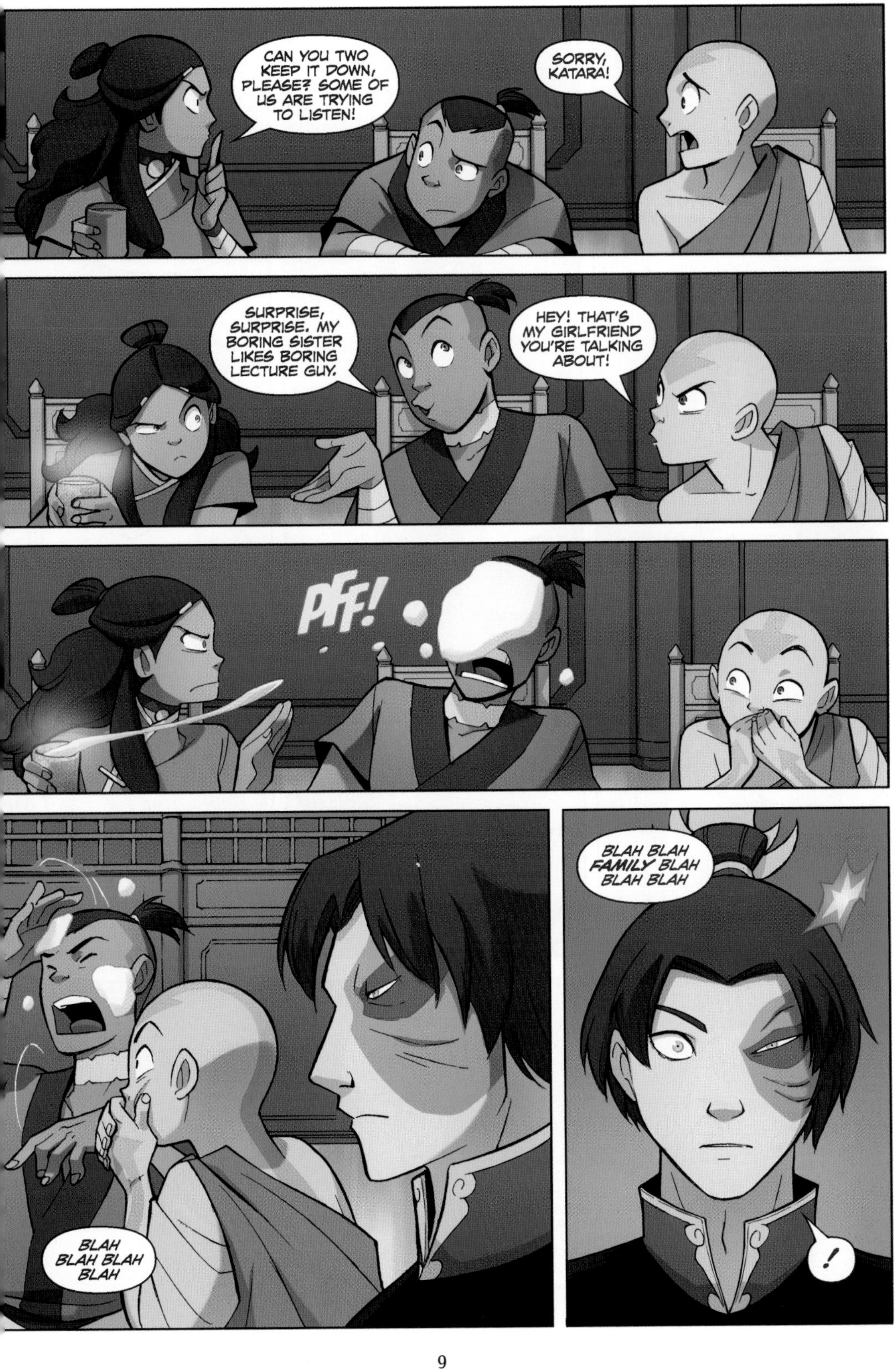
CAN YOU TWO KEEP IT DOWN, PLEASE? SOME OF US ARE TRYING TO LISTEN!
SORRY, KATARA!
SURPRISE, SURPRISE. MY BORING SISTER LIKES BORING LECTURE GUY.
HEY! THAT'S MY GIRLFRIEND YOU'RE TALKING ABOUT!
PFF!
BLAH BLAH BLAH BLAH
BLAH BLAH *FAMILY* BLAH BLAH BLAH
!

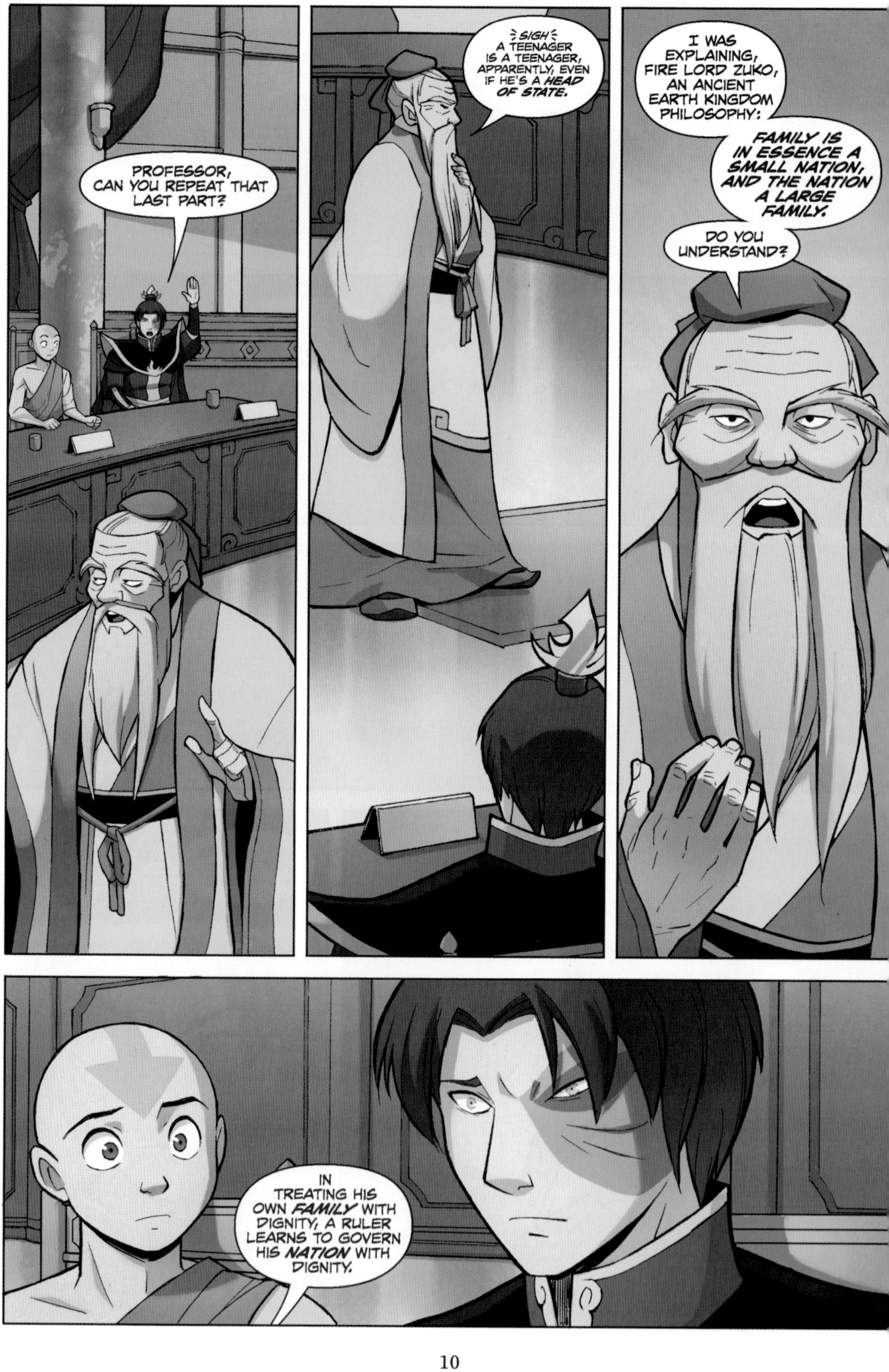
PROFESSOR, CAN YOU REPEAT THAT LAST PART?
SIGH
A TEENAGER IS A TEENAGER, APPARENTLY, EVEN IF HE'S A HEAD OF STATE.
I WAS EXPLAINING, FIRE LORD ZUKO, AN ANCIENT EARTH KINGDOM PHILOSOPHY:
FAMILY IS IN ESSENCE A SMALL NATION, AND THE NATION A LARGE FAMILY.
DO YOU UNDERSTAND?
IN TREATING HIS OWN FAMILY WITH DIGNITY, A RULER LEARNS TO GOVERN HIS NATION WITH DIGNITY.

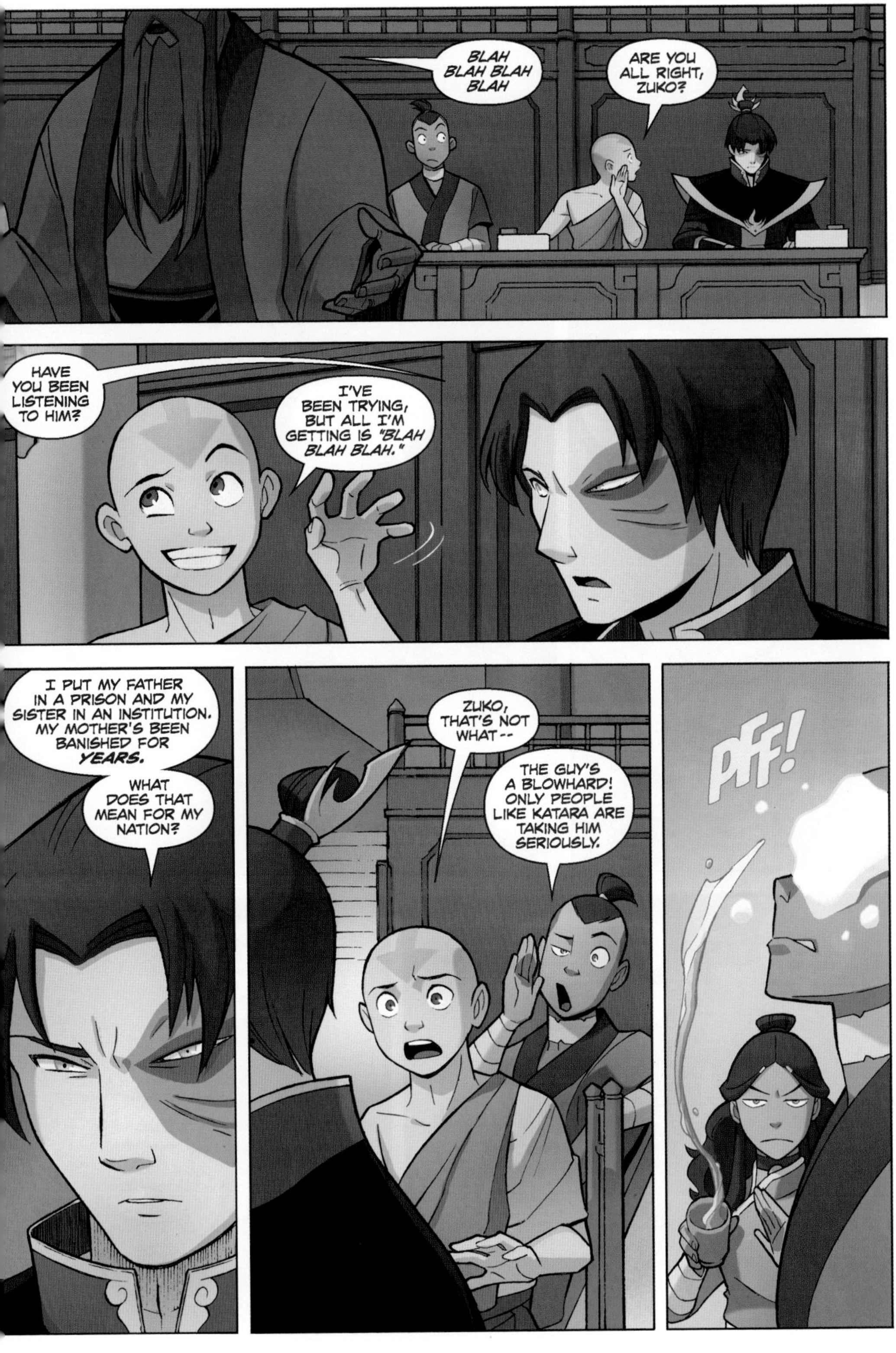
BLAH BLAH BLAH BLAH
ARE YOU ALL RIGHT, ZUKO?
HAVE YOU BEEN LISTENING TO HIM?
I'VE BEEN TRYING, BUT ALL I'M GETTING IS "BLAH BLAH BLAH."
I PUT MY FATHER IN A PRISON AND MY SISTER IN AN INSTITUTION. MY MOTHER'S BEEN BANISHED FOR YEARS.
WHAT DOES THAT MEAN FOR MY NATION?
ZUKO, THAT'S NOT WHAT--
THE GUY'S A BLOWHARD! ONLY PEOPLE LIKE KATARA ARE TAKING HIM SERIOUSLY.
PFF!

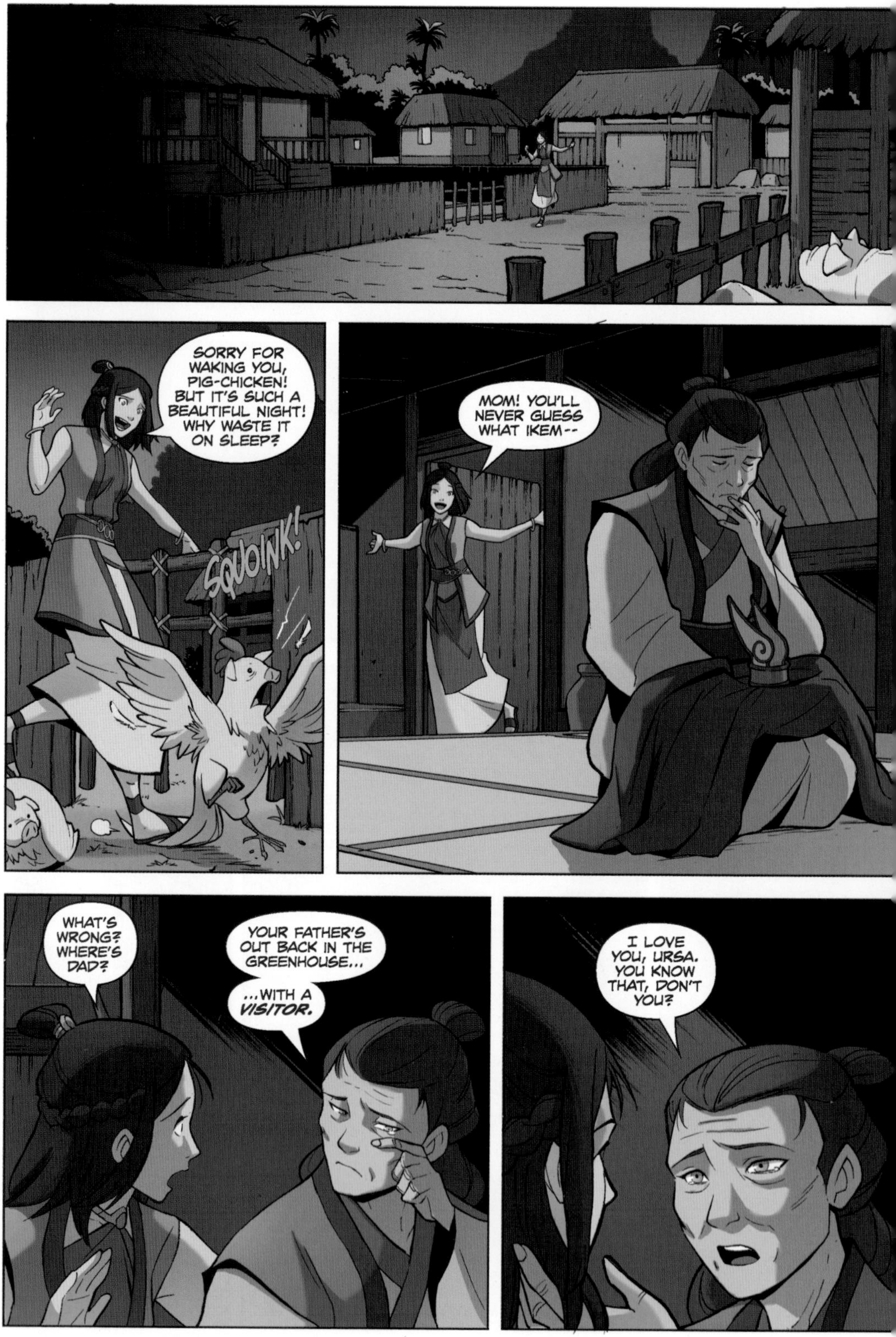
SORRY FOR WAKING YOU, PIG-CHICKEN! BUT IT'S SUCH A BEAUTIFUL NIGHT! WHY WASTE IT ON SLEEP?
SQUOINK!
MOM! YOU'LL NEVER GUESS WHAT IKEM--
WHAT'S WRONG? WHERE'S DAD?
YOUR FATHER'S OUT BACK IN THE GREENHOUSE...
...WITH A *VISITOR*.
I LOVE YOU, URSA. YOU KNOW THAT, DON'T YOU?

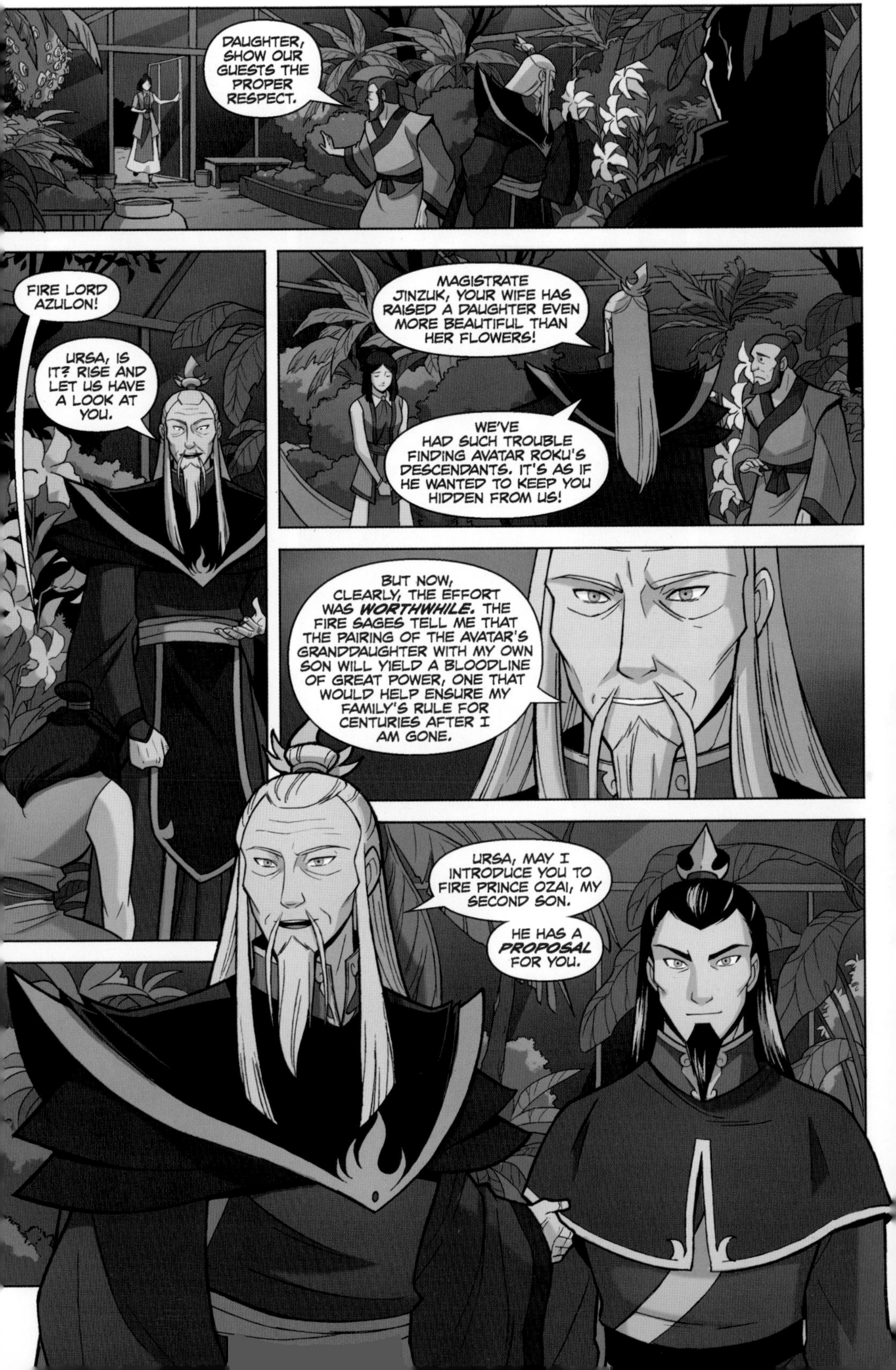
DAUGHTER, SHOW OUR GUESTS THE PROPER RESPECT.
FIRE LORD AZULON!
URSA, IS IT? RISE AND LET US HAVE A LOOK AT YOU.
MAGISTRATE JINZUK, YOUR WIFE HAS RAISED A DAUGHTER EVEN MORE BEAUTIFUL THAN HER FLOWERS!
WE'VE HAD SUCH TROUBLE FINDING AVATAR ROKU'S DESCENDANTS. IT'S AS IF HE WANTED TO KEEP YOU HIDDEN FROM US!
BUT NOW, CLEARLY, THE EFFORT WAS WORTHWHILE. THE FIRE SAGES TELL ME THAT THE PAIRING OF THE AVATAR'S GRANDDAUGHTER WITH MY OWN SON WILL YIELD A BLOODLINE OF GREAT POWER, ONE THAT WOULD HELP ENSURE MY FAMILY'S RULE FOR CENTURIES AFTER I AM GONE.
URSA, MAY I INTRODUCE YOU TO FIRE PRINCE OZAI, MY SECOND SON.
HE HAS A PROPOSAL FOR YOU.

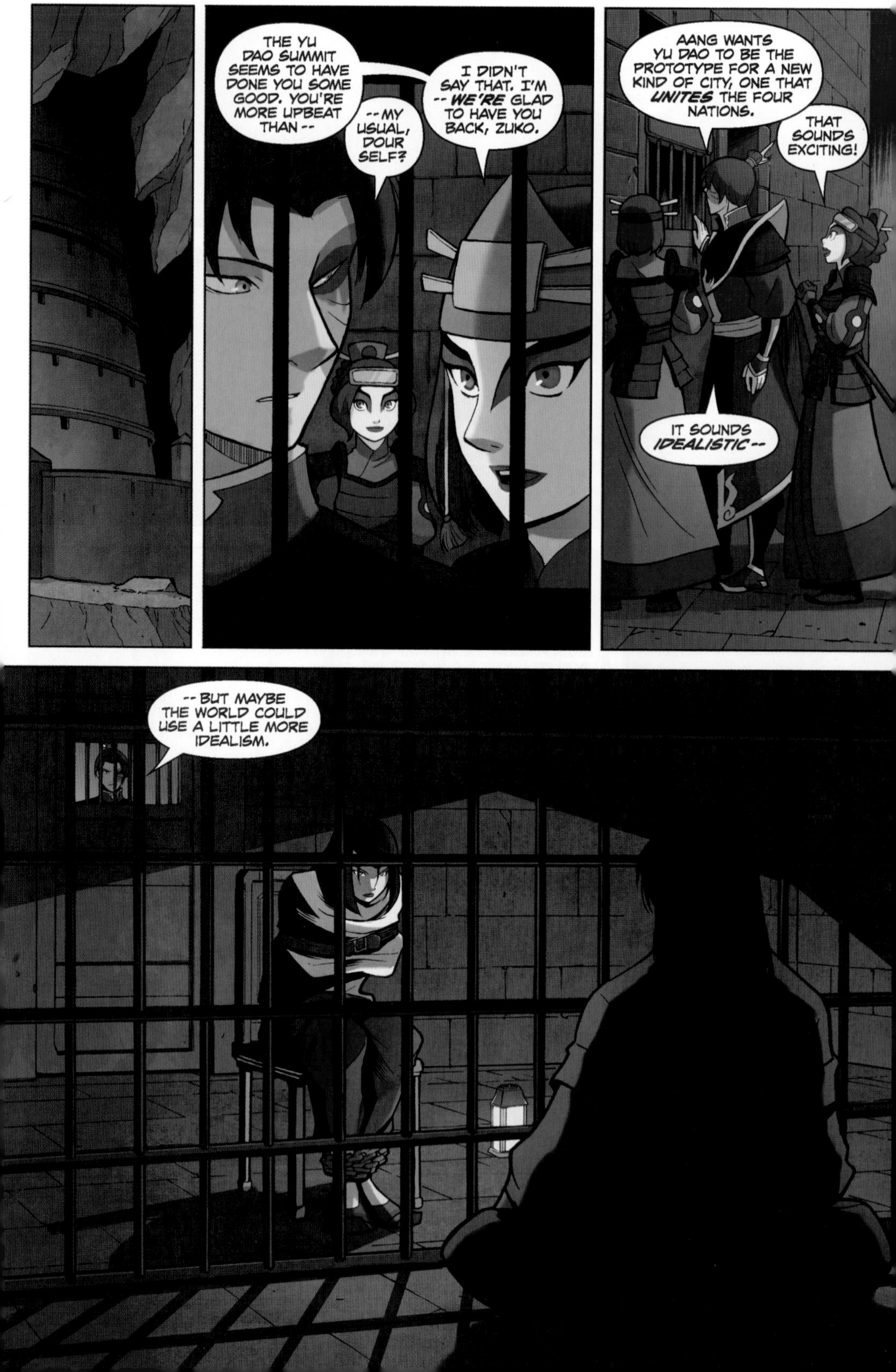
THE YU DAO SUMMIT SEEMS TO HAVE DONE YOU SOME GOOD. YOU'RE MORE UPBEAT THAN --
-- MY USUAL, DOUR SELF?
I DIDN'T SAY THAT. I'M -- WE'RE GLAD TO HAVE YOU BACK, ZUKO.
AANG WANTS YU DAO TO BE THE PROTOTYPE FOR A NEW KIND OF CITY, ONE THAT UNITES THE FOUR NATIONS.
THAT SOUNDS EXCITING!
IT SOUNDS IDEALISTIC --
-- BUT MAYBE THE WORLD COULD USE A LITTLE MORE IDEALISM.

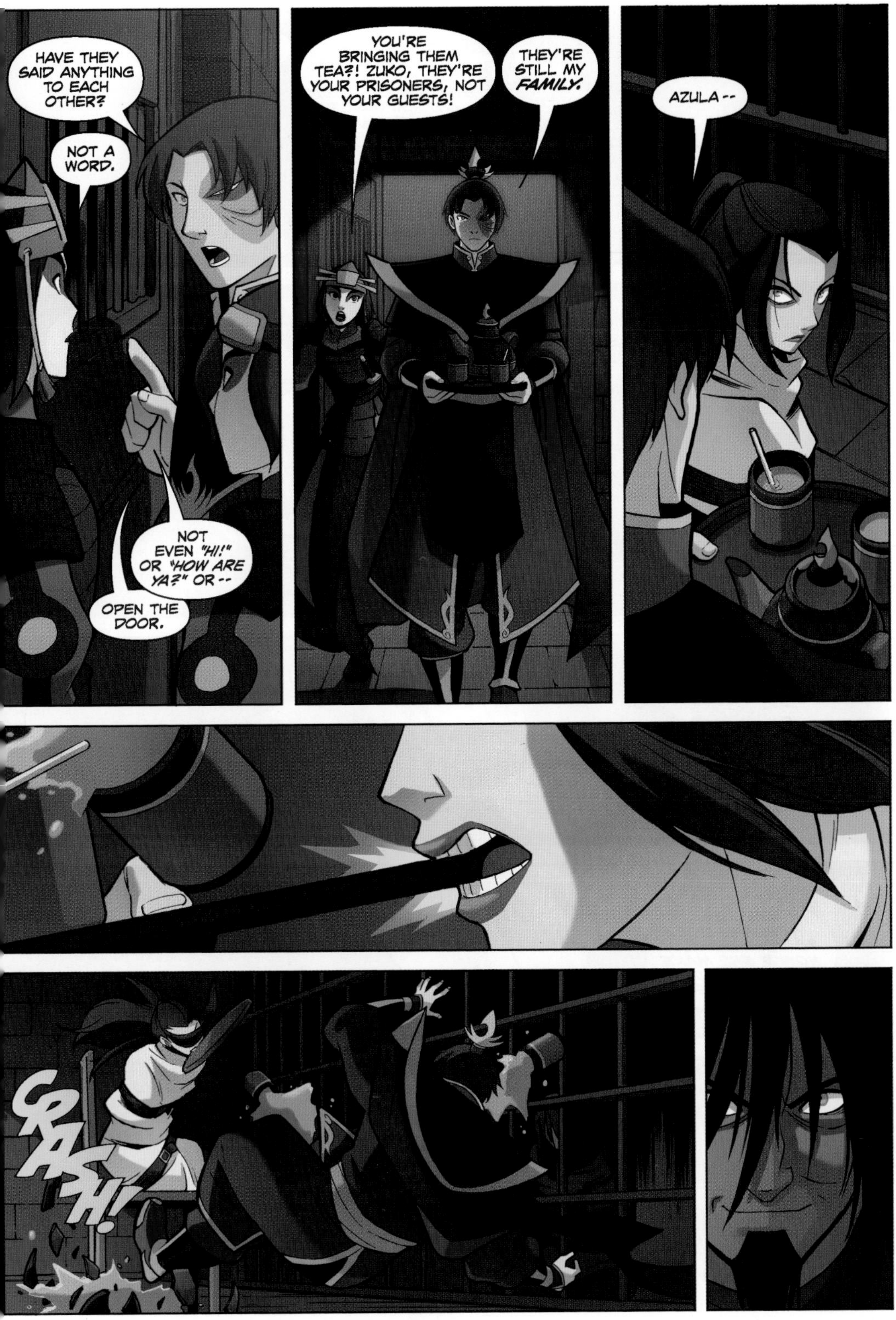
HAVE THEY SAID ANYTHING TO EACH OTHER?
NOT A WORD.
NOT EVEN "HI!" OR "HOW ARE YA?" OR --
OPEN THE DOOR.
YOU'RE BRINGING THEM TEA?! ZUKO, THEY'RE YOUR PRISONERS, NOT YOUR GUESTS!
THEY'RE STILL MY FAMILY.
AZULA --
CRASH!

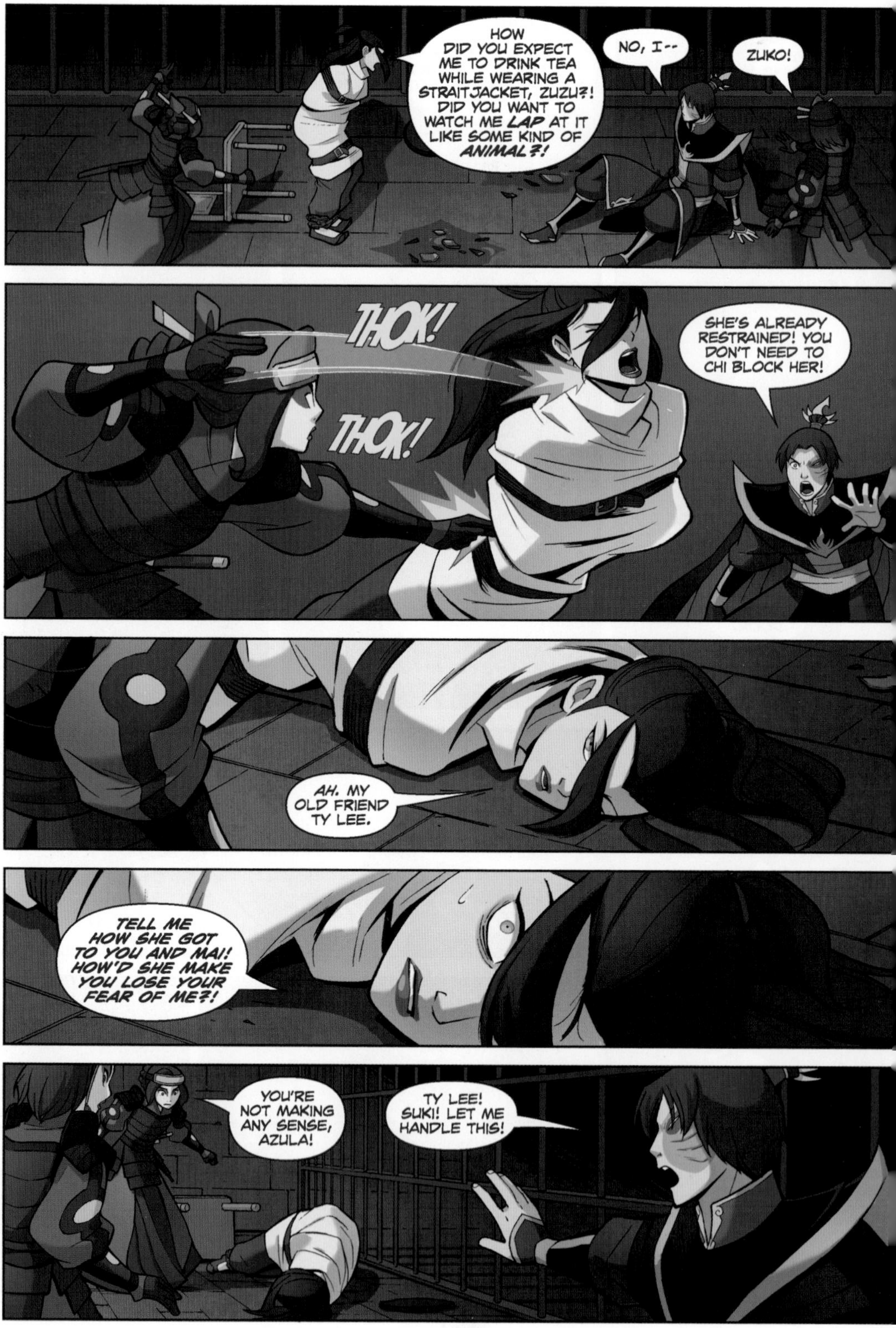
HOW DID YOU EXPECT ME TO DRINK TEA WHILE WEARING A STRAITJACKET, ZUZU?! DID YOU WANT TO WATCH ME LAP AT IT LIKE SOME KIND OF ANIMAL?!
NO, I--
ZUKO!
THOK!
THOK!
SHE'S ALREADY RESTRAINED! YOU DON'T NEED TO CHI BLOCK HER!
AH. MY OLD FRIEND TY LEE.
TELL ME HOW SHE GOT TO YOU AND MAI! HOW'D SHE MAKE YOU LOSE YOUR FEAR OF ME?!
YOU'RE NOT MAKING ANY SENSE, AZULA!
TY LEE! SUKI! LET ME HANDLE THIS!

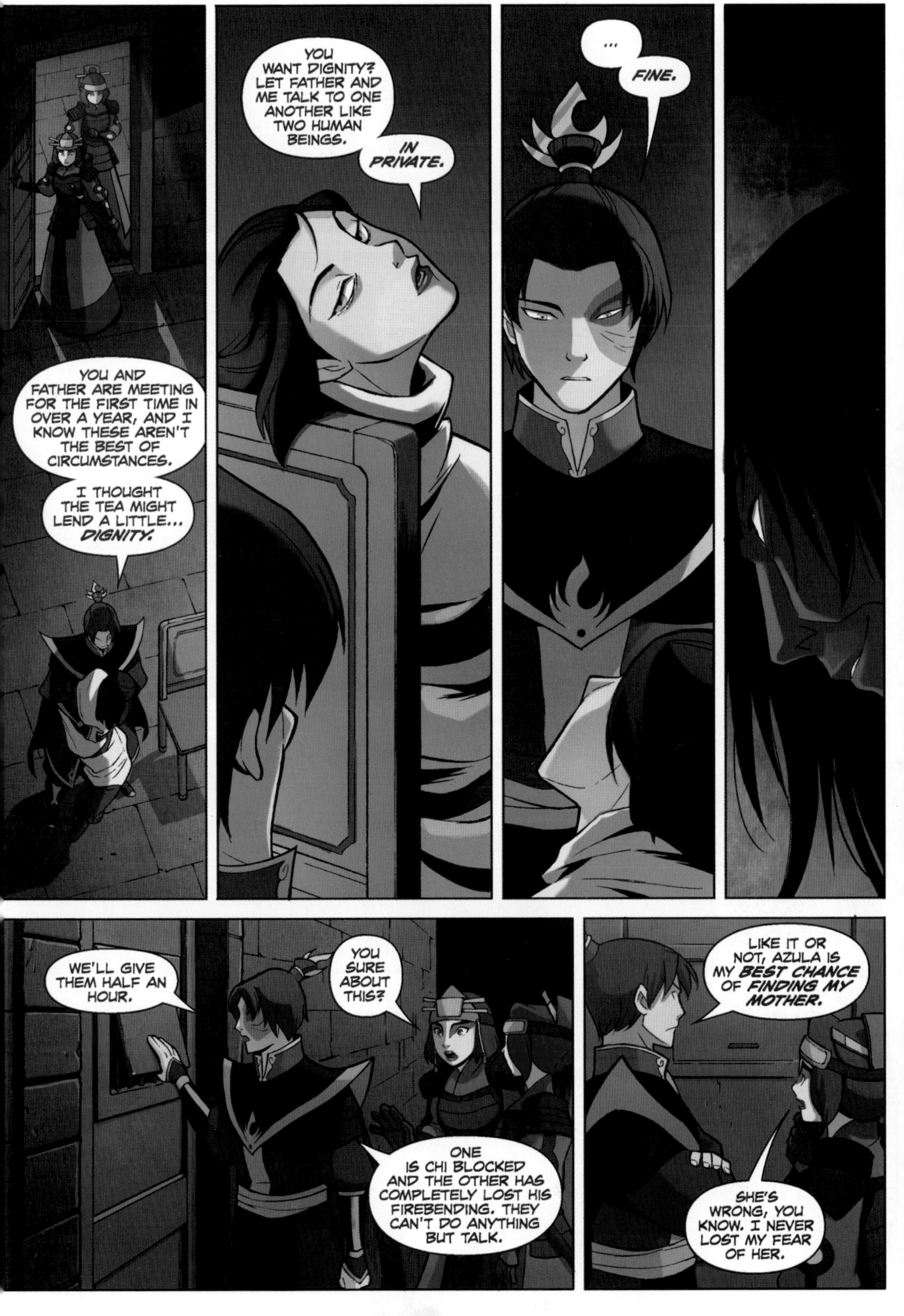
YOU AND FATHER ARE MEETING FOR THE FIRST TIME IN OVER A YEAR, AND I KNOW THESE AREN'T THE BEST OF CIRCUMSTANCES.
I THOUGHT THE TEA MIGHT LEND A LITTLE... DIGNITY.
YOU WANT DIGNITY? LET FATHER AND ME TALK TO ONE ANOTHER LIKE TWO HUMAN BEINGS.
IN PRIVATE.
...
FINE.
WE'LL GIVE THEM HALF AN HOUR.
YOU SURE ABOUT THIS?
ONE IS CHI BLOCKED AND THE OTHER HAS COMPLETELY LOST HIS FIREBENDING. THEY CAN'T DO ANYTHING BUT TALK.
LIKE IT OR NOT, AZULA IS MY BEST CHANCE OF FINDING MY MOTHER.
SHE'S WRONG, YOU KNOW. I NEVER LOST MY FEAR OF HER.

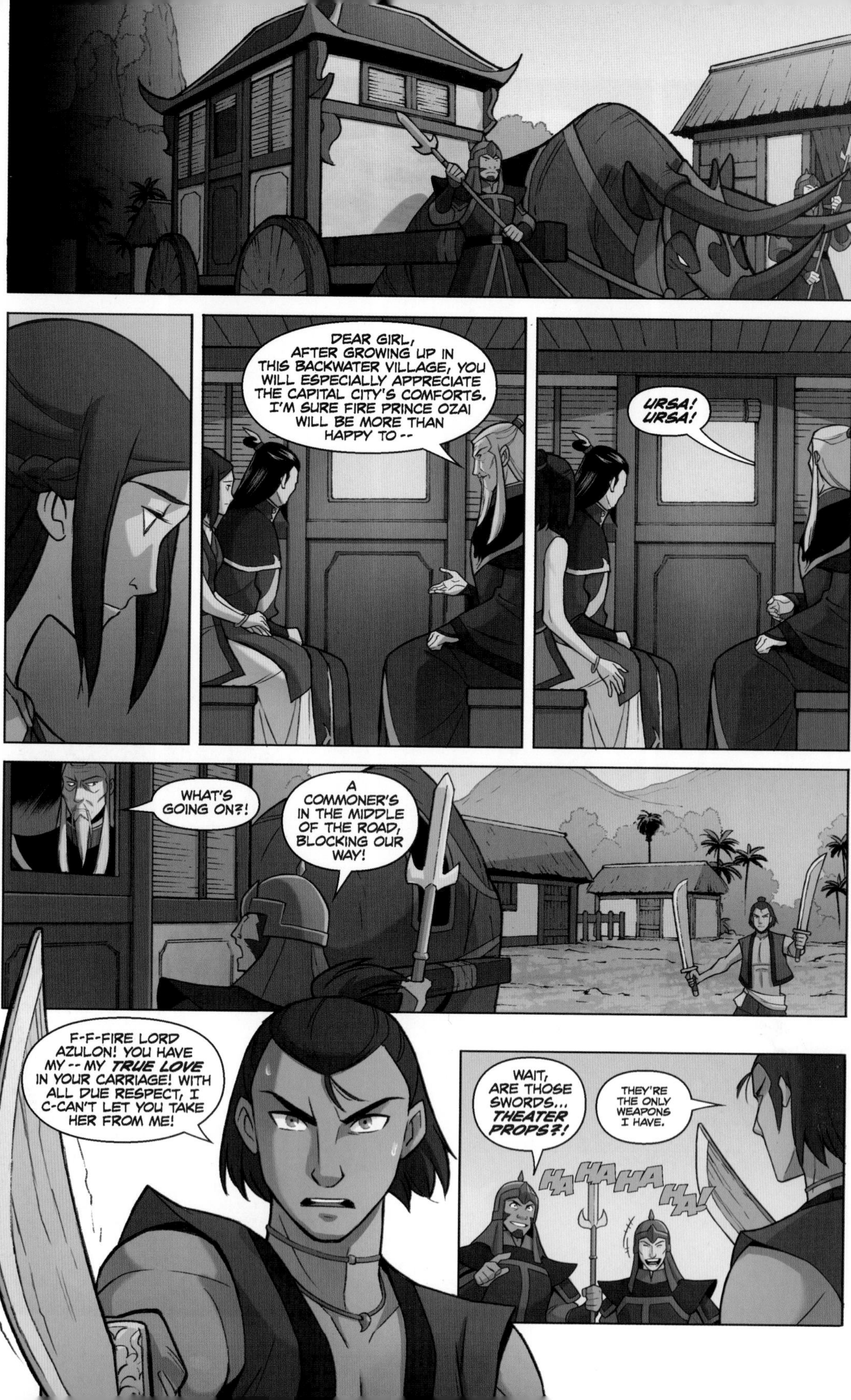
DEAR GIRL, AFTER GROWING UP IN THIS BACKWATER VILLAGE, YOU WILL ESPECIALLY APPRECIATE THE CAPITAL CITY'S COMFORTS. I'M SURE FIRE PRINCE OZAI WILL BE MORE THAN HAPPY TO --
URSA! URSA!
WHAT'S GOING ON?!
A COMMONER'S IN THE MIDDLE OF THE ROAD, BLOCKING OUR WAY!
F-F-FIRE LORD AZULON! YOU HAVE MY -- MY TRUE LOVE IN YOUR CARRIAGE! WITH ALL DUE RESPECT, I C-CAN'T LET YOU TAKE HER FROM ME!
WAIT, ARE THOSE SWORDS... THEATER PROPS?!
THEY'RE THE ONLY WEAPONS I HAVE.
HA HA HA HA HA!

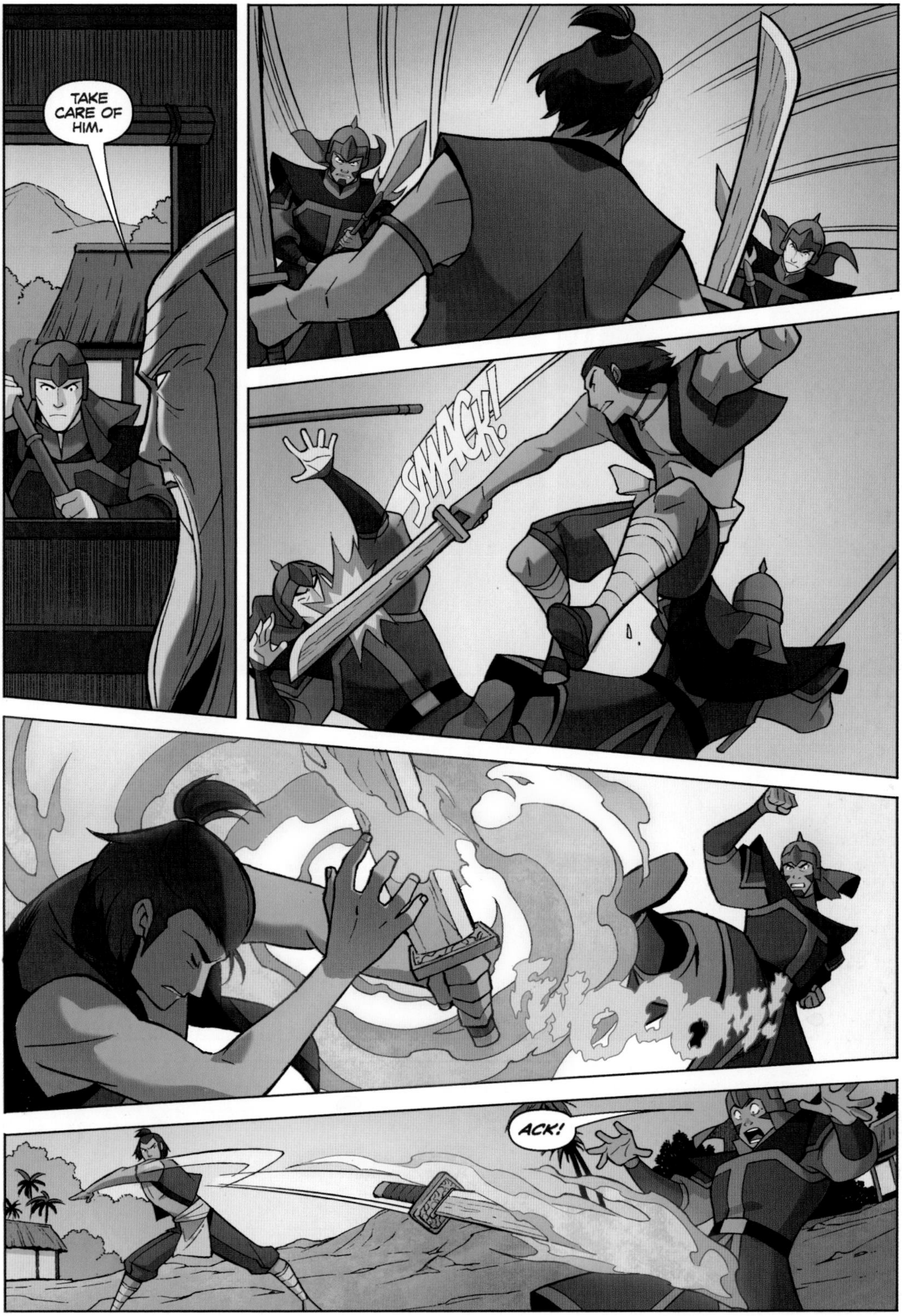
TAKE CARE OF HIM.
SMACK!
ACK!

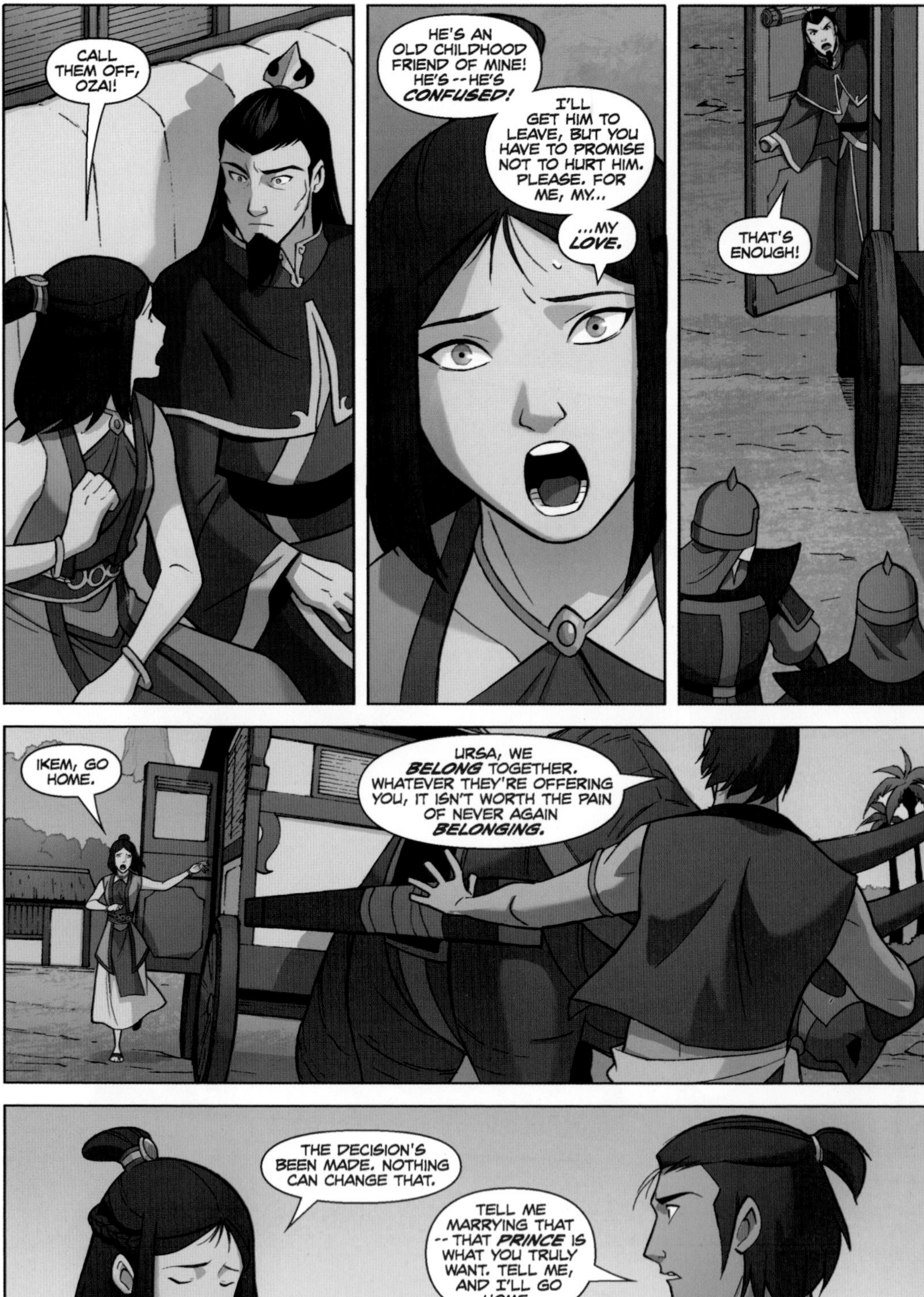

CALL THEM OFF, OZAI!
HE'S AN OLD CHILDHOOD FRIEND OF MINE! HE'S--HE'S CONFUSED!
I'LL GET HIM TO LEAVE, BUT YOU HAVE TO PROMISE NOT TO HURT HIM. PLEASE. FOR ME, MY...
...MY LOVE.
THAT'S ENOUGH!
IKEM, GO HOME.
URSA, WE BELONG TOGETHER. WHATEVER THEY'RE OFFERING YOU, IT ISN'T WORTH THE PAIN OF NEVER AGAIN BELONGING.
THE DECISION'S BEEN MADE. NOTHING CAN CHANGE THAT.
TELL ME MARRYING THAT--THAT PRINCE IS WHAT YOU TRULY WANT. TELL ME, AND I'LL GO HOME.

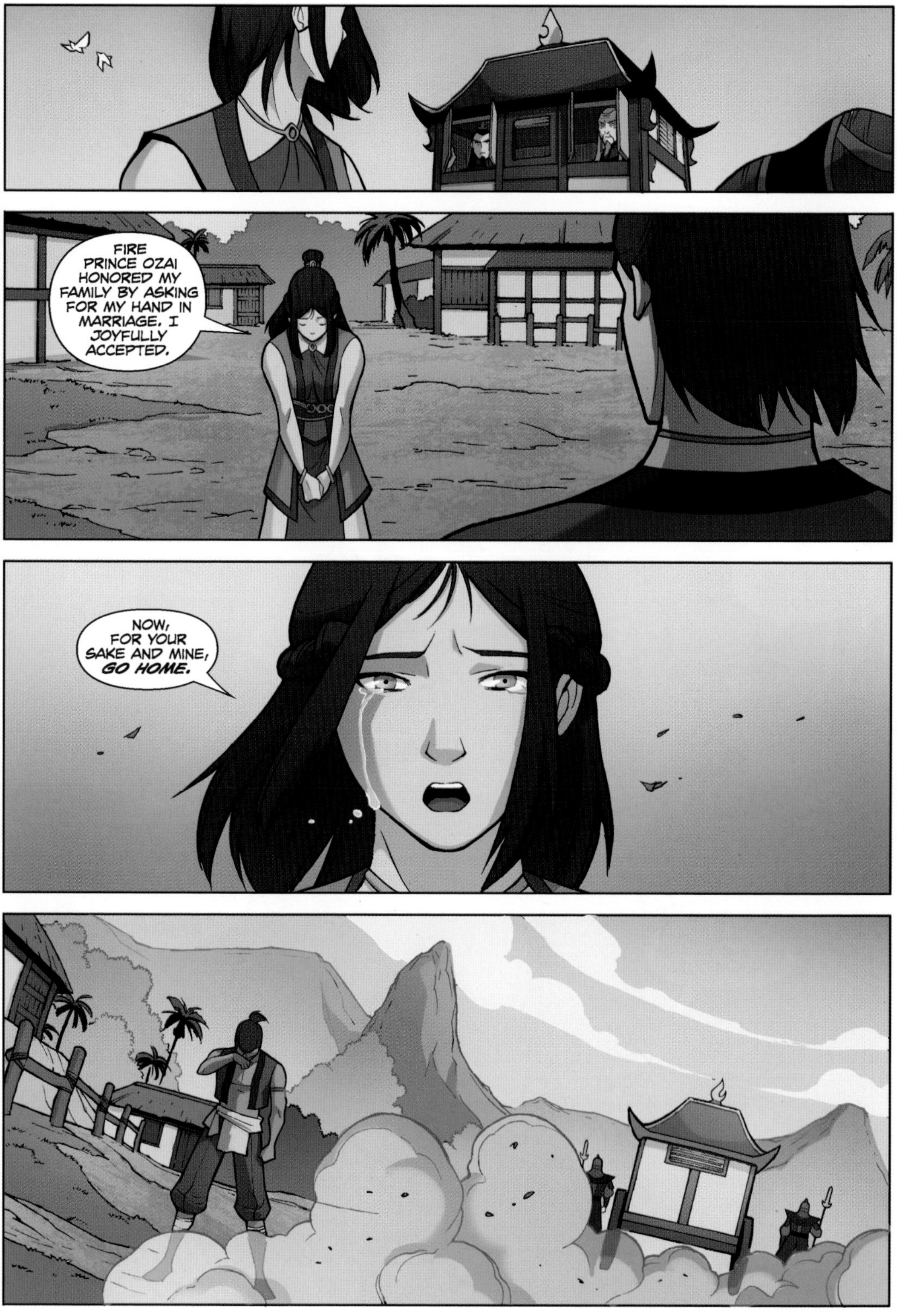
FIRE PRINCE OZAI HONORED MY FAMILY BY ASKING FOR MY HAND IN MARRIAGE. I JOYFULLY ACCEPTED.
NOW, FOR YOUR SAKE AND MINE, *GO HOME.*

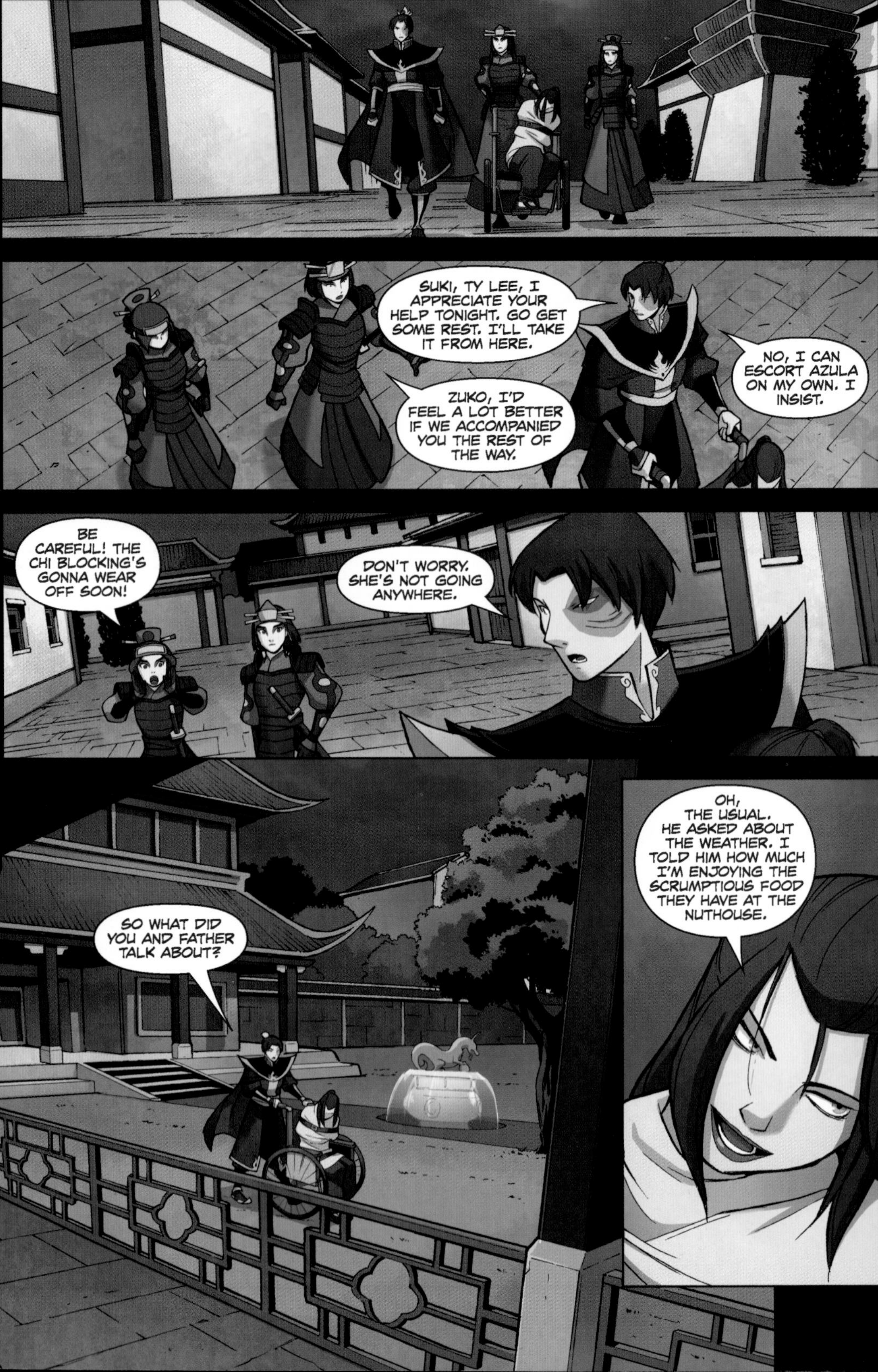
SUKI, TY LEE, I APPRECIATE YOUR HELP TONIGHT. GO GET SOME REST. I'LL TAKE IT FROM HERE.
ZUKO, I'D FEEL A LOT BETTER IF WE ACCOMPANIED YOU THE REST OF THE WAY.
NO, I CAN ESCORT AZULA ON MY OWN. I INSIST.
BE CAREFUL! THE CHI BLOCKING'S GONNA WEAR OFF SOON!
DON'T WORRY. SHE'S NOT GOING ANYWHERE.
SO WHAT DID YOU AND FATHER TALK ABOUT?
OH, THE USUAL. HE ASKED ABOUT THE WEATHER. I TOLD HIM HOW MUCH I'M ENJOYING THE SCRUMPTIOUS FOOD THEY HAVE AT THE NUTHOUSE.

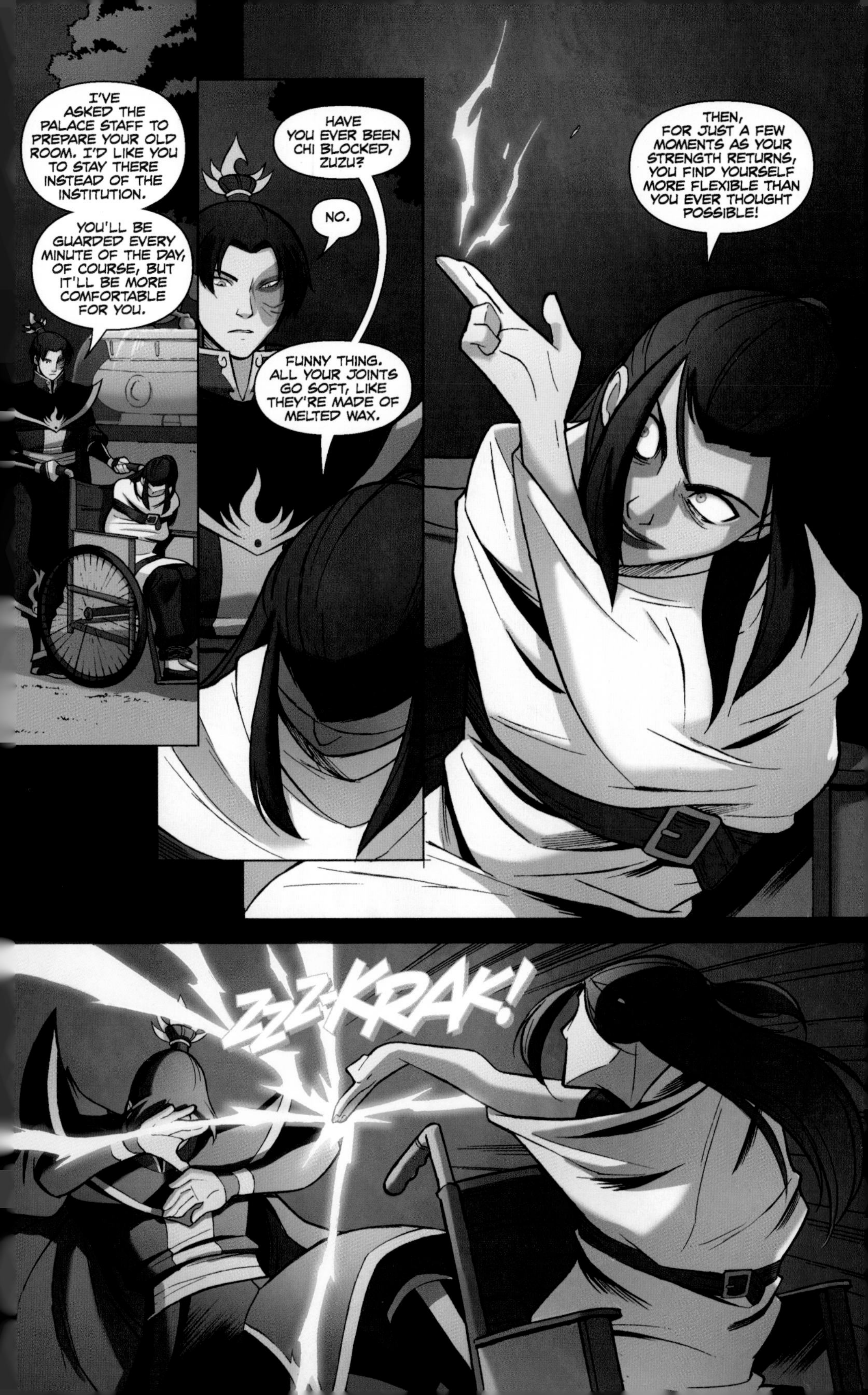

I'VE ASKED THE PALACE STAFF TO PREPARE YOUR OLD ROOM. I'D LIKE YOU TO STAY THERE INSTEAD OF THE INSTITUTION.
YOU'LL BE GUARDED EVERY MINUTE OF THE DAY, OF COURSE, BUT IT'LL BE MORE COMFORTABLE FOR YOU.
HAVE YOU EVER BEEN CHI BLOCKED, ZUZU?
NO.
FUNNY THING. ALL YOUR JOINTS GO SOFT, LIKE THEY'RE MADE OF MELTED WAX.
THEN, FOR JUST A FEW MOMENTS AS YOUR STRENGTH RETURNS, YOU FIND YOURSELF MORE FLEXIBLE THAN YOU EVER THOUGHT POSSIBLE!
ZZZ-KRAK!

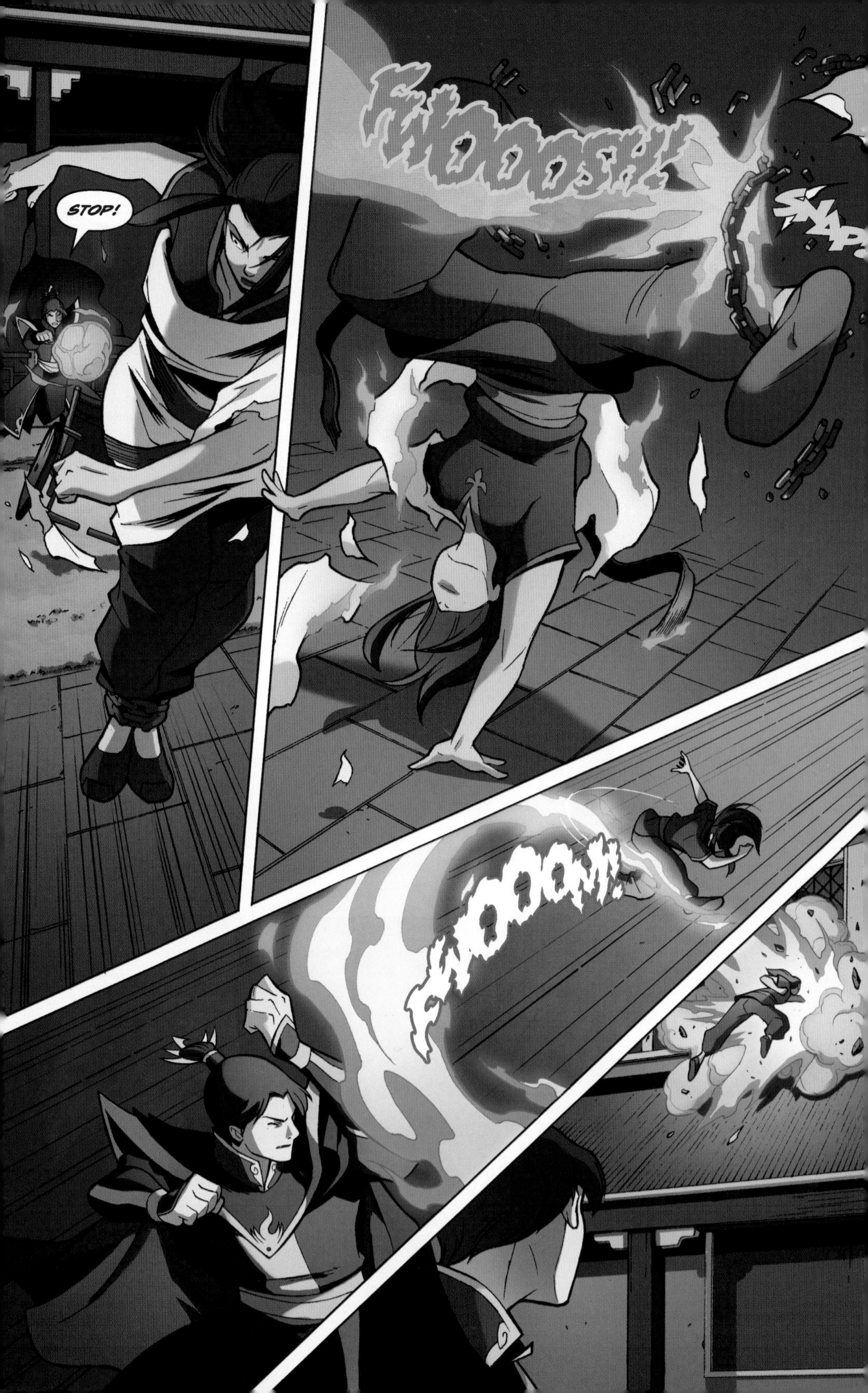
STOP!
FWOOOSH!
SNAP!
FWOOOM!

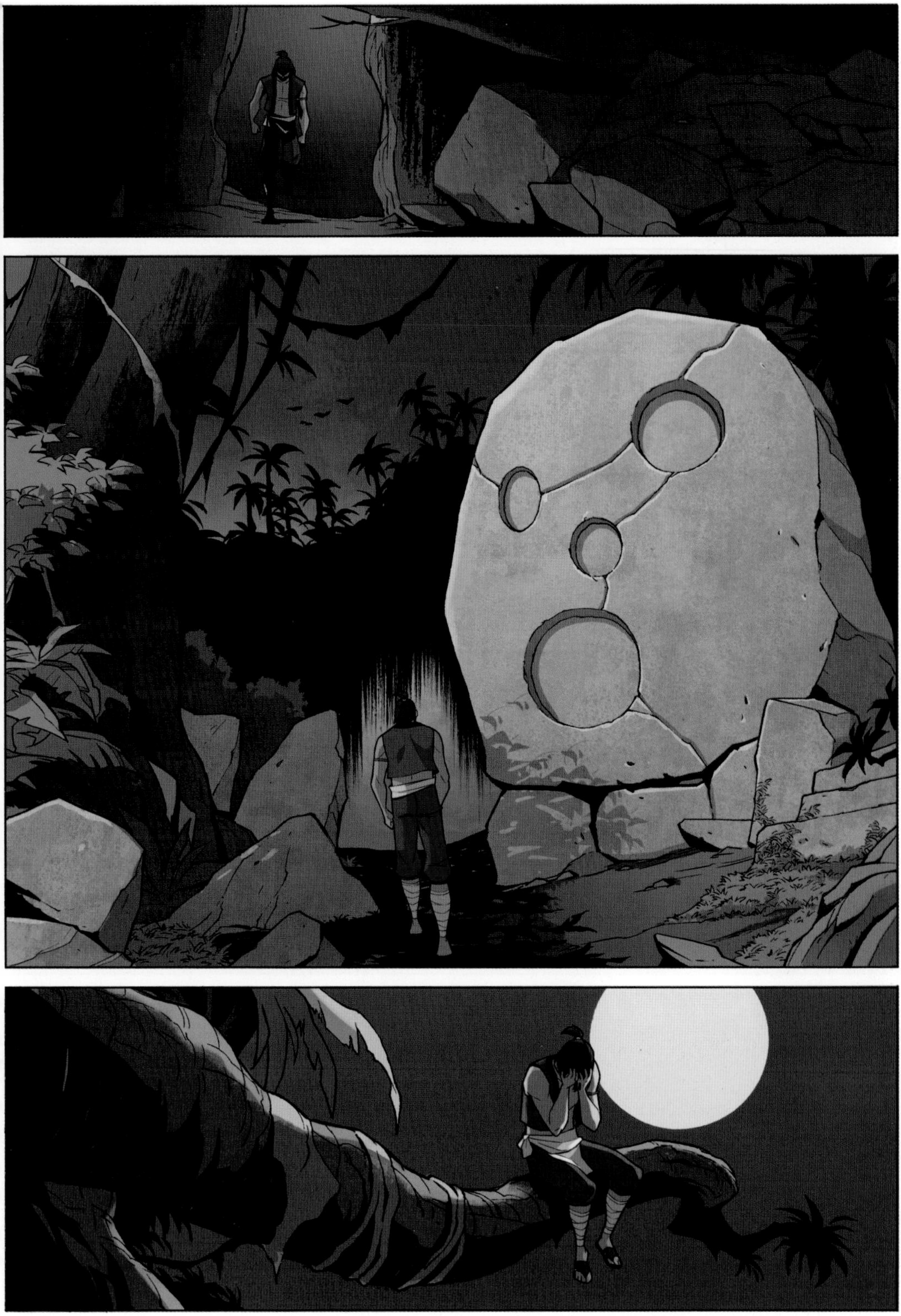

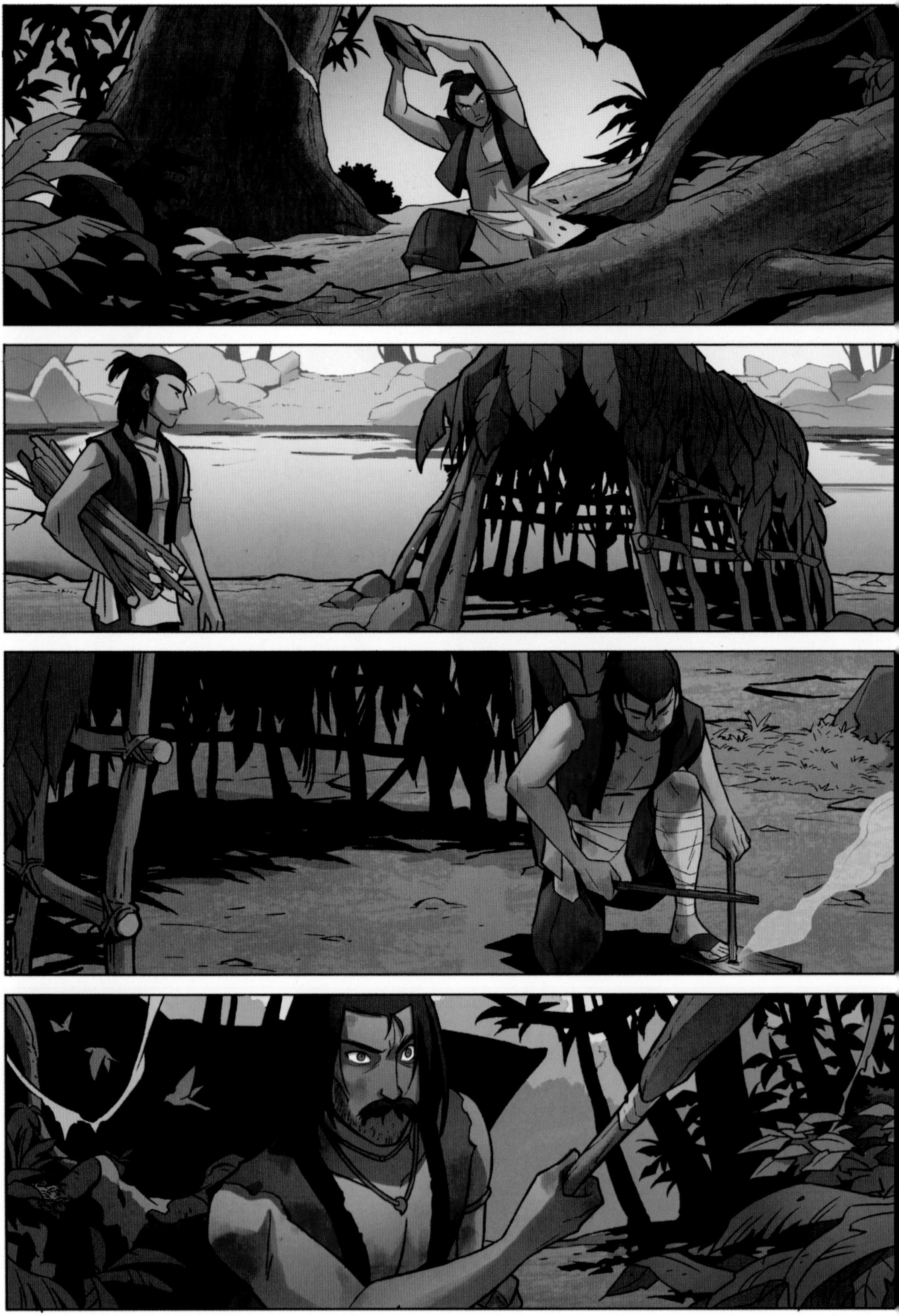

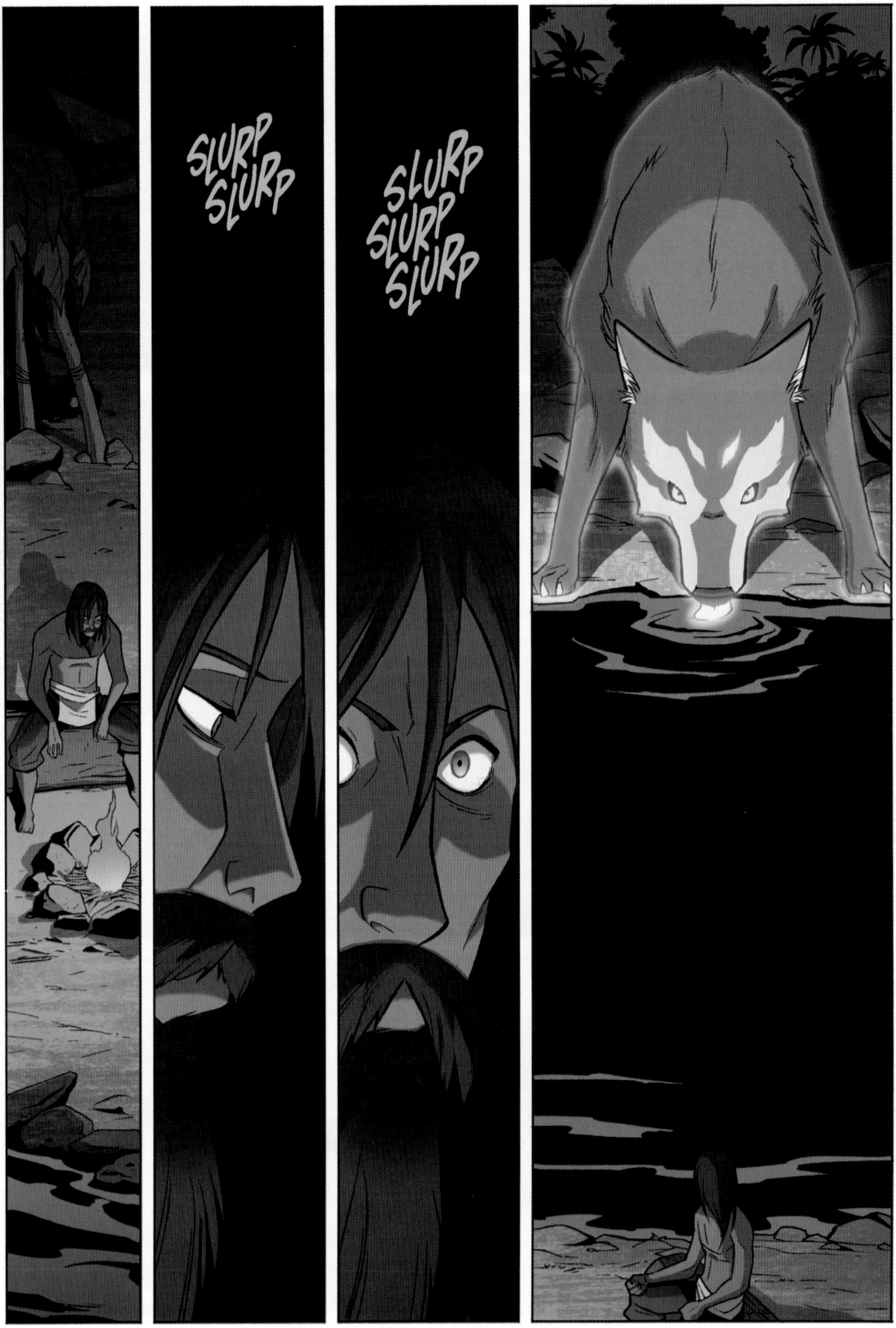
SLURP SLURP
SLURP SLURP SLURP

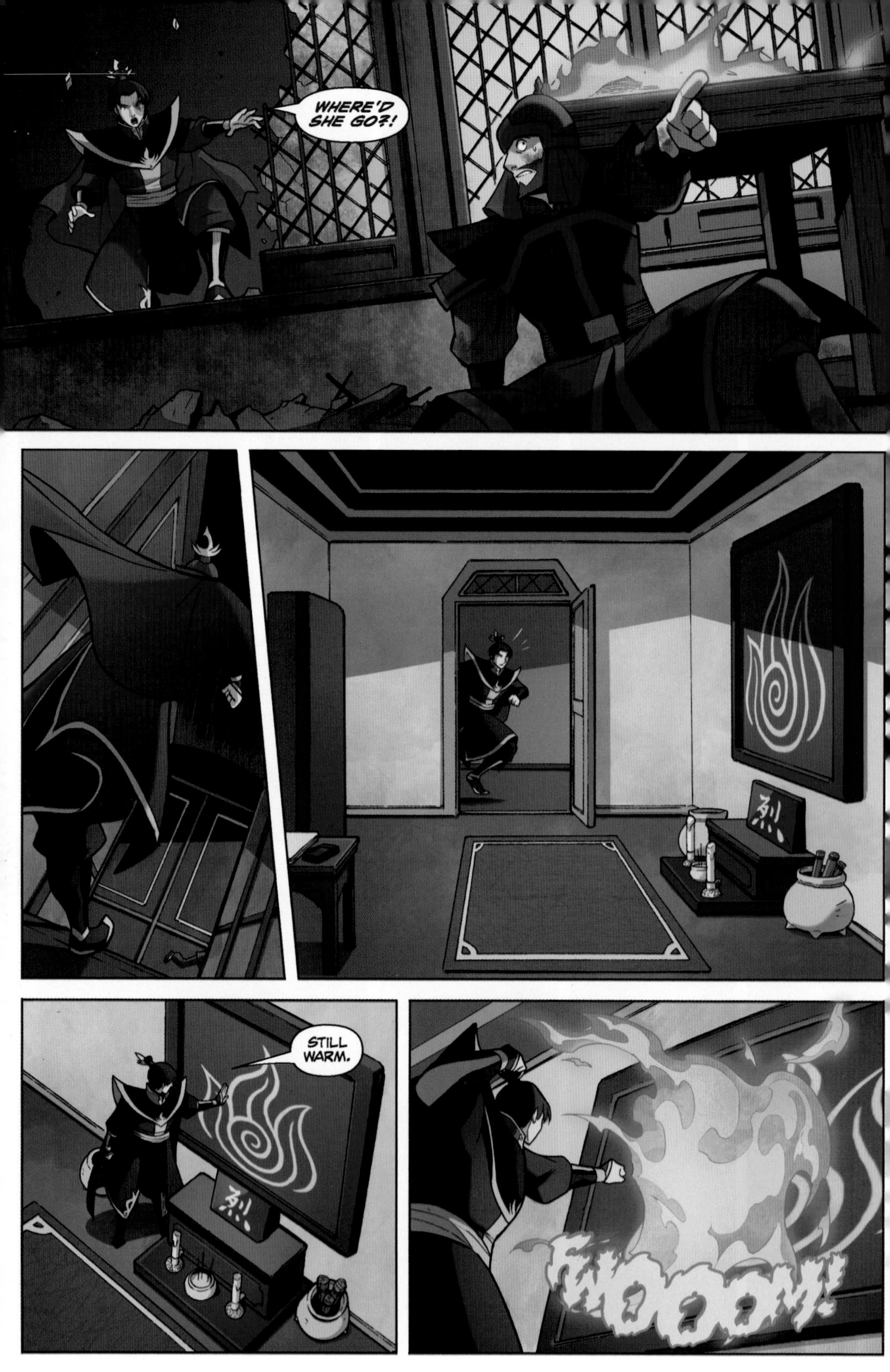
WHERE'D SHE GO?!
STILL WARM.
FOOOOM!

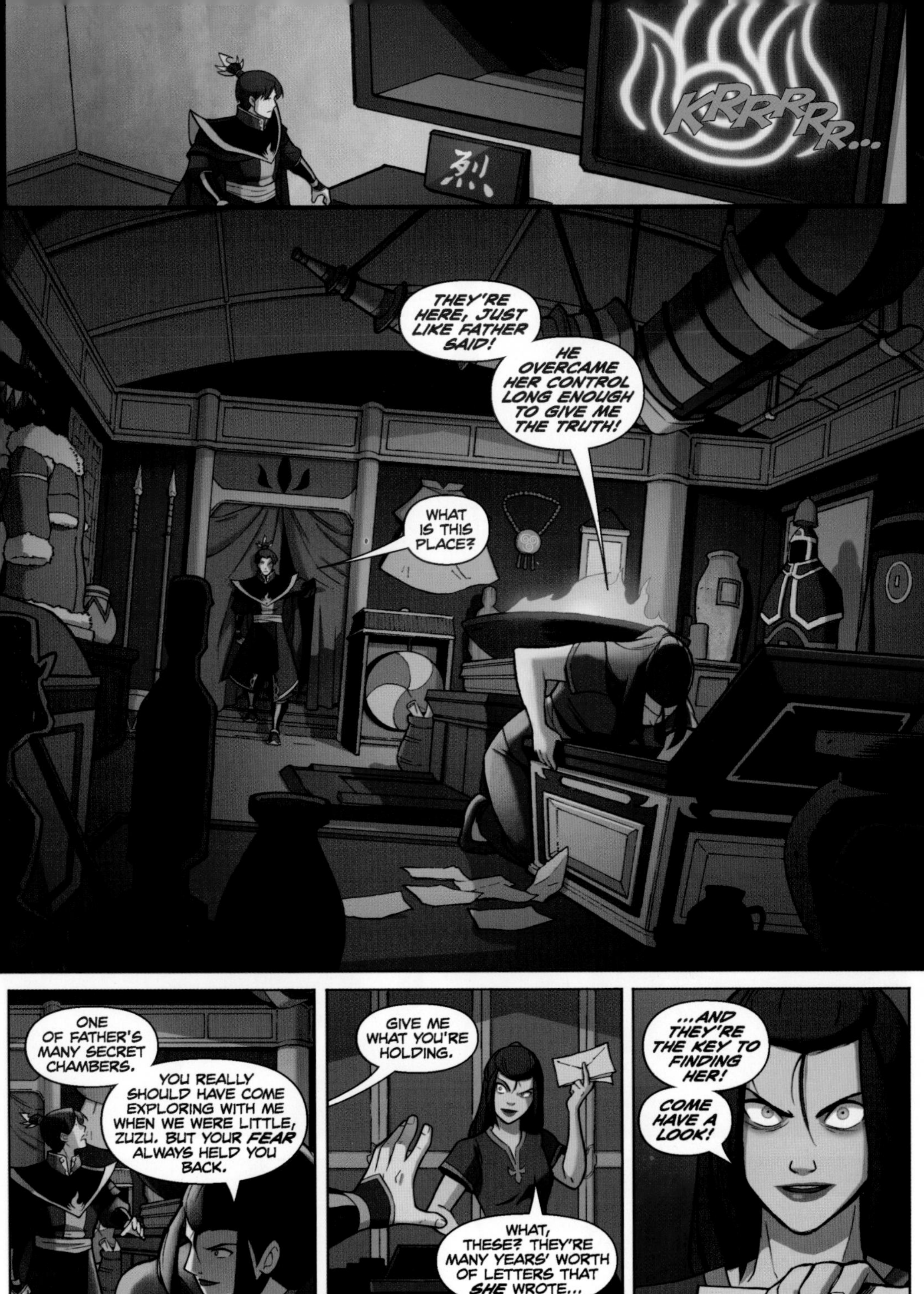

KRRRRR...
THEY'RE HERE, JUST LIKE FATHER SAID!
HE OVERCAME HER CONTROL LONG ENOUGH TO GIVE ME THE TRUTH!
WHAT IS THIS PLACE?
ONE OF FATHER'S MANY SECRET CHAMBERS.
YOU REALLY SHOULD HAVE COME EXPLORING WITH ME WHEN WE WERE LITTLE, ZUZU. BUT YOUR FEAR ALWAYS HELD YOU BACK.
GIVE ME WHAT YOU'RE HOLDING.
WHAT, THESE? THEY'RE MANY YEARS' WORTH OF LETTERS THAT SHE WROTE...
...AND THEY'RE THE KEY TO FINDING HER!
COME HAVE A LOOK!

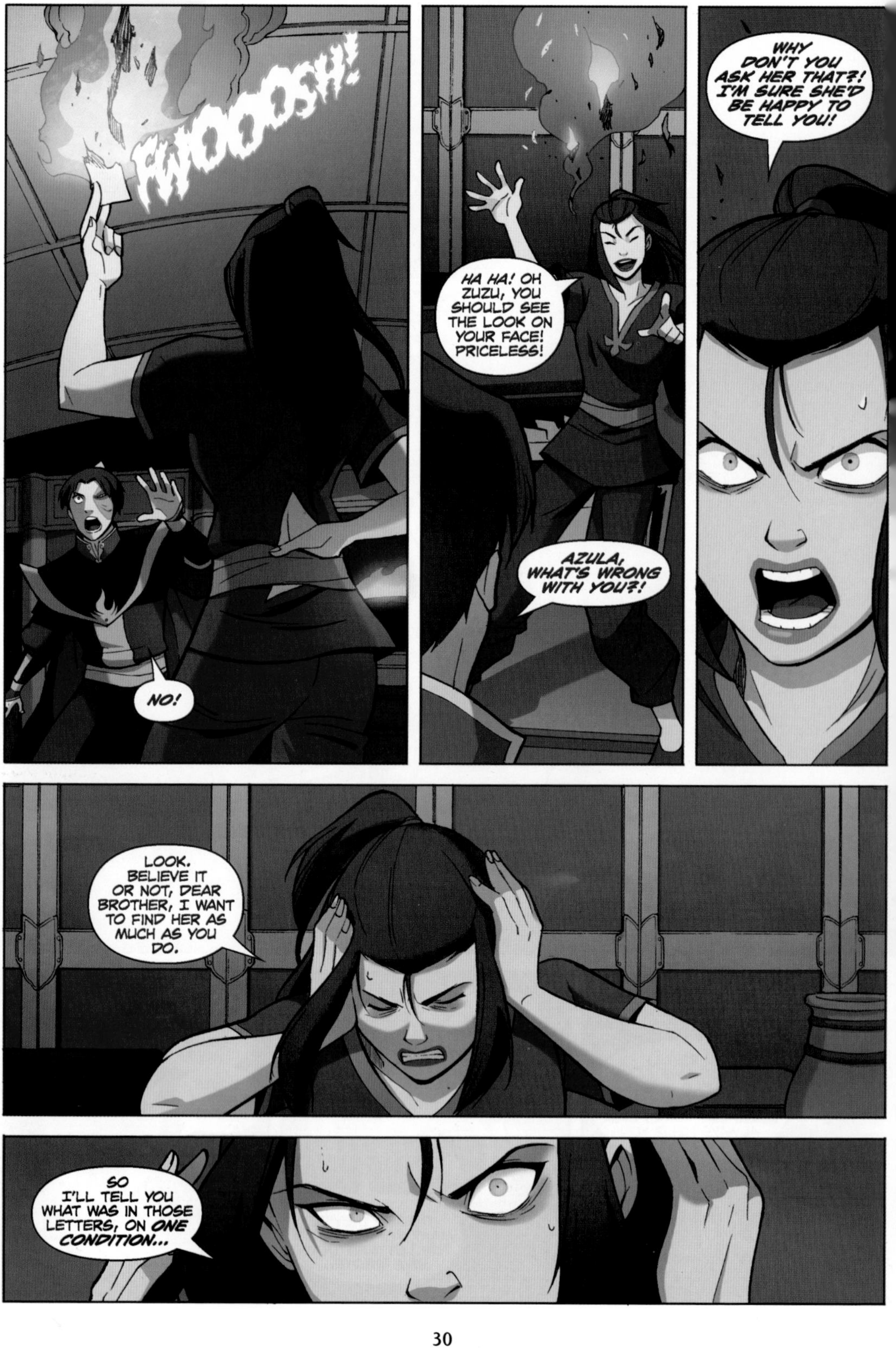
FWOOOSH!
NO!
HA HA! OH ZUZU, YOU SHOULD SEE THE LOOK ON YOUR FACE! PRICELESS!
AZULA, WHAT'S WRONG WITH YOU?!
WHY DON'T YOU ASK HER THAT?! I'M SURE SHE'D BE HAPPY TO TELL YOU!
LOOK. BELIEVE IT OR NOT, DEAR BROTHER, I WANT TO FIND HER AS MUCH AS YOU DO.
SO I'LL TELL YOU WHAT WAS IN THOSE LETTERS, ON ONE CONDITION...

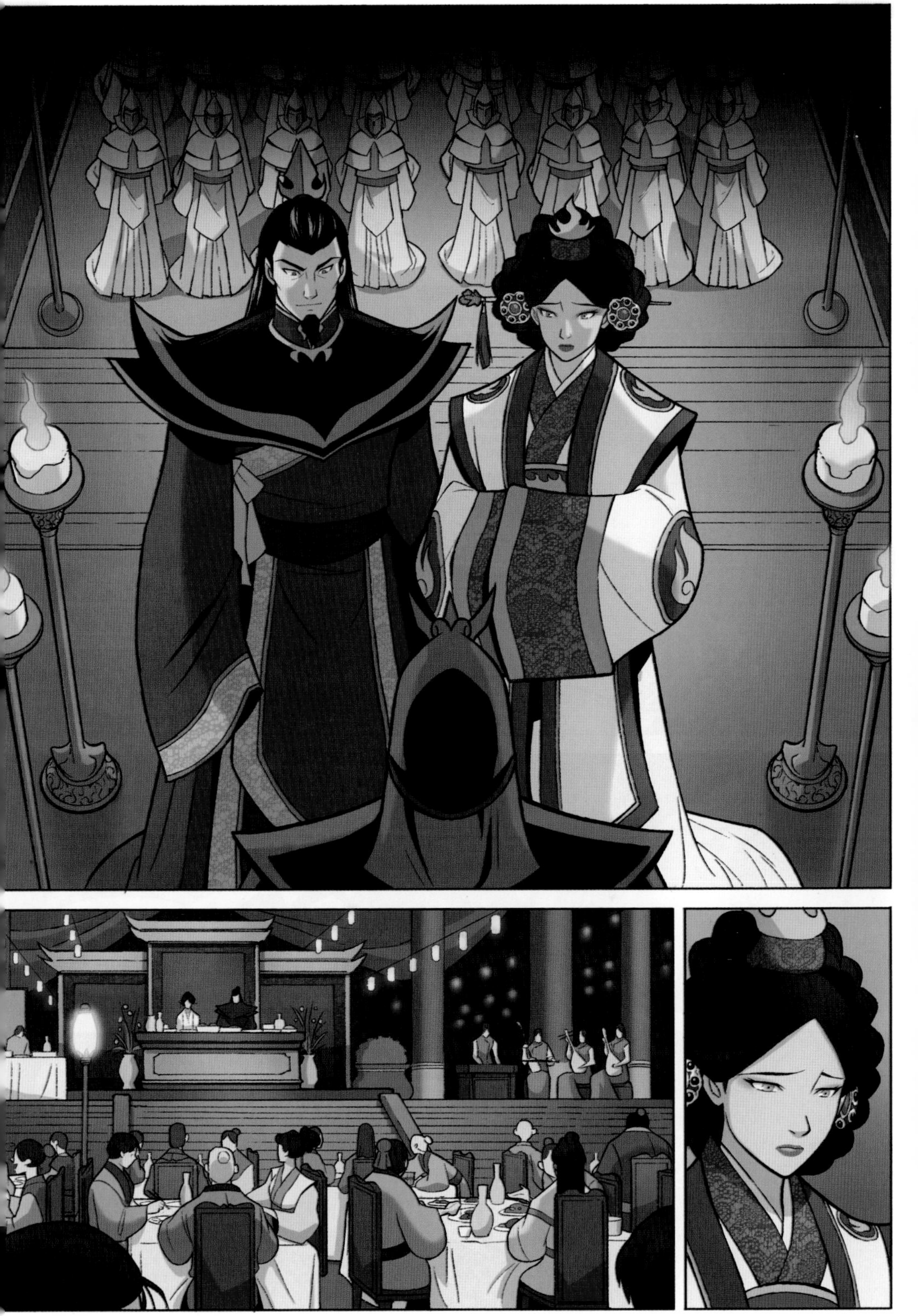

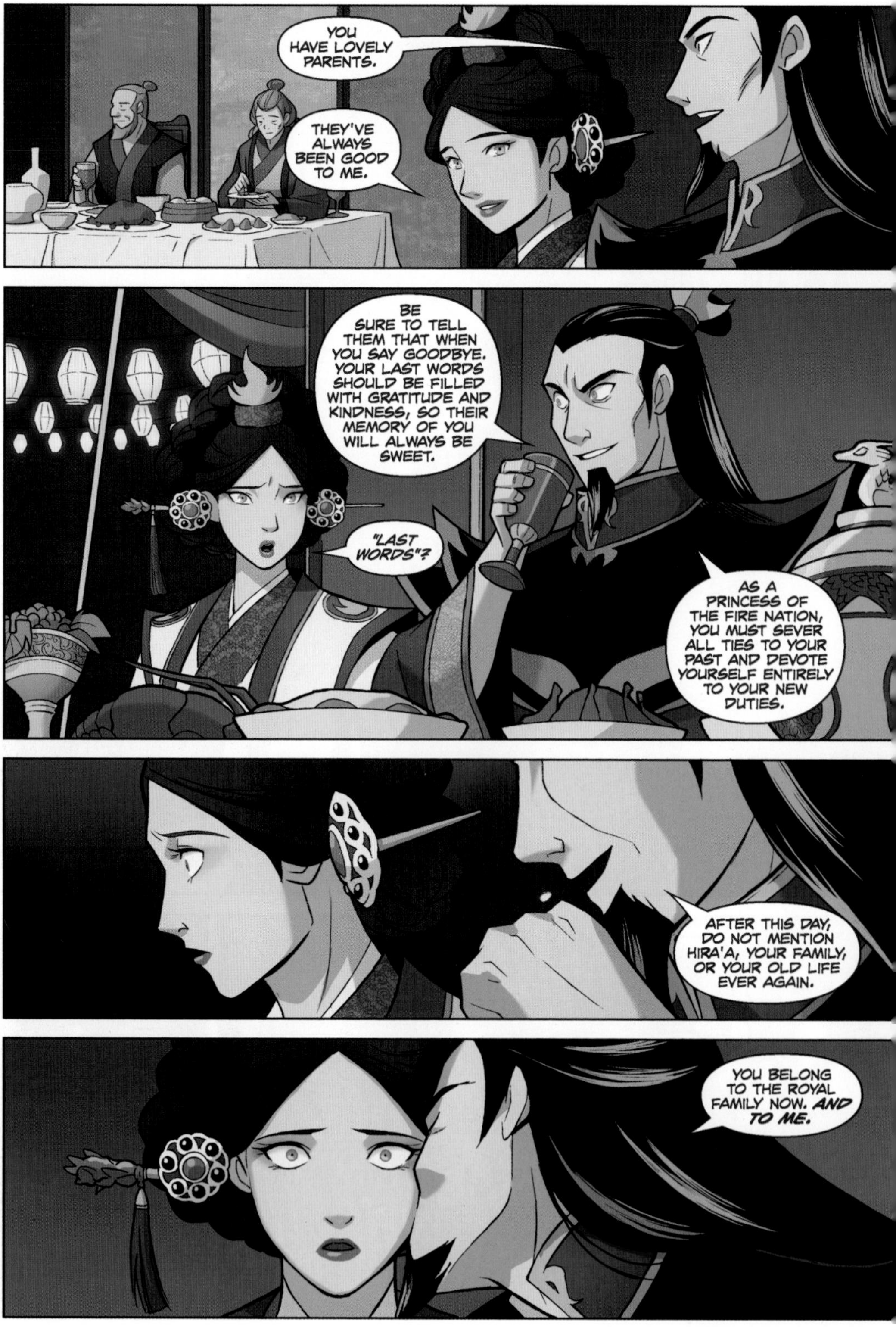
YOU HAVE LOVELY PARENTS.
THEY'VE ALWAYS BEEN GOOD TO ME.
BE SURE TO TELL THEM THAT WHEN YOU SAY GOODBYE. YOUR LAST WORDS SHOULD BE FILLED WITH GRATITUDE AND KINDNESS, SO THEIR MEMORY OF YOU WILL ALWAYS BE SWEET.
"LAST WORDS"?
AS A PRINCESS OF THE FIRE NATION, YOU MUST SEVER ALL TIES TO YOUR PAST AND DEVOTE YOURSELF ENTIRELY TO YOUR NEW DUTIES.
AFTER THIS DAY, DO NOT MENTION HIRA'A, YOUR FAMILY, OR YOUR OLD LIFE EVER AGAIN.
YOU BELONG TO THE ROYAL FAMILY NOW. *AND TO ME.*

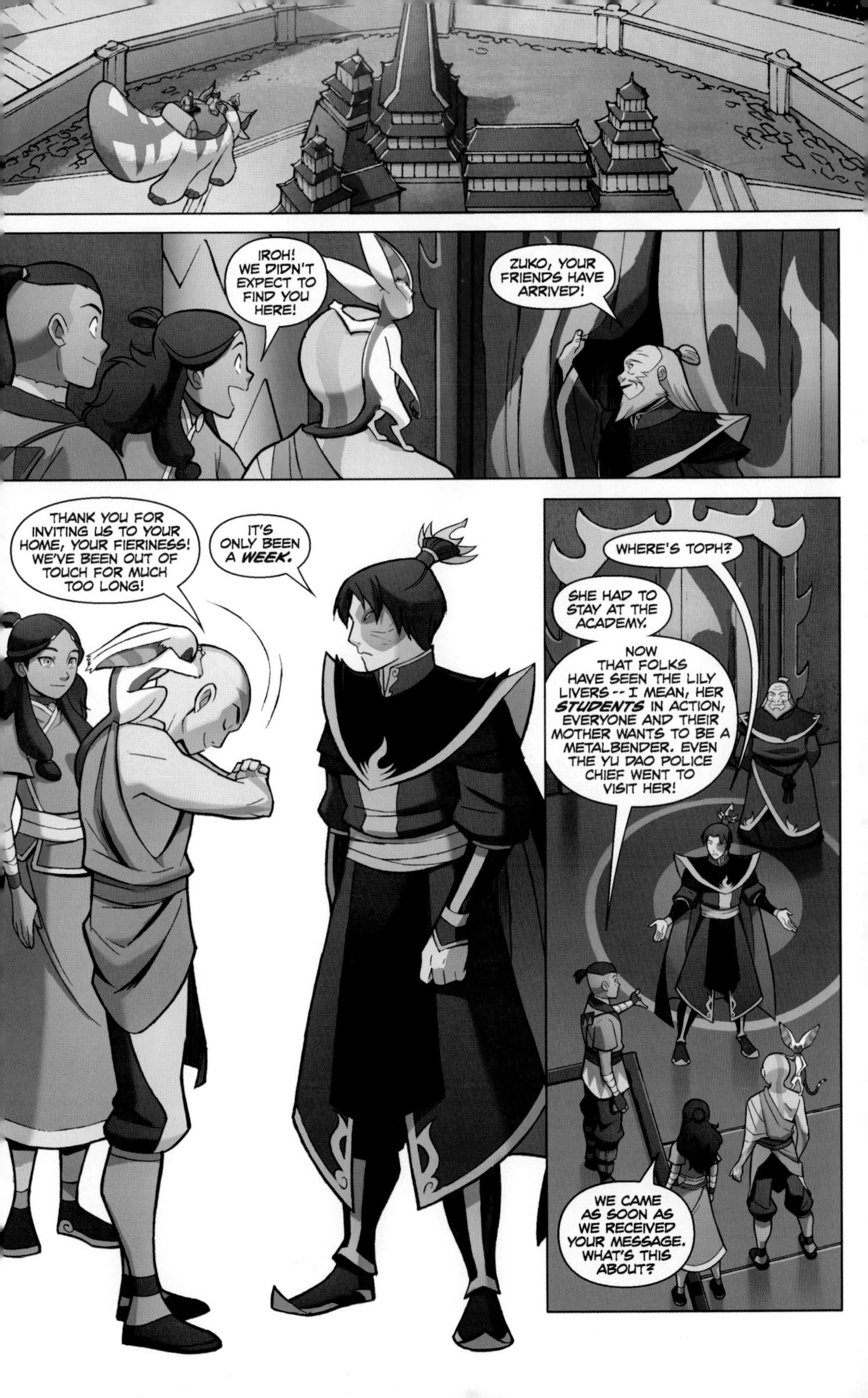
IROH! WE DIDN'T EXPECT TO FIND YOU HERE!
ZUKO, YOUR FRIENDS HAVE ARRIVED!
THANK YOU FOR INVITING US TO YOUR HOME, YOUR FIERINESS! WE'VE BEEN OUT OF TOUCH FOR MUCH TOO LONG!
IT'S ONLY BEEN A WEEK.
WHERE'S TOPH?
SHE HAD TO STAY AT THE ACADEMY.
NOW THAT FOLKS HAVE SEEN THE LILY LIVERS -- I MEAN, HER STUDENTS IN ACTION, EVERYONE AND THEIR MOTHER WANTS TO BE A METALBENDER. EVEN THE YU DAO POLICE CHIEF WENT TO VISIT HER!
WE CAME AS SOON AS WE RECEIVED YOUR MESSAGE. WHAT'S THIS ABOUT?

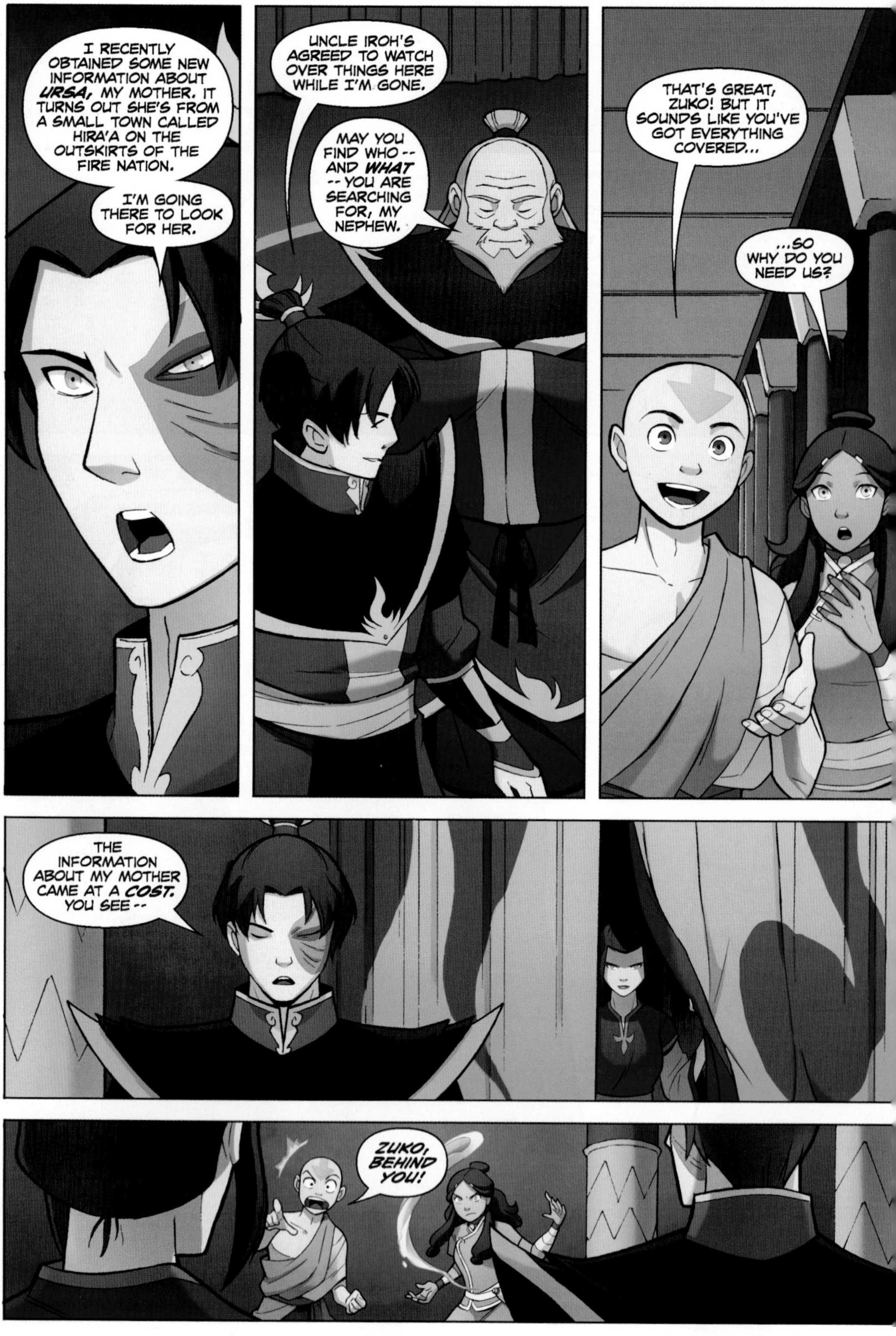
I RECENTLY OBTAINED SOME NEW INFORMATION ABOUT URSA, MY MOTHER. IT TURNS OUT SHE'S FROM A SMALL TOWN CALLED HIRA'A ON THE OUTSKIRTS OF THE FIRE NATION.
I'M GOING THERE TO LOOK FOR HER.
UNCLE IROH'S AGREED TO WATCH OVER THINGS HERE WHILE I'M GONE.
MAY YOU FIND WHO -- AND WHAT -- YOU ARE SEARCHING FOR, MY NEPHEW.
THAT'S GREAT, ZUKO! BUT IT SOUNDS LIKE YOU'VE GOT EVERYTHING COVERED...
...SO WHY DO YOU NEED US?
THE INFORMATION ABOUT MY MOTHER CAME AT A COST. YOU SEE --
ZUKO, BEHIND YOU!

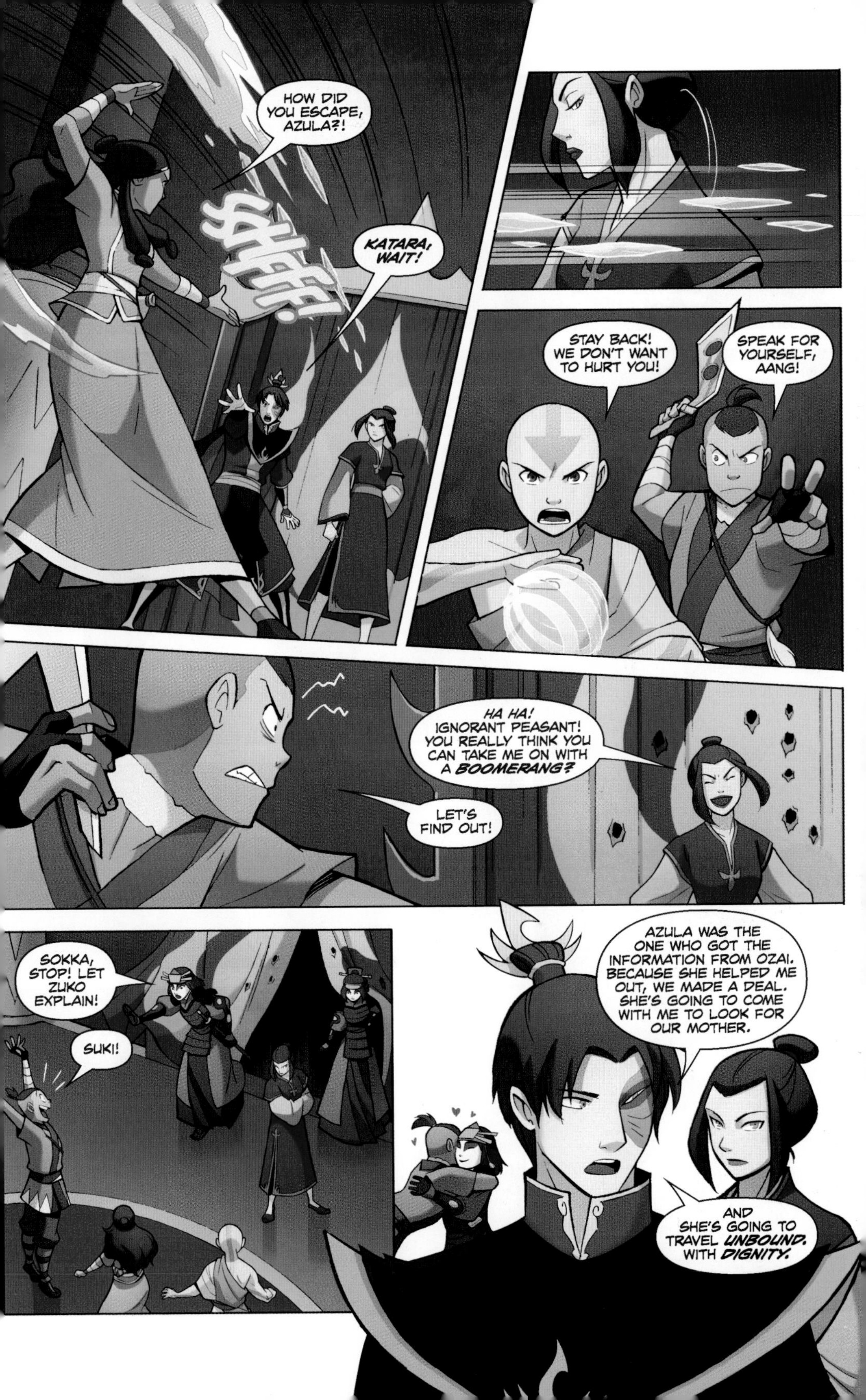
HOW DID YOU ESCAPE, AZULA?!
SHFFF!
KATARA, WAIT!
STAY BACK! WE DON'T WANT TO HURT YOU!
SPEAK FOR YOURSELF, AANG!
HA HA! IGNORANT PEASANT! YOU REALLY THINK YOU CAN TAKE ME ON WITH A BOOMERANG?
LET'S FIND OUT!
SOKKA, STOP! LET ZUKO EXPLAIN!
SUKI!
AZULA WAS THE ONE WHO GOT THE INFORMATION FROM OZAI. BECAUSE SHE HELPED ME OUT, WE MADE A DEAL. SHE'S GOING TO COME WITH ME TO LOOK FOR OUR MOTHER.
AND SHE'S GOING TO TRAVEL UNBOUND. WITH DIGNITY.

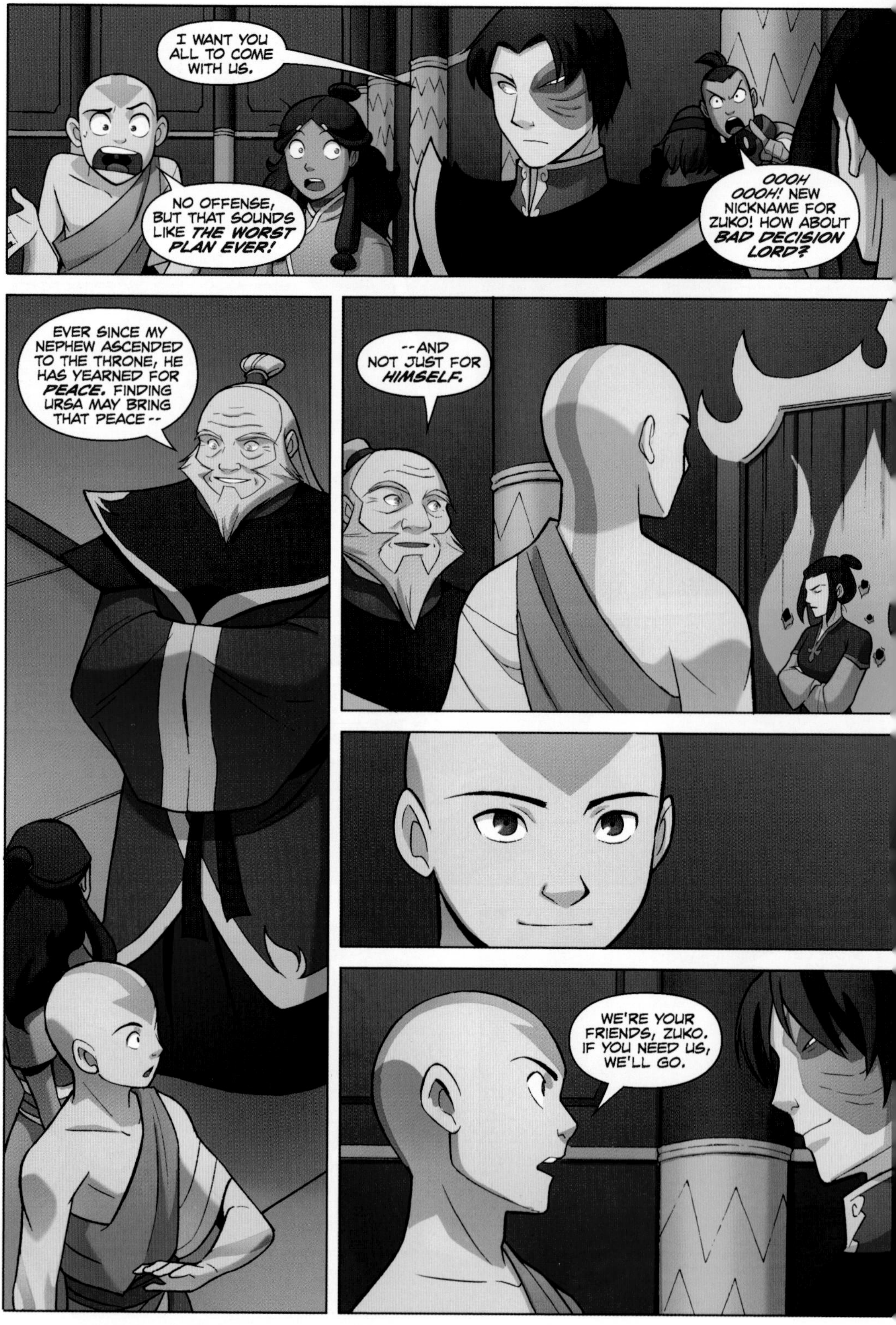
I WANT YOU ALL TO COME WITH US.
NO OFFENSE, BUT THAT SOUNDS LIKE THE WORST PLAN EVER!
OOOH OOOH! NEW NICKNAME FOR ZUKO! HOW ABOUT BAD DECISION LORD?
EVER SINCE MY NEPHEW ASCENDED TO THE THRONE, HE HAS YEARNED FOR PEACE. FINDING URSA MAY BRING THAT PEACE--
--AND NOT JUST FOR HIMSELF.
WE'RE YOUR FRIENDS, ZUKO. IF YOU NEED US, WE'LL GO.

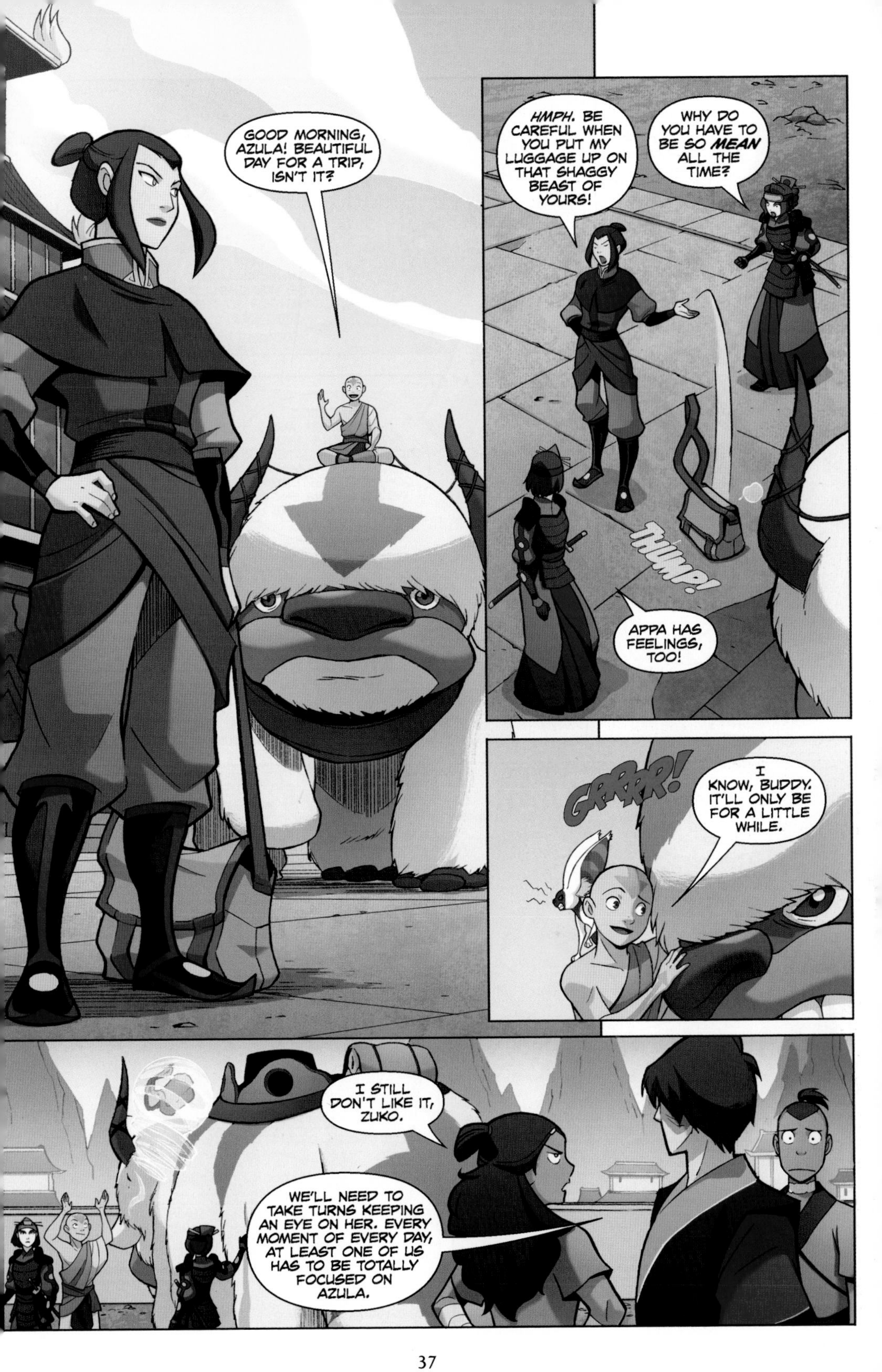
GOOD MORNING, AZULA! BEAUTIFUL DAY FOR A TRIP, ISN'T IT?
HMPH. BE CAREFUL WHEN YOU PUT MY LUGGAGE UP ON THAT SHAGGY BEAST OF YOURS!
WHY DO YOU HAVE TO BE SO MEAN ALL THE TIME?
THUMP!
APPA HAS FEELINGS, TOO!
GRRRR!
I KNOW, BUDDY. IT'LL ONLY BE FOR A LITTLE WHILE.
I STILL DON'T LIKE IT, ZUKO.
WE'LL NEED TO TAKE TURNS KEEPING AN EYE ON HER. EVERY MOMENT OF EVERY DAY, AT LEAST ONE OF US HAS TO BE TOTALLY FOCUSED ON AZULA.

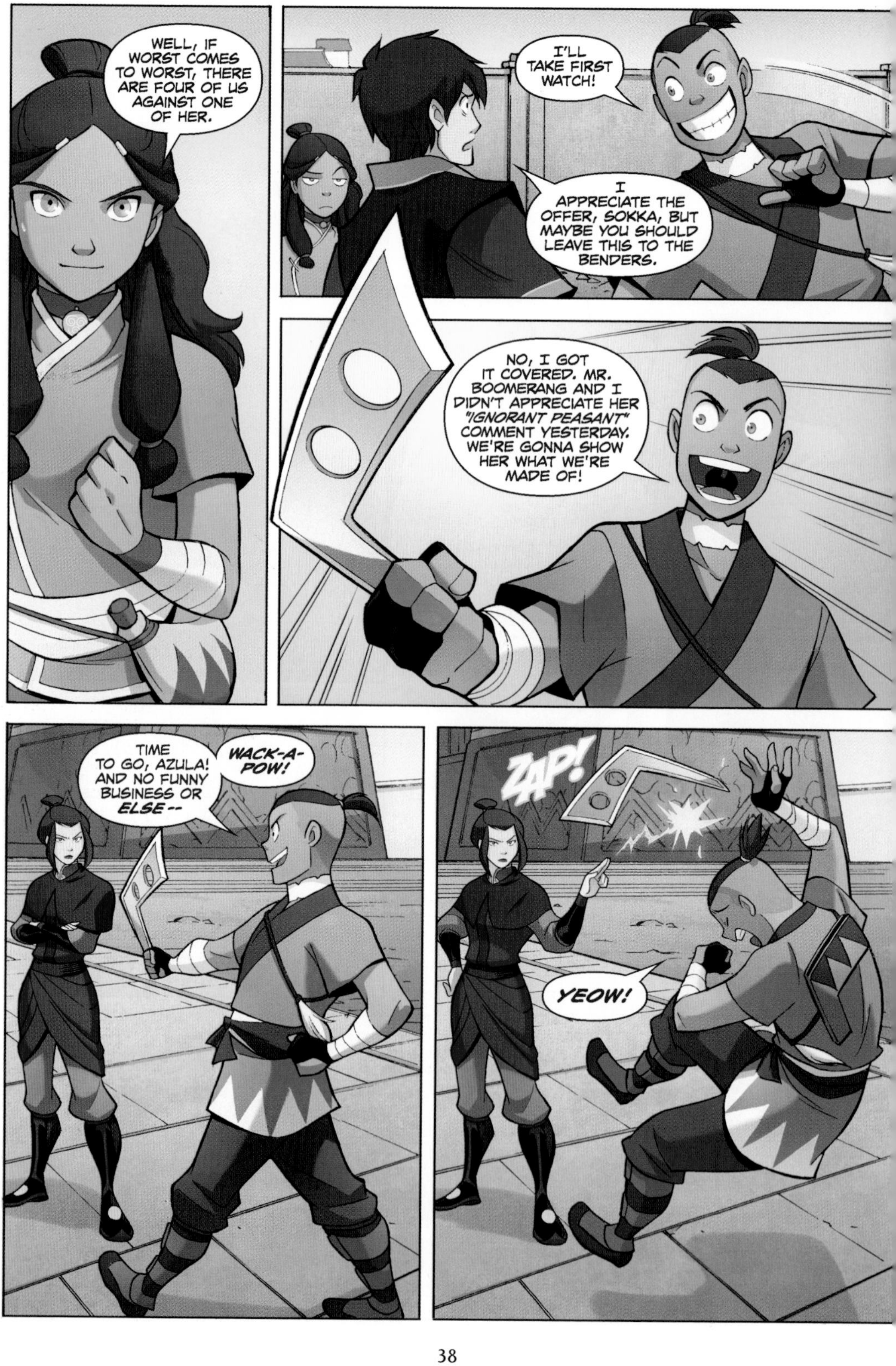
WELL, IF WORST COMES TO WORST, THERE ARE FOUR OF US AGAINST ONE OF HER.
I'LL TAKE FIRST WATCH!
I APPRECIATE THE OFFER, SOKKA, BUT MAYBE YOU SHOULD LEAVE THIS TO THE BENDERS.
NO, I GOT IT COVERED. MR. BOOMERANG AND I DIDN'T APPRECIATE HER *"IGNORANT PEASANT"* COMMENT YESTERDAY. WE'RE GONNA SHOW HER WHAT WE'RE MADE OF!
TIME TO GO, AZULA! AND NO FUNNY BUSINESS OR *ELSE* --
WACK-A-POW!
ZAP!
YEOW!

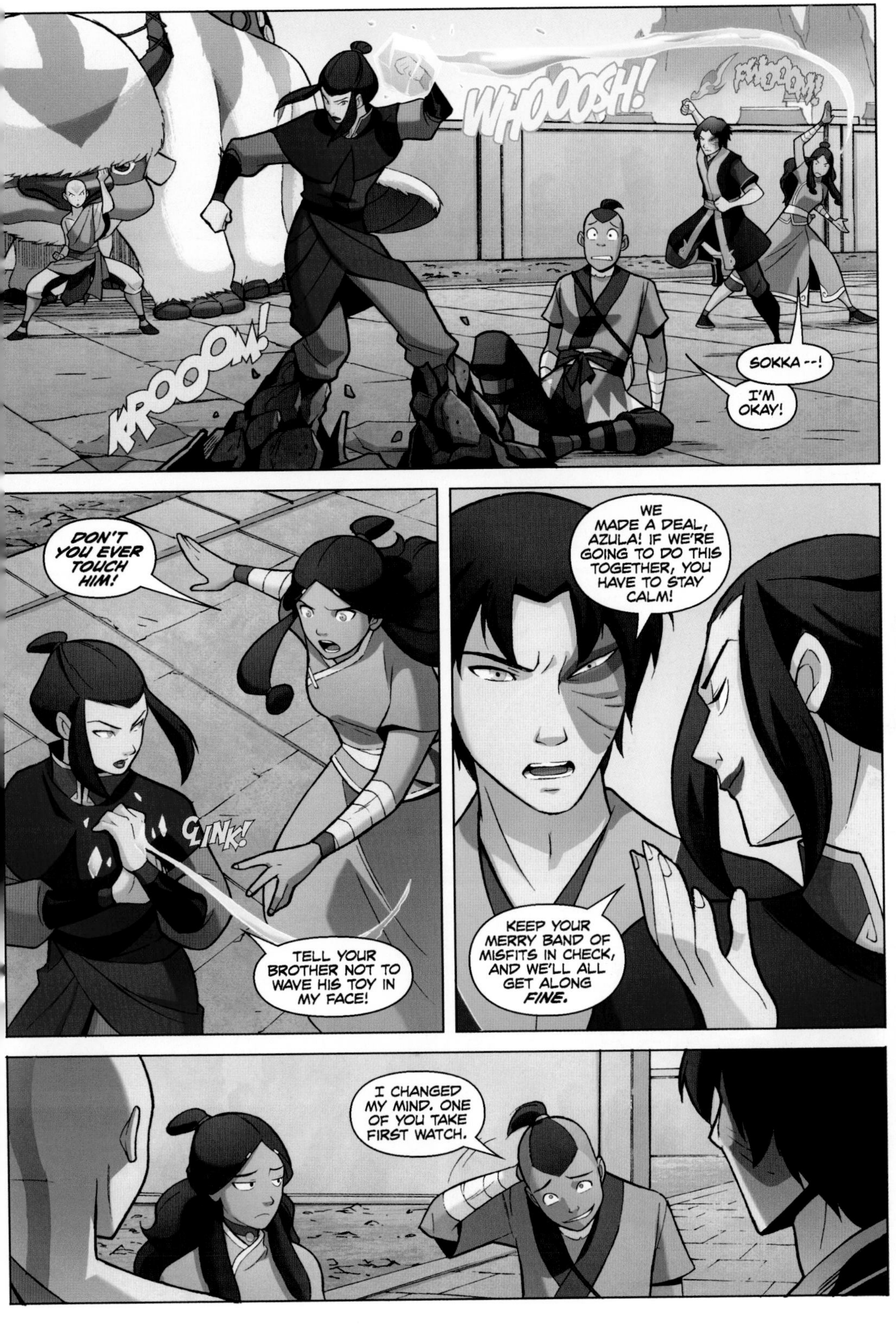
WHOOOSH!
FWOOM!
KROOOM!
SOKKA--!
I'M OKAY!
DON'T YOU EVER TOUCH HIM!
CLINK!
TELL YOUR BROTHER NOT TO WAVE HIS TOY IN MY FACE!
WE MADE A DEAL, AZULA! IF WE'RE GOING TO DO THIS TOGETHER, YOU HAVE TO STAY CALM!
KEEP YOUR MERRY BAND OF MISFITS IN CHECK, AND WE'LL ALL GET ALONG *FINE.*
I CHANGED MY MIND. ONE OF YOU TAKE FIRST WATCH.

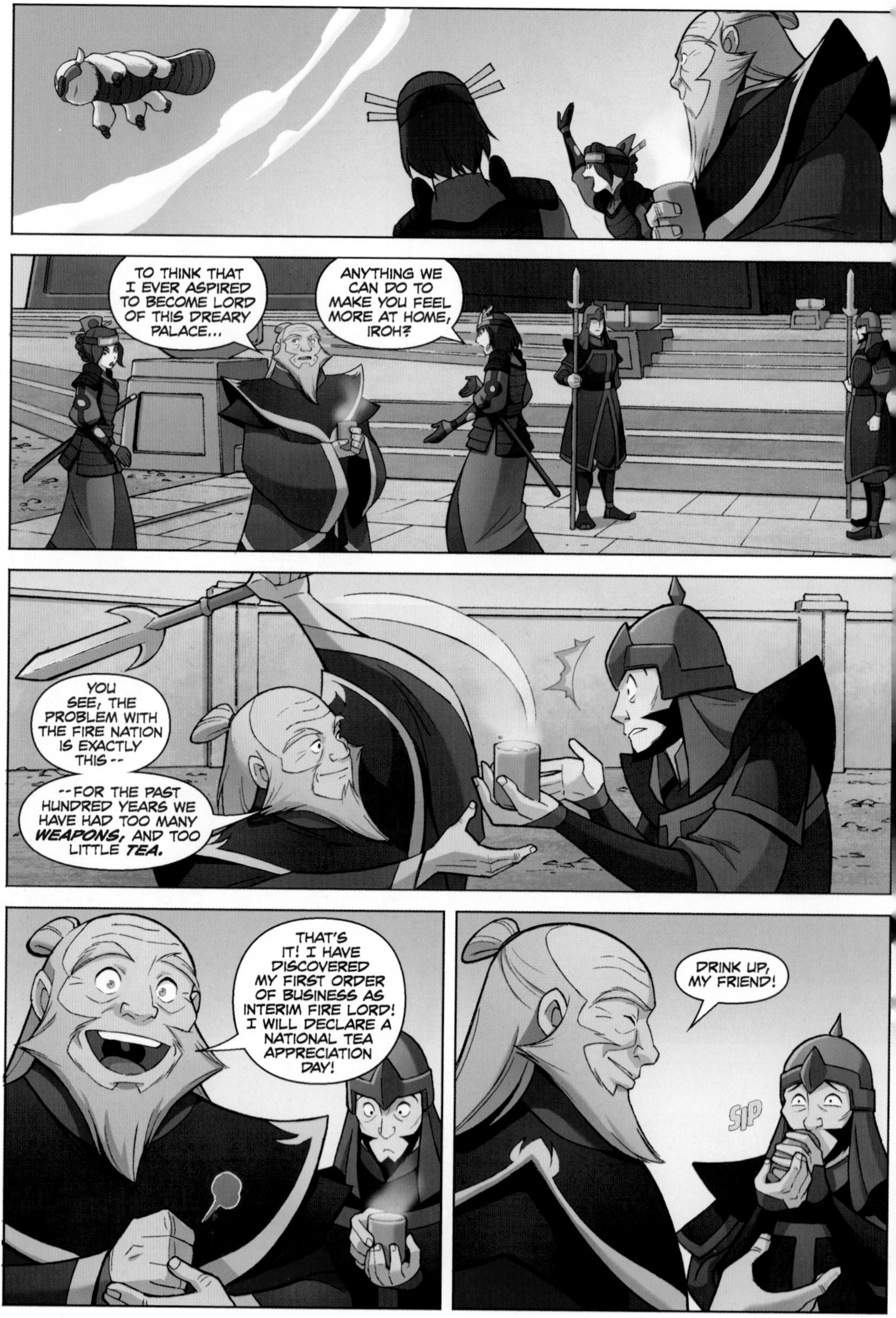
TO THINK THAT I EVER ASPIRED TO BECOME LORD OF THIS DREARY PALACE...
ANYTHING WE CAN DO TO MAKE YOU FEEL MORE AT HOME, IROH?
YOU SEE, THE PROBLEM WITH THE FIRE NATION IS EXACTLY THIS--
--FOR THE PAST HUNDRED YEARS WE HAVE HAD TOO MANY *WEAPONS,* AND TOO LITTLE *TEA.*
THAT'S IT! I HAVE DISCOVERED MY FIRST ORDER OF BUSINESS AS INTERIM FIRE LORD! I WILL DECLARE A NATIONAL TEA APPRECIATION DAY!
DRINK UP, MY FRIEND!
SIP

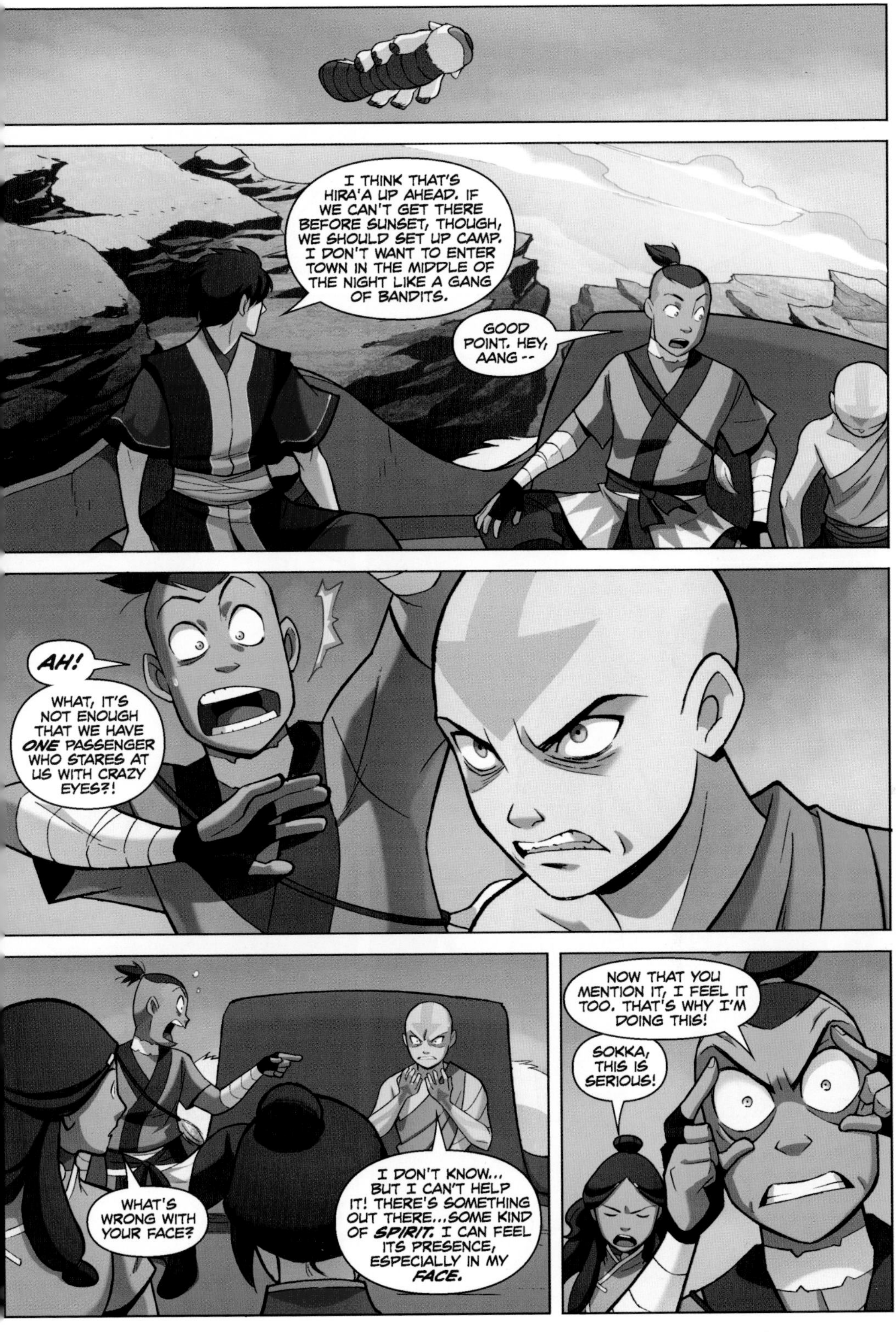
I THINK THAT'S HIRA'A UP AHEAD. IF WE CAN'T GET THERE BEFORE SUNSET, THOUGH, WE SHOULD SET UP CAMP. I DON'T WANT TO ENTER TOWN IN THE MIDDLE OF THE NIGHT LIKE A GANG OF BANDITS.
GOOD POINT. HEY, AANG --
AH!
WHAT, IT'S NOT ENOUGH THAT WE HAVE ONE PASSENGER WHO STARES AT US WITH CRAZY EYES?!
WHAT'S WRONG WITH YOUR FACE?
I DON'T KNOW... BUT I CAN'T HELP IT! THERE'S SOMETHING OUT THERE...SOME KIND OF SPIRIT. I CAN FEEL ITS PRESENCE, ESPECIALLY IN MY FACE.
NOW THAT YOU MENTION IT, I FEEL IT TOO. THAT'S WHY I'M DOING THIS!
SOKKA, THIS IS SERIOUS!

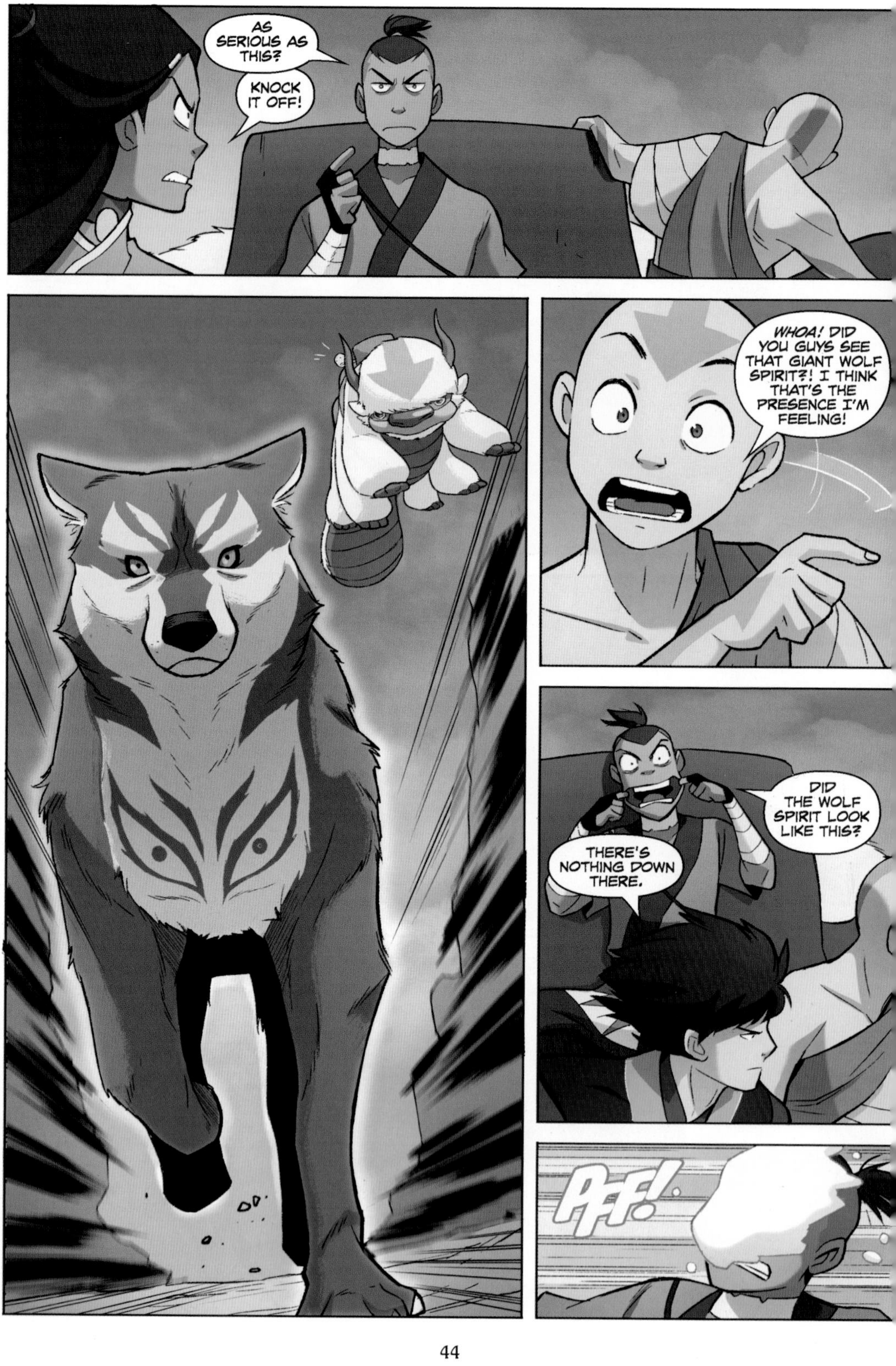
AS SERIOUS AS THIS?
KNOCK IT OFF!
WHOA! DID YOU GUYS SEE THAT GIANT WOLF SPIRIT?! I THINK THAT'S THE PRESENCE I'M FEELING!
DID THE WOLF SPIRIT LOOK LIKE THIS?
THERE'S NOTHING DOWN THERE.
PFF!

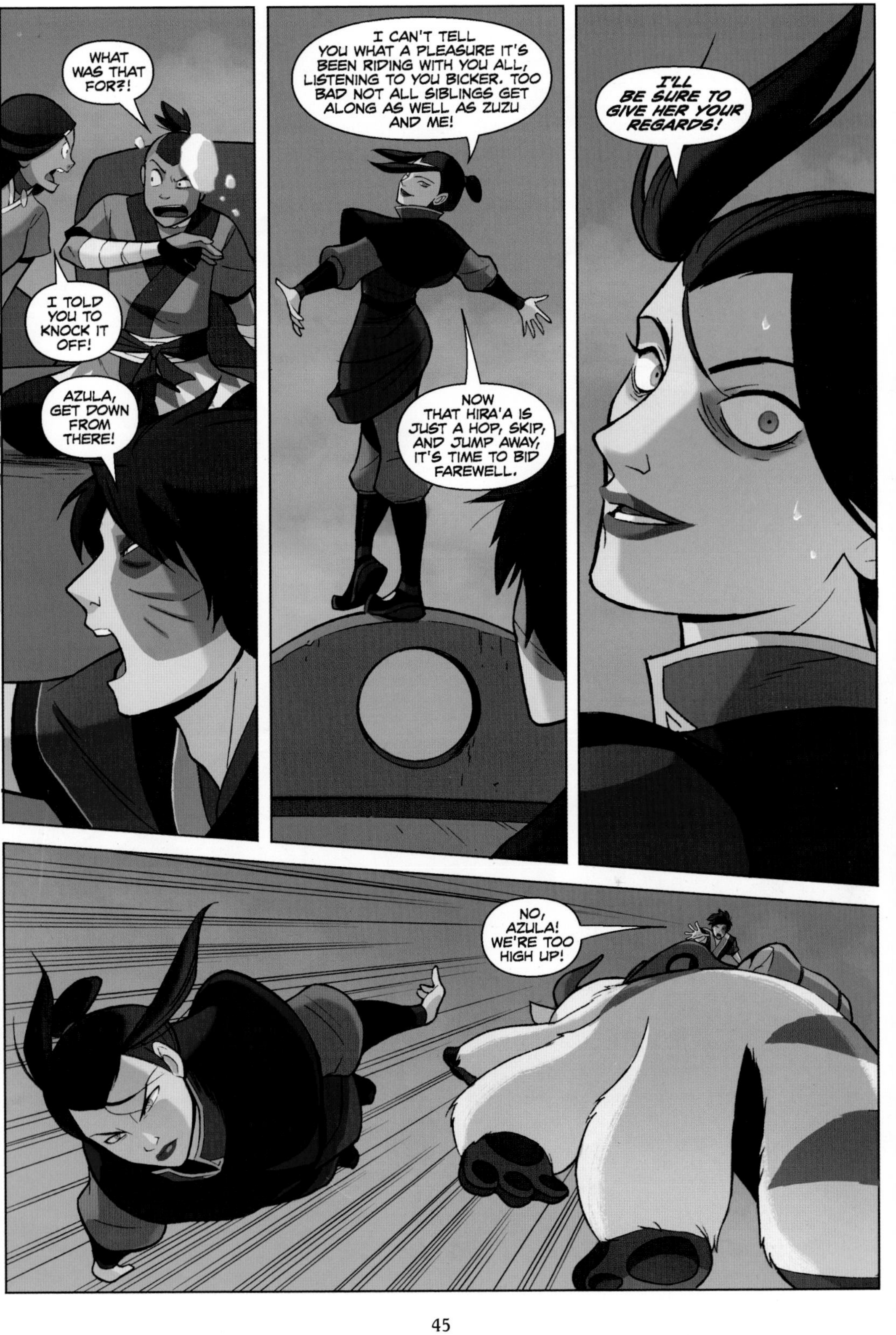
WHAT WAS THAT FOR?!
I TOLD YOU TO KNOCK IT OFF!
AZULA, GET DOWN FROM THERE!
I CAN'T TELL YOU WHAT A PLEASURE IT'S BEEN RIDING WITH YOU ALL, LISTENING TO YOU BICKER. TOO BAD NOT ALL SIBLINGS GET ALONG AS WELL AS ZUZU AND ME!
NOW THAT HIRA'A IS JUST A HOP, SKIP, AND JUMP AWAY, IT'S TIME TO BID FAREWELL.
I'LL BE SURE TO GIVE HER YOUR REGARDS!
NO, AZULA! WE'RE TOO HIGH UP!

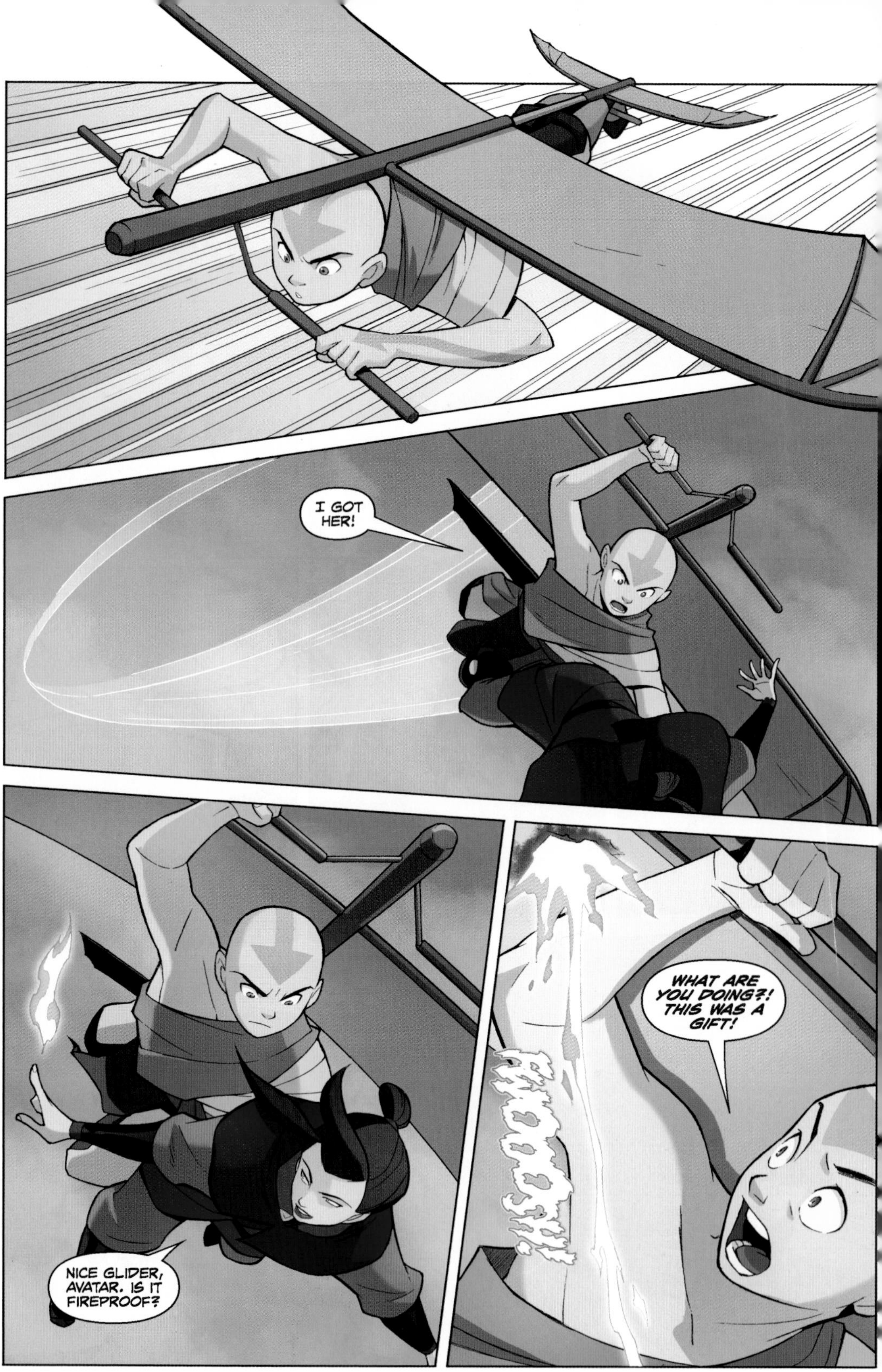
I GOT HER!
NICE GLIDER, AVATAR. IS IT FIREPROOF?
FWOOSH!
WHAT ARE YOU DOING?! THIS WAS A GIFT!

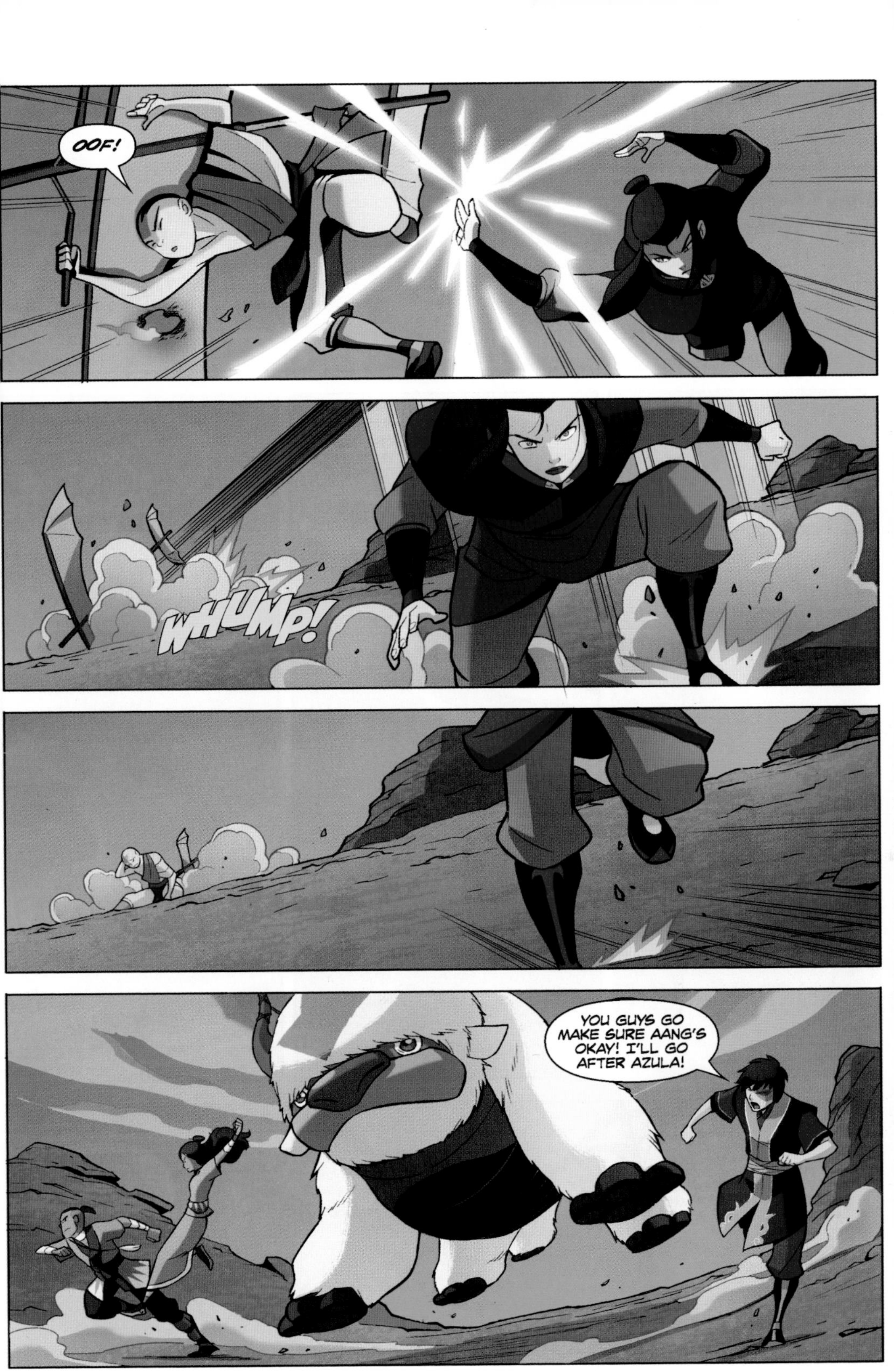
OOF!
WHUMP!
YOU GUYS GO MAKE SURE AANG'S OKAY! I'LL GO AFTER AZULA!

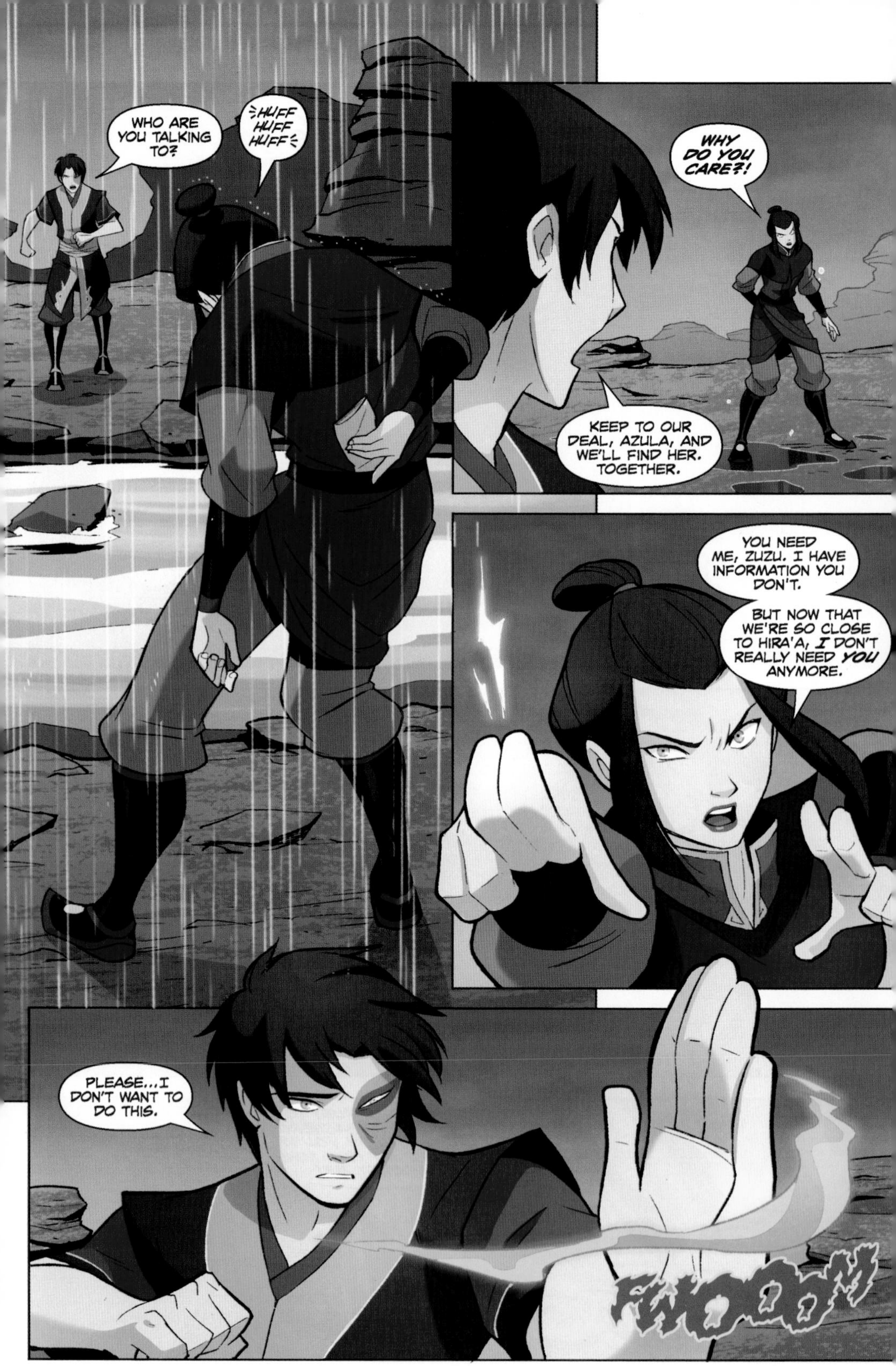
WHO ARE YOU TALKING TO?
HUFF HUFF HUFF
WHY DO YOU CARE?!
KEEP TO OUR DEAL, AZULA, AND WE'LL FIND HER. TOGETHER.
YOU NEED ME, ZUZU. I HAVE INFORMATION YOU DON'T.
BUT NOW THAT WE'RE SO CLOSE TO HIRA'A, I DON'T REALLY NEED YOU ANYMORE.
PLEASE...I DON'T WANT TO DO THIS.
FWOOOM

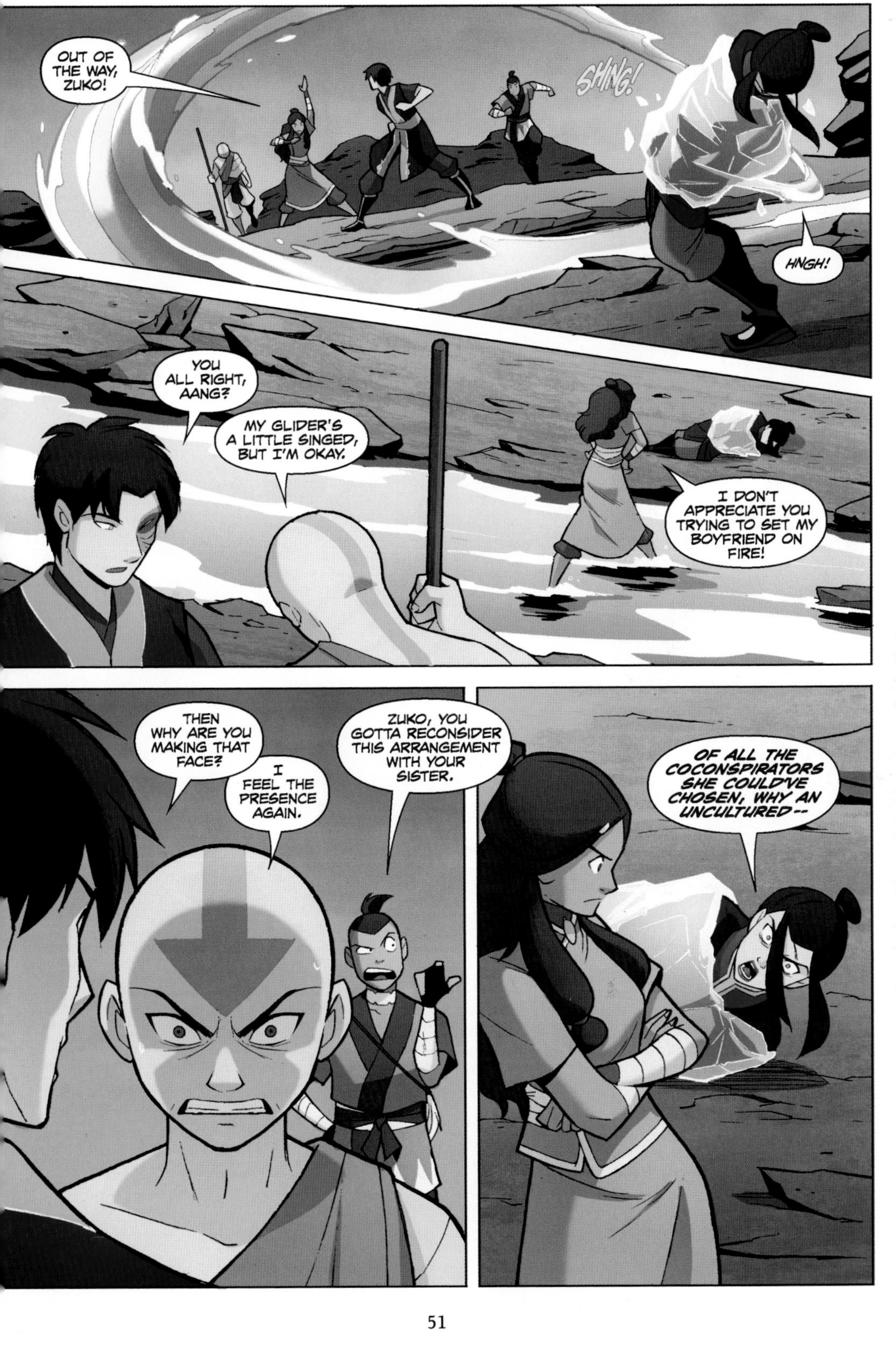
OUT OF THE WAY, ZUKO!
SHING!
HNGH!
YOU ALL RIGHT, AANG?
MY GLIDER'S A LITTLE SINGED, BUT I'M OKAY.
I DON'T APPRECIATE YOU TRYING TO SET MY BOYFRIEND ON FIRE!
THEN WHY ARE YOU MAKING THAT FACE?
I FEEL THE PRESENCE AGAIN.
ZUKO, YOU GOTTA RECONSIDER THIS ARRANGEMENT WITH YOUR SISTER.
OF ALL THE COCONSPIRATORS SHE COULD'VE CHOSEN, WHY AN UNCULTURED--

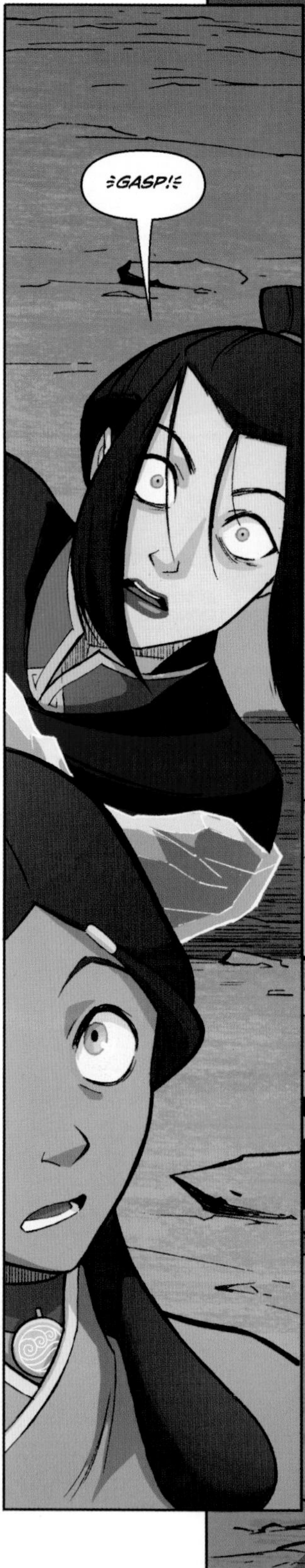
GASP!

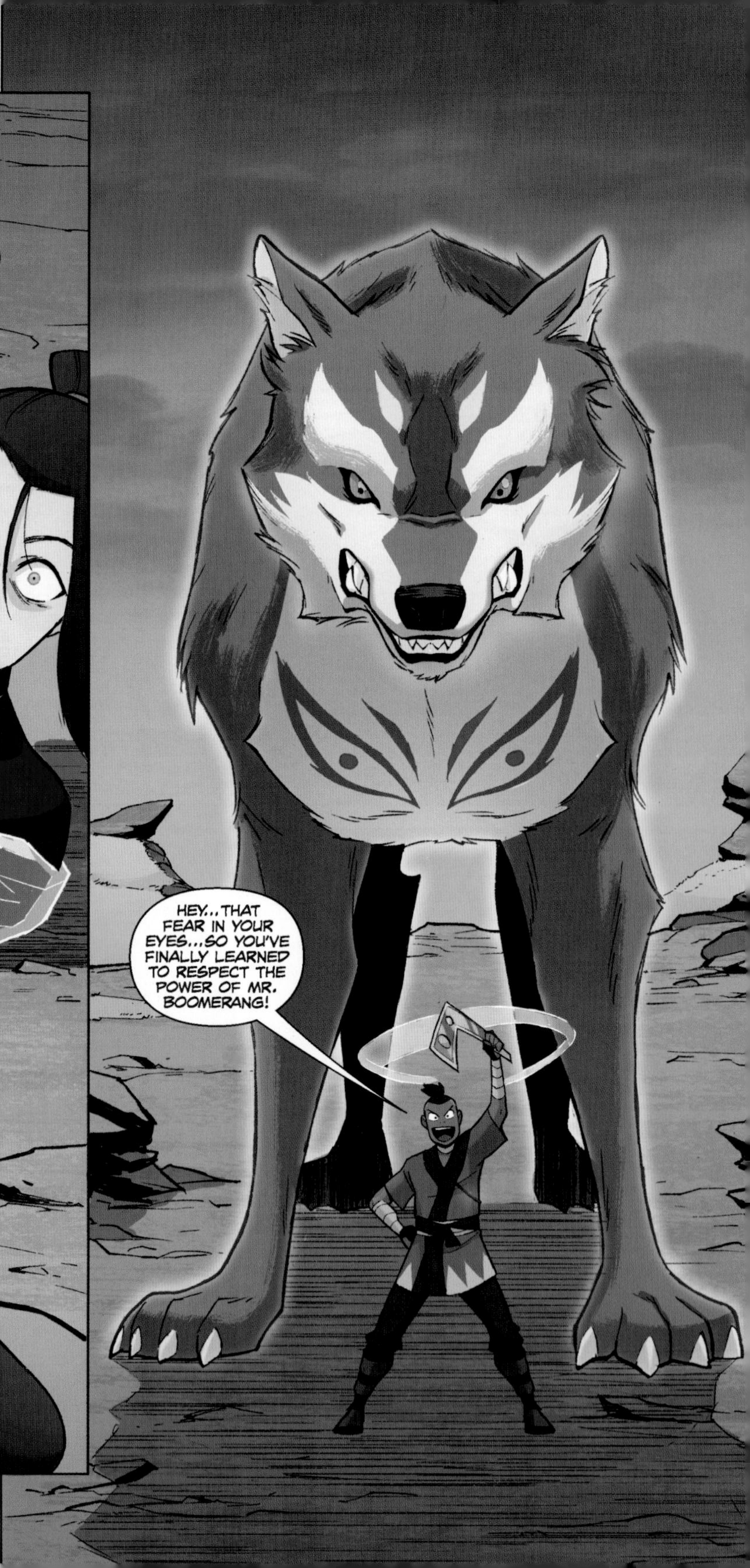
HEY... THAT FEAR IN YOUR EYES... SO YOU'VE FINALLY LEARNED TO RESPECT THE POWER OF MR. BOOMERANG!

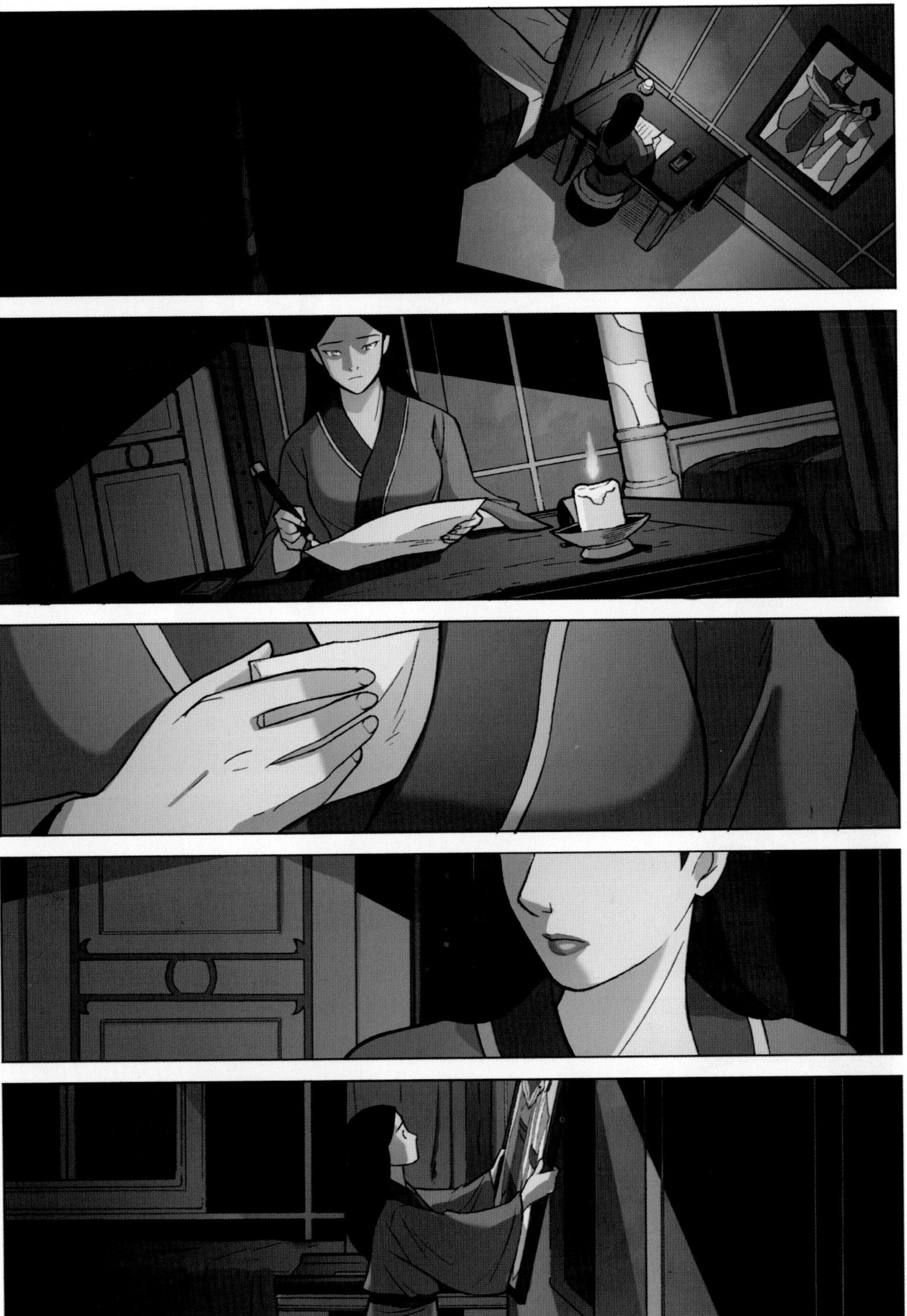

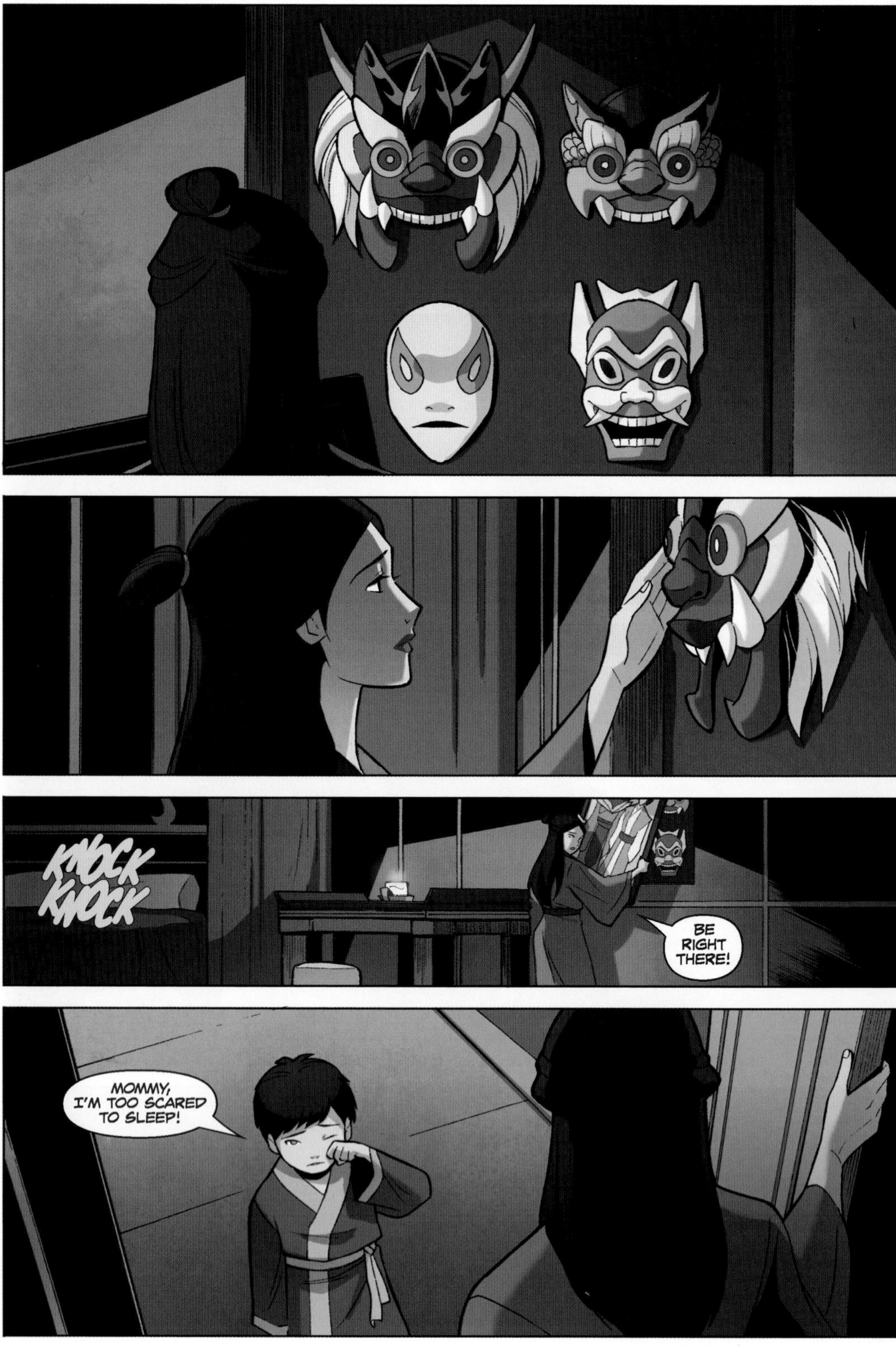
KNOCK KNOCK
BE RIGHT THERE!
MOMMY, I'M TOO SCARED TO SLEEP!

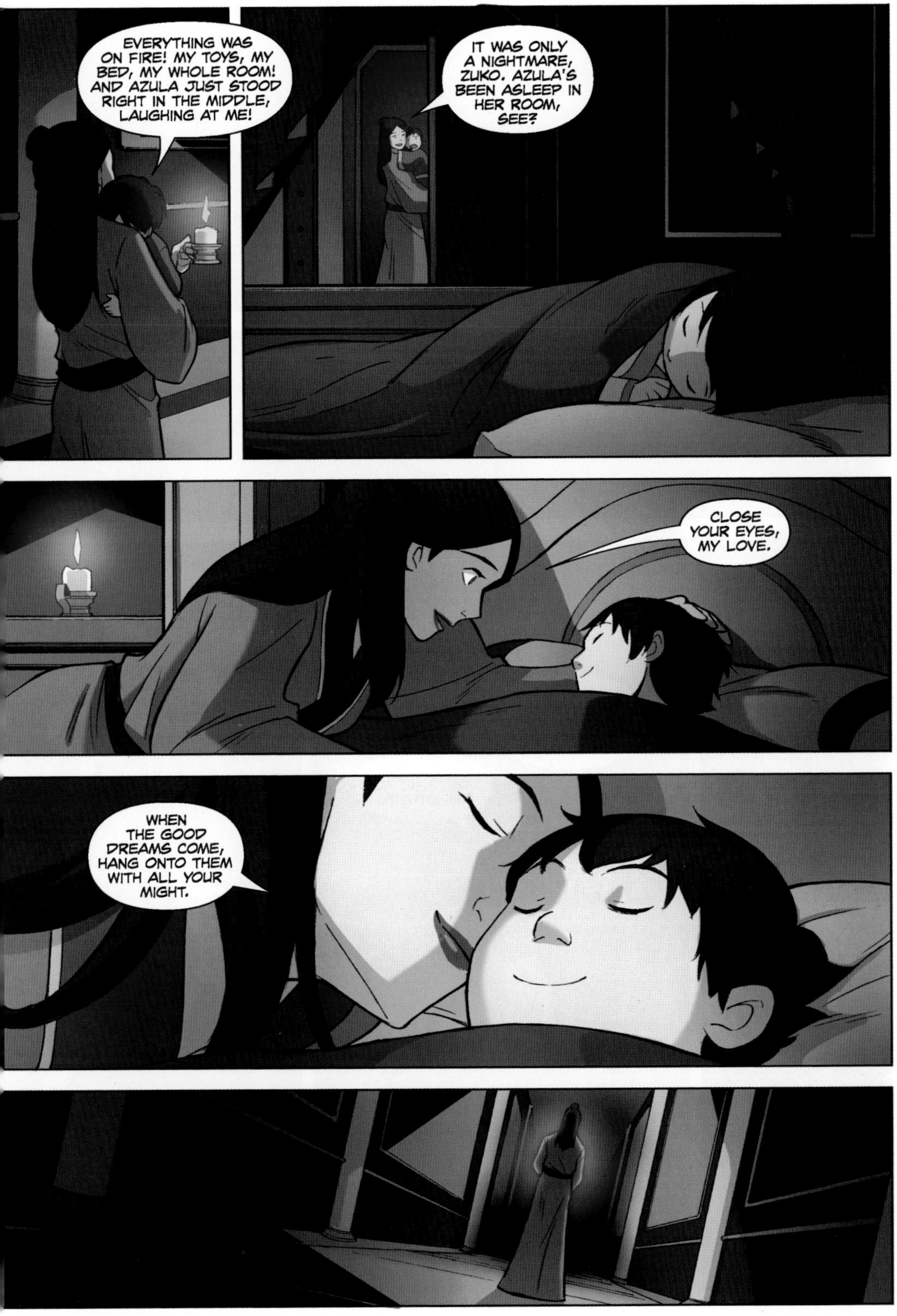
EVERYTHING WAS ON FIRE! MY TOYS, MY BED, MY WHOLE ROOM! AND AZULA JUST STOOD RIGHT IN THE MIDDLE, LAUGHING AT ME!
IT WAS ONLY A NIGHTMARE, ZUKO. AZULA'S BEEN ASLEEP IN HER ROOM, SEE?
CLOSE YOUR EYES, MY LOVE.
WHEN THE GOOD DREAMS COME, HANG ONTO THEM WITH ALL YOUR MIGHT.

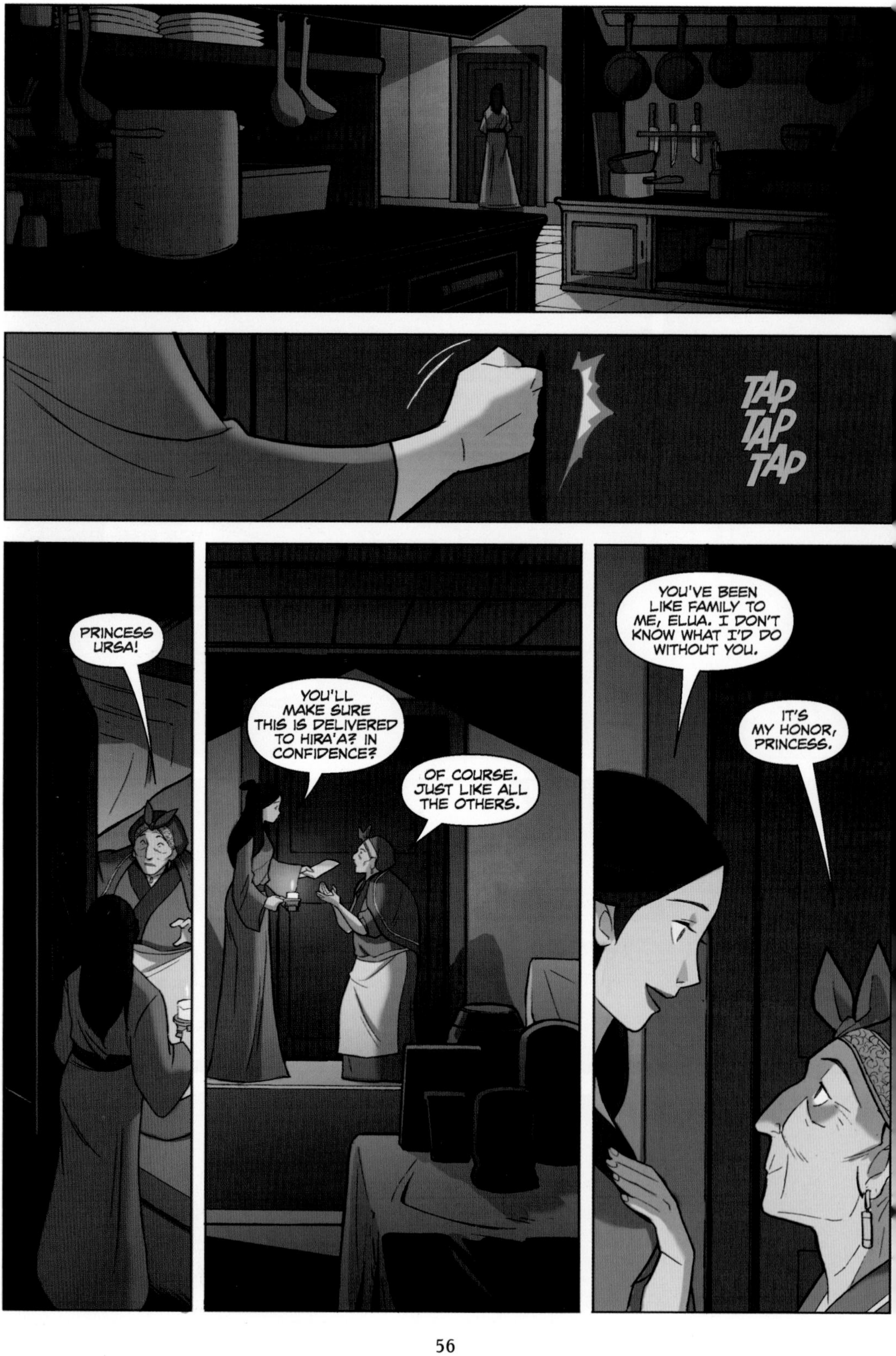
TAP TAP TAP
PRINCESS URSA!
YOU'LL MAKE SURE THIS IS DELIVERED TO HIRA'A? IN CONFIDENCE?
OF COURSE. JUST LIKE ALL THE OTHERS.
YOU'VE BEEN LIKE FAMILY TO ME, ELUA. I DON'T KNOW WHAT I'D DO WITHOUT YOU.
IT'S MY HONOR, PRINCESS.

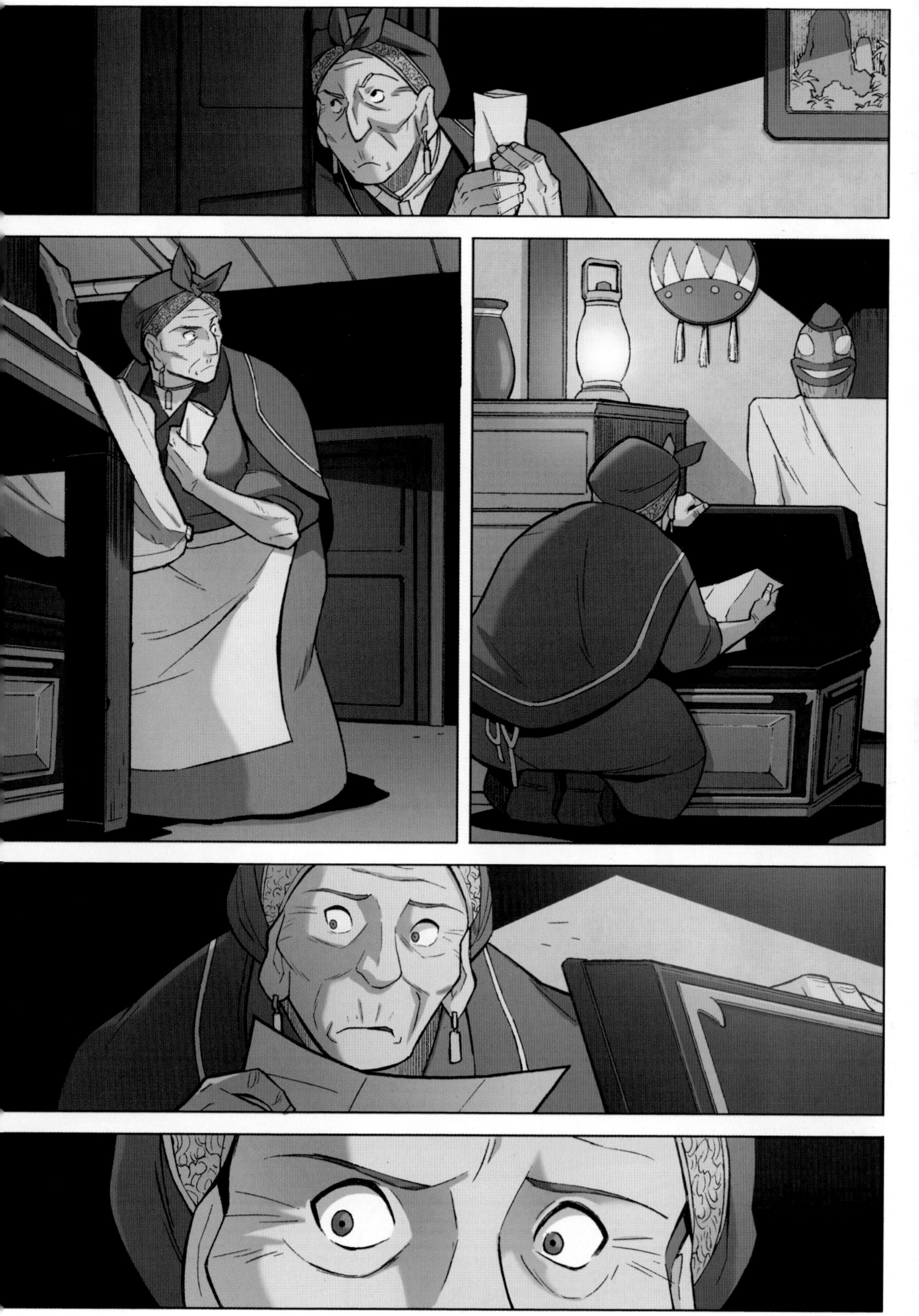

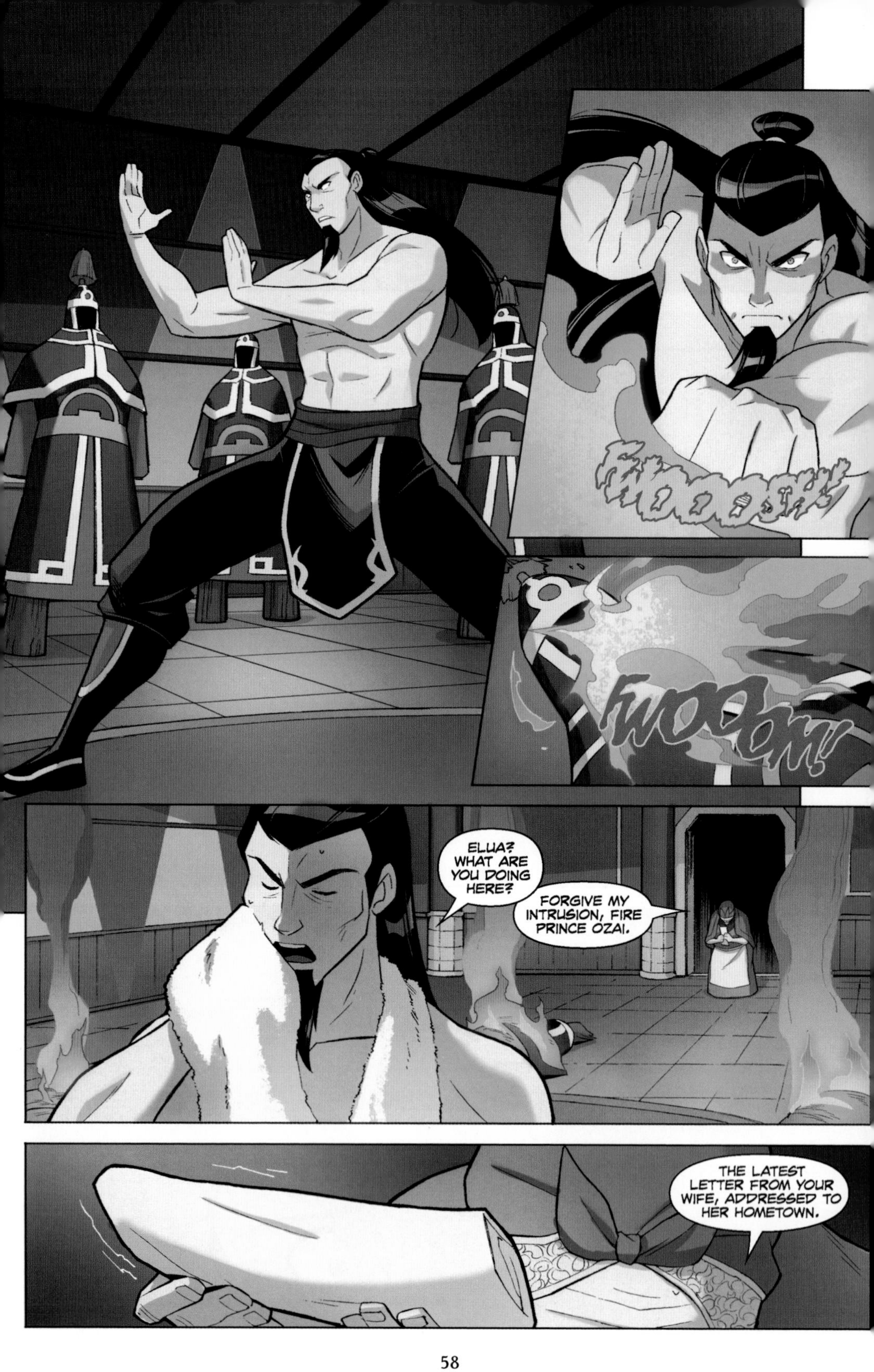
FWOOOSH!
FWOOOM!
ELUA? WHAT ARE YOU DOING HERE?
FORGIVE MY INTRUSION, FIRE PRINCE OZAI.
THE LATEST LETTER FROM YOUR WIFE, ADDRESSED TO HER HOMETOWN.

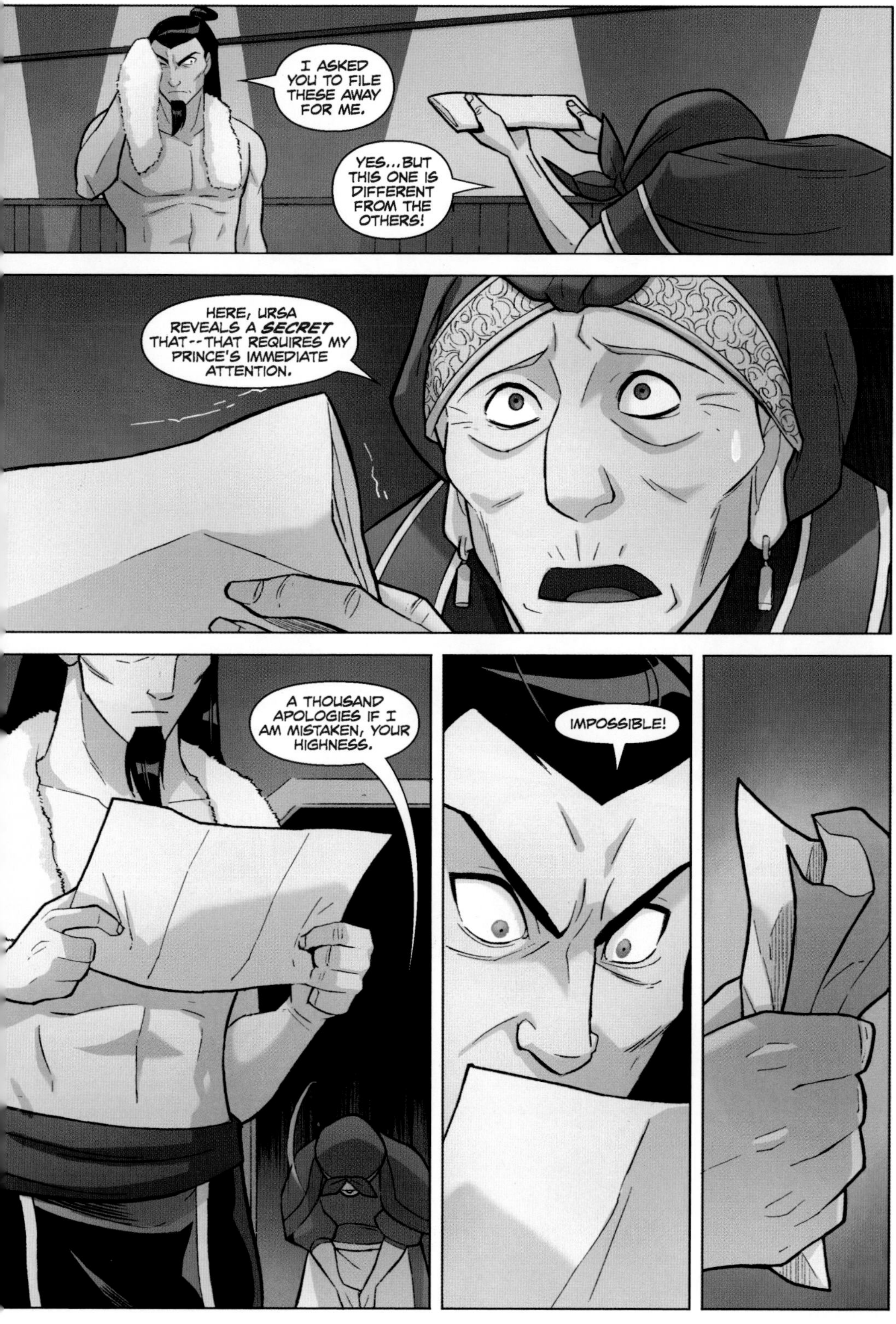
I ASKED YOU TO FILE THESE AWAY FOR ME.
YES...BUT THIS ONE IS DIFFERENT FROM THE OTHERS!
HERE, URSA REVEALS A *SECRET* THAT--THAT REQUIRES MY PRINCE'S IMMEDIATE ATTENTION.
A THOUSAND APOLOGIES IF I AM MISTAKEN, YOUR HIGHNESS.
IMPOSSIBLE!

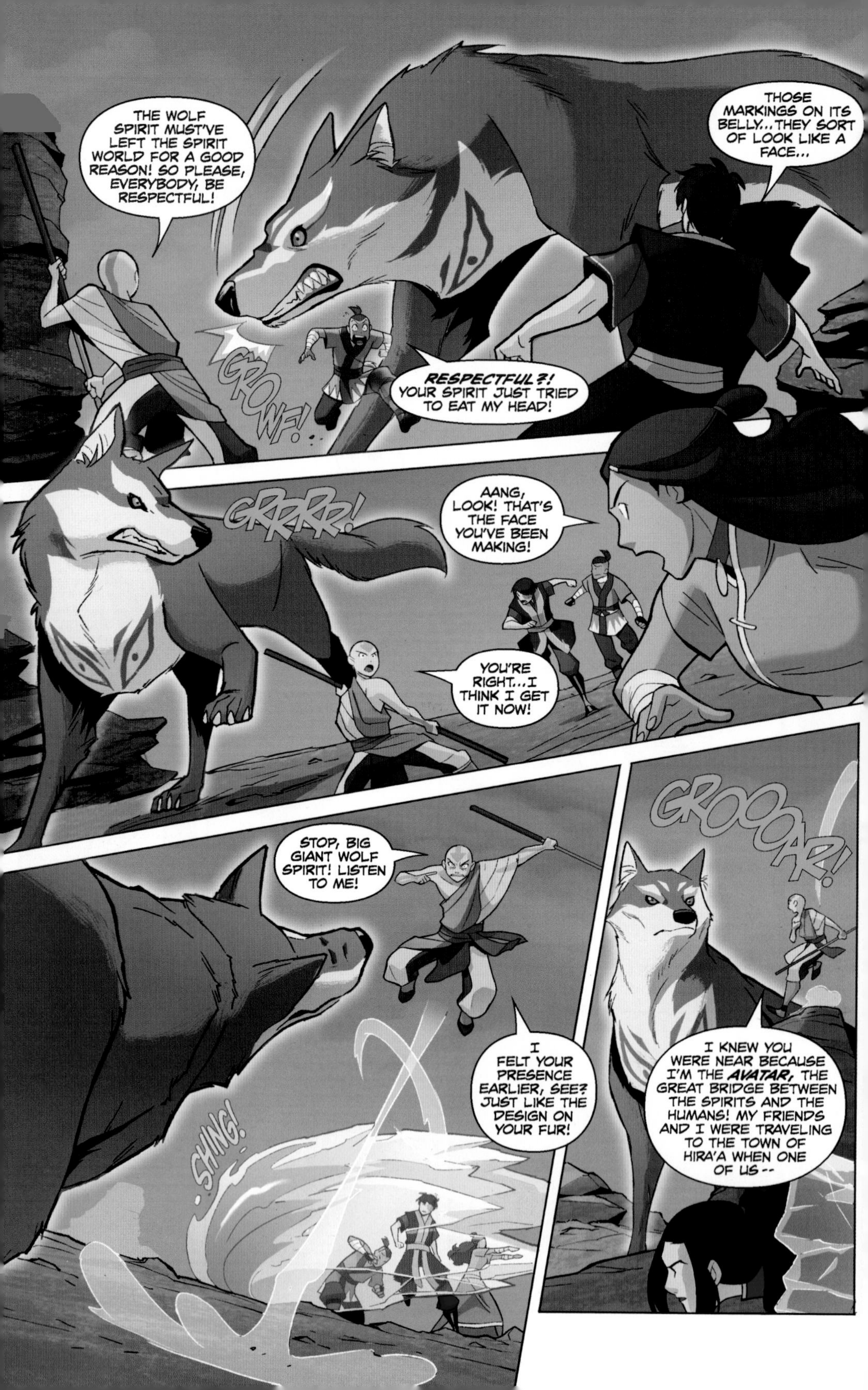
THE WOLF SPIRIT MUST'VE LEFT THE SPIRIT WORLD FOR A GOOD REASON! SO PLEASE, EVERYBODY, BE RESPECTFUL!
THOSE MARKINGS ON ITS BELLY...THEY SORT OF LOOK LIKE A FACE...
GROWF!
RESPECTFUL?! YOUR SPIRIT JUST TRIED TO EAT MY HEAD!
GRRRR!
AANG, LOOK! THAT'S THE FACE YOU'VE BEEN MAKING!
YOU'RE RIGHT...I THINK I GET IT NOW!
STOP, BIG GIANT WOLF SPIRIT! LISTEN TO ME!
SHING!
I FELT YOUR PRESENCE EARLIER, SEE? JUST LIKE THE DESIGN ON YOUR FUR!
GROOOAR!
I KNEW YOU WERE NEAR BECAUSE I'M THE AVATAR, THE GREAT BRIDGE BETWEEN THE SPIRITS AND THE HUMANS! MY FRIENDS AND I WERE TRAVELING TO THE TOWN OF HIRA'A WHEN ONE OF US--

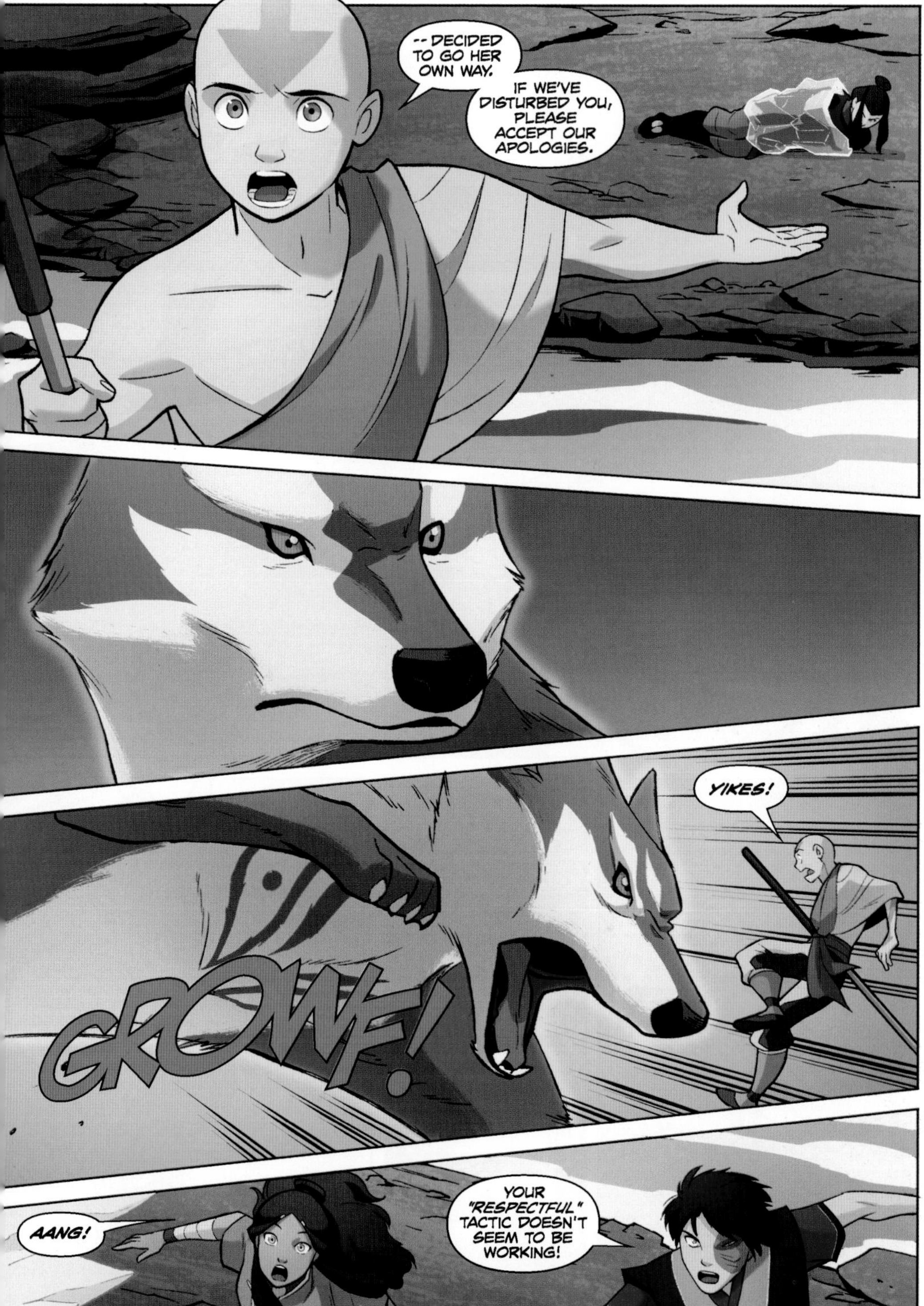

-- DECIDED TO GO HER OWN WAY.
IF WE'VE DISTURBED YOU, PLEASE ACCEPT OUR APOLOGIES.
YIKES!
GROWF!
AANG!
YOUR "RESPECTFUL" TACTIC DOESN'T SEEM TO BE WORKING!

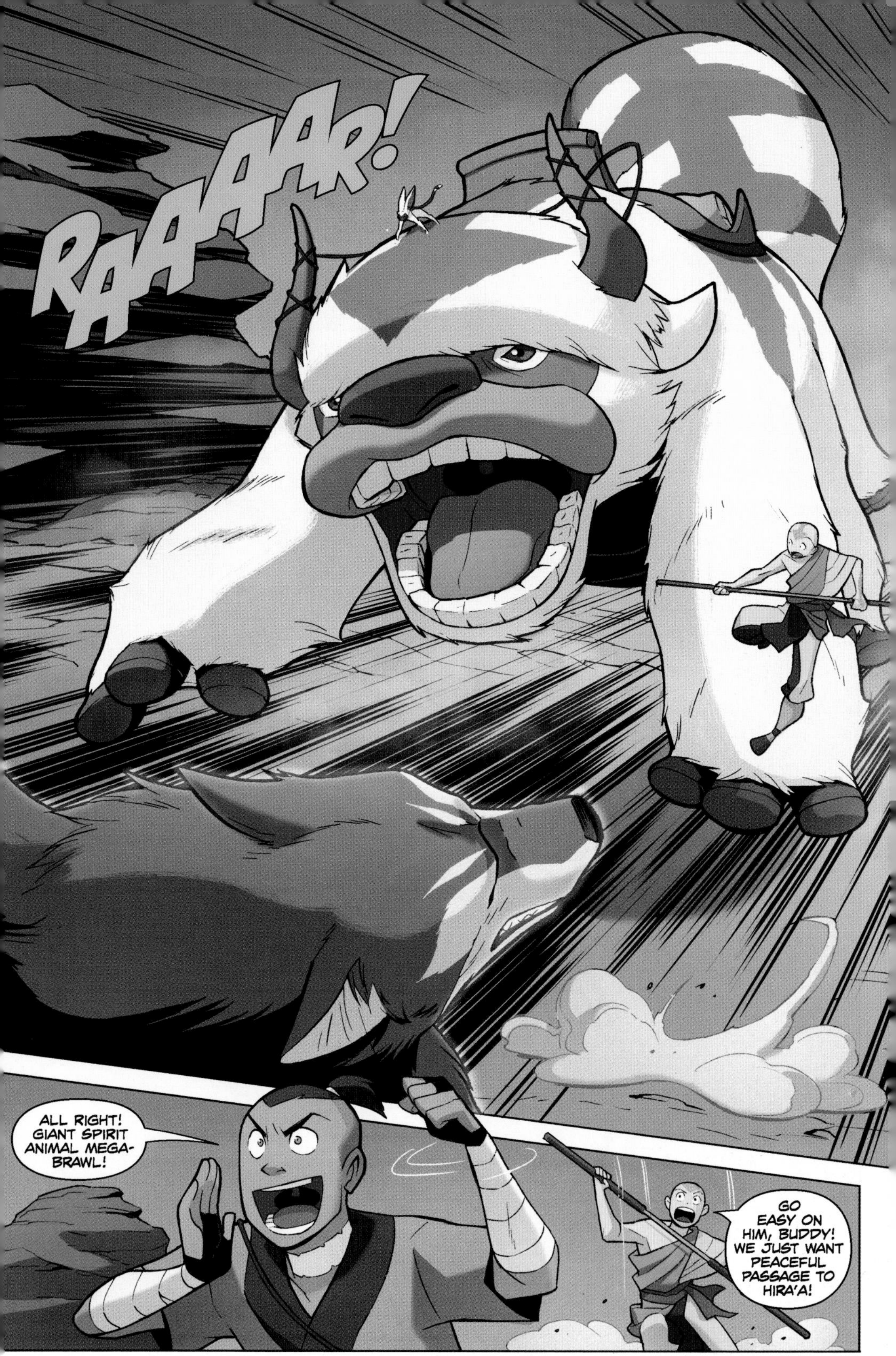
RAAAAAR!
ALL RIGHT! GIANT SPIRIT ANIMAL MEGA-BRAWL!
GO EASY ON HIM, BUDDY! WE JUST WANT PEACEFUL PASSAGE TO HIRA'A!

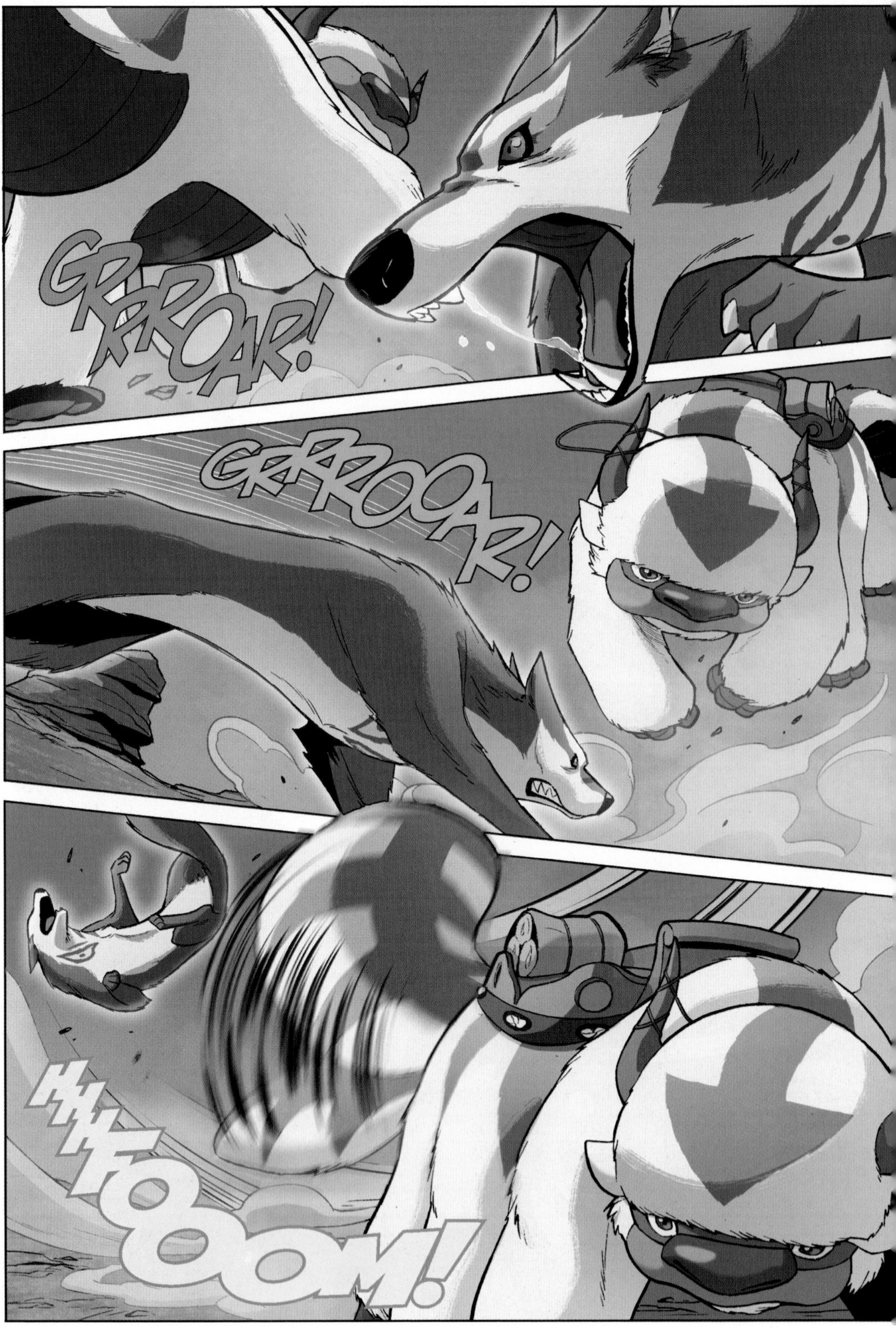
GRRROAR!
GRRROOAR!
HHFOOOM!

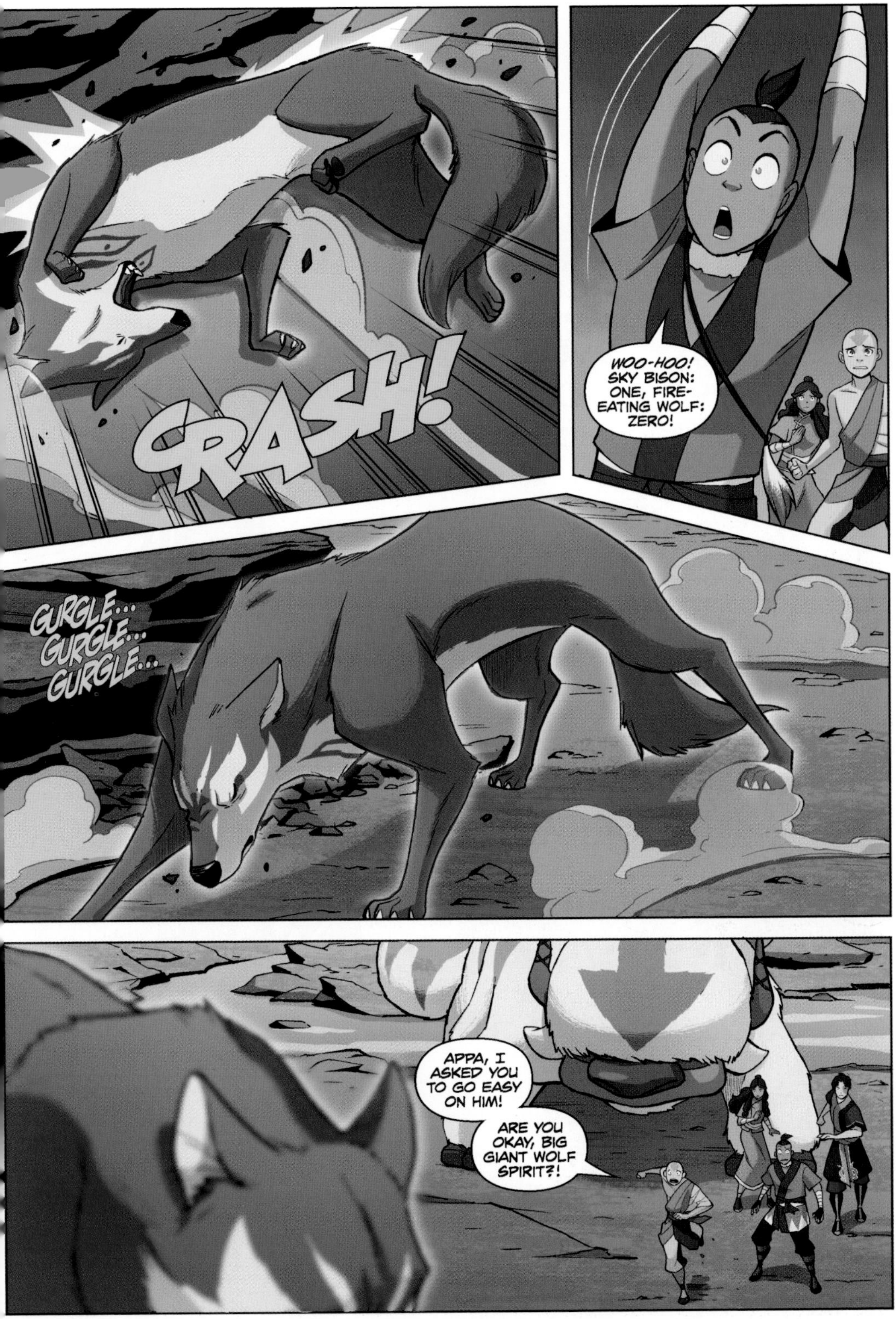
CRASH!
WOO-HOO! SKY BISON: ONE, FIRE-EATING WOLF: ZERO!
GURGLE... GURGLE... GURGLE...
APPA, I ASKED YOU TO GO EASY ON HIM!
ARE YOU OKAY, BIG GIANT WOLF SPIRIT?!

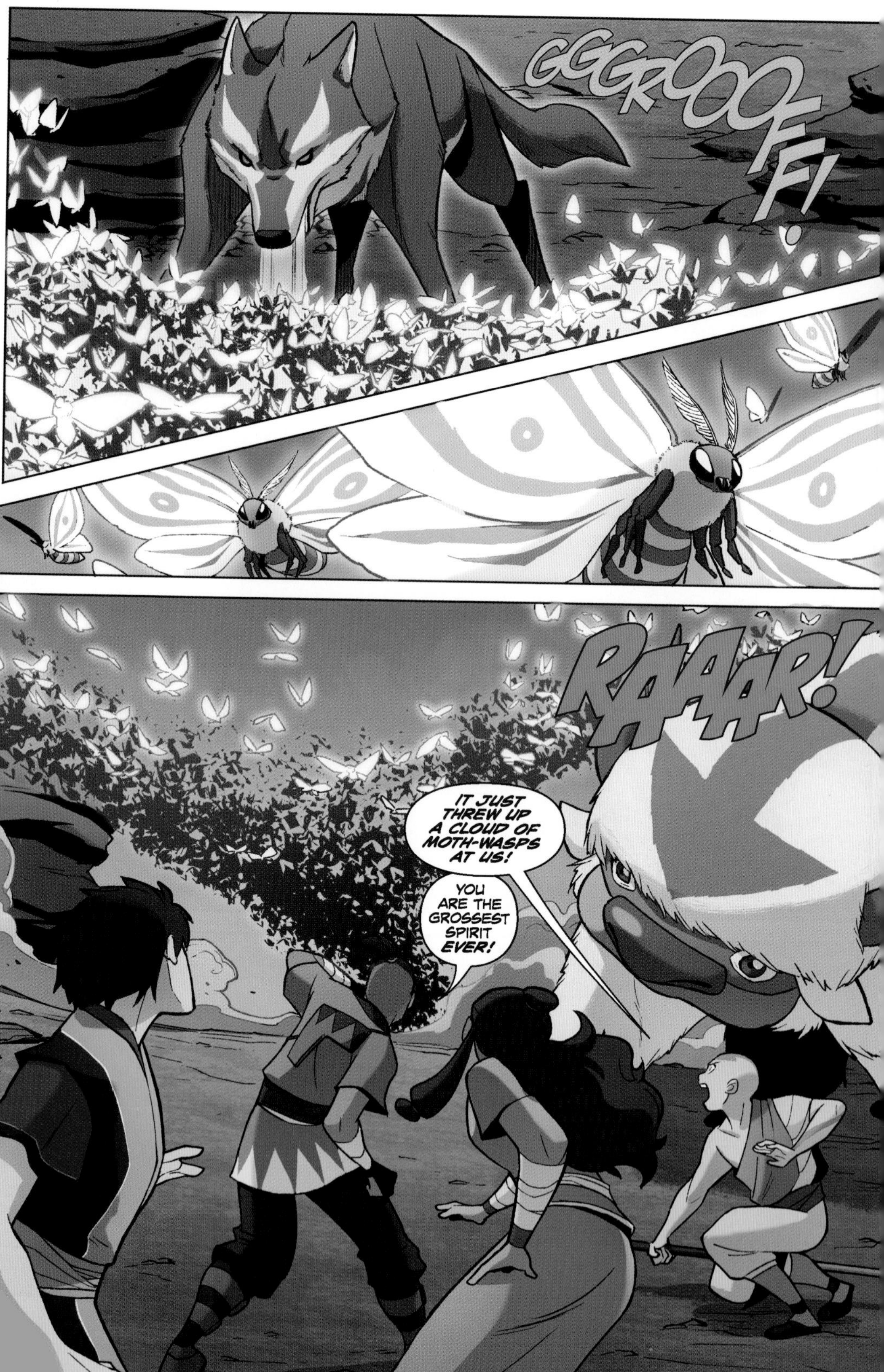
GGGROOOOFF!
RAAAR!
IT JUST THREW UP A CLOUD OF MOTH-WASPS AT US!
YOU ARE THE GROSSEST SPIRIT EVER!

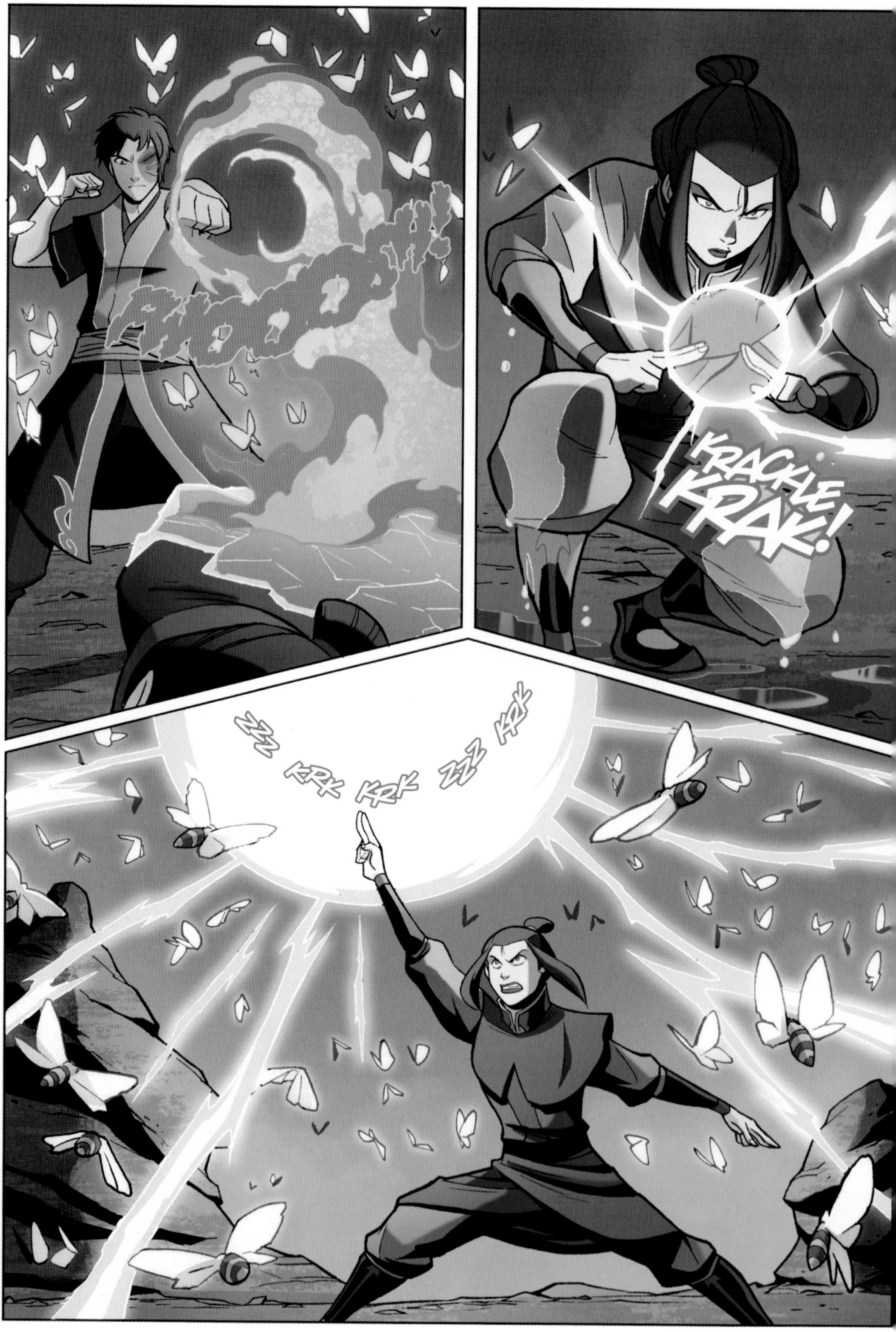
FWOOOOOSH!
KRACKLE
KRAK!
ZZZ
KRK
KRK
ZZZ
KRK

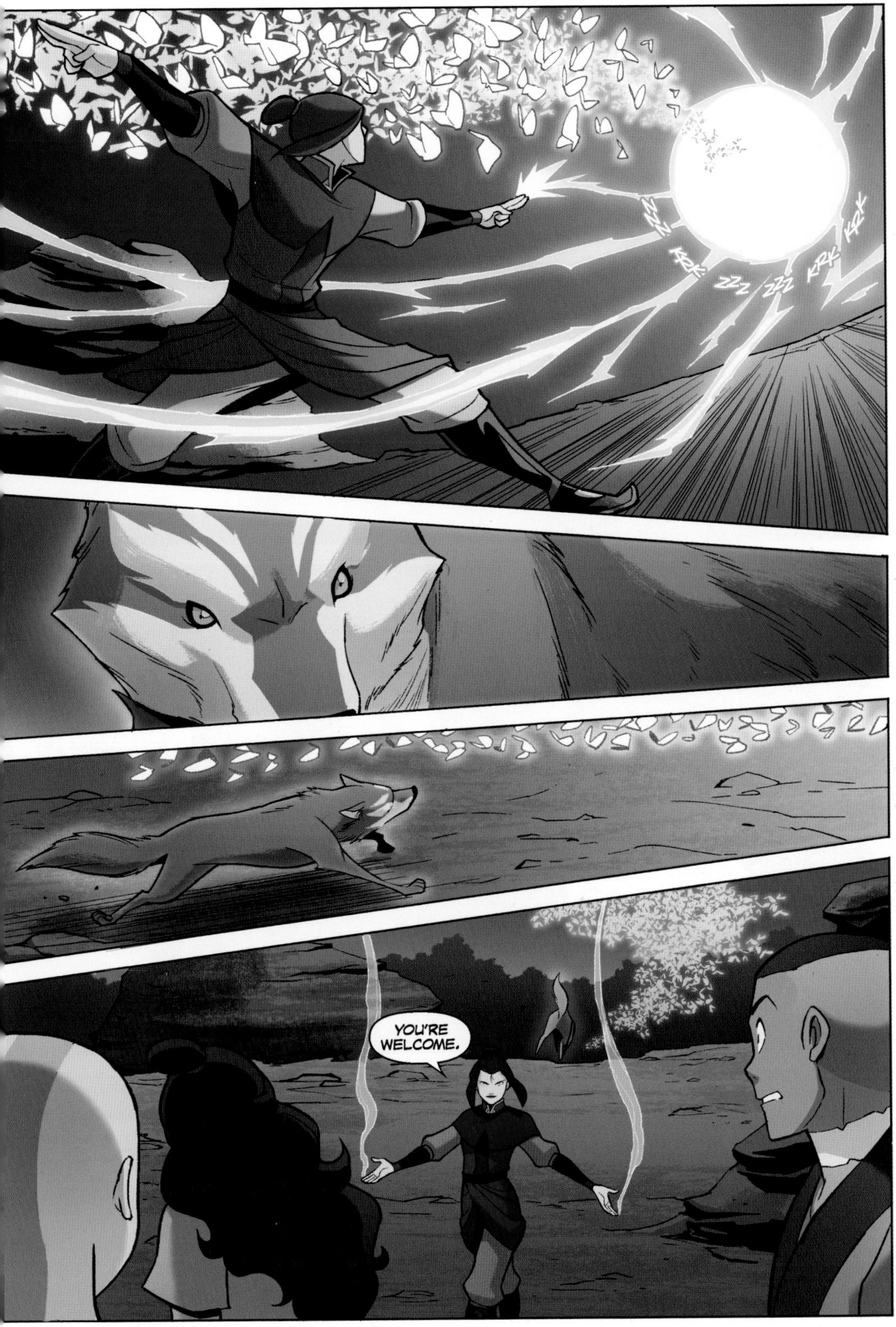
ZZZ
KRK
ZZZ
ZZZ
KRK
KRK
YOU'RE WELCOME.

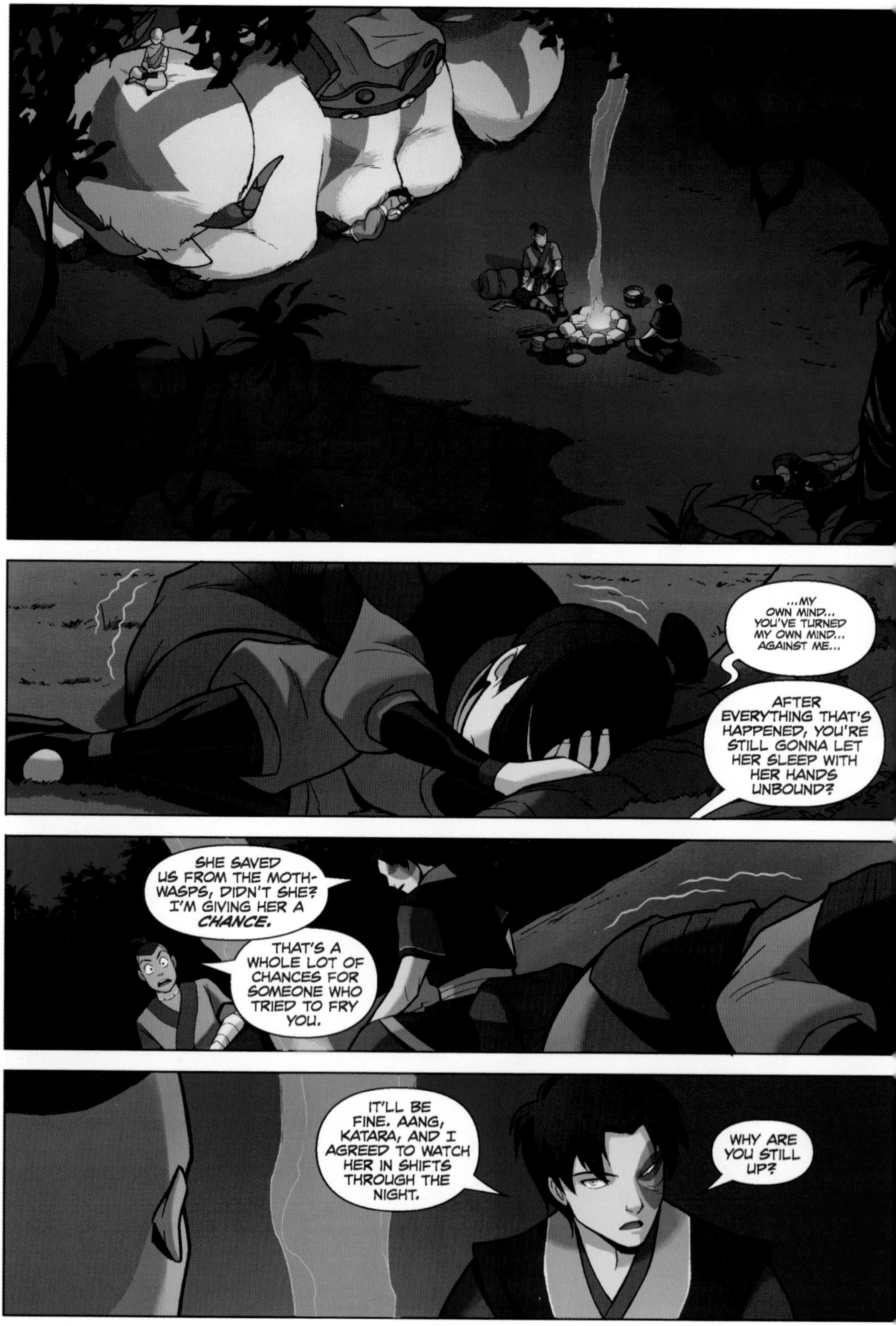

...MY OWN MIND... YOU'VE TURNED MY OWN MIND... AGAINST ME...
AFTER EVERYTHING THAT'S HAPPENED, YOU'RE STILL GONNA LET HER SLEEP WITH HER HANDS UNBOUND?
SHE SAVED US FROM THE MOTH-WASPS, DIDN'T SHE? I'M GIVING HER A CHANCE.
THAT'S A WHOLE LOT OF CHANCES FOR SOMEONE WHO TRIED TO FRY YOU.
IT'LL BE FINE. AANG, KATARA, AND I AGREED TO WATCH HER IN SHIFTS THROUGH THE NIGHT.
WHY ARE YOU STILL UP?

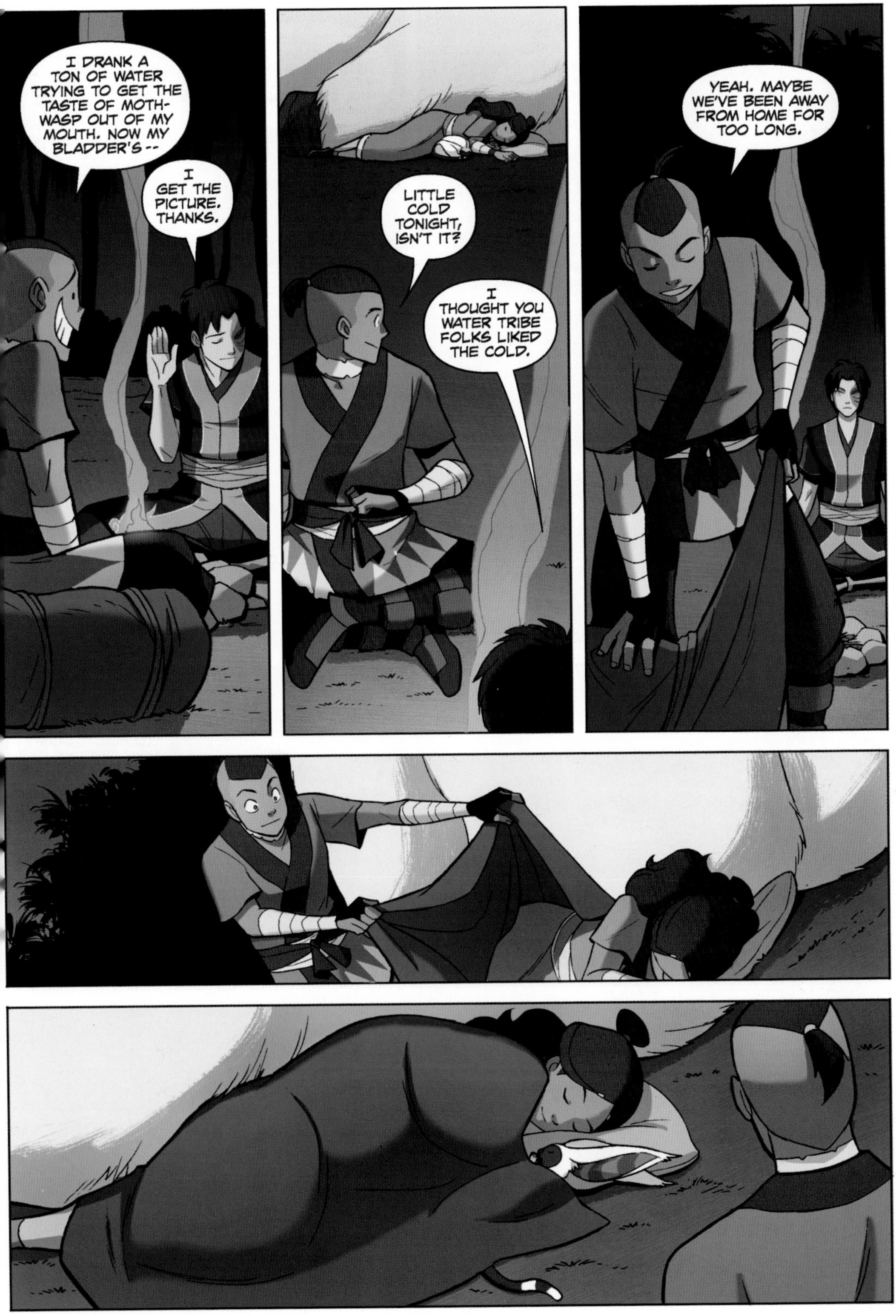
I DRANK A TON OF WATER TRYING TO GET THE TASTE OF MOTH-WASP OUT OF MY MOUTH. NOW MY BLADDER'S --
I GET THE PICTURE. THANKS.
LITTLE COLD TONIGHT, ISN'T IT?
I THOUGHT YOU WATER TRIBE FOLKS LIKED THE COLD.
YEAH. MAYBE WE'VE BEEN AWAY FROM HOME FOR TOO LONG.

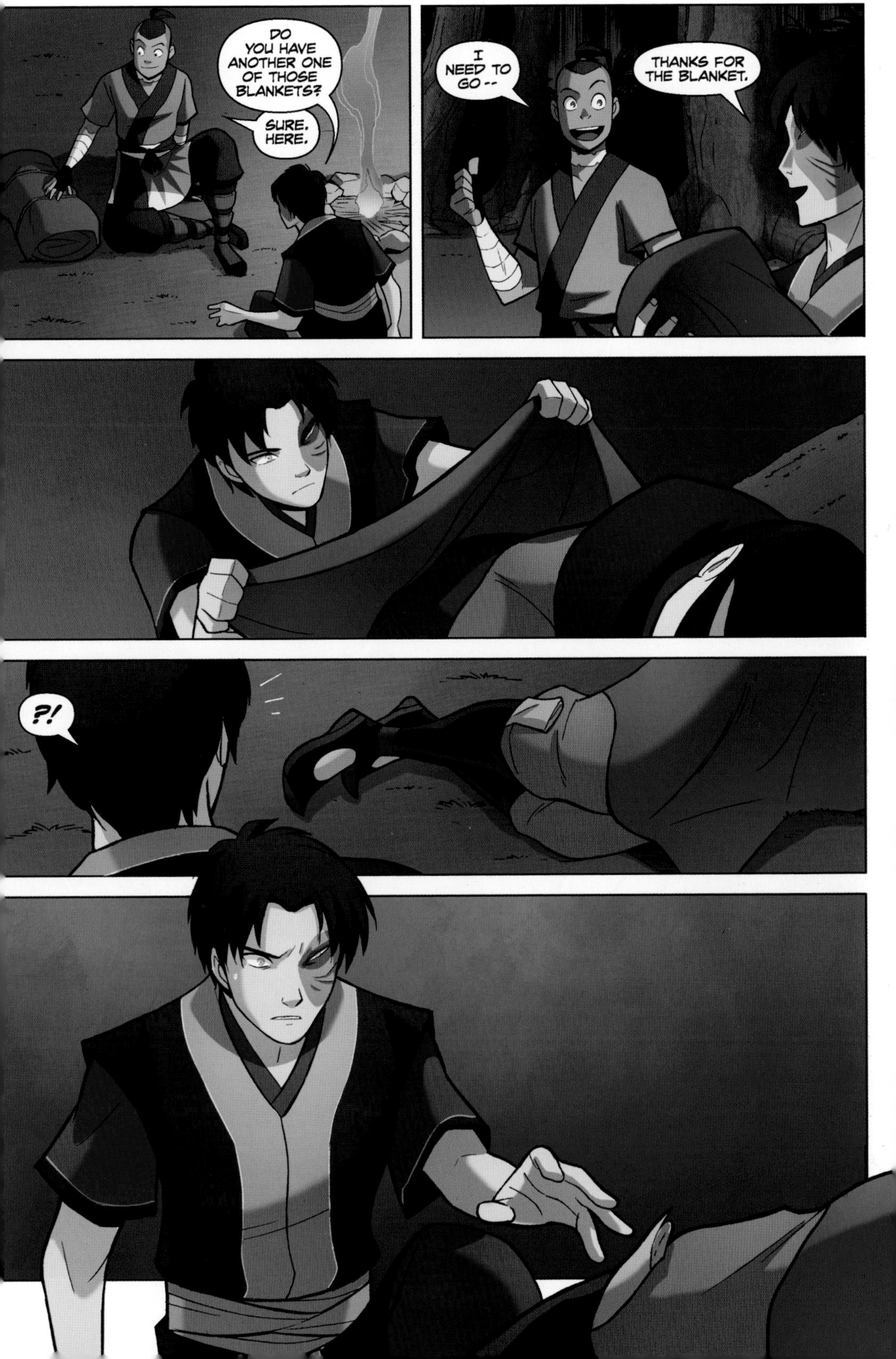
DO YOU HAVE ANOTHER ONE OF THOSE BLANKETS?
SURE. HERE.
I NEED TO GO --
THANKS FOR THE BLANKET.
?!

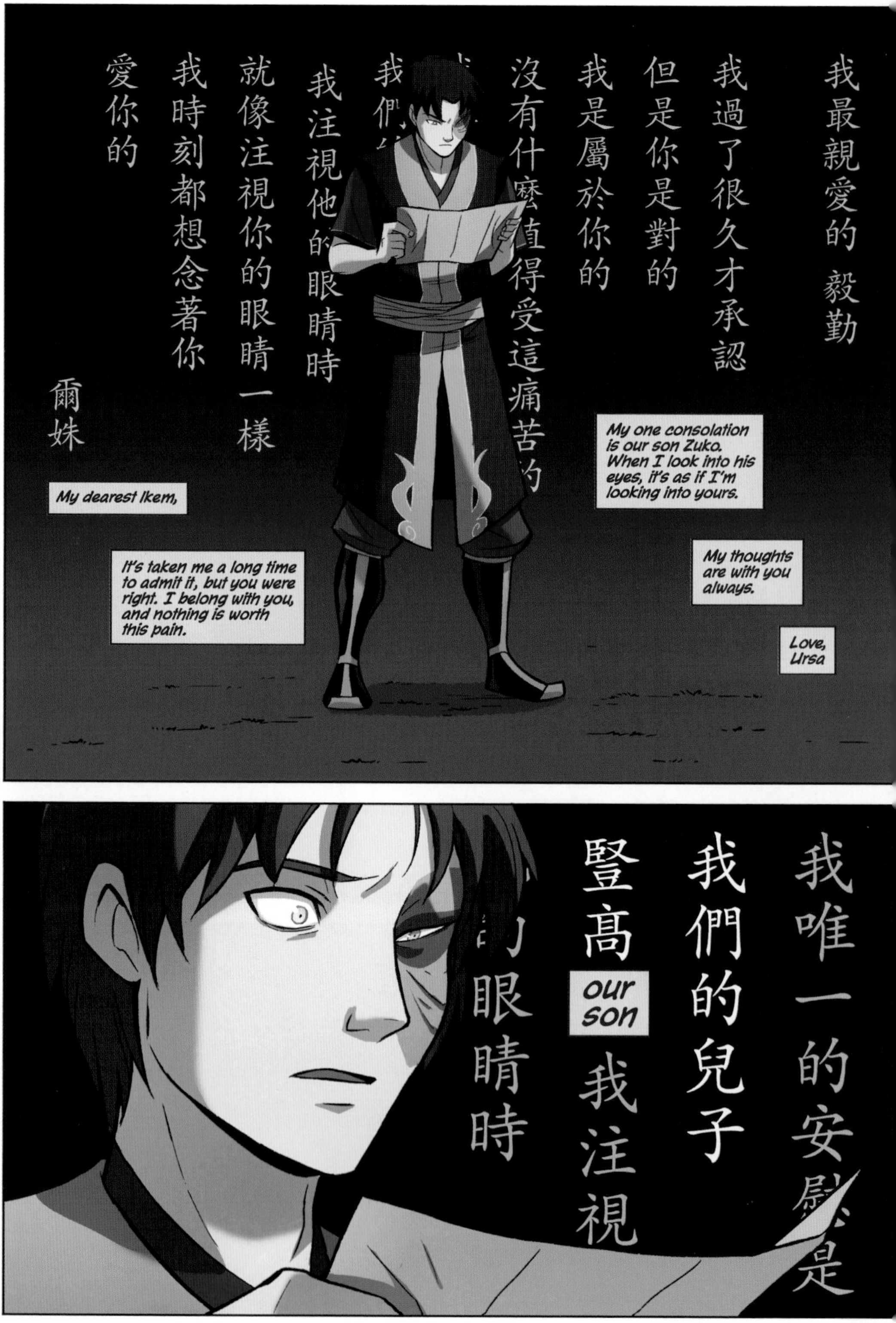
我最親愛的 毅勤
我過了很久才承認
但是你是對的
我是屬於你的
沒有什麼值得受這痛苦的
我注視他的眼睛時
就像注視你的眼睛一樣
我時刻都想念著你
愛你的
爾姝
My dearest Ikem,
It's taken me a long time to admit it, but you were right. I belong with you, and nothing is worth this pain.
My one consolation is our son Zuko. When I look into his eyes, it's as if I'm looking into yours.
My thoughts are with you always.
Love, Ursa
我唯一的安慰是
我們的兒子
暨高
our son
我注視
眼睛時

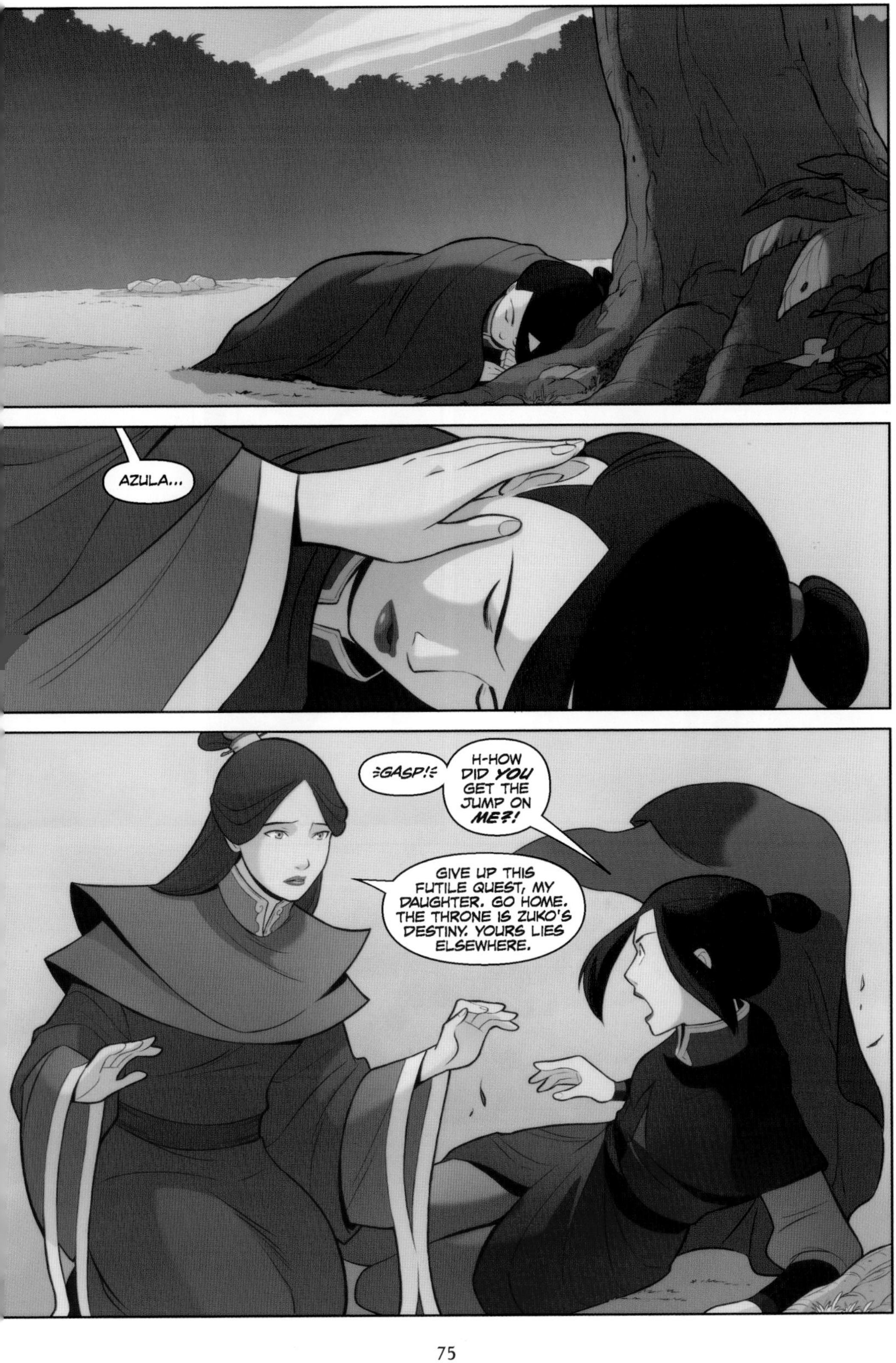

AZULA...
GASP!
H-HOW DID YOU GET THE JUMP ON ME?!
GIVE UP THIS FUTILE QUEST, MY DAUGHTER. GO HOME. THE THRONE IS ZUKO'S DESTINY. YOURS LIES ELSEWHERE.

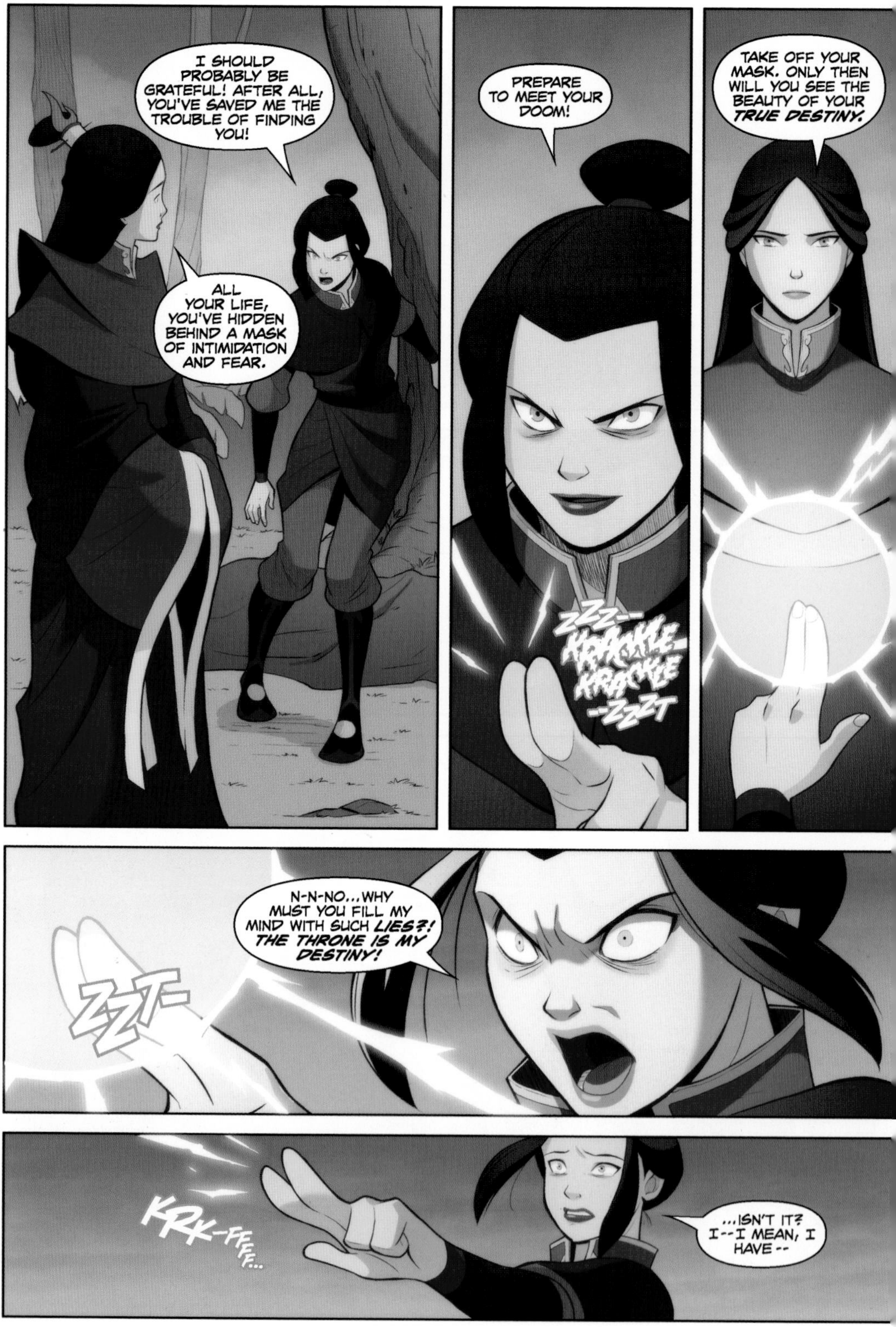
I SHOULD PROBABLY BE GRATEFUL! AFTER ALL, YOU'VE SAVED ME THE TROUBLE OF FINDING YOU!
ALL YOUR LIFE, YOU'VE HIDDEN BEHIND A MASK OF INTIMIDATION AND FEAR.
PREPARE TO MEET YOUR DOOM!
ZZZ-- KRACKLE-KRACKLE --ZZZT
TAKE OFF YOUR MASK. ONLY THEN WILL YOU SEE THE BEAUTY OF YOUR TRUE DESTINY.
N-N-NO...WHY MUST YOU FILL MY MIND WITH SUCH LIES?! THE THRONE IS MY DESTINY!
ZZT-
KRK-FFFF...
...ISN'T IT? I--I MEAN, I HAVE --

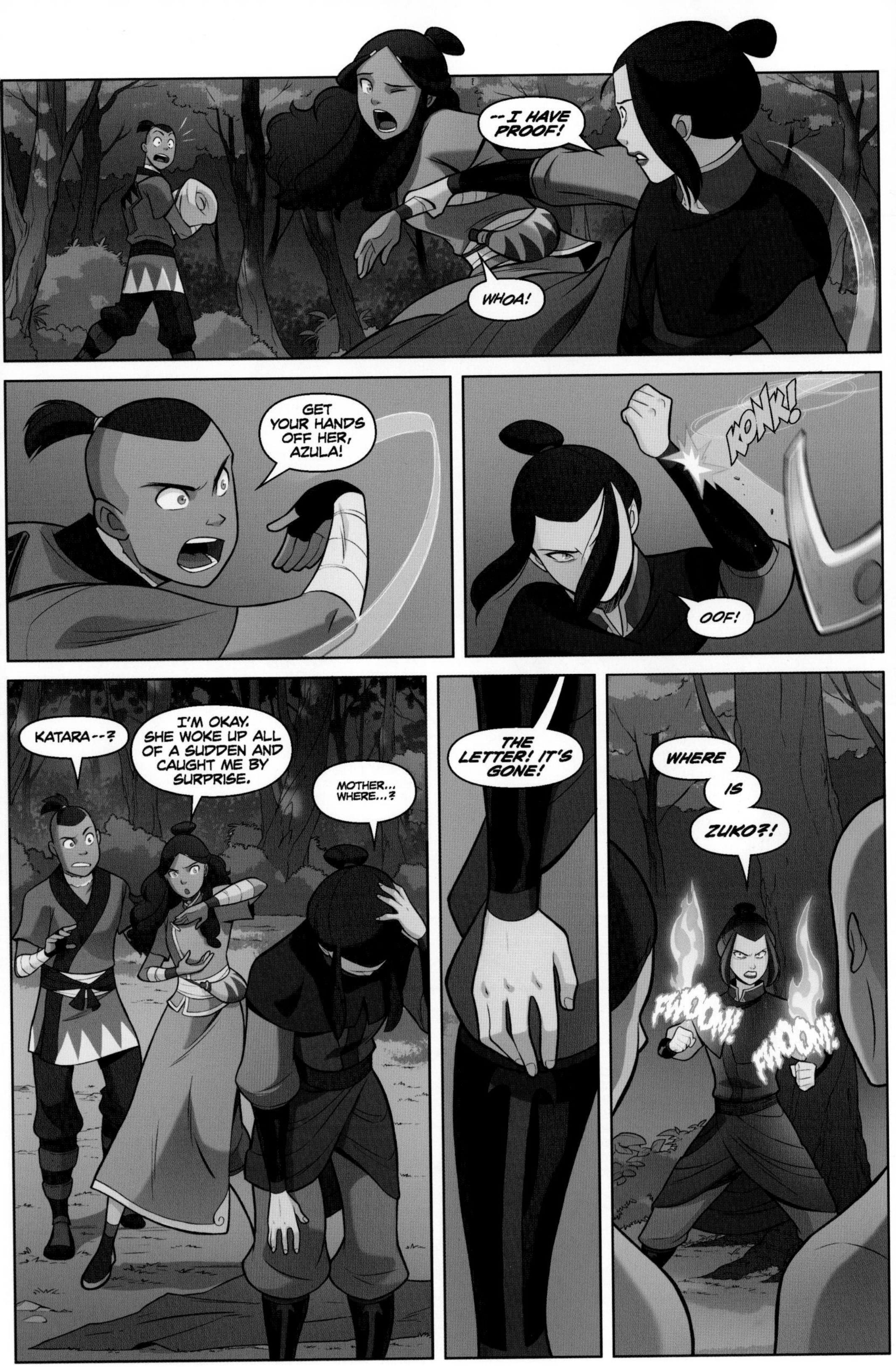
--I HAVE PROOF!
WHOA!
GET YOUR HANDS OFF HER, AZULA!
KONK!
OOF!
KATARA--?
I'M OKAY. SHE WOKE UP ALL OF A SUDDEN AND CAUGHT ME BY SURPRISE.
MOTHER... WHERE...?
THE LETTER! IT'S GONE!
WHERE IS ZUKO?!
FWOOM!
FWOOM!

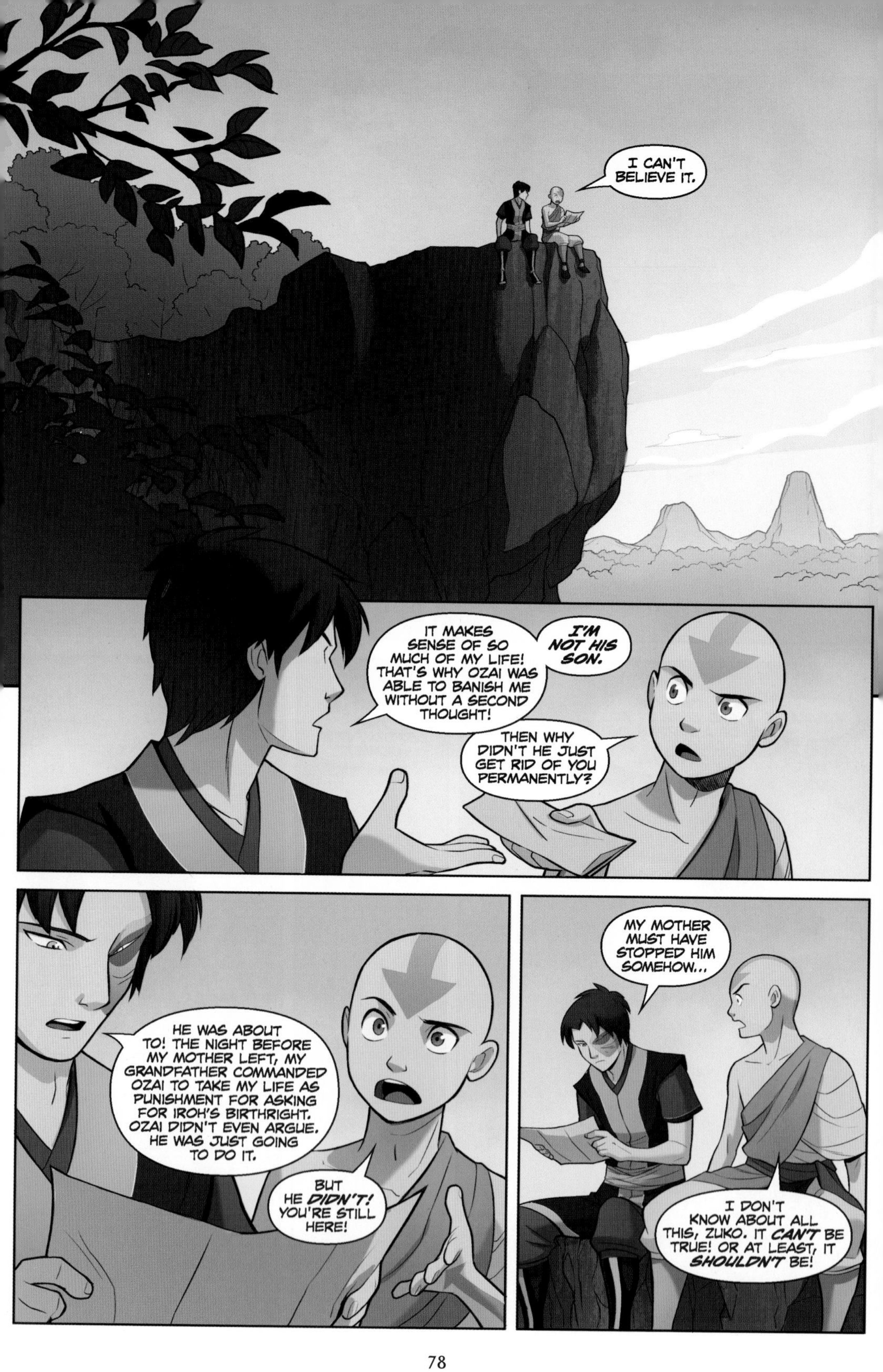
I CAN'T BELIEVE IT.
IT MAKES SENSE OF SO MUCH OF MY LIFE! THAT'S WHY OZAI WAS ABLE TO BANISH ME WITHOUT A SECOND THOUGHT!
I'M NOT HIS SON.
THEN WHY DIDN'T HE JUST GET RID OF YOU PERMANENTLY?
HE WAS ABOUT TO! THE NIGHT BEFORE MY MOTHER LEFT, MY GRANDFATHER COMMANDED OZAI TO TAKE MY LIFE AS PUNISHMENT FOR ASKING FOR IROH'S BIRTHRIGHT. OZAI DIDN'T EVEN ARGUE. HE WAS JUST GOING TO DO IT.
BUT HE DIDN'T! YOU'RE STILL HERE!
MY MOTHER MUST HAVE STOPPED HIM SOMEHOW...
I DON'T KNOW ABOUT ALL THIS, ZUKO. IT CAN'T BE TRUE! OR AT LEAST, IT SHOULDN'T BE!

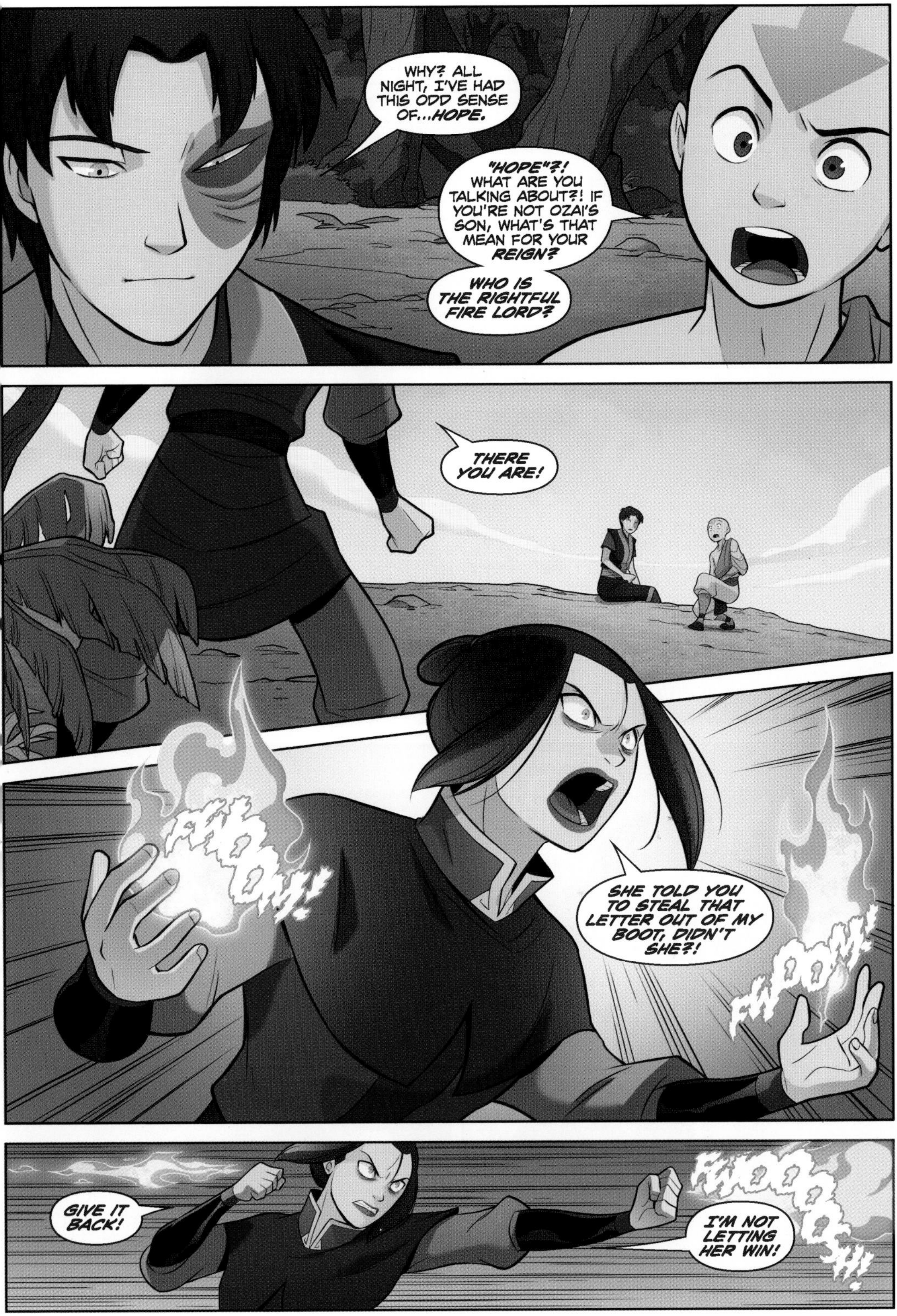
WHY? ALL NIGHT, I'VE HAD THIS ODD SENSE OF...HOPE.
"HOPE"?! WHAT ARE YOU TALKING ABOUT?! IF YOU'RE NOT OZAI'S SON, WHAT'S THAT MEAN FOR YOUR REIGN?
WHO IS THE RIGHTFUL FIRE LORD?
THERE YOU ARE!
FWOOM!
SHE TOLD YOU TO STEAL THAT LETTER OUT OF MY BOOT, DIDN'T SHE?!
FWOOM!
GIVE IT BACK!
FWOOOOSH!
I'M NOT LETTING HER WIN!

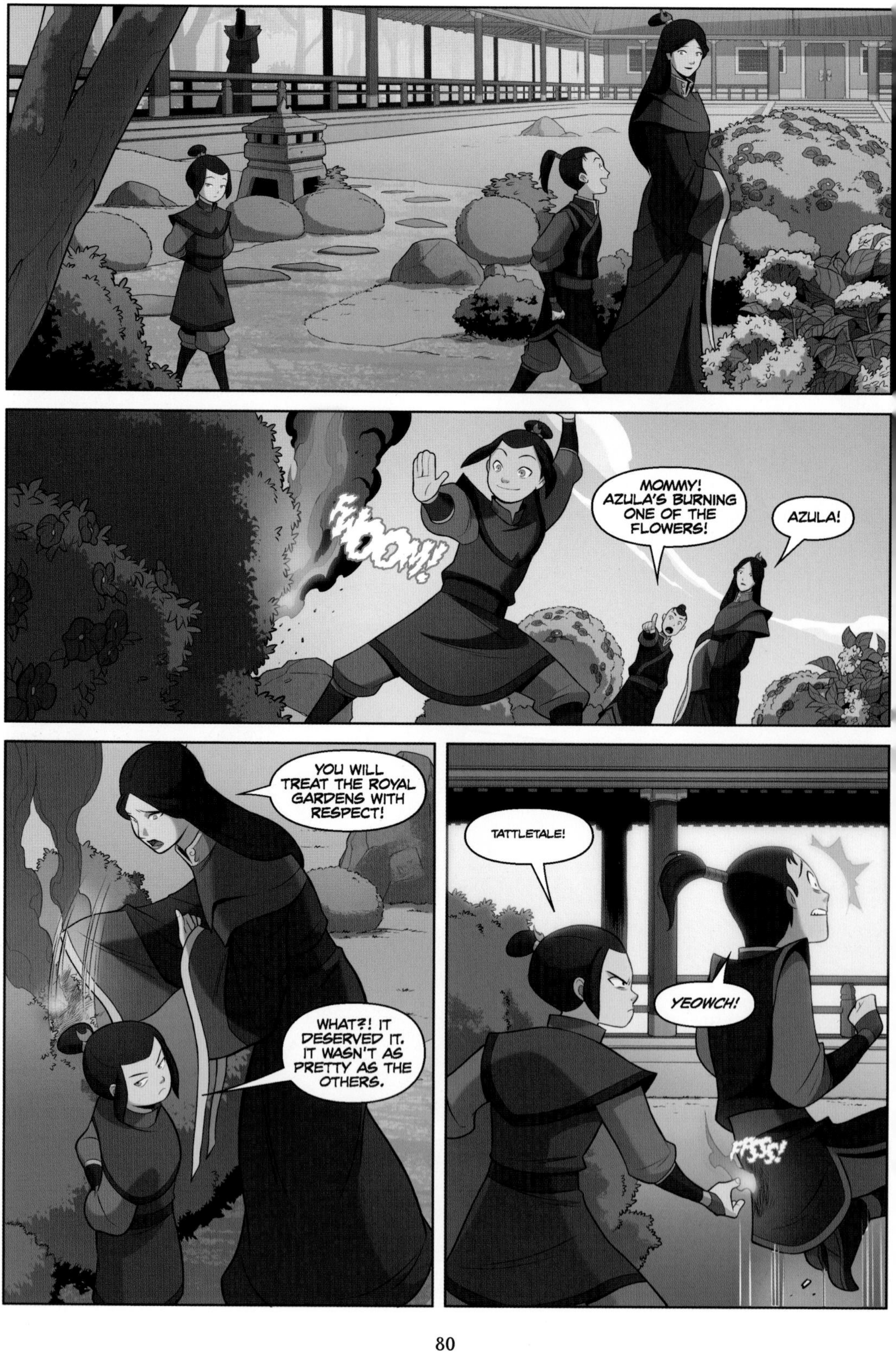
FWOOM!
MOMMY! AZULA'S BURNING ONE OF THE FLOWERS!
AZULA!
YOU WILL TREAT THE ROYAL GARDENS WITH RESPECT!
WHAT?! IT DESERVED IT. IT WASN'T AS PRETTY AS THE OTHERS.
TATTLETALE!
YEOWCH!
FFSSS!

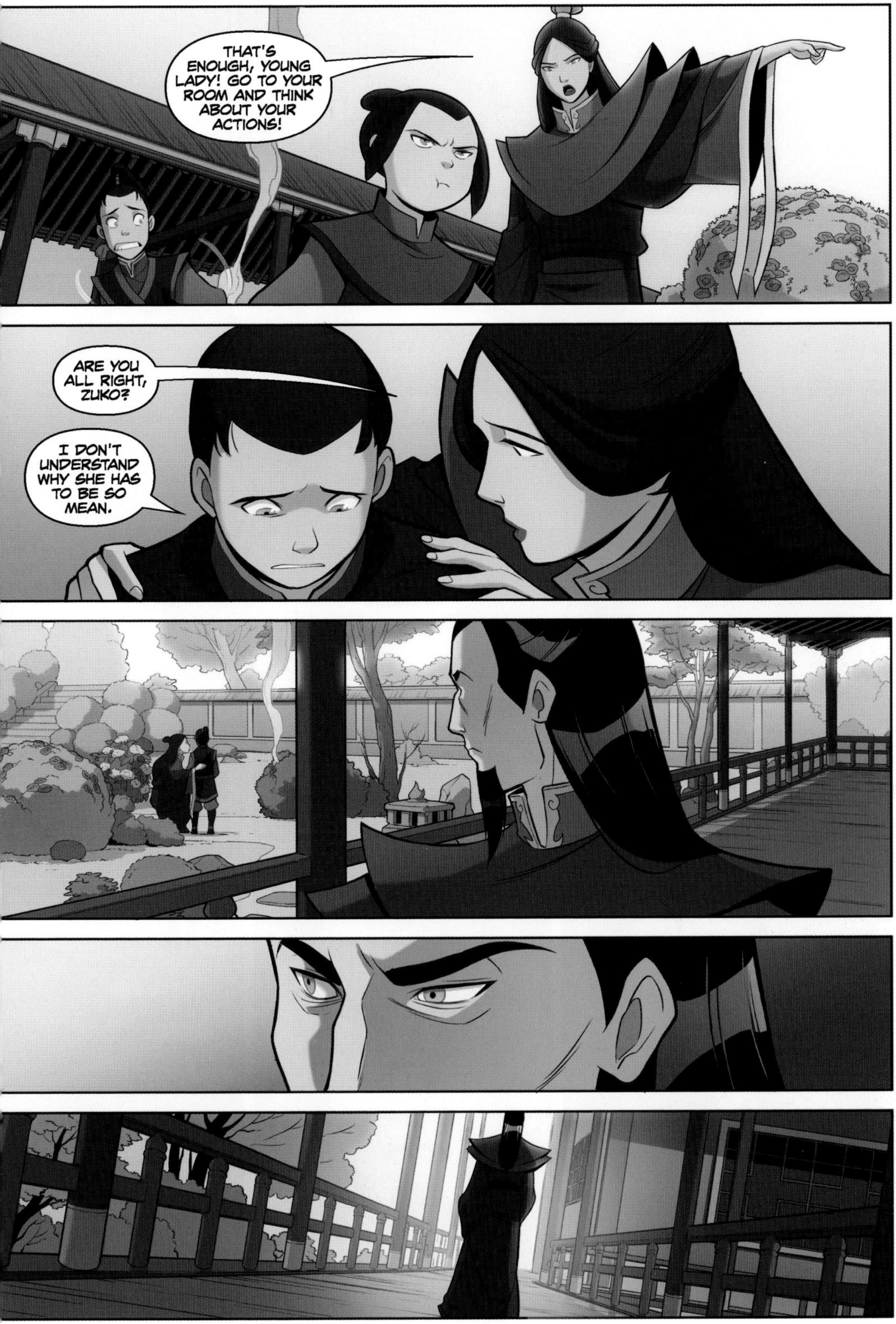
THAT'S ENOUGH, YOUNG LADY! GO TO YOUR ROOM AND THINK ABOUT YOUR ACTIONS!
ARE YOU ALL RIGHT, ZUKO?
I DON'T UNDERSTAND WHY SHE HAS TO BE SO MEAN.

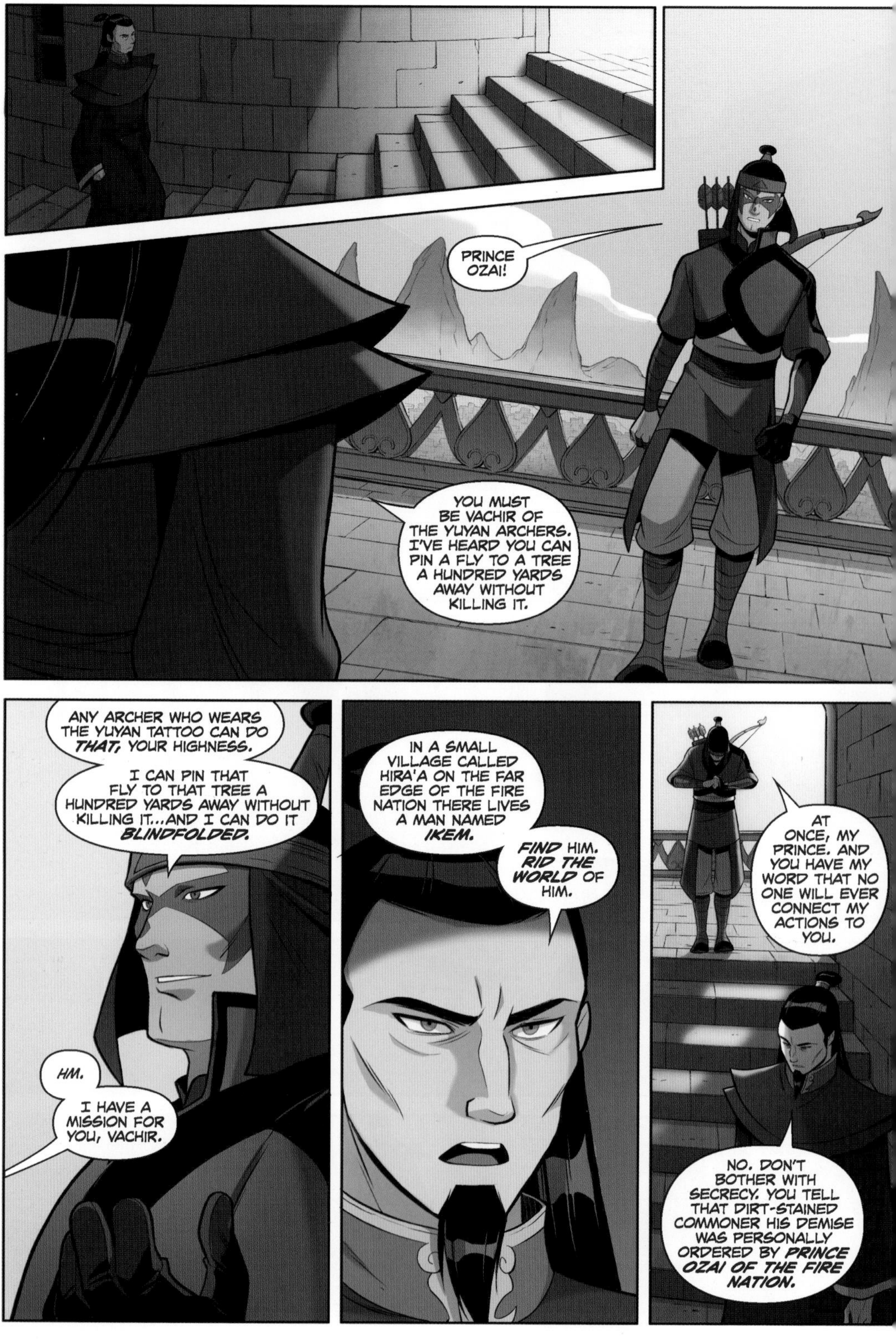
PRINCE OZAI!
YOU MUST BE VACHIR OF THE YUYAN ARCHERS. I'VE HEARD YOU CAN PIN A FLY TO A TREE A HUNDRED YARDS AWAY WITHOUT KILLING IT.
ANY ARCHER WHO WEARS THE YUYAN TATTOO CAN DO THAT, YOUR HIGHNESS.
I CAN PIN THAT FLY TO THAT TREE A HUNDRED YARDS AWAY WITHOUT KILLING IT...AND I CAN DO IT BLINDFOLDED.
HM.
I HAVE A MISSION FOR YOU, VACHIR.
IN A SMALL VILLAGE CALLED HIRA'A ON THE FAR EDGE OF THE FIRE NATION THERE LIVES A MAN NAMED IKEM.
FIND HIM. RID THE WORLD OF HIM.
AT ONCE, MY PRINCE. AND YOU HAVE MY WORD THAT NO ONE WILL EVER CONNECT MY ACTIONS TO YOU.
NO. DON'T BOTHER WITH SECRECY. YOU TELL THAT DIRT-STAINED COMMONER HIS DEMISE WAS PERSONALLY ORDERED BY PRINCE OZAI OF THE FIRE NATION.

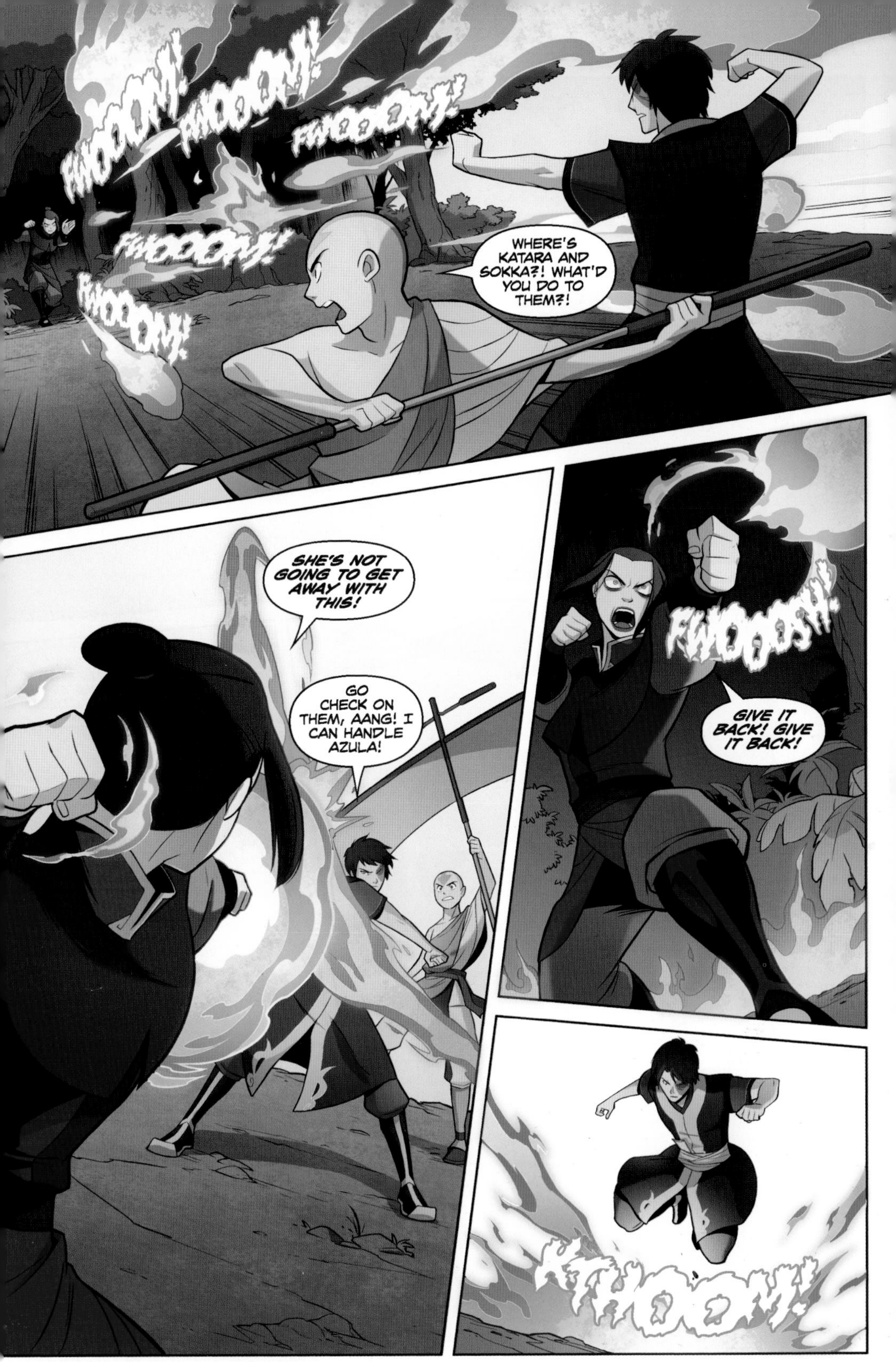
FWOOOM! FWOOOM! FWOOOM!
FWOOOM!
FWOOOM!
WHERE'S KATARA AND SOKKA?! WHAT'D YOU DO TO THEM?!
SHE'S NOT GOING TO GET AWAY WITH THIS!
GO CHECK ON THEM, AANG! I CAN HANDLE AZULA!
FWOOOSH!
GIVE IT BACK! GIVE IT BACK!
FHOOM!

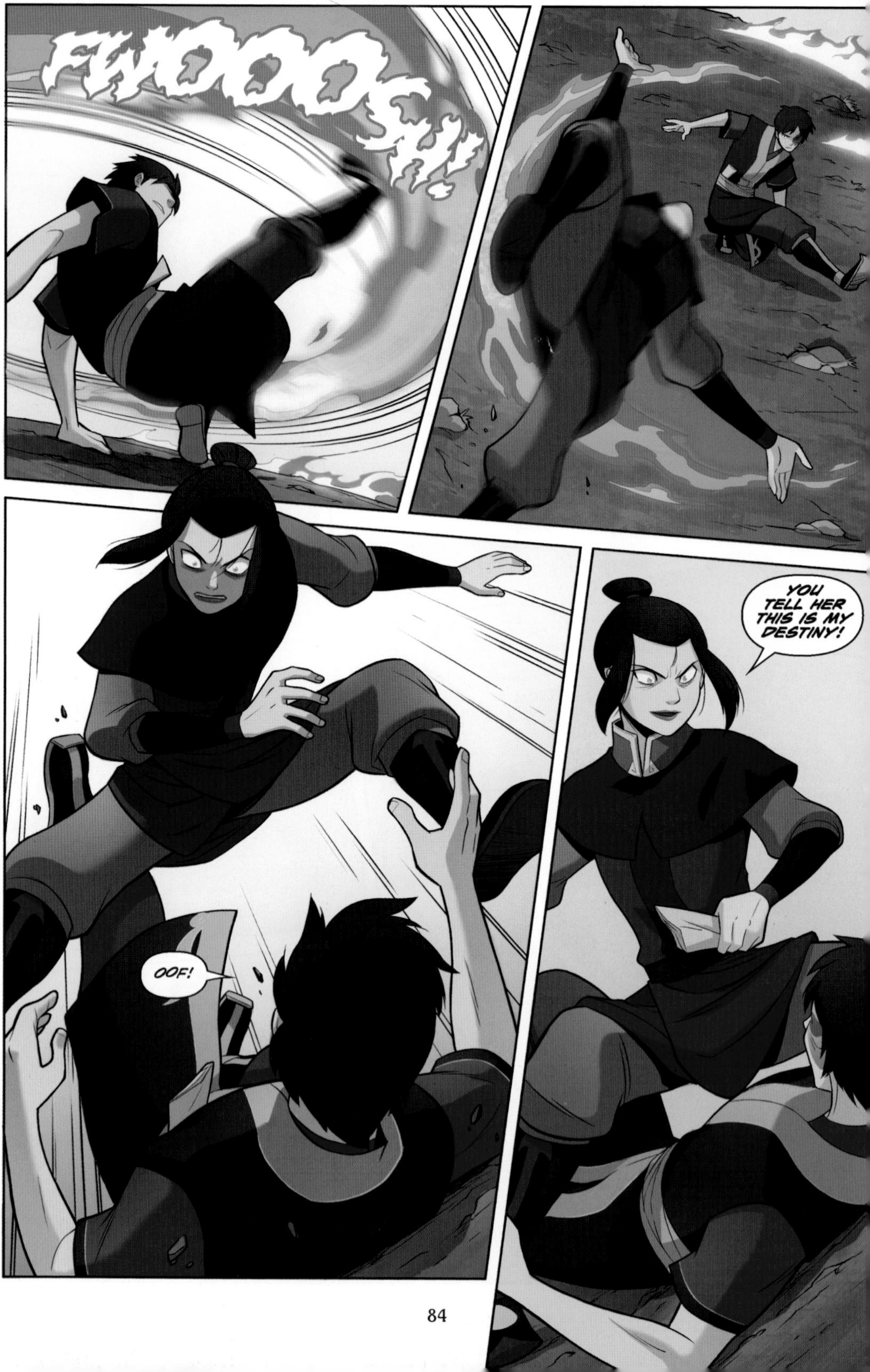
FWOOOSH!
OOF!
YOU TELL HER THIS IS MY DESTINY!

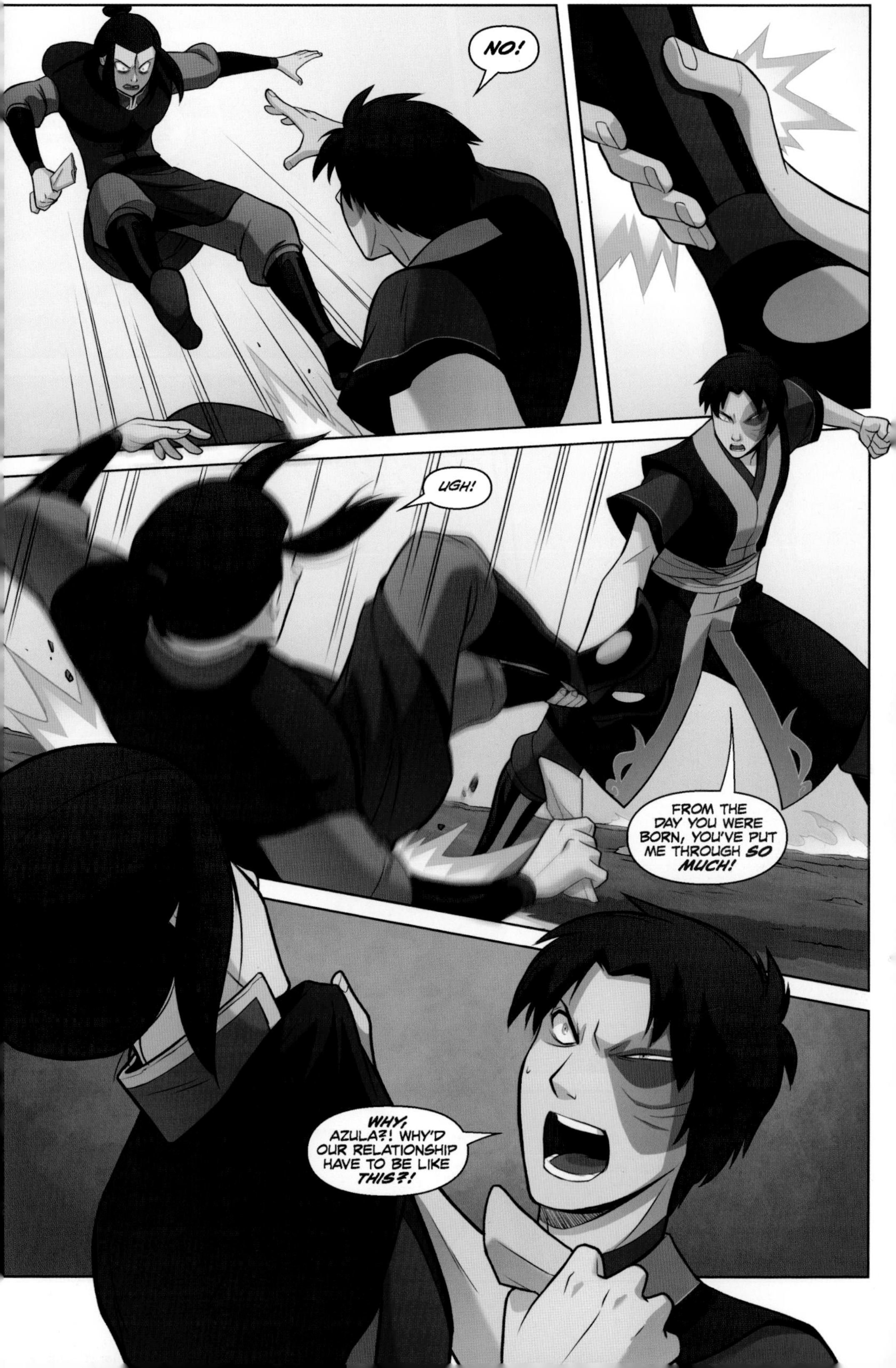
NO!
UGH!
FROM THE DAY YOU WERE BORN, YOU'VE PUT ME THROUGH SO MUCH!
WHY, AZULA?! WHY'D OUR RELATIONSHIP HAVE TO BE LIKE THIS?!

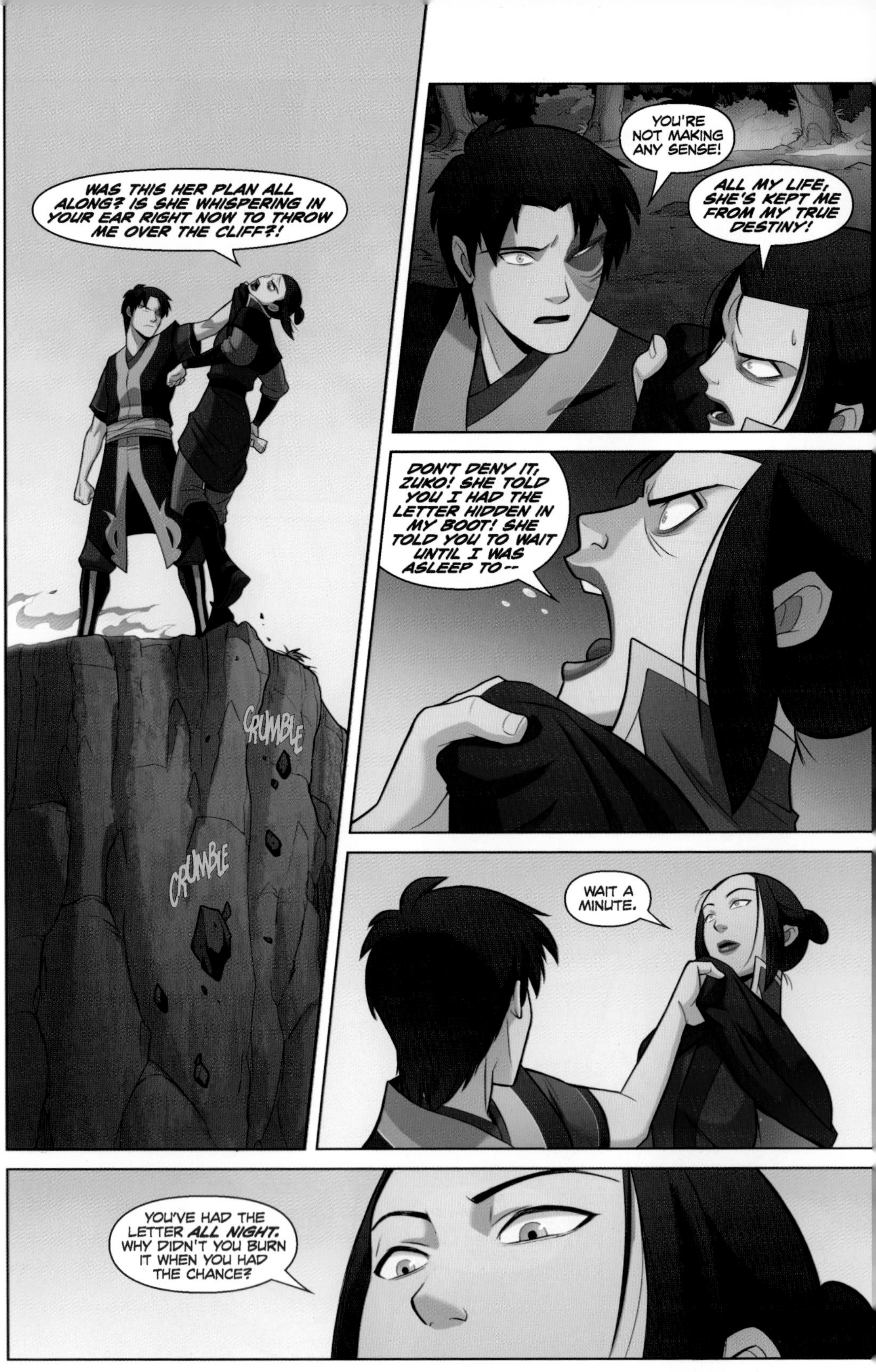
WAS THIS HER PLAN ALL ALONG? IS SHE WHISPERING IN YOUR EAR RIGHT NOW TO THROW ME OVER THE CLIFF?!
CRUMBLE
CRUMBLE
YOU'RE NOT MAKING ANY SENSE!
ALL MY LIFE, SHE'S KEPT ME FROM MY TRUE DESTINY!
DON'T DENY IT, ZUKO! SHE TOLD YOU I HAD THE LETTER HIDDEN IN MY BOOT! SHE TOLD YOU TO WAIT UNTIL I WAS ASLEEP TO--
WAIT A MINUTE.
YOU'VE HAD THE LETTER ALL NIGHT. WHY DIDN'T YOU BURN IT WHEN YOU HAD THE CHANCE?

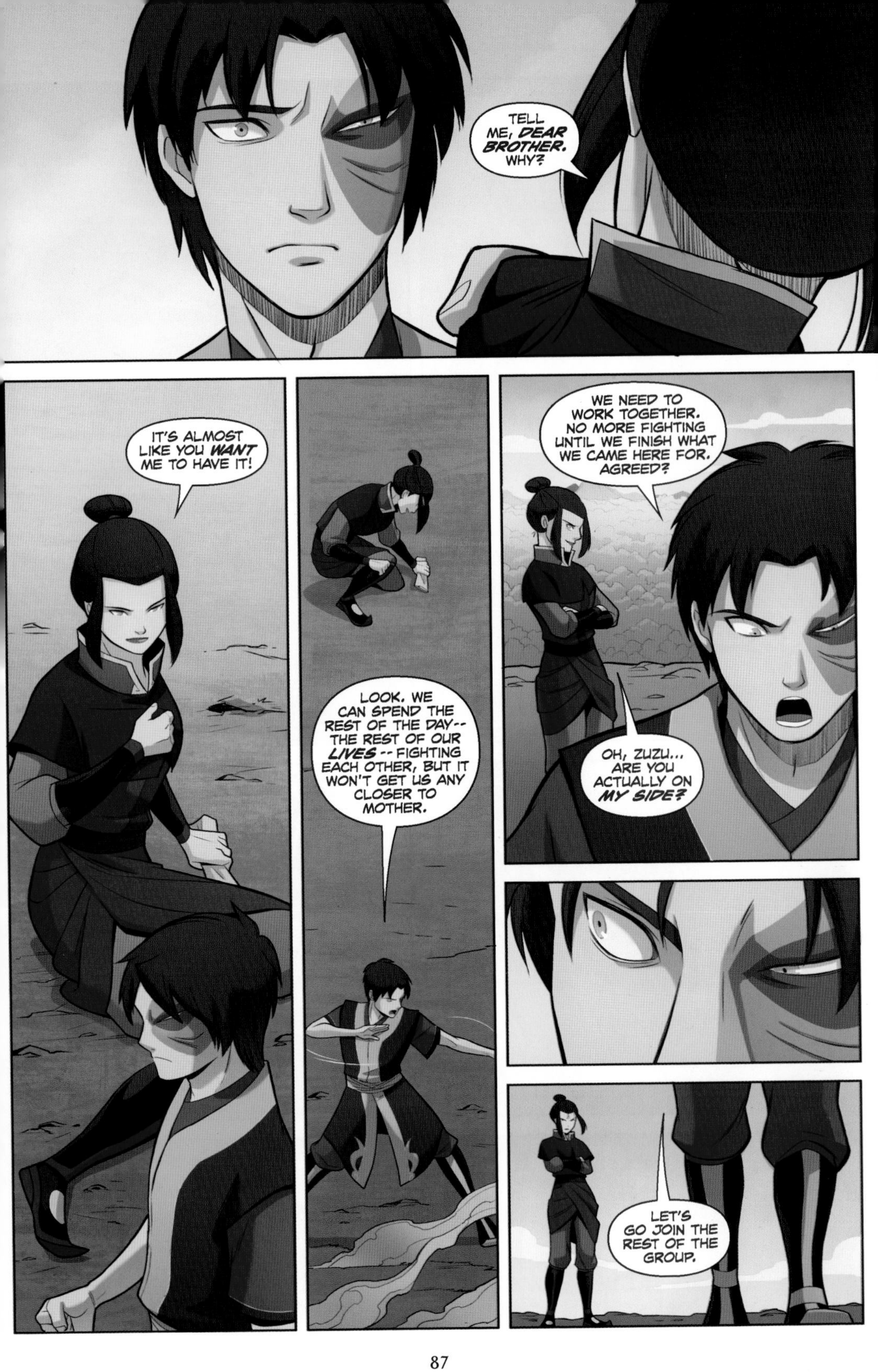
TELL ME, DEAR BROTHER. WHY?
IT'S ALMOST LIKE YOU WANT ME TO HAVE IT!
LOOK. WE CAN SPEND THE REST OF THE DAY-- THE REST OF OUR LIVES -- FIGHTING EACH OTHER, BUT IT WON'T GET US ANY CLOSER TO MOTHER.
WE NEED TO WORK TOGETHER. NO MORE FIGHTING UNTIL WE FINISH WHAT WE CAME HERE FOR. AGREED?
OH, ZUZU... ARE YOU ACTUALLY ON MY SIDE?
LET'S GO JOIN THE REST OF THE GROUP.

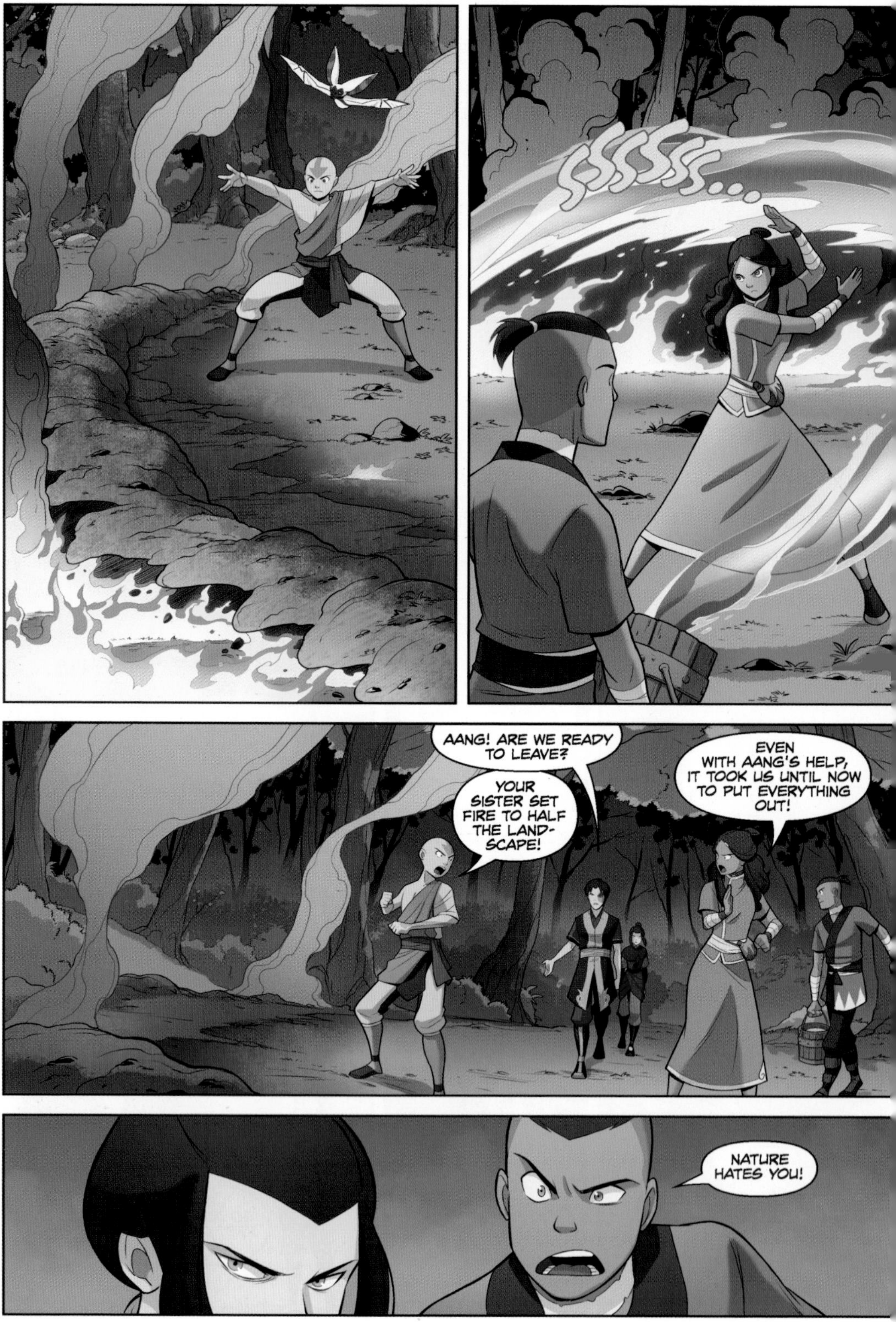
SSSSSS...
AANG! ARE WE READY TO LEAVE?
YOUR SISTER SET FIRE TO HALF THE LAND-SCAPE!
EVEN WITH AANG'S HELP, IT TOOK US UNTIL NOW TO PUT EVERYTHING OUT!
NATURE HATES YOU!

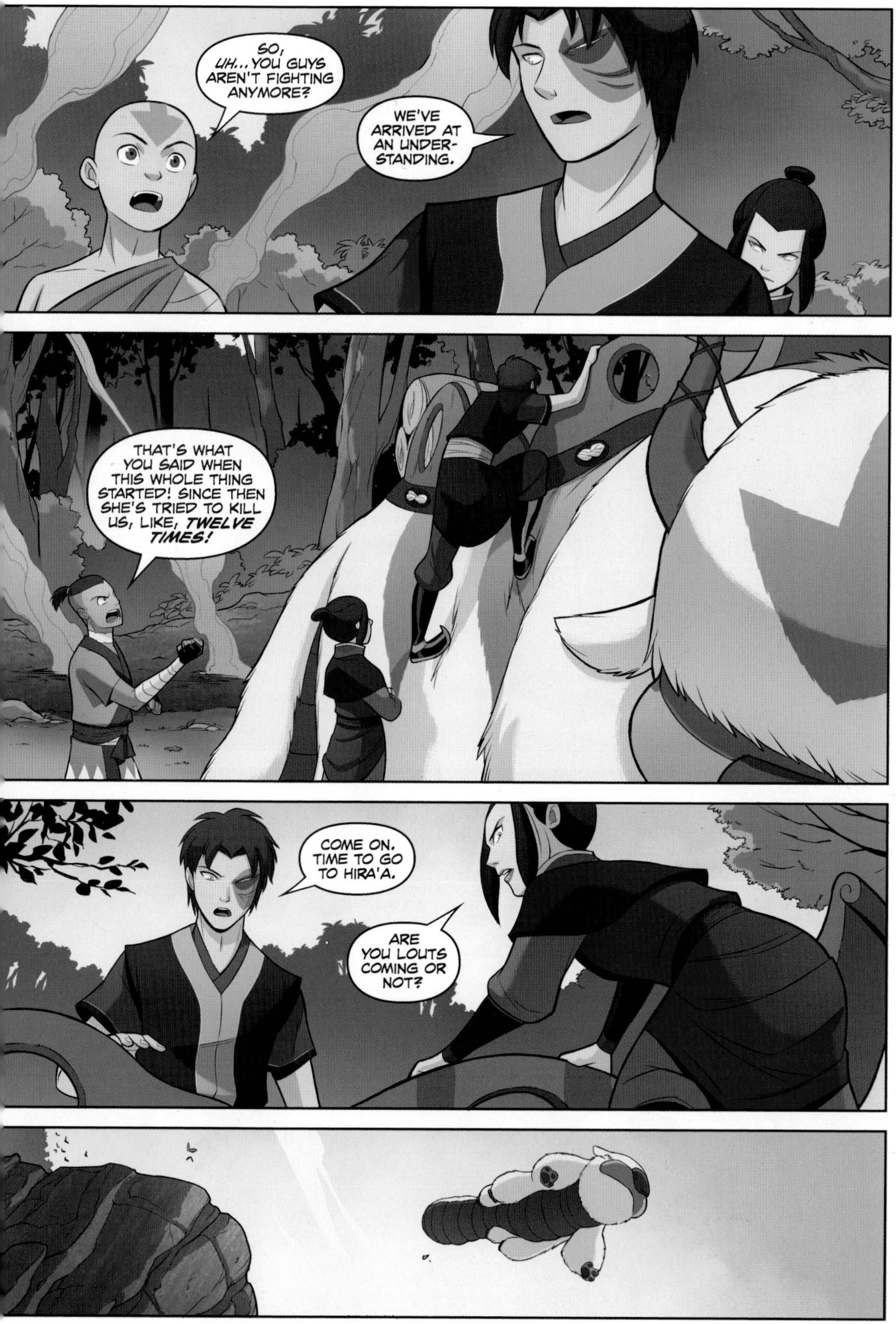
SO, UH...YOU GUYS AREN'T FIGHTING ANYMORE?
WE'VE ARRIVED AT AN UNDER-STANDING.
THAT'S WHAT YOU SAID WHEN THIS WHOLE THING STARTED! SINCE THEN SHE'S TRIED TO KILL US, LIKE, *TWELVE TIMES!*
COME ON. TIME TO GO TO HIRA'A.
ARE YOU LOUTS COMING OR NOT?

DURING TRAINING TODAY, MASTER KUNYO SAID I WAS HOLDING MY ARMS TOO FAR APART FOR ONE OF MY FORMS.

I TOLD HIM THAT'S HOW YOU GET THE BIGGEST FIRE BLAST! HE DIDN'T CARE. HE WANTED ME TO DO THE FORM THE WAY HE DOES IT. THE DUMB WAY.

SO WHEN HE HAD HIS BACK TURNED, I SET HIS PANTS ON FIRE!

HM. YOUR TEACHER SOUNDS LIKE A FOOL. I'LL HAVE HIM SENT TO THE COLONIES.

SERVES HIM RIGHT! WHAT A DUMMY!

HE'S NOT A DUMMY! HE JUST THINKS THAT PROPER FIREBENDING HAS TO START--

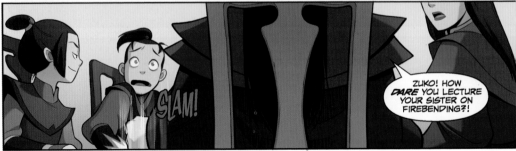

SLAM!

ZUKO! HOW *DARE* YOU LECTURE YOUR SISTER ON FIREBENDING?!

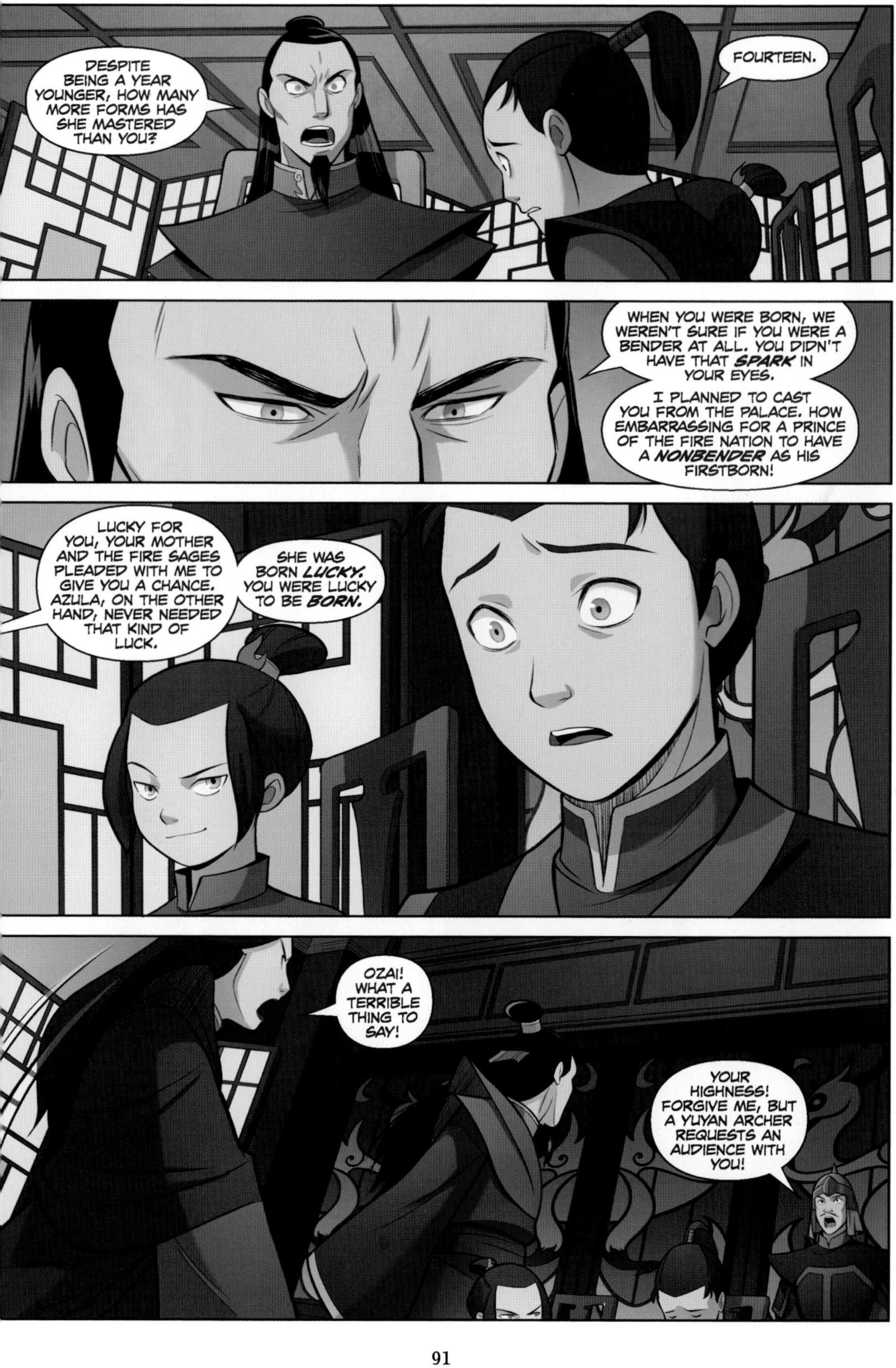
DESPITE BEING A YEAR YOUNGER, HOW MANY MORE FORMS HAS SHE MASTERED THAN YOU?
FOURTEEN.
WHEN YOU WERE BORN, WE WEREN'T SURE IF YOU WERE A BENDER AT ALL. YOU DIDN'T HAVE THAT SPARK IN YOUR EYES.
I PLANNED TO CAST YOU FROM THE PALACE. HOW EMBARRASSING FOR A PRINCE OF THE FIRE NATION TO HAVE A NONBENDER AS HIS FIRSTBORN!
LUCKY FOR YOU, YOUR MOTHER AND THE FIRE SAGES PLEADED WITH ME TO GIVE YOU A CHANCE. AZULA, ON THE OTHER HAND, NEVER NEEDED THAT KIND OF LUCK.
SHE WAS BORN LUCKY. YOU WERE LUCKY TO BE BORN.
OZAI! WHAT A TERRIBLE THING TO SAY!
YOUR HIGHNESS! FORGIVE ME, BUT A YUYAN ARCHER REQUESTS AN AUDIENCE WITH YOU!

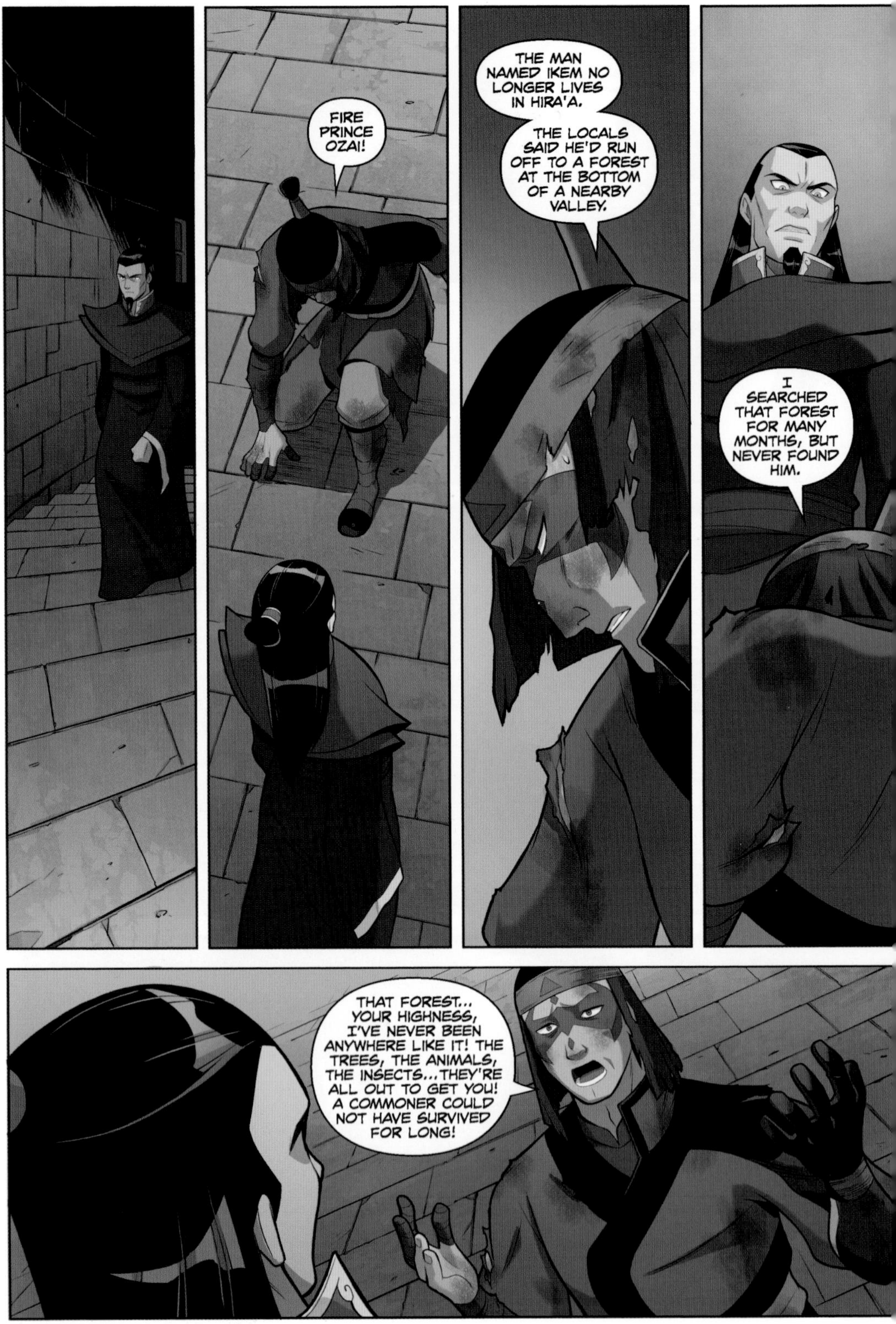
FIRE PRINCE OZAI!
THE MAN NAMED IKEM NO LONGER LIVES IN HIRA'A.
THE LOCALS SAID HE'D RUN OFF TO A FOREST AT THE BOTTOM OF A NEARBY VALLEY.
I SEARCHED THAT FOREST FOR MANY MONTHS, BUT NEVER FOUND HIM.
THAT FOREST... YOUR HIGHNESS, I'VE NEVER BEEN ANYWHERE LIKE IT! THE TREES, THE ANIMALS, THE INSECTS...THEY'RE ALL OUT TO GET YOU! A COMMONER COULD NOT HAVE SURVIVED FOR LONG!

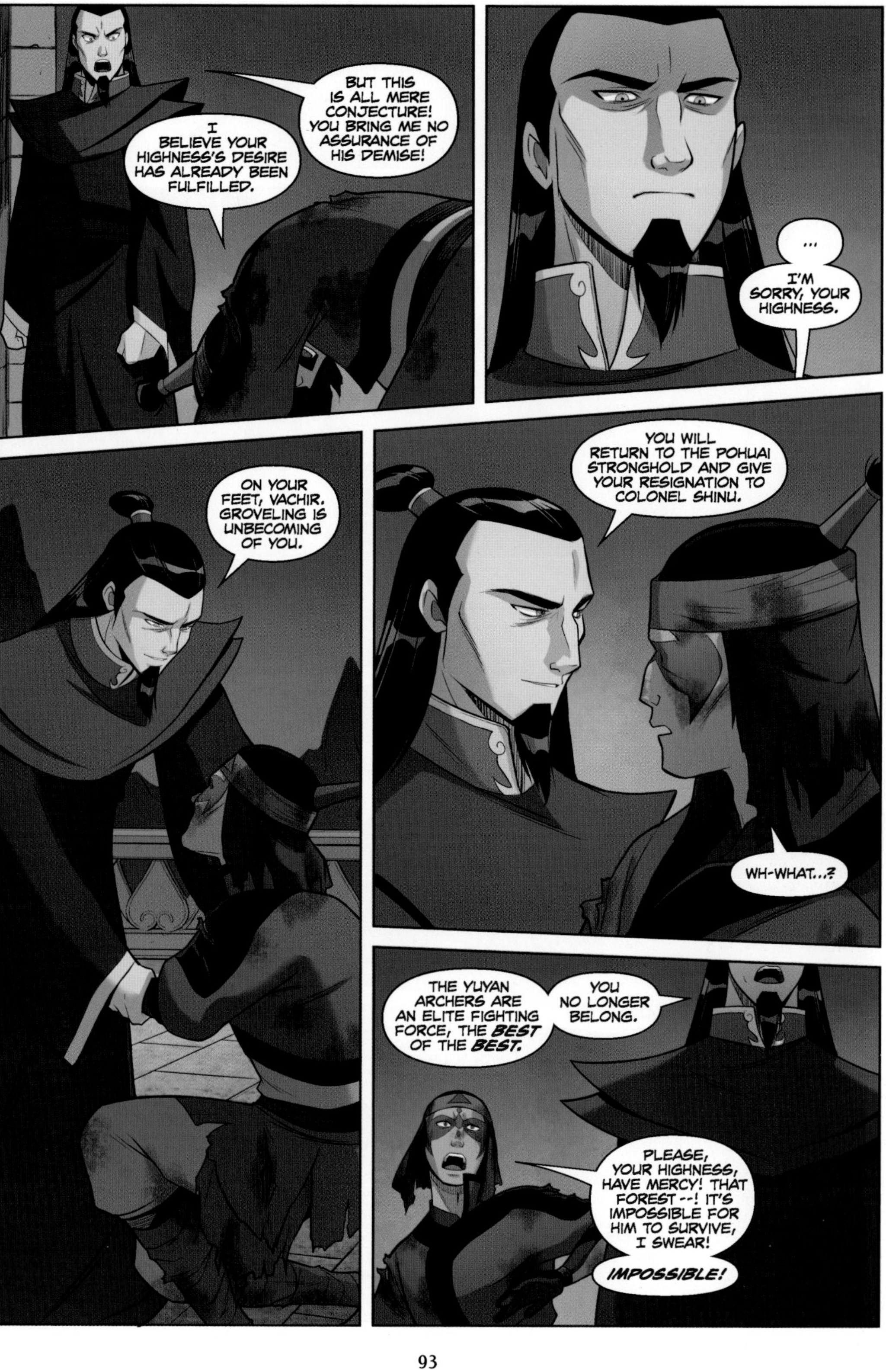
I BELIEVE YOUR HIGHNESS'S DESIRE HAS ALREADY BEEN FULFILLED.
BUT THIS IS ALL MERE CONJECTURE! YOU BRING ME NO ASSURANCE OF HIS DEMISE!
...
I'M SORRY, YOUR HIGHNESS.
ON YOUR FEET, VACHIR. GROVELING IS UNBECOMING OF YOU.
YOU WILL RETURN TO THE POHUAI STRONGHOLD AND GIVE YOUR RESIGNATION TO COLONEL SHINU.
WH-WHAT...?
THE YUYAN ARCHERS ARE AN ELITE FIGHTING FORCE, THE BEST OF THE BEST.
YOU NO LONGER BELONG.
PLEASE, YOUR HIGHNESS, HAVE MERCY! THAT FOREST --! IT'S IMPOSSIBLE FOR HIM TO SURVIVE, I SWEAR!
IMPOSSIBLE!

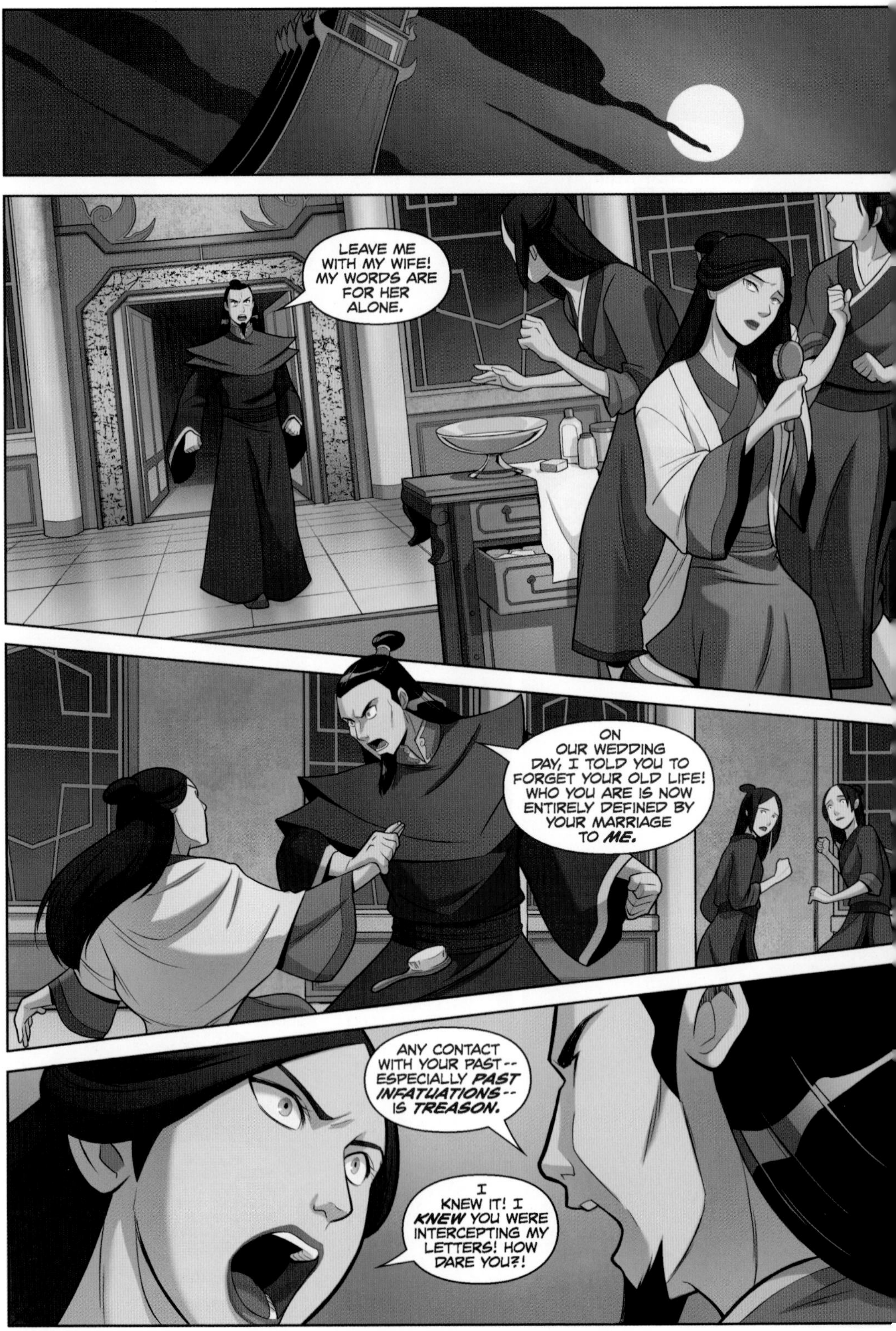
LEAVE ME WITH MY WIFE! MY WORDS ARE FOR HER ALONE.
ON OUR WEDDING DAY, I TOLD YOU TO FORGET YOUR OLD LIFE! WHO YOU ARE IS NOW ENTIRELY DEFINED BY YOUR MARRIAGE TO ***ME.***
ANY CONTACT WITH YOUR PAST-- ESPECIALLY ***PAST INFATUATIONS***-- IS ***TREASON.***
I KNEW IT! I ***KNEW*** YOU WERE INTERCEPTING MY LETTERS! HOW DARE YOU?!

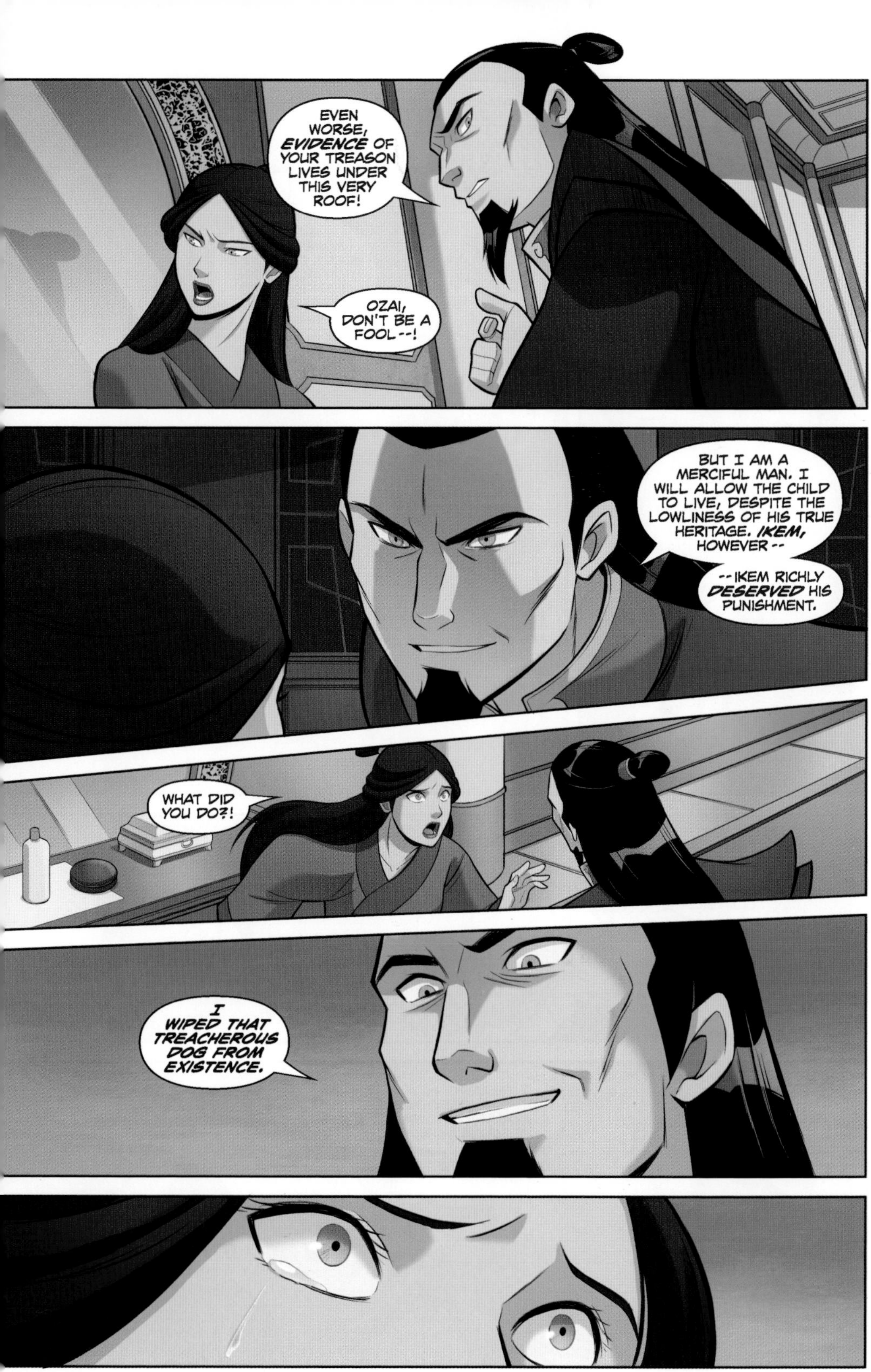
EVEN WORSE, *EVIDENCE* OF YOUR TREASON LIVES UNDER THIS VERY ROOF!
OZAI, DON'T BE A FOOL--!
BUT I AM A MERCIFUL MAN. I WILL ALLOW THE CHILD TO LIVE, DESPITE THE LOWLINESS OF HIS TRUE HERITAGE. *IKEM,* HOWEVER--
--IKEM RICHLY *DESERVED* HIS PUNISHMENT.
WHAT DID YOU DO?!
I WIPED THAT TREACHEROUS DOG FROM EXISTENCE.

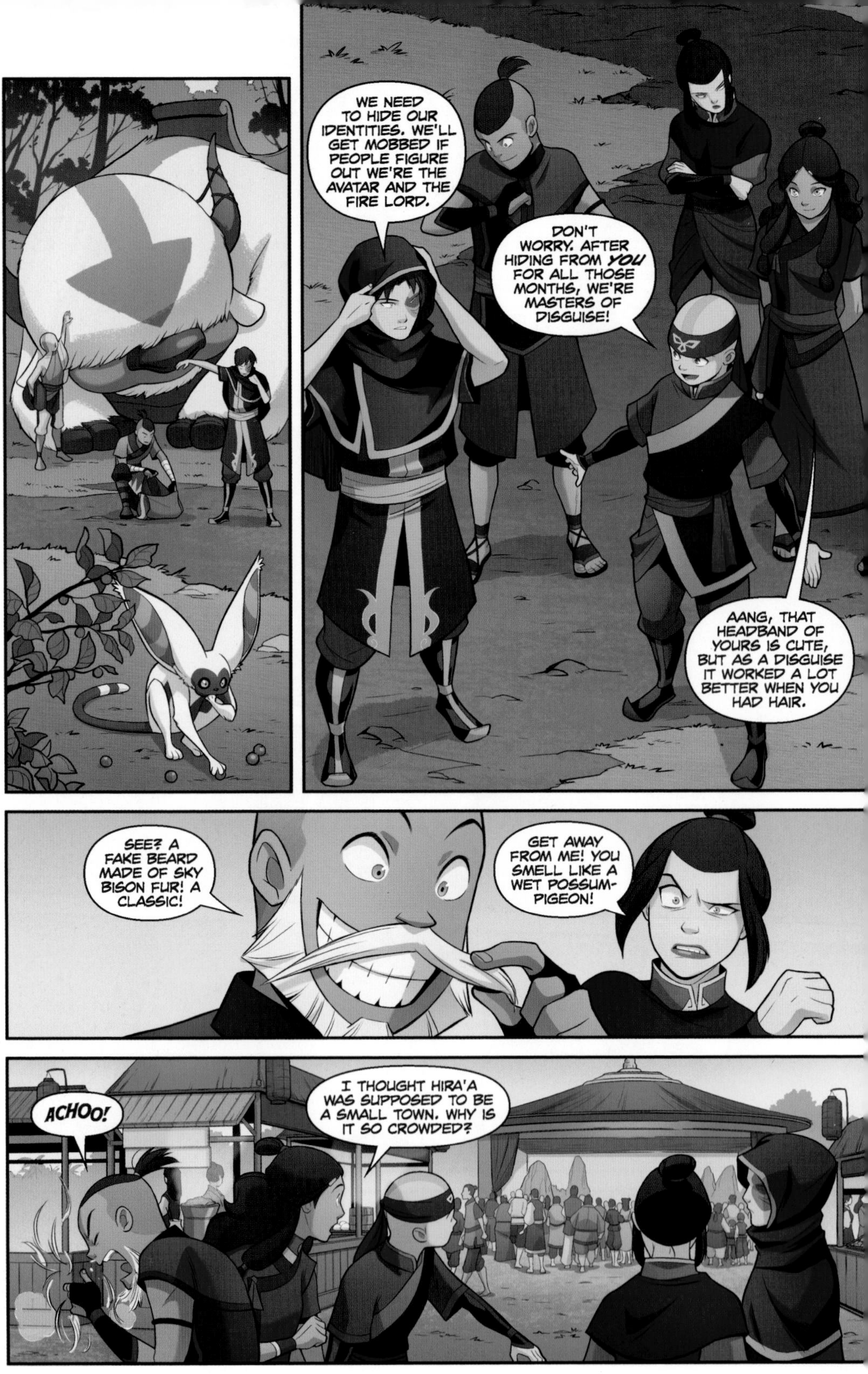
WE NEED TO HIDE OUR IDENTITIES. WE'LL GET MOBBED IF PEOPLE FIGURE OUT WE'RE THE AVATAR AND THE FIRE LORD.
DON'T WORRY. AFTER HIDING FROM *YOU* FOR ALL THOSE MONTHS, WE'RE MASTERS OF DISGUISE!
AANG, THAT HEADBAND OF YOURS IS CUTE, BUT AS A DISGUISE IT WORKED A LOT BETTER WHEN YOU HAD HAIR.
SEE? A FAKE BEARD MADE OF SKY BISON FUR! A CLASSIC!
GET AWAY FROM ME! YOU SMELL LIKE A WET POSSUM-PIGEON!
ACHOO!
I THOUGHT HIRA'A WAS SUPPOSED TO BE A SMALL TOWN. WHY IS IT SO CROWDED?

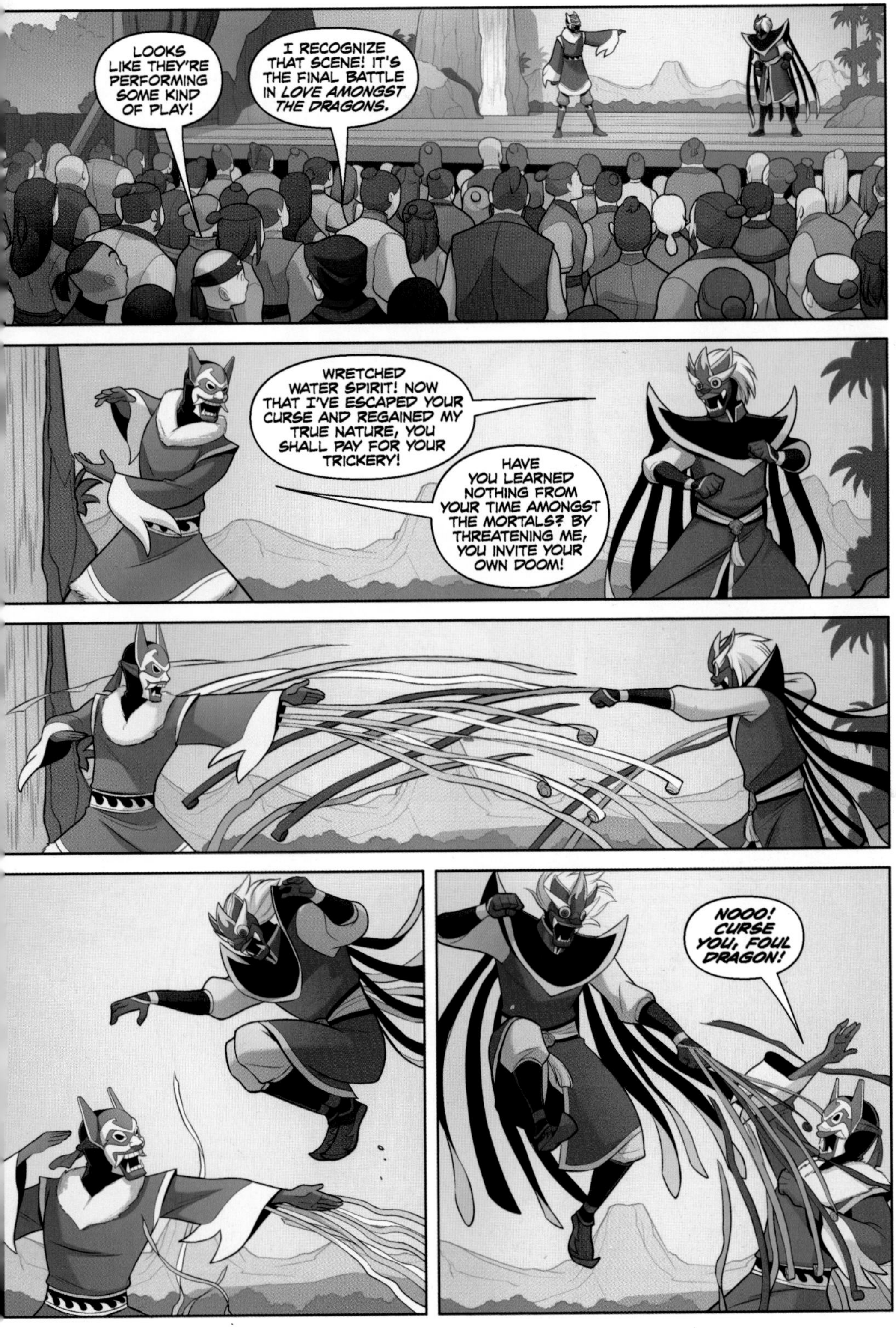
LOOKS LIKE THEY'RE PERFORMING SOME KIND OF PLAY!
I RECOGNIZE THAT SCENE! IT'S THE FINAL BATTLE IN *LOVE AMONGST THE DRAGONS.*
WRETCHED WATER SPIRIT! NOW THAT I'VE ESCAPED YOUR CURSE AND REGAINED MY TRUE NATURE, YOU SHALL PAY FOR YOUR TRICKERY!
HAVE YOU LEARNED NOTHING FROM YOUR TIME AMONGST THE MORTALS? BY THREATENING ME, YOU INVITE YOUR OWN DOOM!
NOOO! CURSE YOU, FOUL DRAGON!

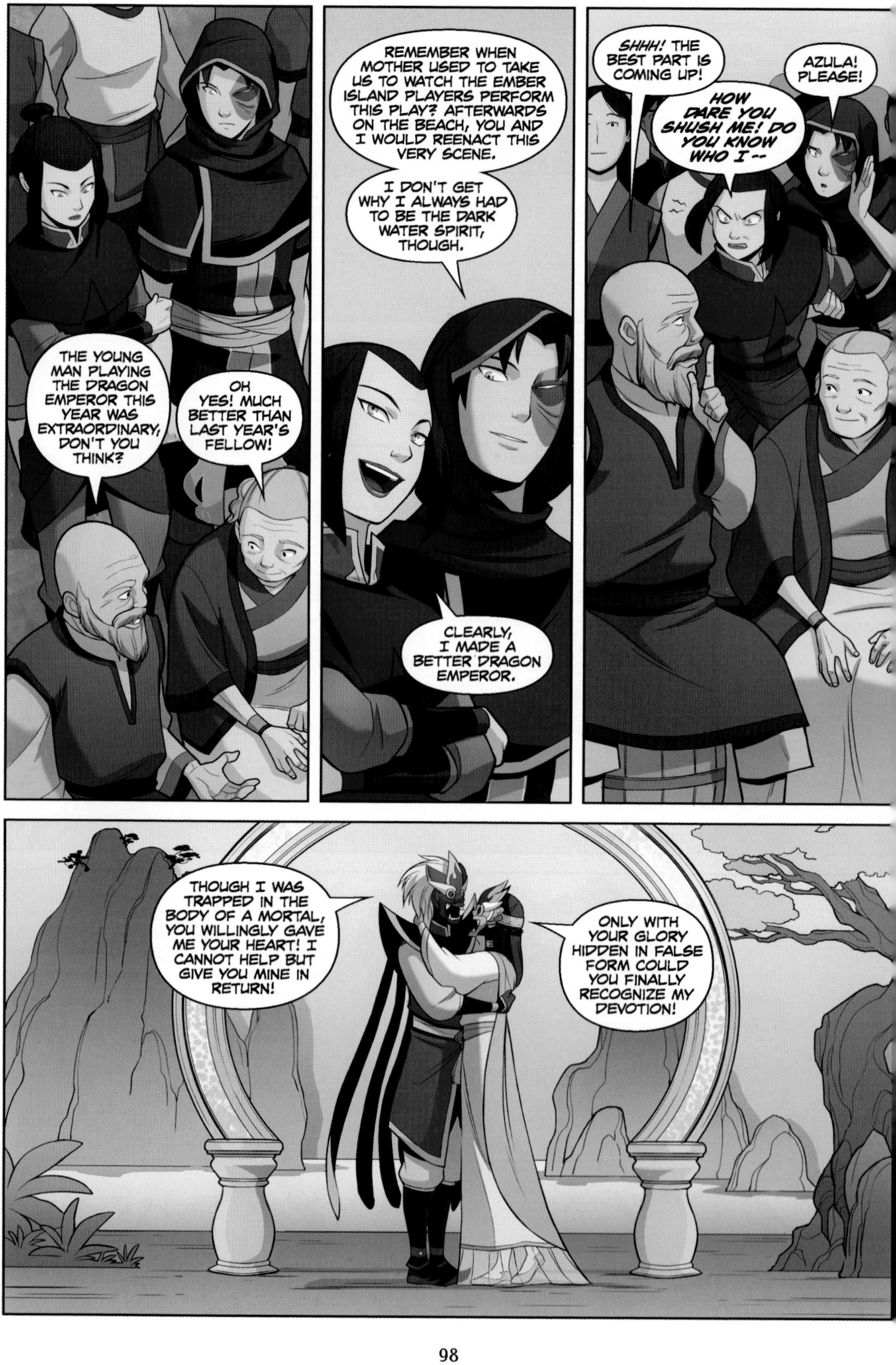
THE YOUNG MAN PLAYING THE DRAGON EMPEROR THIS YEAR WAS EXTRAORDINARY, DON'T YOU THINK?
OH YES! MUCH BETTER THAN LAST YEAR'S FELLOW!
REMEMBER WHEN MOTHER USED TO TAKE US TO WATCH THE EMBER ISLAND PLAYERS PERFORM THIS PLAY? AFTERWARDS ON THE BEACH, YOU AND I WOULD REENACT THIS VERY SCENE.
I DON'T GET WHY I ALWAYS HAD TO BE THE DARK WATER SPIRIT, THOUGH.
CLEARLY, I MADE A BETTER DRAGON EMPEROR.
SHHH! THE BEST PART IS COMING UP!
HOW DARE YOU SHUSH ME! DO YOU KNOW WHO I --
AZULA! PLEASE!
THOUGH I WAS TRAPPED IN THE BODY OF A MORTAL, YOU WILLINGLY GAVE ME YOUR HEART! I CANNOT HELP BUT GIVE YOU MINE IN RETURN!
ONLY WITH YOUR GLORY HIDDEN IN FALSE FORM COULD YOU FINALLY RECOGNIZE MY DEVOTION!

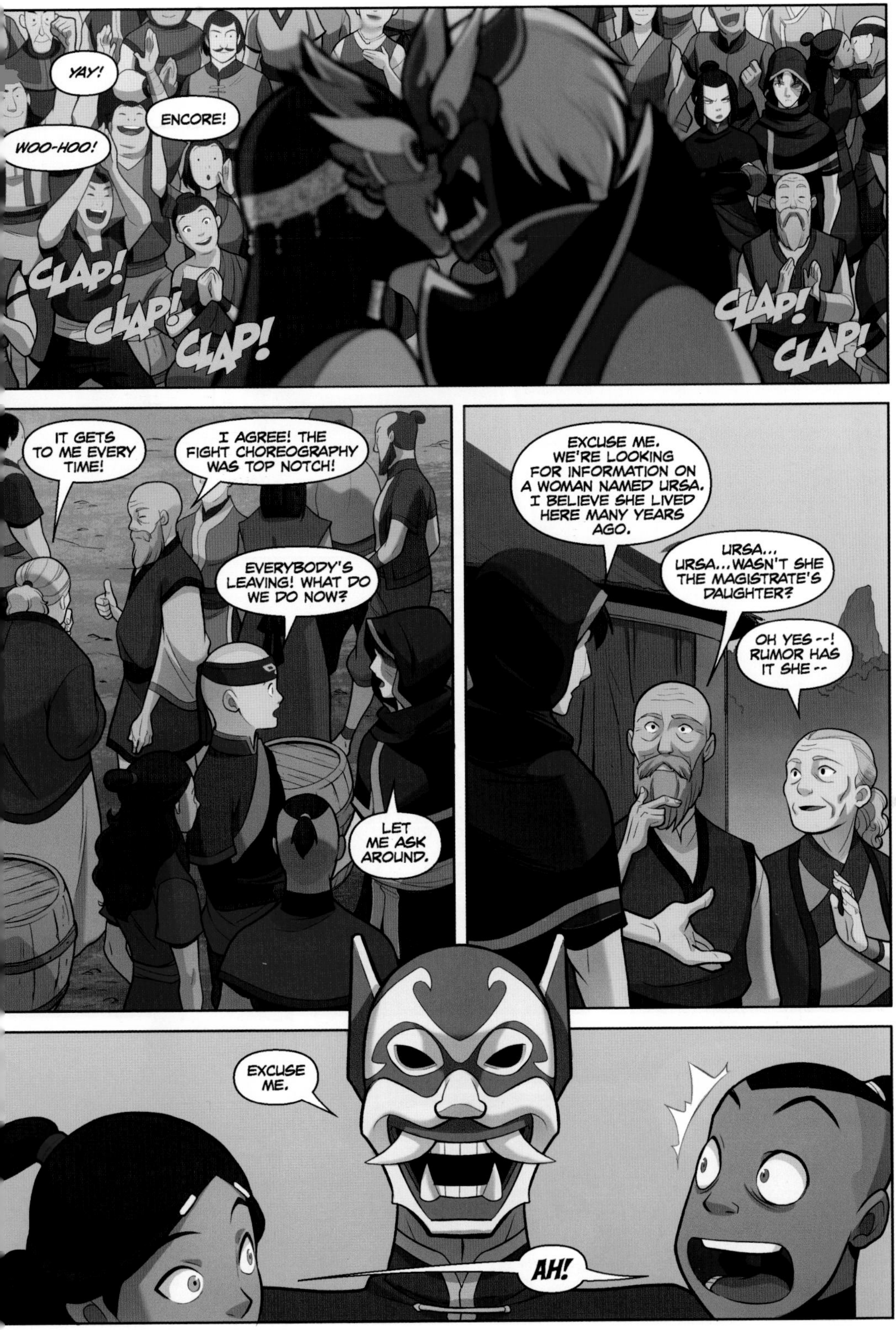
YAY!
ENCORE!
WOO-HOO!
CLAP!
CLAP!
CLAP!
CLAP!
CLAP!
IT GETS TO ME EVERY TIME!
I AGREE! THE FIGHT CHOREOGRAPHY WAS TOP NOTCH!
EVERYBODY'S LEAVING! WHAT DO WE DO NOW?
LET ME ASK AROUND.
EXCUSE ME. WE'RE LOOKING FOR INFORMATION ON A WOMAN NAMED URSA. I BELIEVE SHE LIVED HERE MANY YEARS AGO.
URSA... URSA...WASN'T SHE THE MAGISTRATE'S DAUGHTER?
OH YES --! RUMOR HAS IT SHE --
EXCUSE ME.
AH!

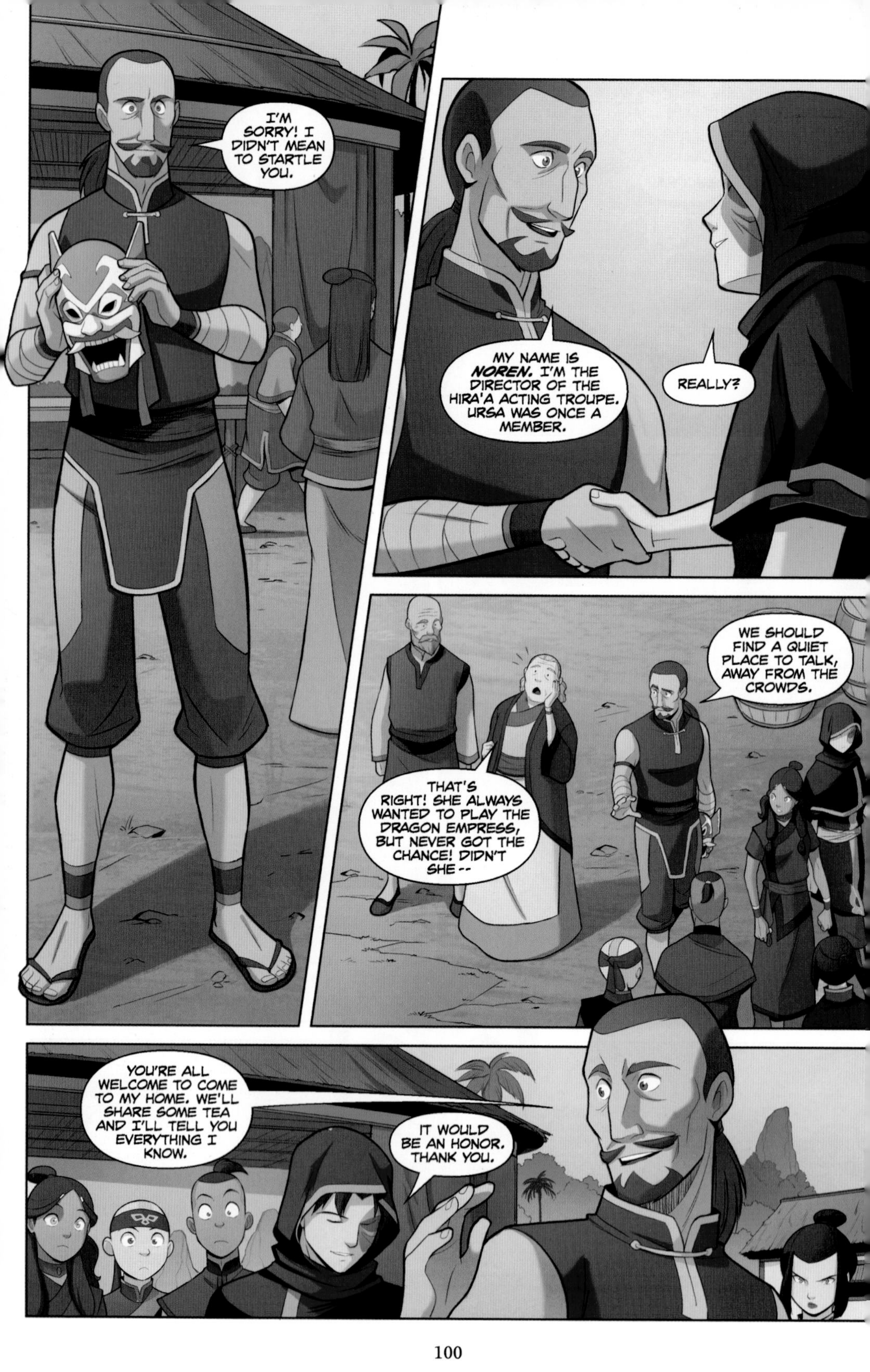
I'M SORRY! I DIDN'T MEAN TO STARTLE YOU.
MY NAME IS NOREN. I'M THE DIRECTOR OF THE HIRA'A ACTING TROUPE. URSA WAS ONCE A MEMBER.
REALLY?
WE SHOULD FIND A QUIET PLACE TO TALK, AWAY FROM THE CROWDS.
THAT'S RIGHT! SHE ALWAYS WANTED TO PLAY THE DRAGON EMPRESS, BUT NEVER GOT THE CHANCE! DIDN'T SHE --
YOU'RE ALL WELCOME TO COME TO MY HOME. WE'LL SHARE SOME TEA AND I'LL TELL YOU EVERYTHING I KNOW.
IT WOULD BE AN HONOR. THANK YOU.

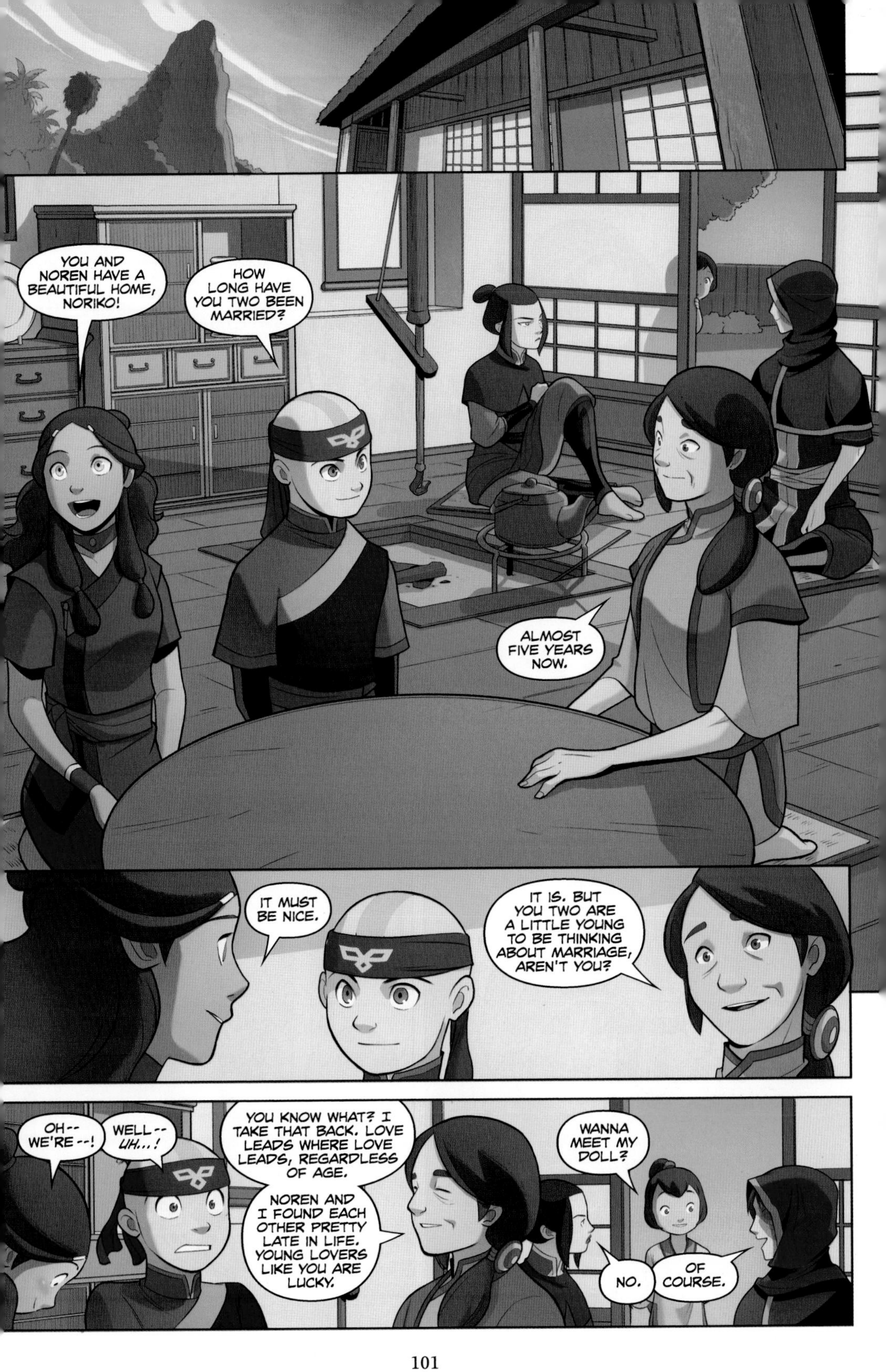

YOU AND NOREN HAVE A BEAUTIFUL HOME, NORIKO!
HOW LONG HAVE YOU TWO BEEN MARRIED?
ALMOST FIVE YEARS NOW.
IT MUST BE NICE.
IT IS. BUT YOU TWO ARE A LITTLE YOUNG TO BE THINKING ABOUT MARRIAGE, AREN'T YOU?
OH-- WE'RE--!
WELL-- UH...!
YOU KNOW WHAT? I TAKE THAT BACK. LOVE LEADS WHERE LOVE LEADS, REGARDLESS OF AGE.
NOREN AND I FOUND EACH OTHER PRETTY LATE IN LIFE. YOUNG LOVERS LIKE YOU ARE LUCKY.
WANNA MEET MY DOLL?
NO.
OF COURSE.

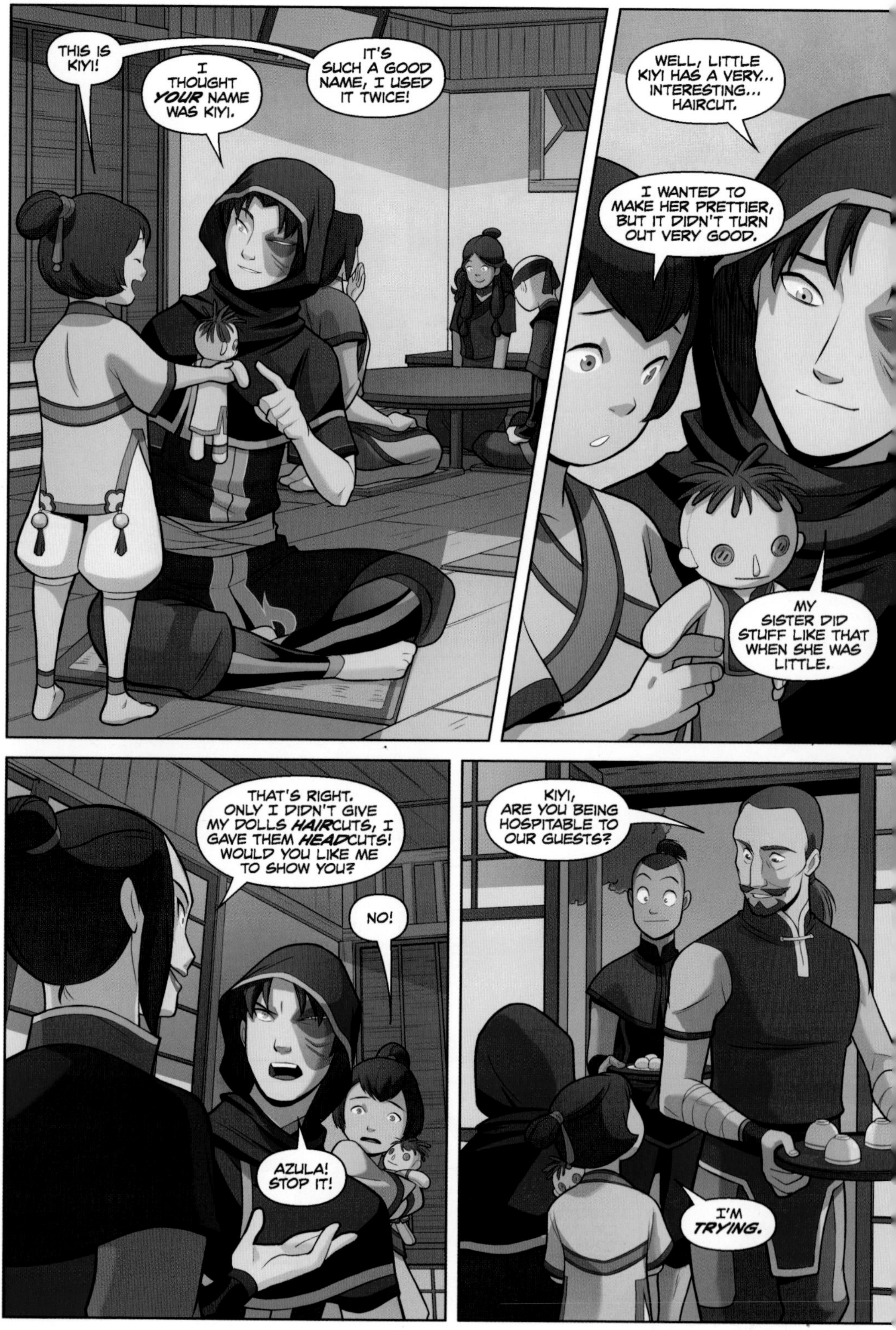
THIS IS KIYI!
I THOUGHT YOUR NAME WAS KIYI.
IT'S SUCH A GOOD NAME, I USED IT TWICE!
WELL, LITTLE KIYI HAS A VERY... INTERESTING... HAIRCUT.
I WANTED TO MAKE HER PRETTIER, BUT IT DIDN'T TURN OUT VERY GOOD.
MY SISTER DID STUFF LIKE THAT WHEN SHE WAS LITTLE.
THAT'S RIGHT. ONLY I DIDN'T GIVE MY DOLLS HAIRCUTS, I GAVE THEM HEADCUTS! WOULD YOU LIKE ME TO SHOW YOU?
NO!
AZULA! STOP IT!
KIYI, ARE YOU BEING HOSPITABLE TO OUR GUESTS?
I'M TRYING.

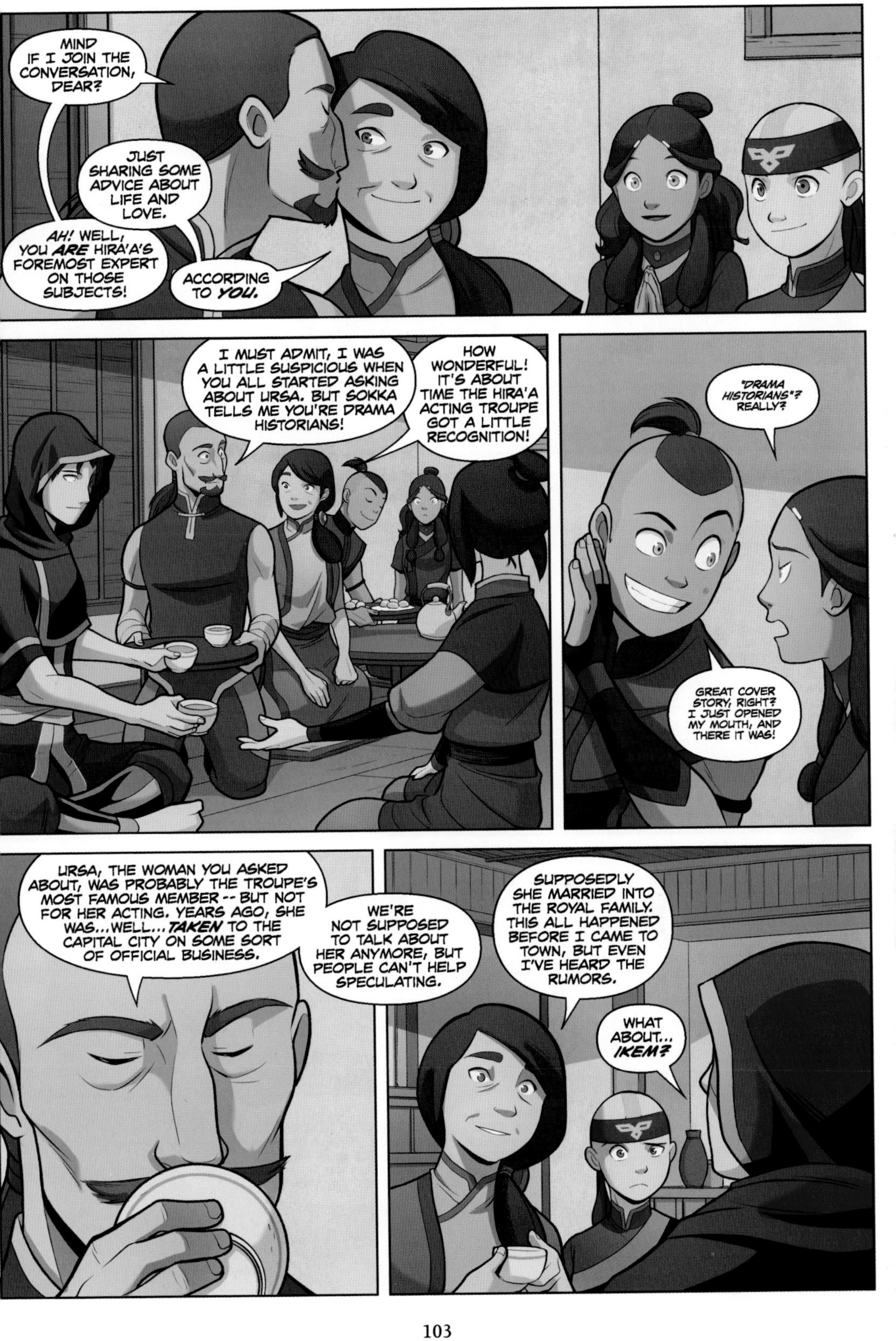
MIND IF I JOIN THE CONVERSATION, DEAR?
JUST SHARING SOME ADVICE ABOUT LIFE AND LOVE.
AH! WELL, YOU ARE HIRA'A'S FOREMOST EXPERT ON THOSE SUBJECTS!
ACCORDING TO YOU.
I MUST ADMIT, I WAS A LITTLE SUSPICIOUS WHEN YOU ALL STARTED ASKING ABOUT URSA. BUT SOKKA TELLS ME YOU'RE DRAMA HISTORIANS!
HOW WONDERFUL! IT'S ABOUT TIME THE HIRA'A ACTING TROUPE GOT A LITTLE RECOGNITION!
"DRAMA HISTORIANS"? REALLY?
GREAT COVER STORY, RIGHT? I JUST OPENED MY MOUTH, AND THERE IT WAS!
URSA, THE WOMAN YOU ASKED ABOUT, WAS PROBABLY THE TROUPE'S MOST FAMOUS MEMBER -- BUT NOT FOR HER ACTING. YEARS AGO, SHE WAS...WELL...TAKEN TO THE CAPITAL CITY ON SOME SORT OF OFFICIAL BUSINESS.
WE'RE NOT SUPPOSED TO TALK ABOUT HER ANYMORE, BUT PEOPLE CAN'T HELP SPECULATING.
SUPPOSEDLY SHE MARRIED INTO THE ROYAL FAMILY. THIS ALL HAPPENED BEFORE I CAME TO TOWN, BUT EVEN I'VE HEARD THE RUMORS.
WHAT ABOUT... IKEM?

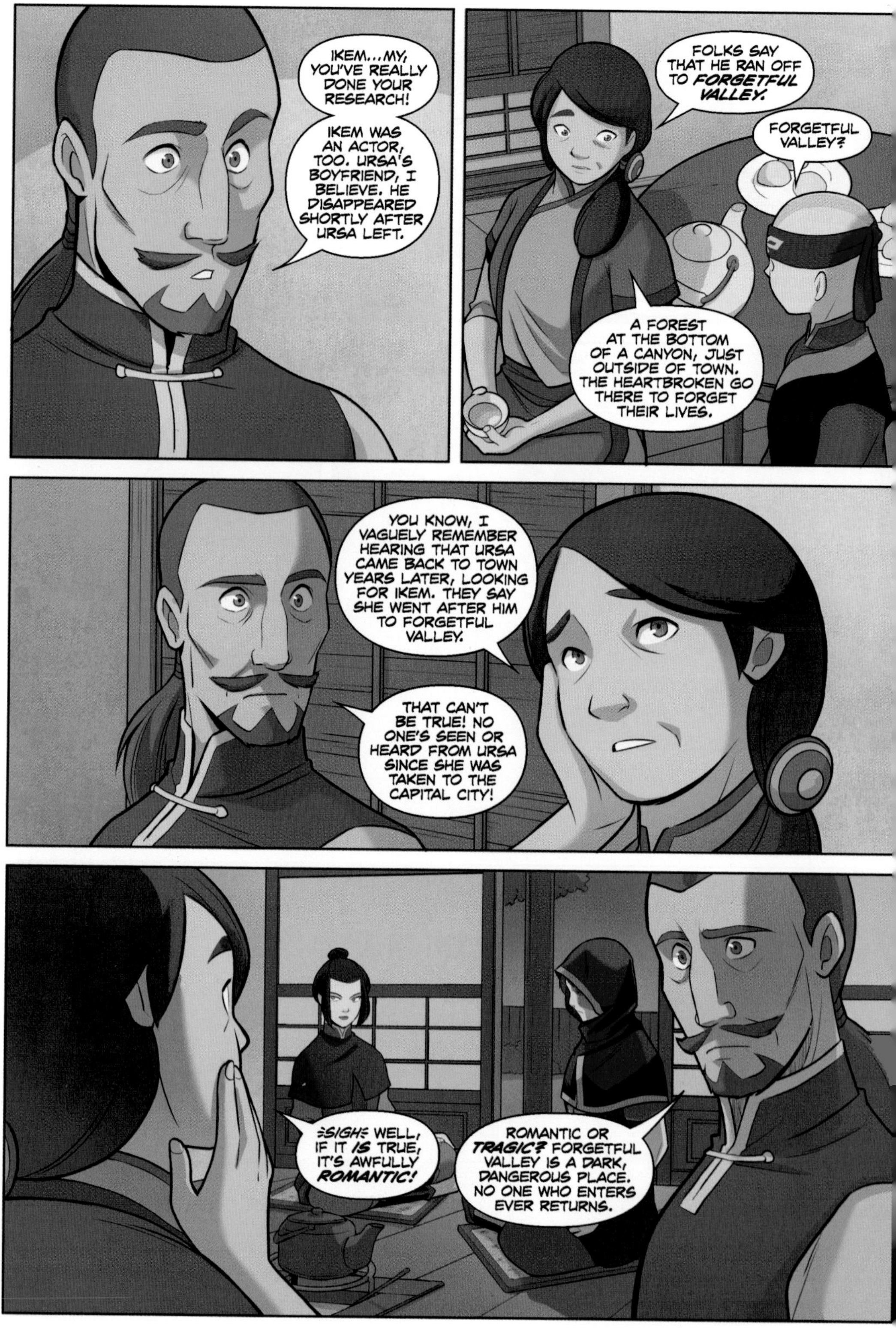
IKEM...MY, YOU'VE REALLY DONE YOUR RESEARCH!
IKEM WAS AN ACTOR, TOO. URSA'S BOYFRIEND, I BELIEVE. HE DISAPPEARED SHORTLY AFTER URSA LEFT.
FOLKS SAY THAT HE RAN OFF TO FORGETFUL VALLEY.
FORGETFUL VALLEY?
A FOREST AT THE BOTTOM OF A CANYON, JUST OUTSIDE OF TOWN. THE HEARTBROKEN GO THERE TO FORGET THEIR LIVES.
YOU KNOW, I VAGUELY REMEMBER HEARING THAT URSA CAME BACK TO TOWN YEARS LATER, LOOKING FOR IKEM. THEY SAY SHE WENT AFTER HIM TO FORGETFUL VALLEY.
THAT CAN'T BE TRUE! NO ONE'S SEEN OR HEARD FROM URSA SINCE SHE WAS TAKEN TO THE CAPITAL CITY!
=SIGH= WELL, IF IT IS TRUE, IT'S AWFULLY ROMANTIC!
ROMANTIC OR TRAGIC? FORGETFUL VALLEY IS A DARK, DANGEROUS PLACE. NO ONE WHO ENTERS EVER RETURNS.

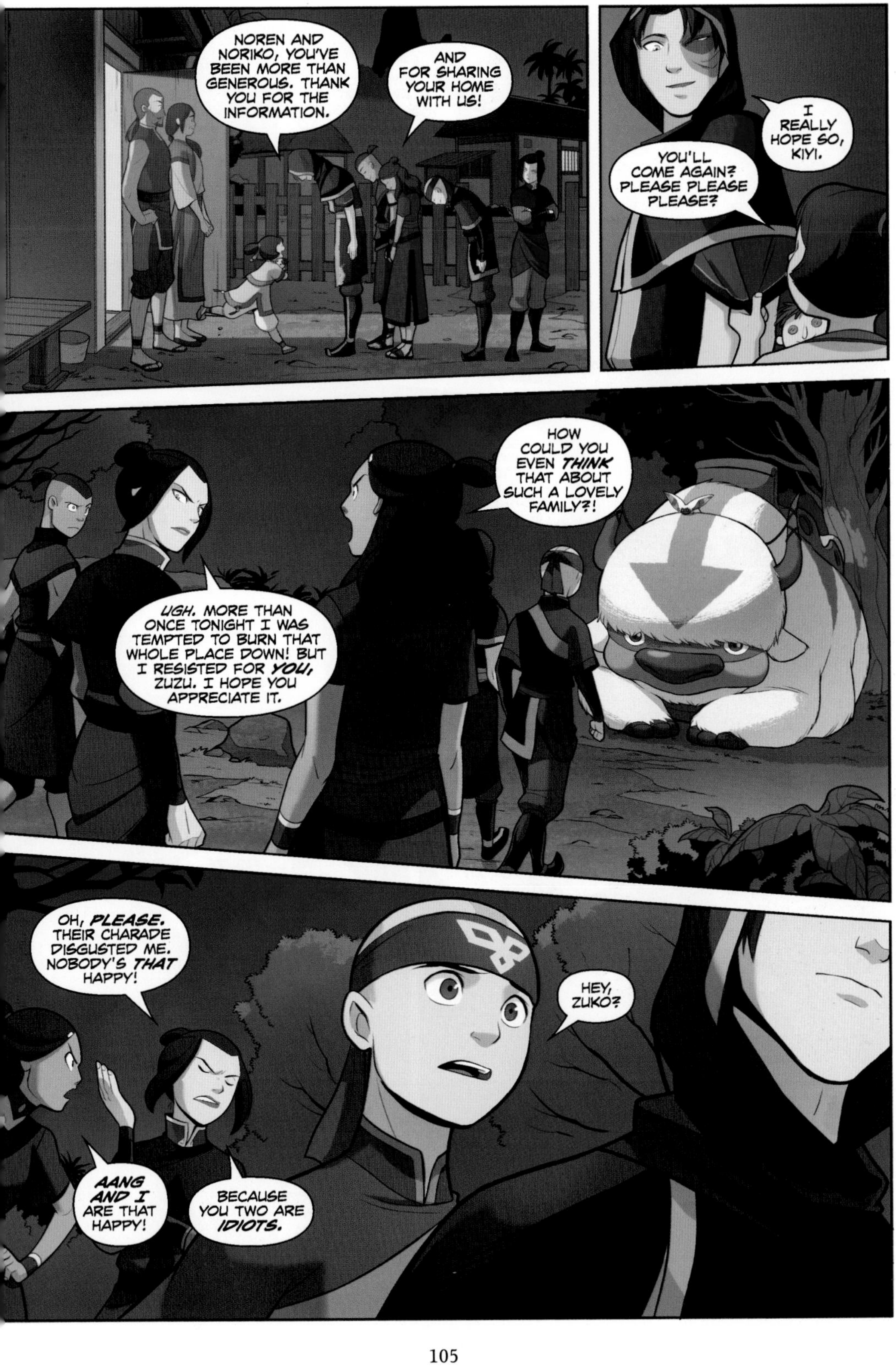
NOREN AND NORIKO, YOU'VE BEEN MORE THAN GENEROUS. THANK YOU FOR THE INFORMATION.
AND FOR SHARING YOUR HOME WITH US!
YOU'LL COME AGAIN? PLEASE PLEASE PLEASE?
I REALLY HOPE SO, KIYI.
UGH. MORE THAN ONCE TONIGHT I WAS TEMPTED TO BURN THAT WHOLE PLACE DOWN! BUT I RESISTED FOR YOU, ZUZU. I HOPE YOU APPRECIATE IT.
HOW COULD YOU EVEN THINK THAT ABOUT SUCH A LOVELY FAMILY?!
OH, PLEASE. THEIR CHARADE DISGUSTED ME. NOBODY'S THAT HAPPY!
AANG AND I ARE THAT HAPPY!
BECAUSE YOU TWO ARE IDIOTS.
HEY, ZUKO?

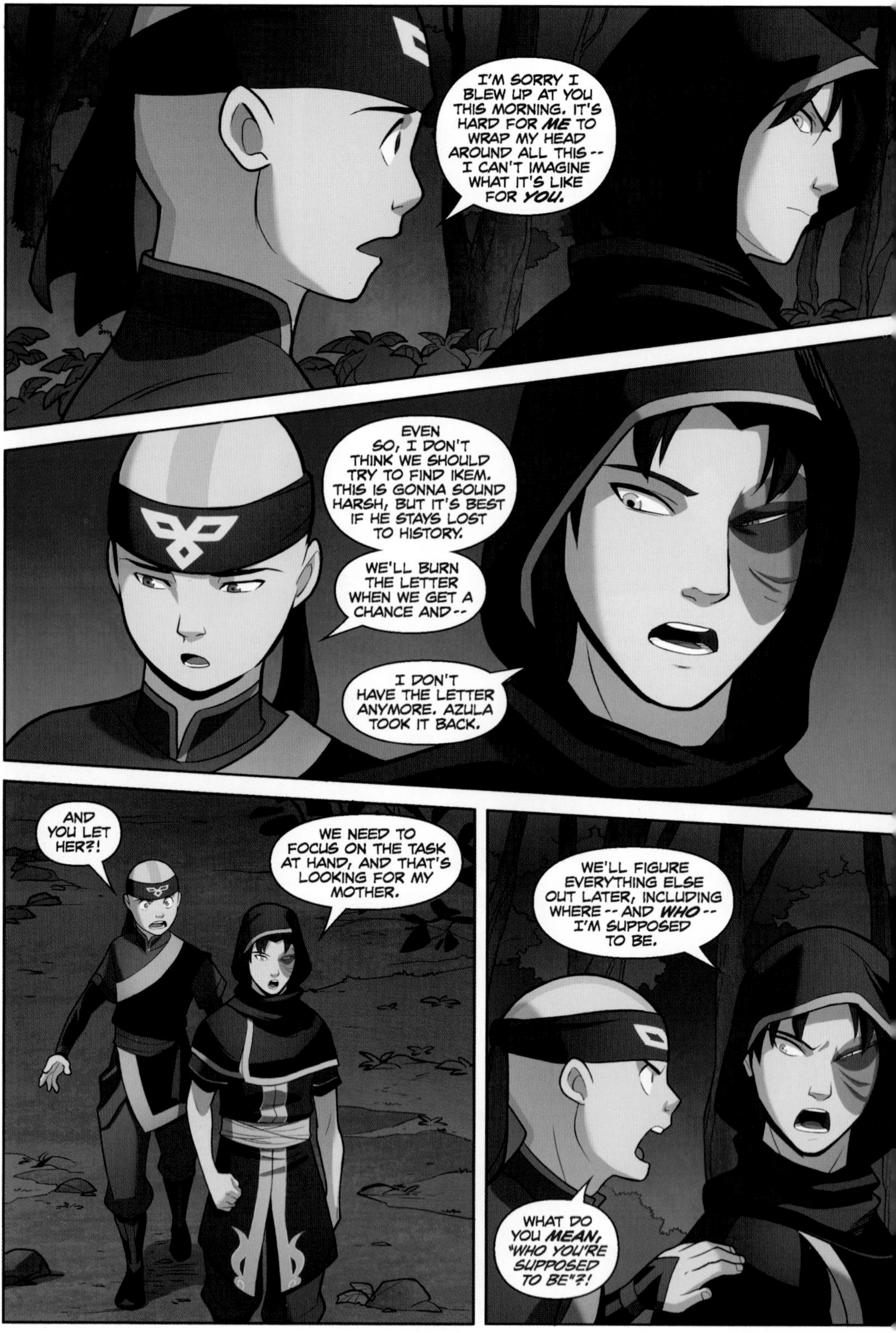
I'M SORRY I BLEW UP AT YOU THIS MORNING. IT'S HARD FOR *ME* TO WRAP MY HEAD AROUND ALL THIS -- I CAN'T IMAGINE WHAT IT'S LIKE FOR *YOU.*
EVEN SO, I DON'T THINK WE SHOULD TRY TO FIND IKEM. THIS IS GONNA SOUND HARSH, BUT IT'S BEST IF HE STAYS LOST TO HISTORY.
WE'LL BURN THE LETTER WHEN WE GET A CHANCE AND --
I DON'T HAVE THE LETTER ANYMORE. AZULA TOOK IT BACK.
AND YOU LET HER?!
WE NEED TO FOCUS ON THE TASK AT HAND, AND THAT'S LOOKING FOR MY MOTHER.
WE'LL FIGURE EVERYTHING ELSE OUT LATER, INCLUDING WHERE -- AND *WHO* -- I'M SUPPOSED TO BE.
WHAT DO YOU *MEAN, "WHO YOU'RE SUPPOSED TO BE"?!*

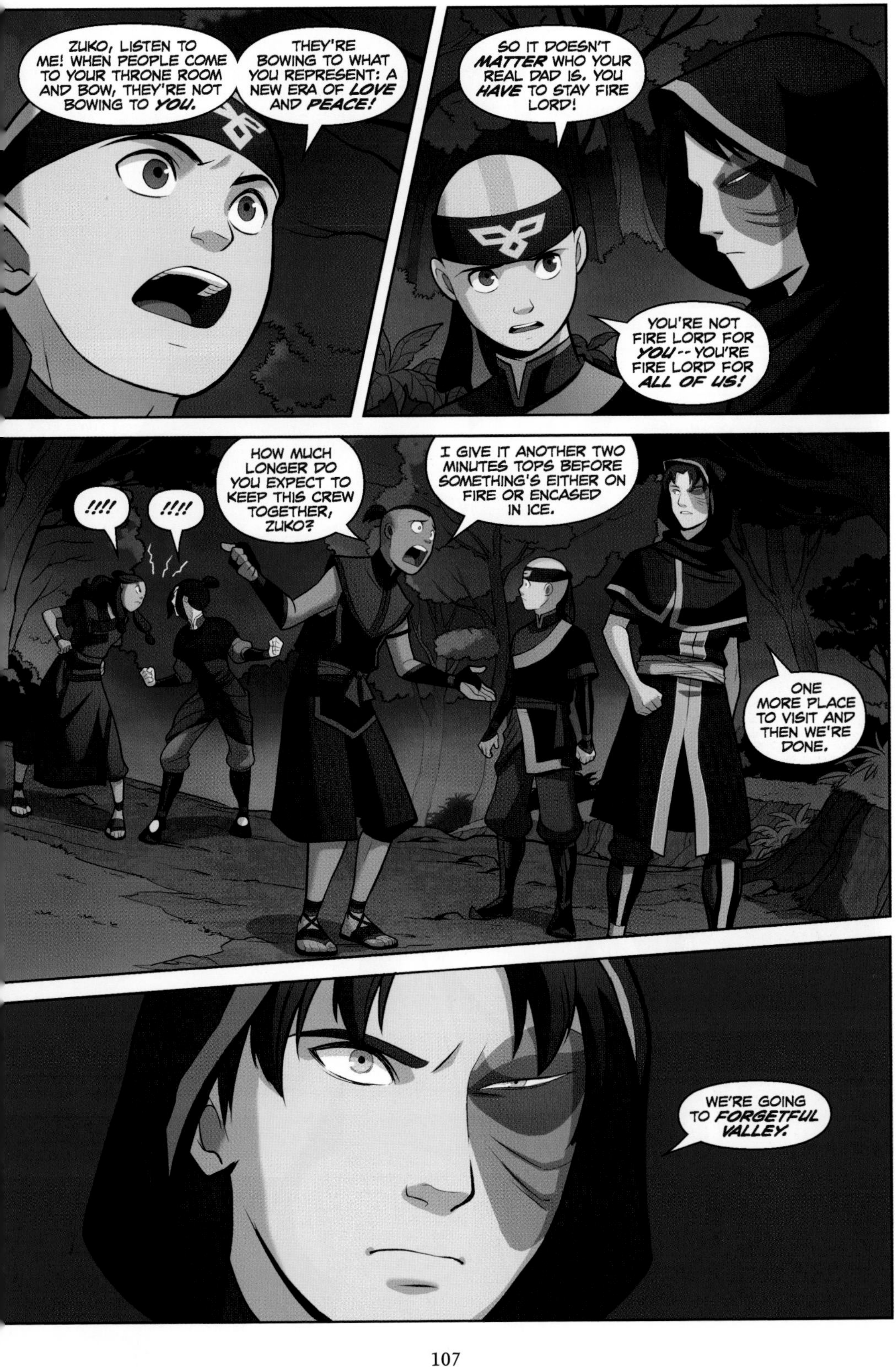
ZUKO, LISTEN TO ME! WHEN PEOPLE COME TO YOUR THRONE ROOM AND BOW, THEY'RE NOT BOWING TO *YOU.*
THEY'RE BOWING TO WHAT YOU REPRESENT: A NEW ERA OF *LOVE* AND *PEACE!*
SO IT DOESN'T *MATTER* WHO YOUR REAL DAD IS. YOU *HAVE* TO STAY FIRE LORD!
YOU'RE NOT FIRE LORD FOR *YOU*-- YOU'RE FIRE LORD FOR *ALL OF US!*
!!!!
!!!!
HOW MUCH LONGER DO YOU EXPECT TO KEEP THIS CREW TOGETHER, ZUKO?
I GIVE IT ANOTHER TWO MINUTES TOPS BEFORE SOMETHING'S EITHER ON FIRE OR ENCASED IN ICE.
ONE MORE PLACE TO VISIT AND THEN WE'RE DONE.
WE'RE GOING TO *FORGETFUL VALLEY.*

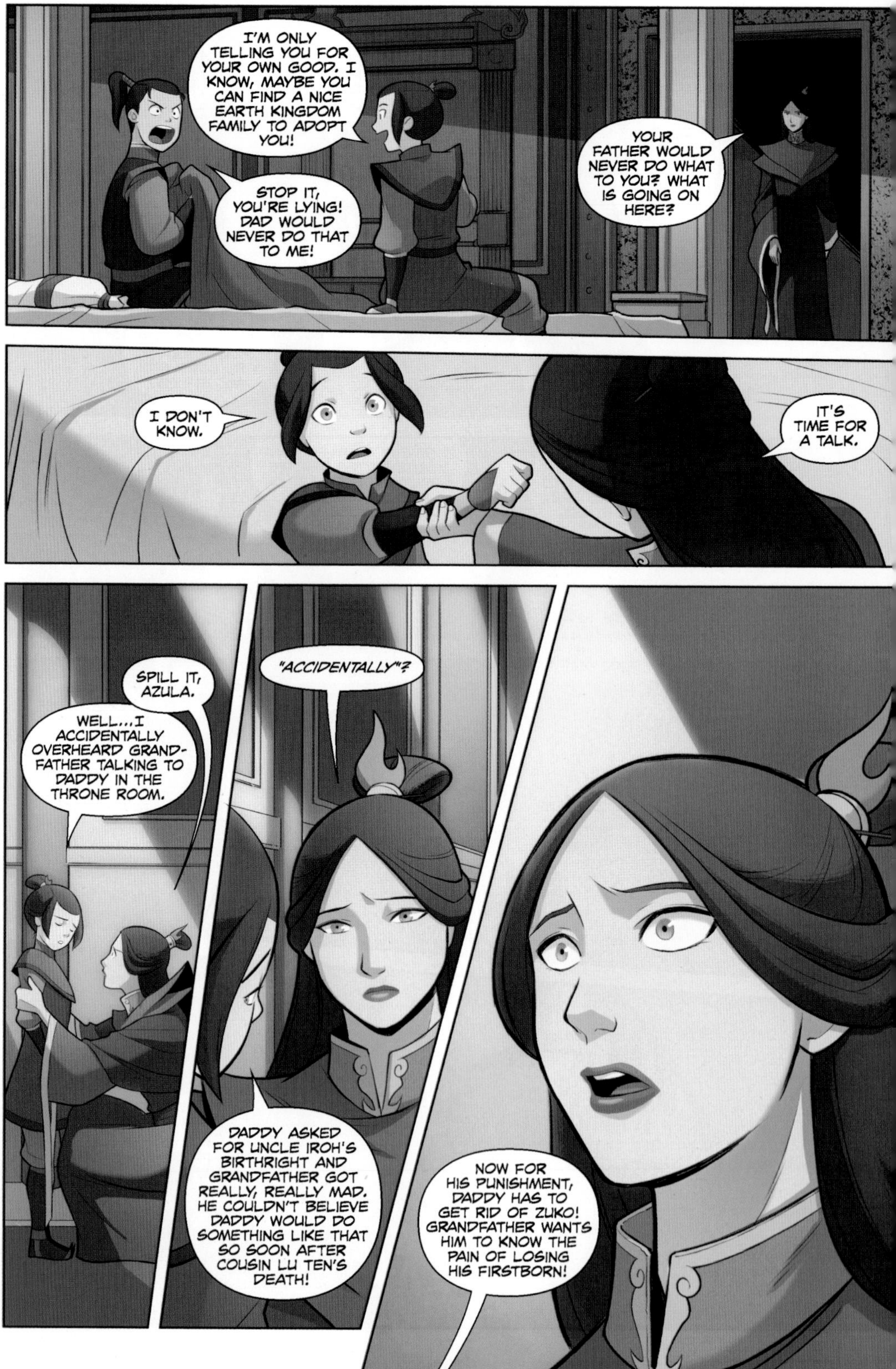
I'M ONLY TELLING YOU FOR YOUR OWN GOOD. I KNOW, MAYBE YOU CAN FIND A NICE EARTH KINGDOM FAMILY TO ADOPT YOU!
STOP IT, YOU'RE LYING! DAD WOULD NEVER DO THAT TO ME!
YOUR FATHER WOULD NEVER DO WHAT TO YOU? WHAT IS GOING ON HERE?
I DON'T KNOW.
IT'S TIME FOR A TALK.
SPILL IT, AZULA.
WELL...I ACCIDENTALLY OVERHEARD GRAND-FATHER TALKING TO DADDY IN THE THRONE ROOM.
"ACCIDENTALLY"?
DADDY ASKED FOR UNCLE IROH'S BIRTHRIGHT AND GRANDFATHER GOT REALLY, REALLY MAD. HE COULDN'T BELIEVE DADDY WOULD DO SOMETHING LIKE THAT SO SOON AFTER COUSIN LU TEN'S DEATH!
NOW FOR HIS PUNISHMENT, DADDY HAS TO GET RID OF ZUKO! GRANDFATHER WANTS HIM TO KNOW THE PAIN OF LOSING HIS FIRSTBORN!

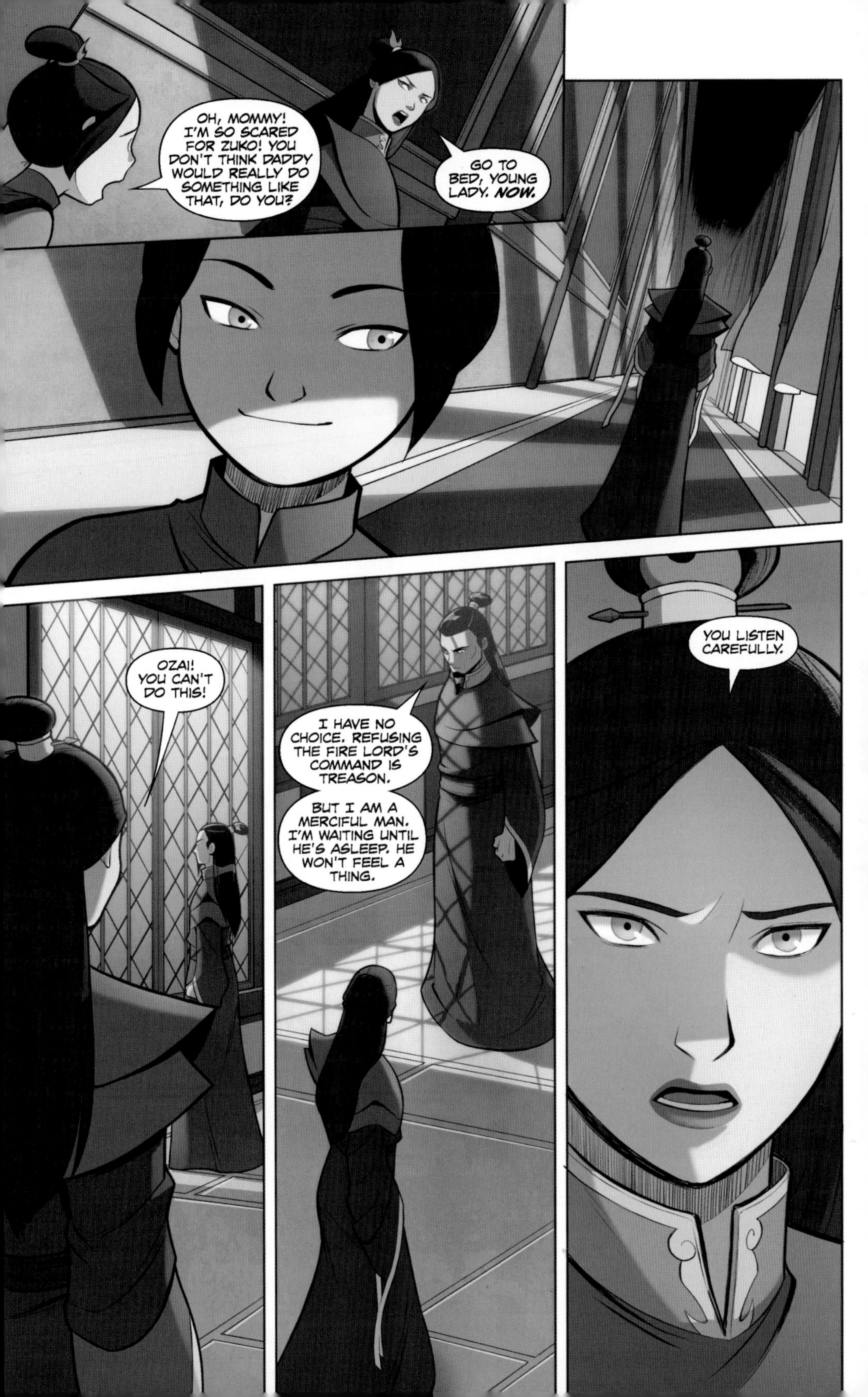
OH, MOMMY! I'M SO SCARED FOR ZUKO! YOU DON'T THINK DADDY WOULD REALLY DO SOMETHING LIKE THAT, DO YOU?
GO TO BED, YOUNG LADY. ***NOW.***
OZAI! YOU CAN'T DO THIS!
I HAVE NO CHOICE. REFUSING THE FIRE LORD'S COMMAND IS TREASON.
BUT I AM A MERCIFUL MAN. I'M WAITING UNTIL HE'S ASLEEP. HE WON'T FEEL A THING.
YOU LISTEN CAREFULLY.

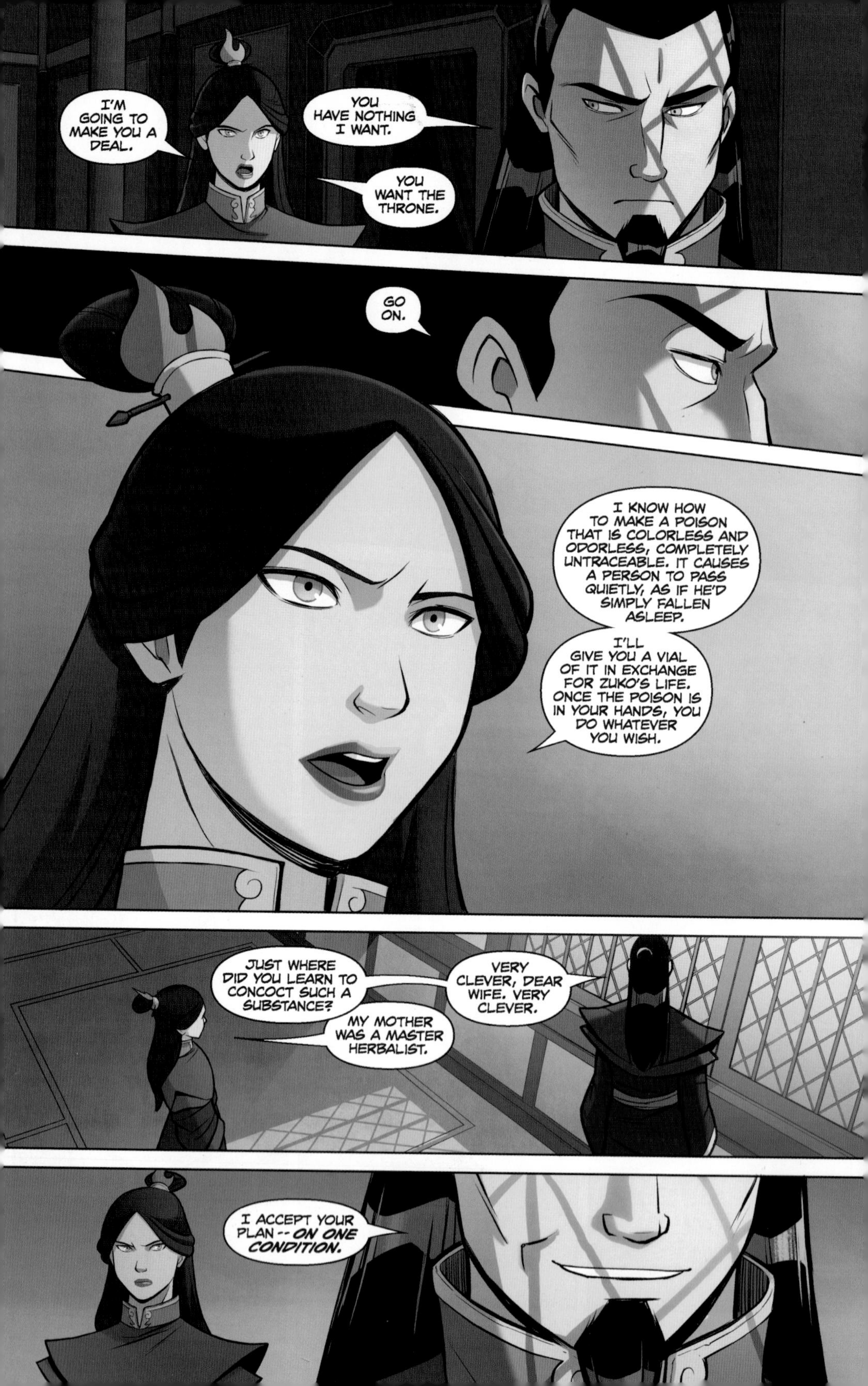
I'M GOING TO MAKE YOU A DEAL.
YOU HAVE NOTHING I WANT.
YOU WANT THE THRONE.
GO ON.
I KNOW HOW TO MAKE A POISON THAT IS COLORLESS AND ODORLESS, COMPLETELY UNTRACEABLE. IT CAUSES A PERSON TO PASS QUIETLY, AS IF HE'D SIMPLY FALLEN ASLEEP.
I'LL GIVE YOU A VIAL OF IT IN EXCHANGE FOR ZUKO'S LIFE. ONCE THE POISON IS IN YOUR HANDS, YOU DO WHATEVER YOU WISH.
VERY CLEVER, DEAR WIFE. VERY CLEVER.
JUST WHERE DID YOU LEARN TO CONCOCT SUCH A SUBSTANCE?
MY MOTHER WAS A MASTER HERBALIST.
I ACCEPT YOUR PLAN -- ON ONE CONDITION.

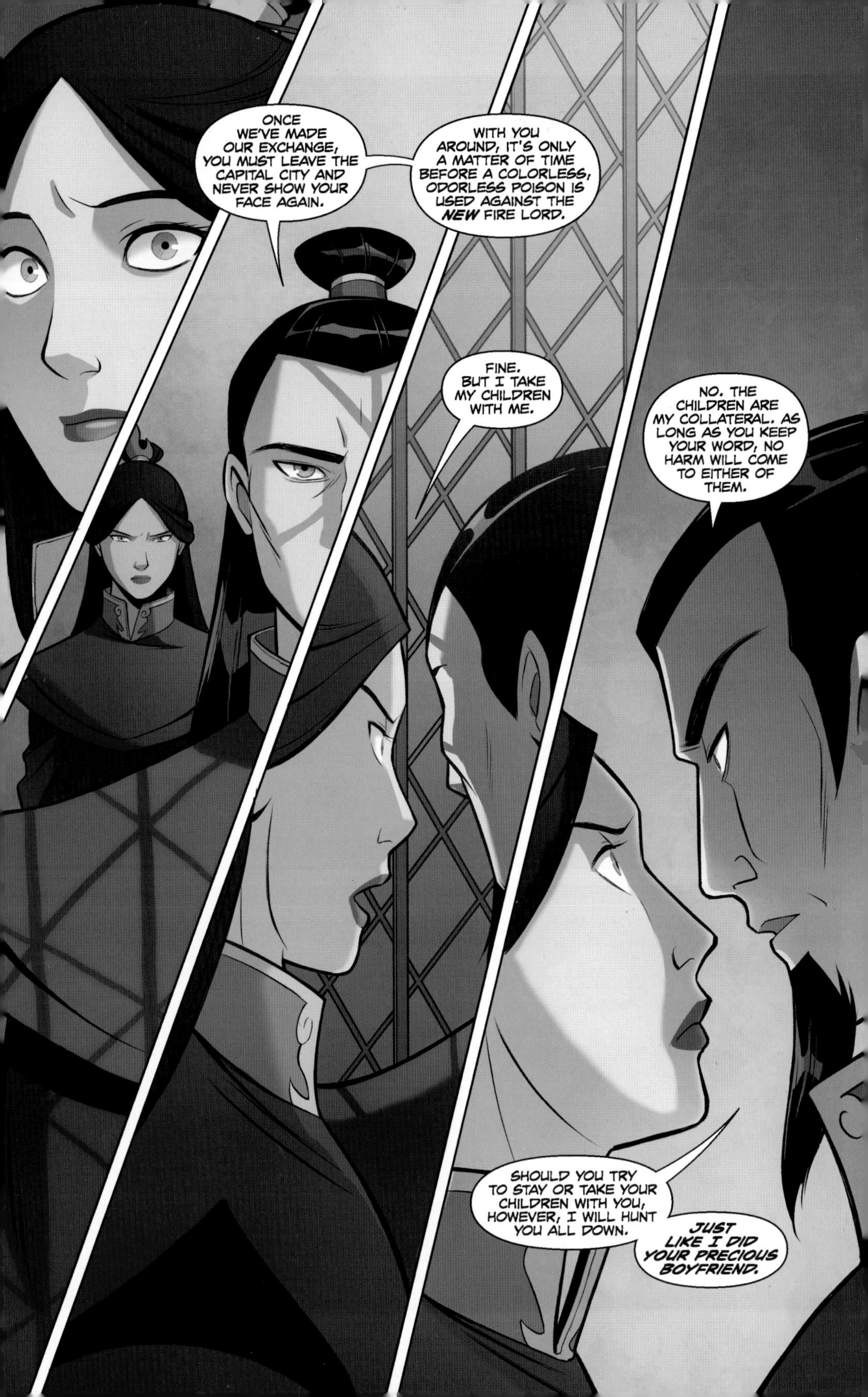
ONCE WE'VE MADE OUR EXCHANGE, YOU MUST LEAVE THE CAPITAL CITY AND NEVER SHOW YOUR FACE AGAIN.
WITH YOU AROUND, IT'S ONLY A MATTER OF TIME BEFORE A COLORLESS, ODORLESS POISON IS USED AGAINST THE *NEW* FIRE LORD.
FINE. BUT I TAKE MY CHILDREN WITH ME.
NO. THE CHILDREN ARE MY COLLATERAL. AS LONG AS YOU KEEP YOUR WORD, NO HARM WILL COME TO EITHER OF THEM.
SHOULD YOU TRY TO STAY OR TAKE YOUR CHILDREN WITH YOU, HOWEVER, I WILL HUNT YOU ALL DOWN.
JUST LIKE I DID YOUR PRECIOUS BOYFRIEND.

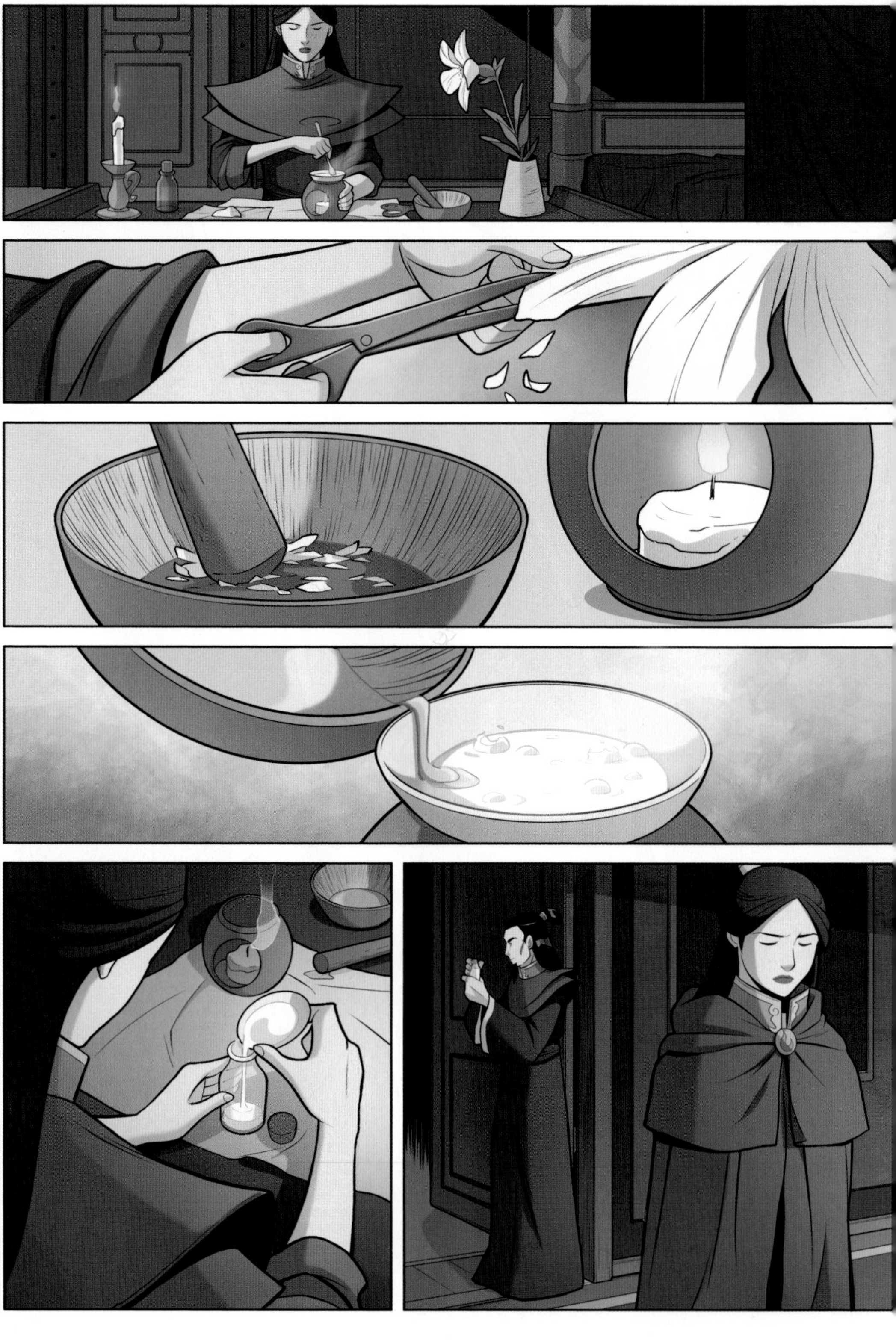

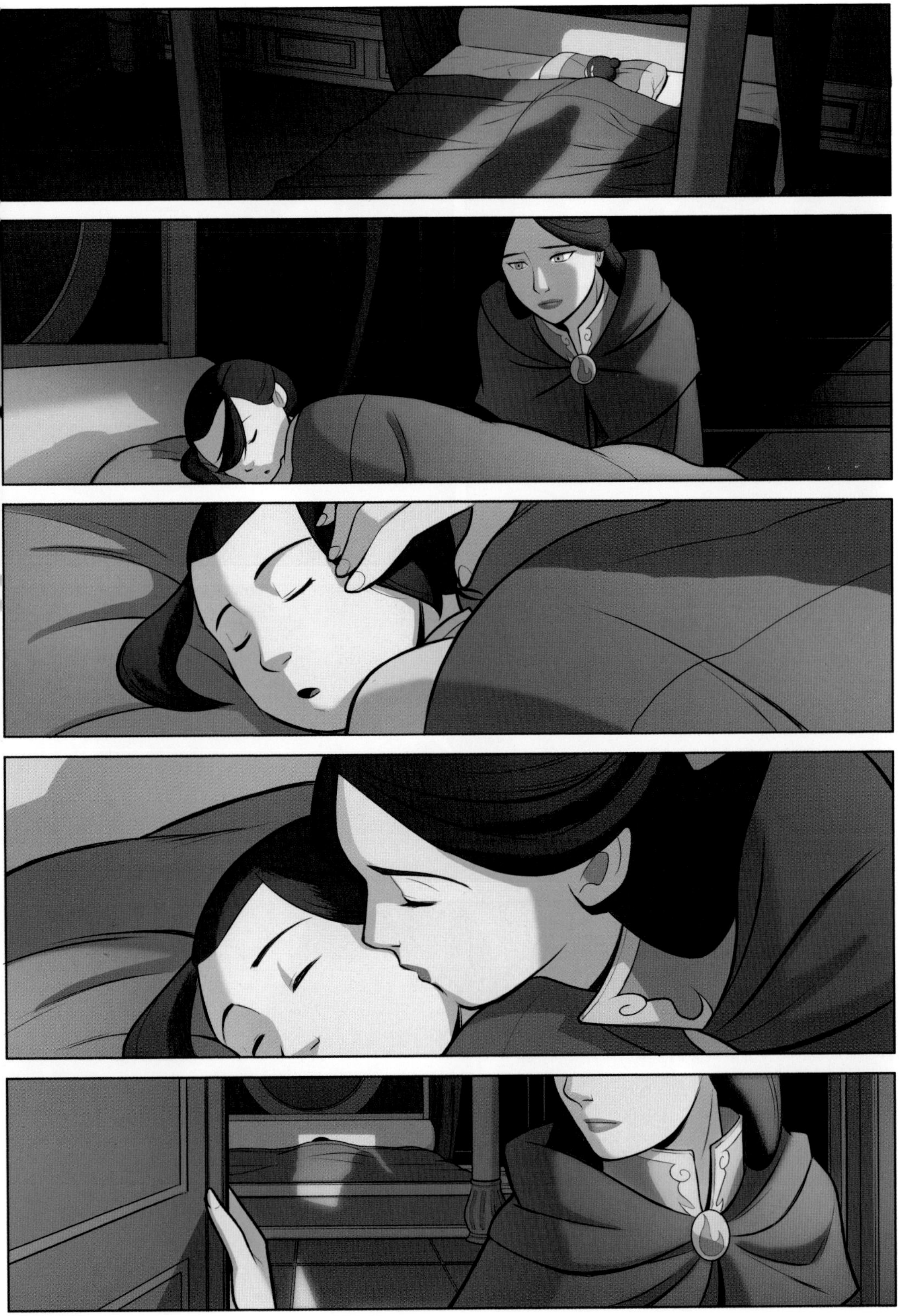

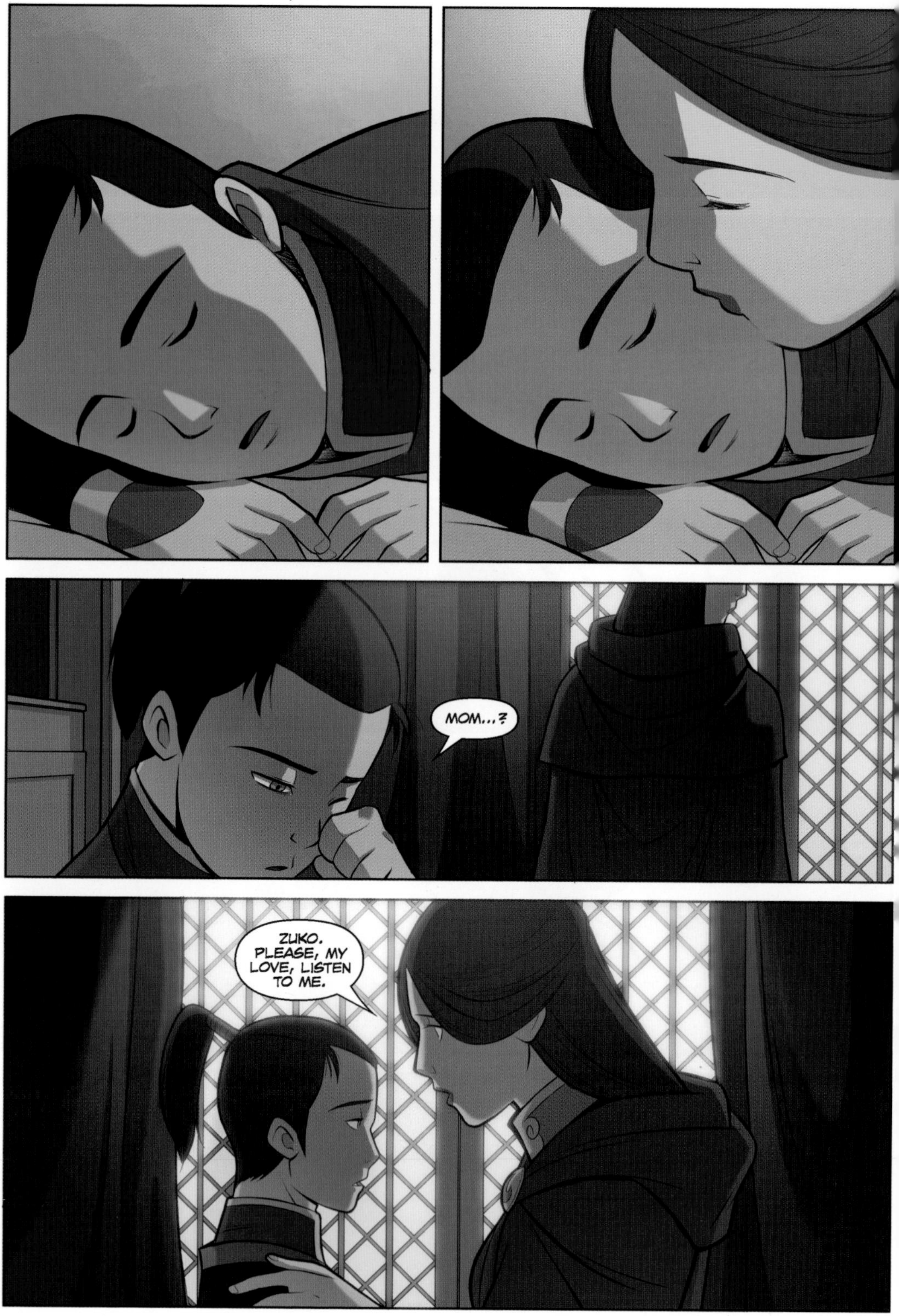
MOM...?
ZUKO. PLEASE, MY LOVE, LISTEN TO ME.

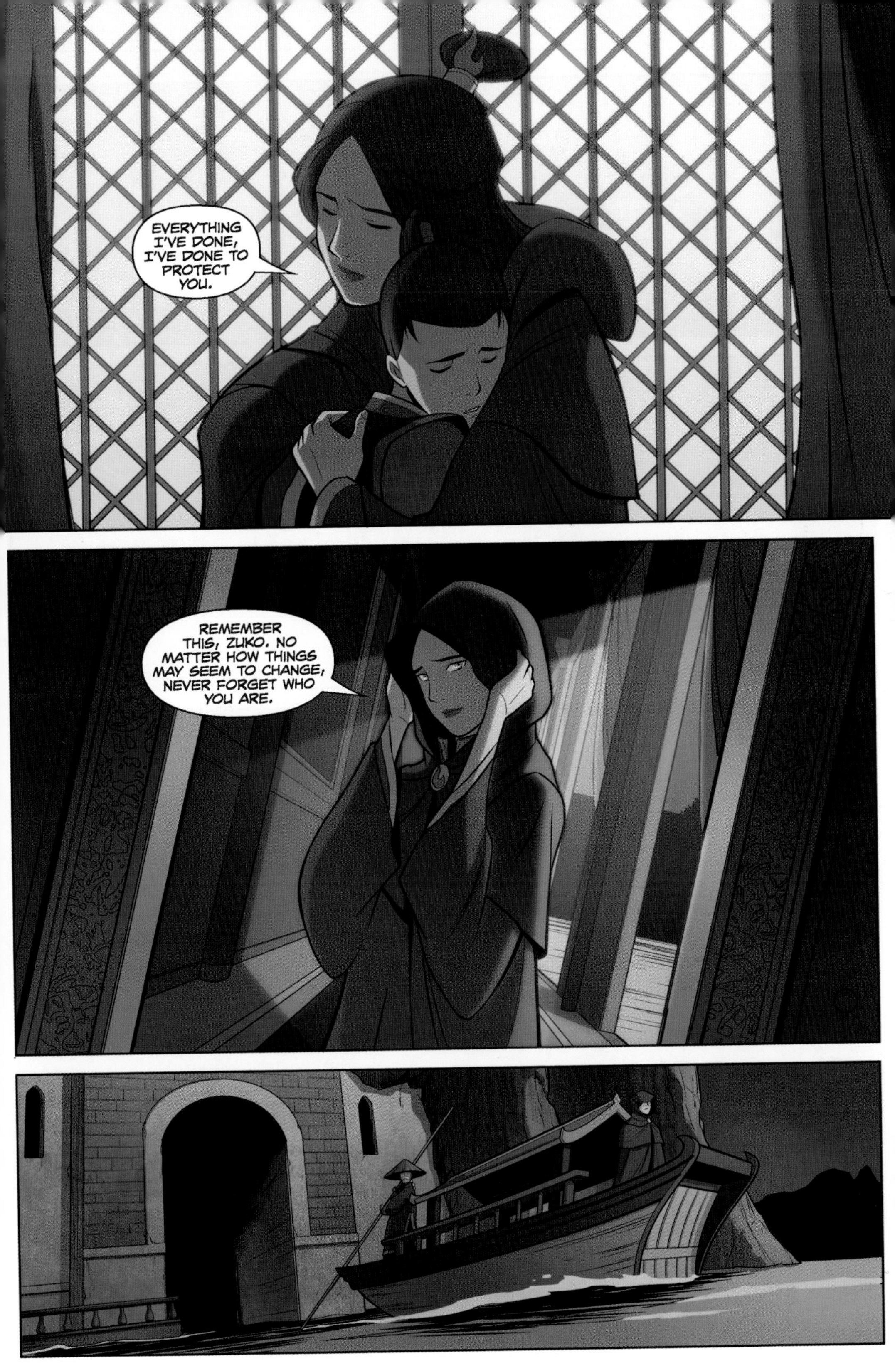
EVERYTHING I'VE DONE, I'VE DONE TO PROTECT YOU.
REMEMBER THIS, ZUKO. NO MATTER HOW THINGS MAY SEEM TO CHANGE, NEVER FORGET WHO YOU ARE.

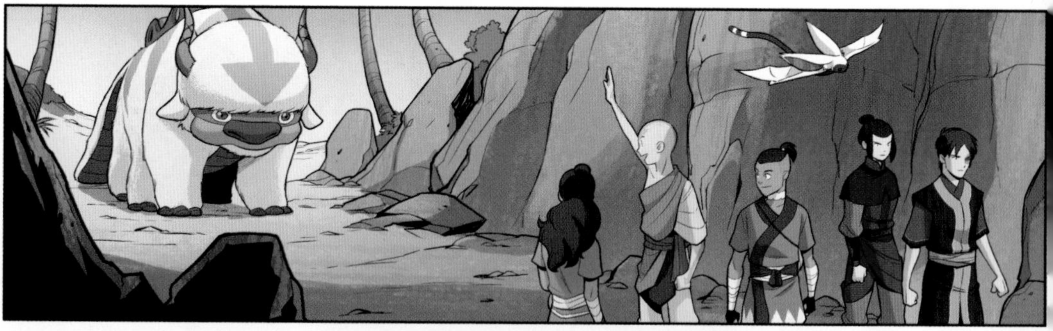

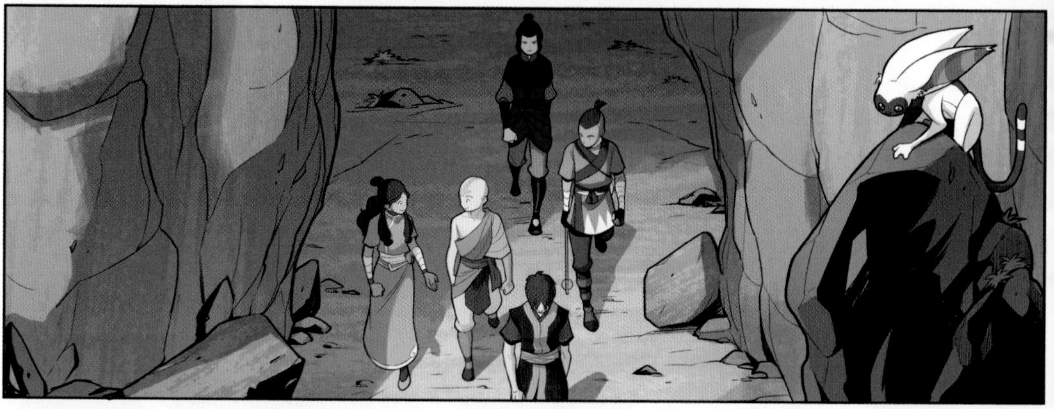

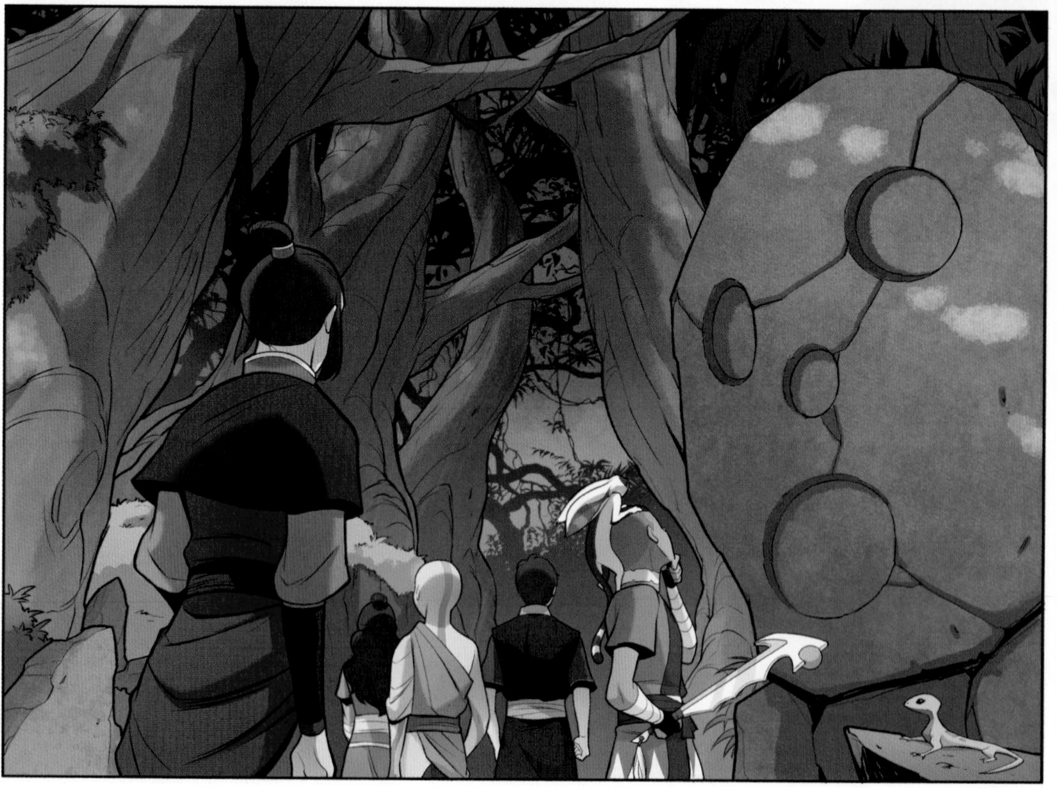

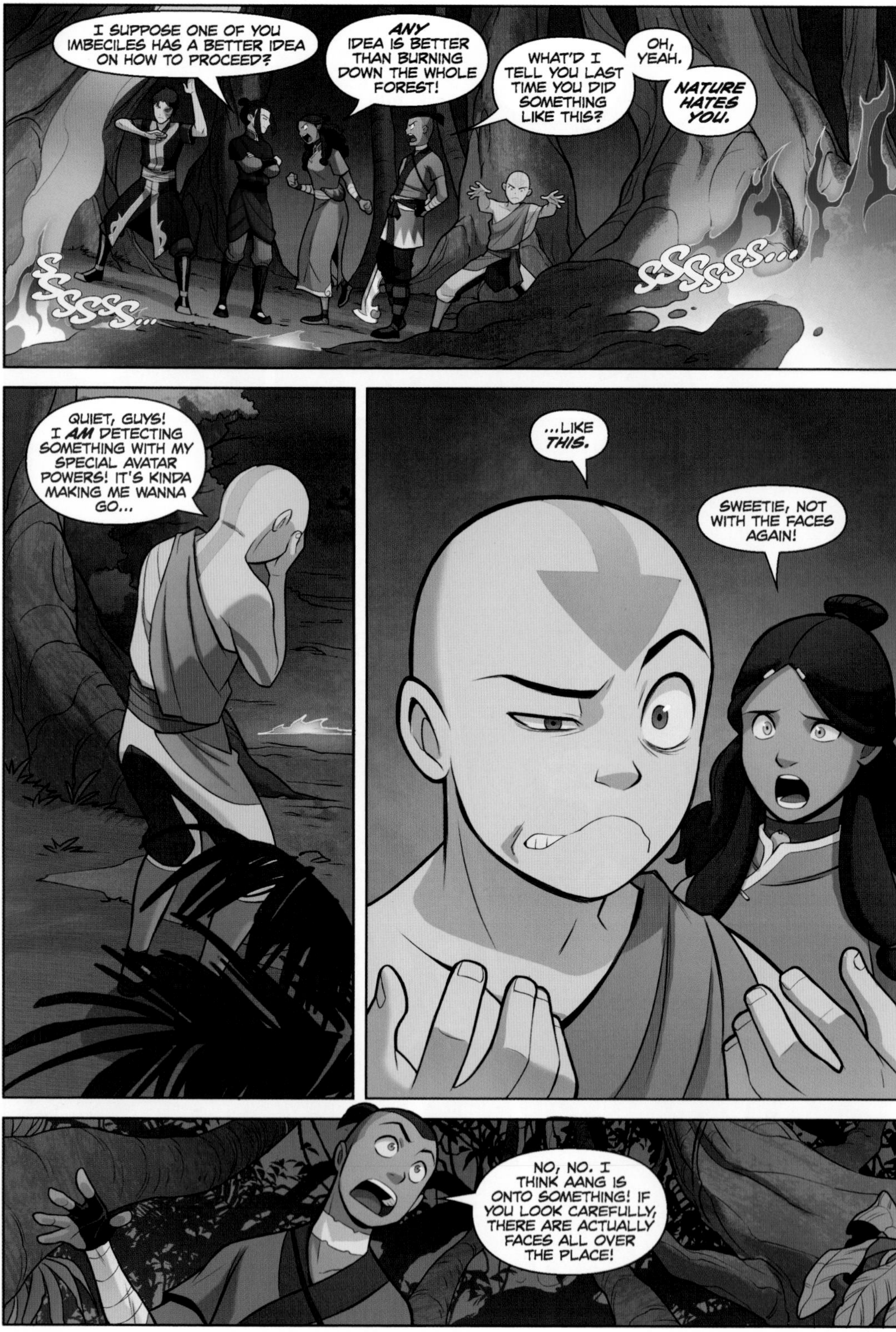
I SUPPOSE ONE OF YOU IMBECILES HAS A BETTER IDEA ON HOW TO PROCEED?
ANY IDEA IS BETTER THAN BURNING DOWN THE WHOLE FOREST!
WHAT'D I TELL YOU LAST TIME YOU DID SOMETHING LIKE THIS?
OH, YEAH.
NATURE HATES YOU.
SSSSS...
SSSSSS...
QUIET, GUYS! I AM DETECTING SOMETHING WITH MY SPECIAL AVATAR POWERS! IT'S KINDA MAKING ME WANNA GO...
...LIKE THIS.
SWEETIE, NOT WITH THE FACES AGAIN!
NO, NO. I THINK AANG IS ONTO SOMETHING! IF YOU LOOK CAREFULLY, THERE ARE ACTUALLY FACES ALL OVER THE PLACE!

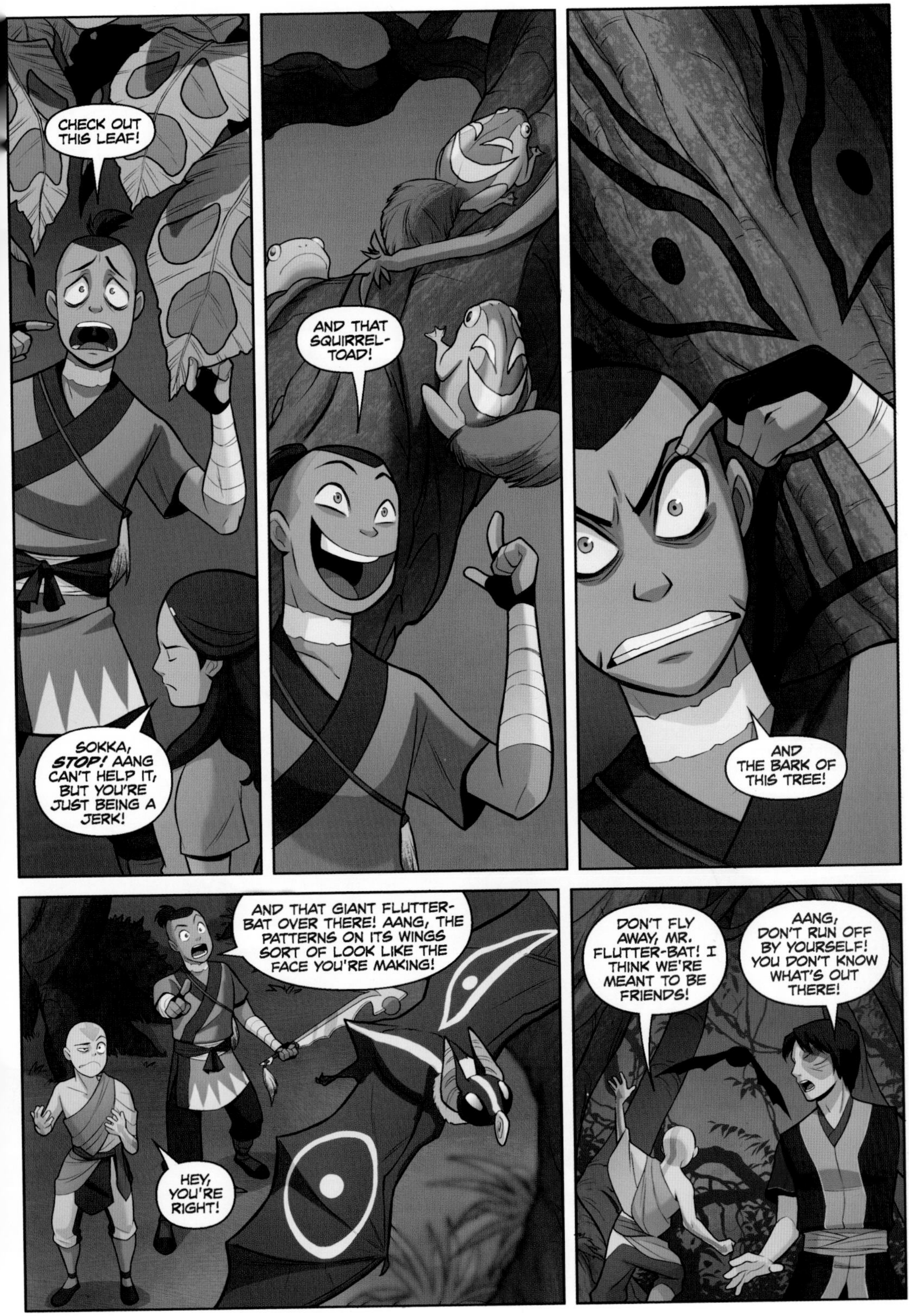
CHECK OUT THIS LEAF!
SOKKA, STOP! AANG CAN'T HELP IT, BUT YOU'RE JUST BEING A JERK!
AND THAT SQUIRREL-TOAD!
AND THE BARK OF THIS TREE!
AND THAT GIANT FLUTTER-BAT OVER THERE! AANG, THE PATTERNS ON ITS WINGS SORT OF LOOK LIKE THE FACE YOU'RE MAKING!
HEY, YOU'RE RIGHT!
DON'T FLY AWAY, MR. FLUTTER-BAT! I THINK WE'RE MEANT TO BE FRIENDS!
AANG, DON'T RUN OFF BY YOURSELF! YOU DON'T KNOW WHAT'S OUT THERE!

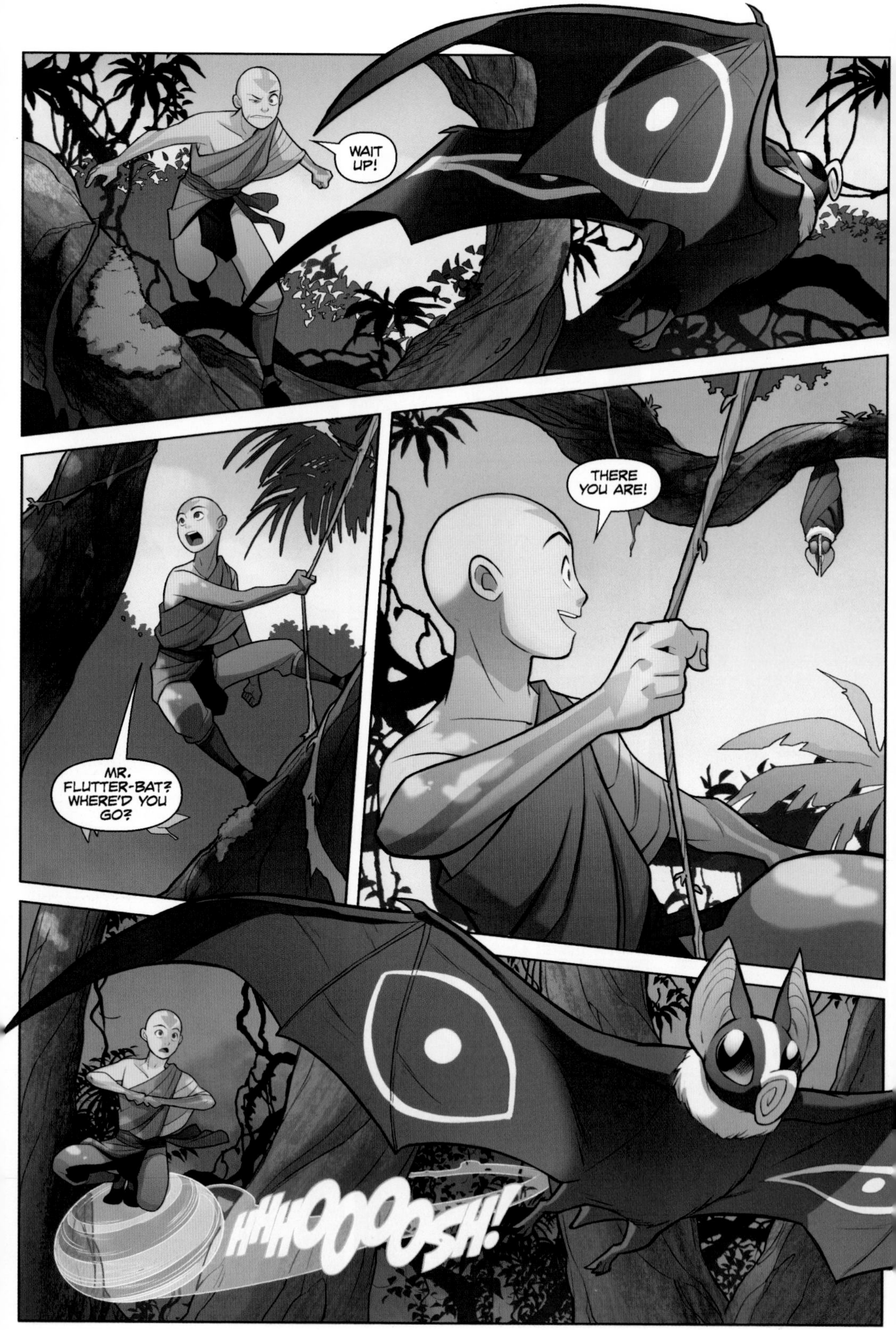
WAIT UP!
MR. FLUTTER-BAT? WHERE'D YOU GO?
THERE YOU ARE!
HHHOOOOOSH!

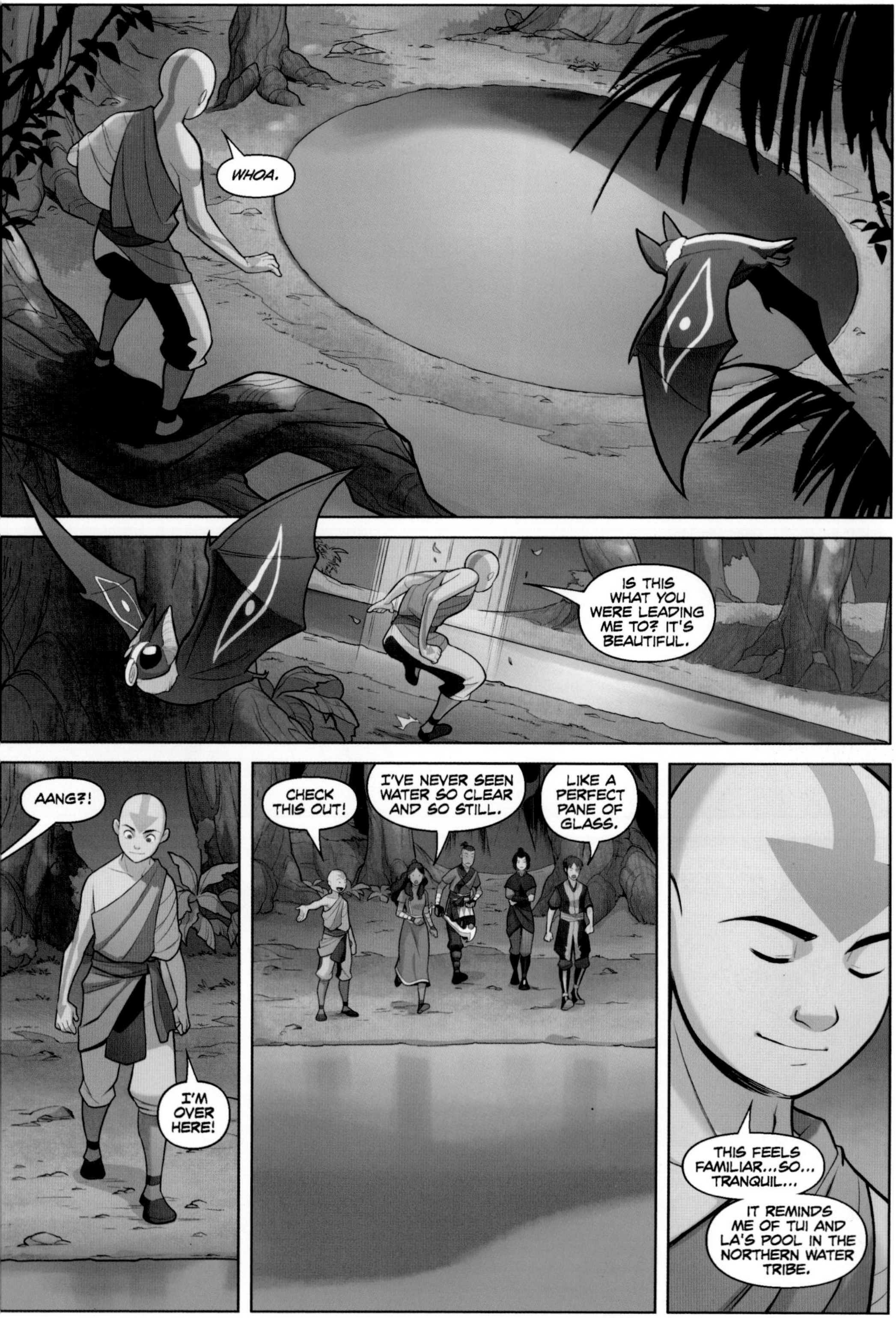
WHOA.
IS THIS WHAT YOU WERE LEADING ME TO? IT'S BEAUTIFUL.
AANG?!
I'M OVER HERE!
CHECK THIS OUT!
I'VE NEVER SEEN WATER SO CLEAR AND SO STILL.
LIKE A PERFECT PANE OF GLASS.
THIS FEELS FAMILIAR...SO... TRANQUIL...
IT REMINDS ME OF TUI AND LA'S POOL IN THE NORTHERN WATER TRIBE.

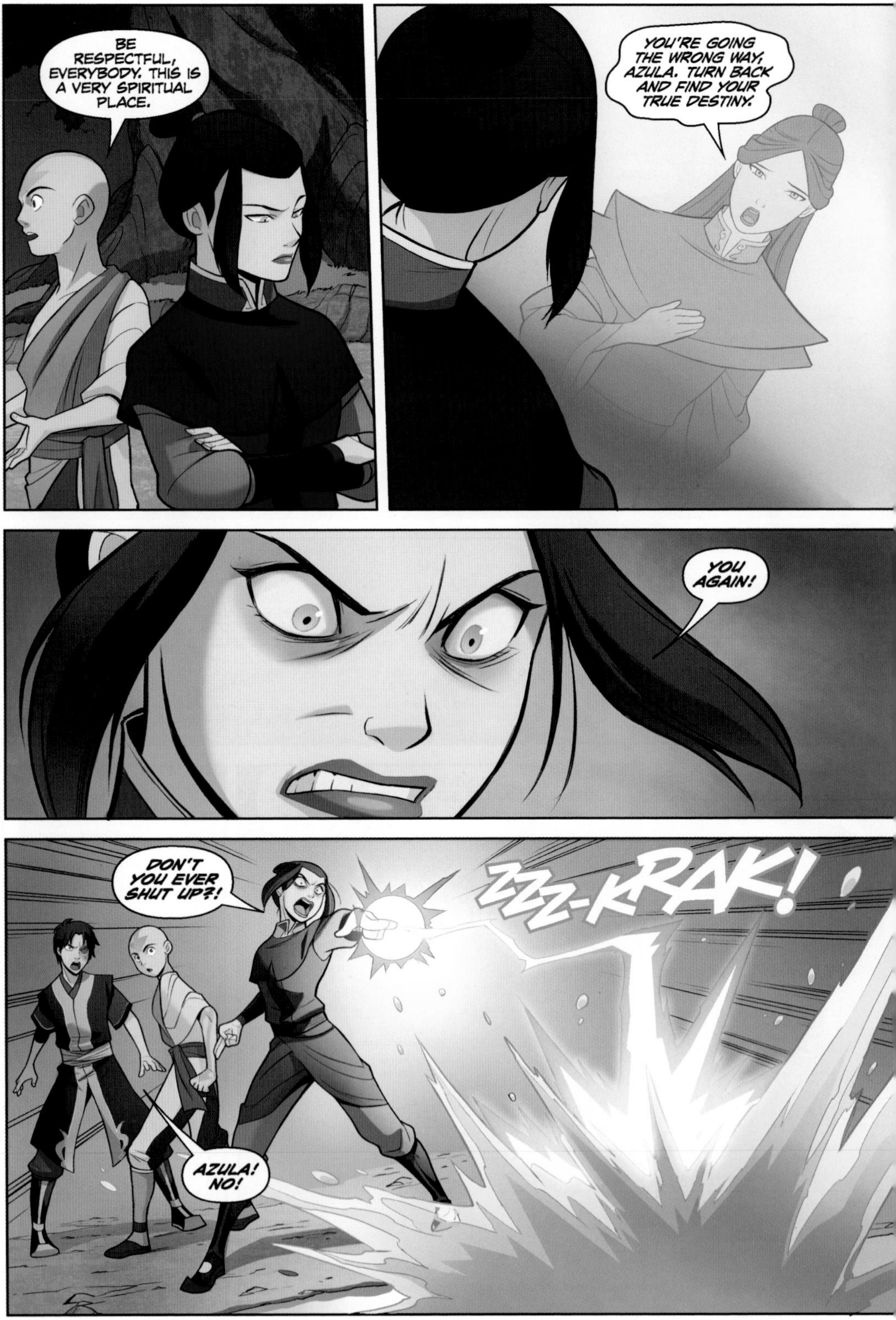
BE RESPECTFUL, EVERYBODY. THIS IS A VERY SPIRITUAL PLACE.
YOU'RE GOING THE WRONG WAY, AZULA. TURN BACK AND FIND YOUR TRUE DESTINY.
YOU AGAIN!
DON'T YOU EVER SHUT UP?!
ZZZ-KRAK!
AZULA! NO!

123

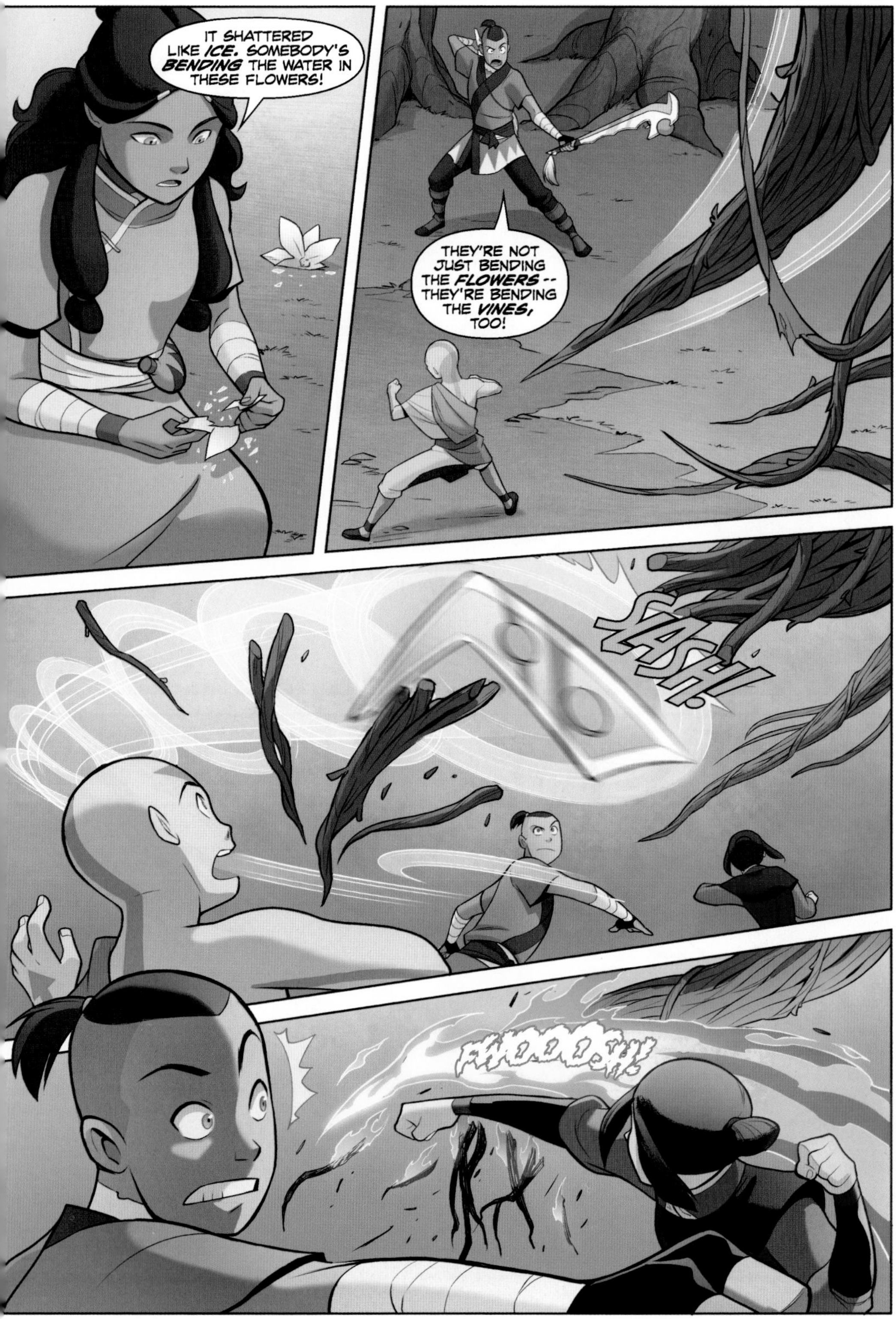
IT SHATTERED LIKE ICE. SOMEBODY'S BENDING THE WATER IN THESE FLOWERS!
THEY'RE NOT JUST BENDING THE FLOWERS -- THEY'RE BENDING THE VINES, TOO!
SASH!
FWOOOSH!

126

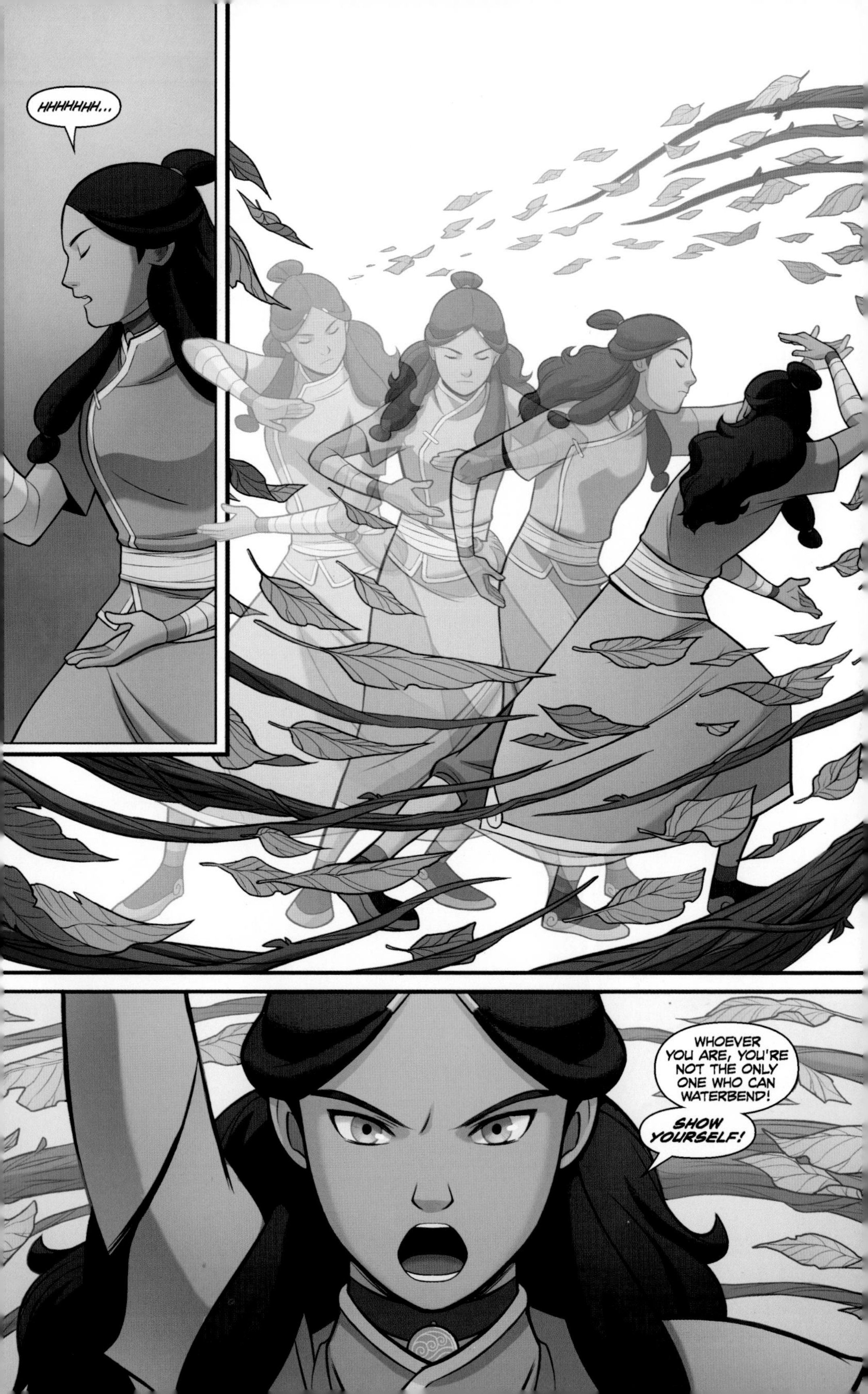
HHHHHHH...
WHOEVER YOU ARE, YOU'RE NOT THE ONLY ONE WHO CAN WATERBEND!
SHOW YOURSELF!

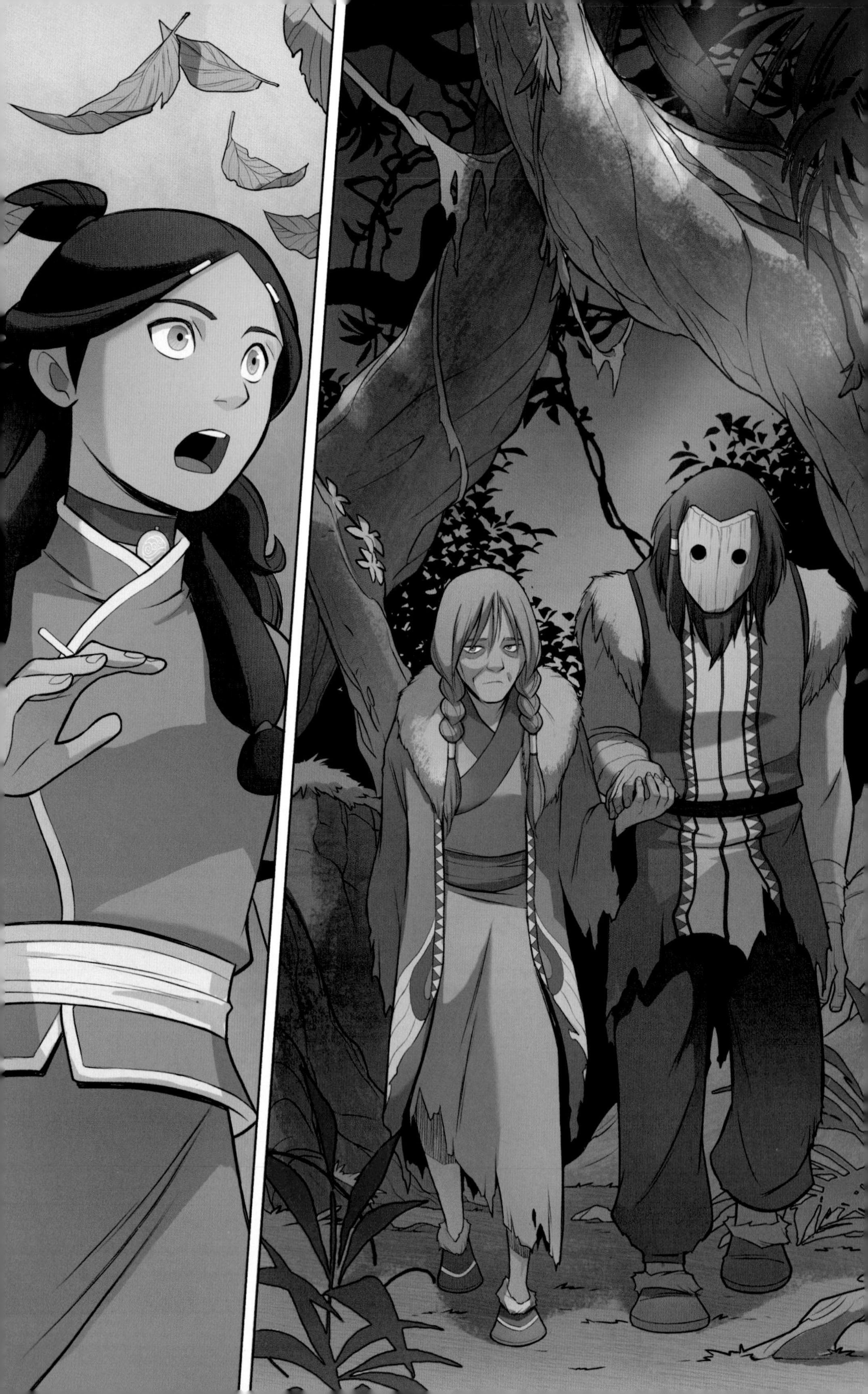

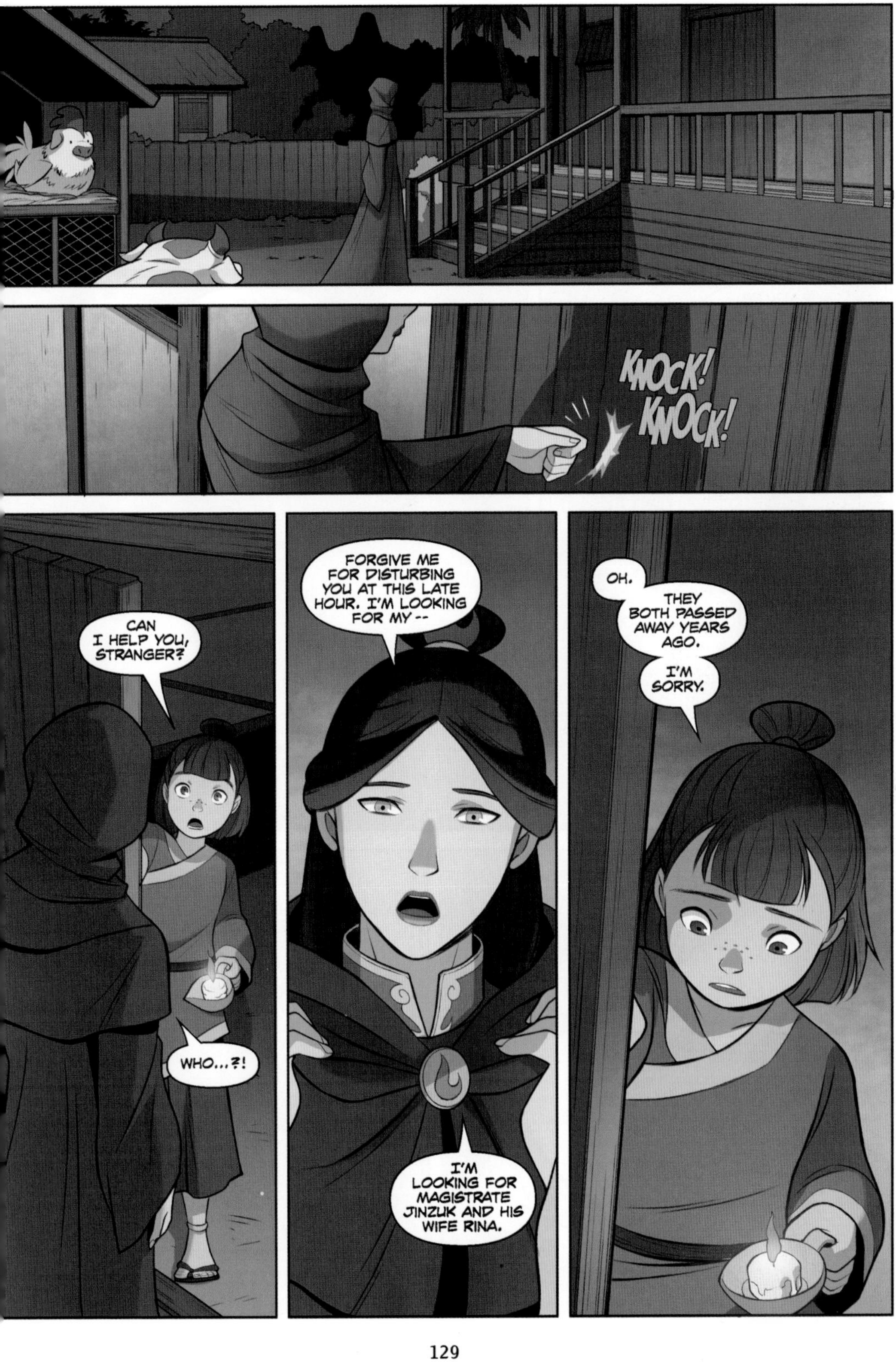
KNOCK! KNOCK!
CAN I HELP YOU, STRANGER?
WHO...?!
FORGIVE ME FOR DISTURBING YOU AT THIS LATE HOUR. I'M LOOKING FOR MY --
I'M LOOKING FOR MAGISTRATE JINZUK AND HIS WIFE RINA.
OH.
THEY BOTH PASSED AWAY YEARS AGO.
I'M SORRY.

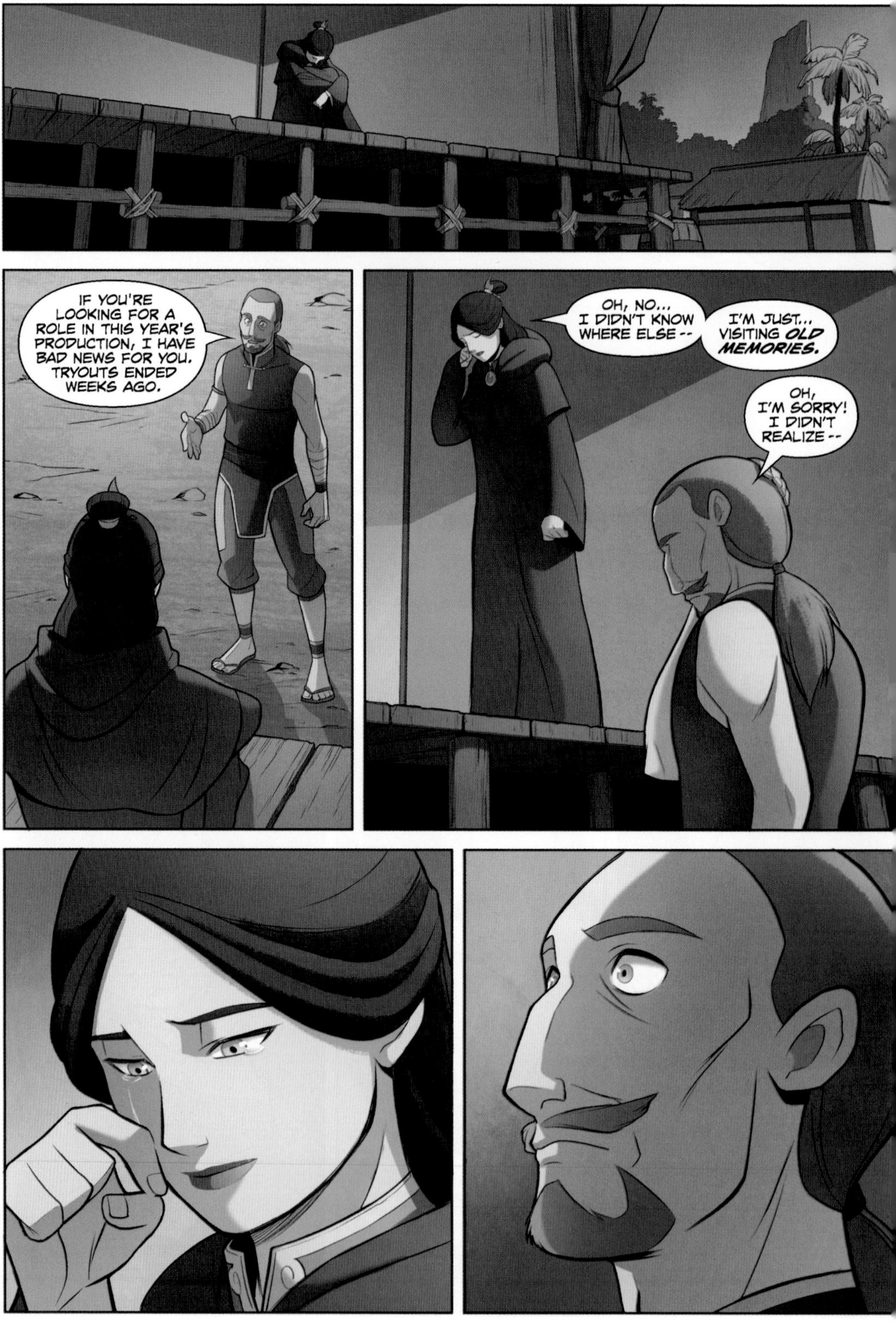
IF YOU'RE LOOKING FOR A ROLE IN THIS YEAR'S PRODUCTION, I HAVE BAD NEWS FOR YOU. TRYOUTS ENDED WEEKS AGO.
OH, NO... I DIDN'T KNOW WHERE ELSE --
I'M JUST... VISITING OLD MEMORIES.
OH, I'M SORRY! I DIDN'T REALIZE --

132

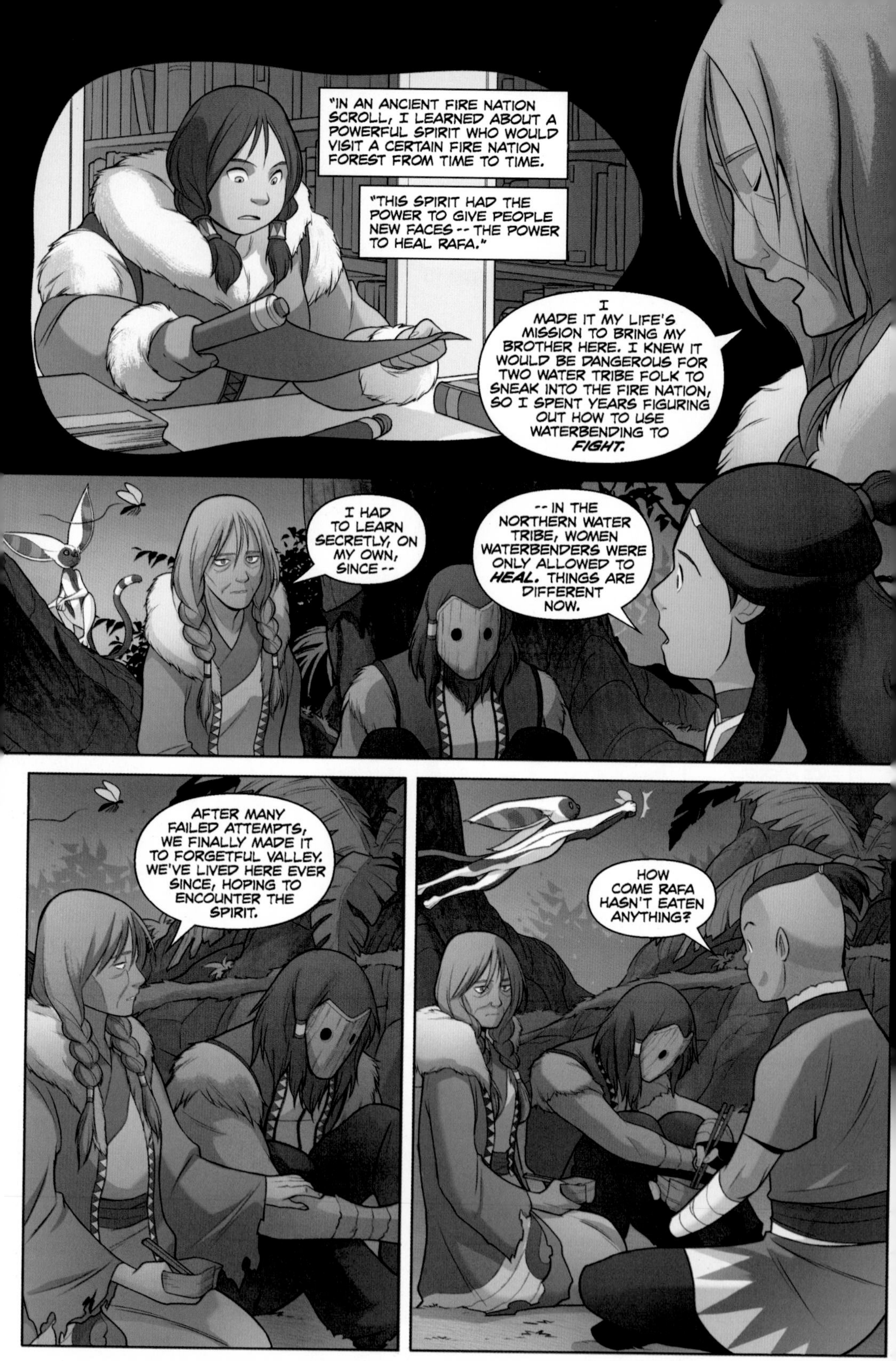
"IN AN ANCIENT FIRE NATION SCROLL, I LEARNED ABOUT A POWERFUL SPIRIT WHO WOULD VISIT A CERTAIN FIRE NATION FOREST FROM TIME TO TIME.
"THIS SPIRIT HAD THE POWER TO GIVE PEOPLE NEW FACES -- THE POWER TO HEAL RAFA."
I MADE IT MY LIFE'S MISSION TO BRING MY BROTHER HERE. I KNEW IT WOULD BE DANGEROUS FOR TWO WATER TRIBE FOLK TO SNEAK INTO THE FIRE NATION, SO I SPENT YEARS FIGURING OUT HOW TO USE WATERBENDING TO *FIGHT*.
I HAD TO LEARN SECRETLY, ON MY OWN, SINCE --
-- IN THE NORTHERN WATER TRIBE, WOMEN WATERBENDERS WERE ONLY ALLOWED TO *HEAL*. THINGS ARE DIFFERENT NOW.
AFTER MANY FAILED ATTEMPTS, WE FINALLY MADE IT TO FORGETFUL VALLEY. WE'VE LIVED HERE EVER SINCE, HOPING TO ENCOUNTER THE SPIRIT.
HOW COME RAFA HASN'T EATEN ANYTHING?

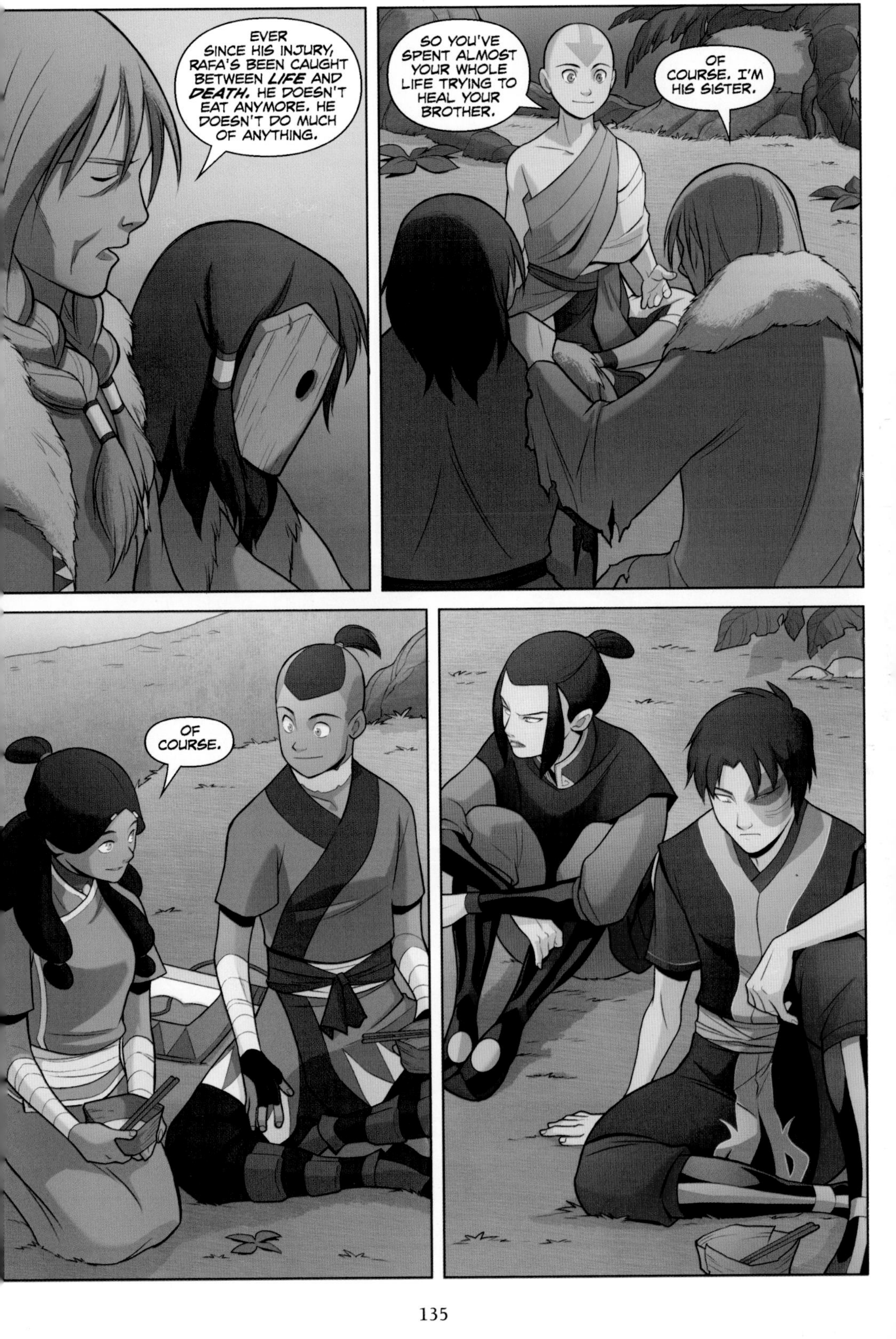
EVER SINCE HIS INJURY, RAFA'S BEEN CAUGHT BETWEEN *LIFE* AND *DEATH*. HE DOESN'T EAT ANYMORE. HE DOESN'T DO MUCH OF ANYTHING.
SO YOU'VE SPENT ALMOST YOUR WHOLE LIFE TRYING TO HEAL YOUR BROTHER.
OF COURSE. I'M HIS SISTER.
OF COURSE.

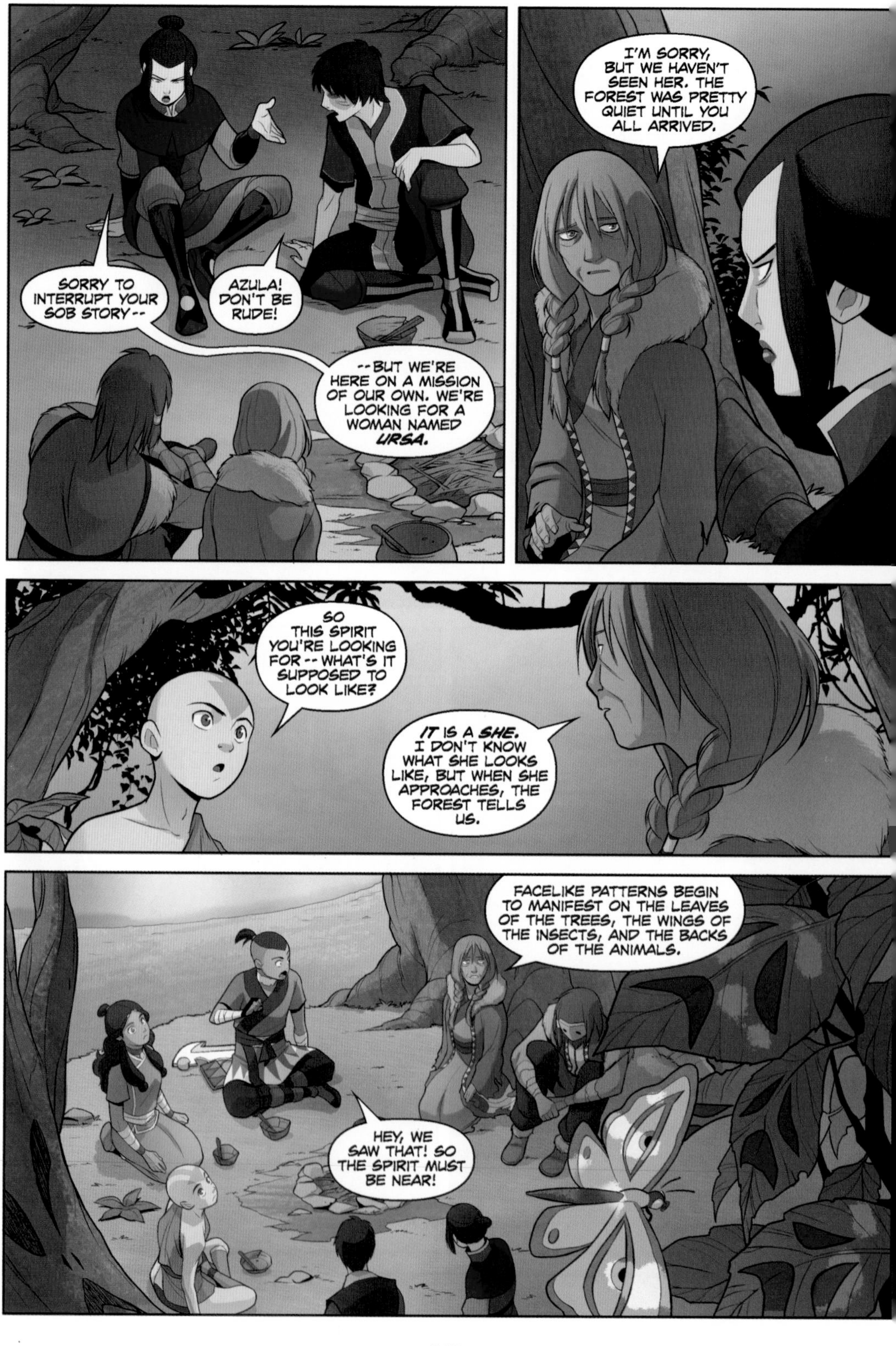
SORRY TO INTERRUPT YOUR SOB STORY--
AZULA! DON'T BE RUDE!
--BUT WE'RE HERE ON A MISSION OF OUR OWN. WE'RE LOOKING FOR A WOMAN NAMED *URSA.*
I'M SORRY, BUT WE HAVEN'T SEEN HER. THE FOREST WAS PRETTY QUIET UNTIL YOU ALL ARRIVED.
SO THIS SPIRIT YOU'RE LOOKING FOR--WHAT'S IT SUPPOSED TO LOOK LIKE?
IT IS A *SHE.* I DON'T KNOW WHAT SHE LOOKS LIKE, BUT WHEN SHE APPROACHES, THE FOREST TELLS US.
FACELIKE PATTERNS BEGIN TO MANIFEST ON THE LEAVES OF THE TREES, THE WINGS OF THE INSECTS, AND THE BACKS OF THE ANIMALS.
HEY, WE SAW THAT! SO THE SPIRIT MUST BE NEAR!

137

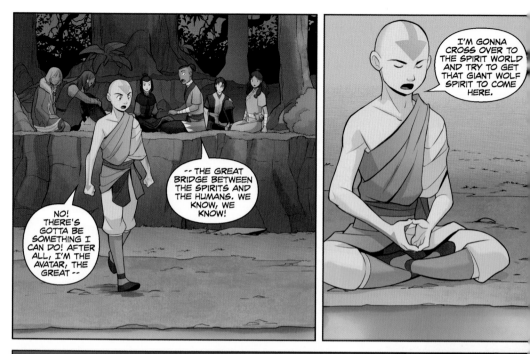

I'M GONNA CROSS OVER TO THE SPIRIT WORLD AND TRY TO GET THAT GIANT WOLF SPIRIT TO COME HERE.

NO! THERE'S GOTTA BE SOMETHING I CAN DO! AFTER ALL, I'M THE AVATAR, THE GREAT --

-- THE GREAT BRIDGE BETWEEN THE SPIRITS AND THE HUMANS. WE KNOW, WE KNOW!

BAH! THIS IS A WASTE OF TIME!

WHERE ARE YOU GOING?

AZULA!

DID WE TRAVEL ALL THIS WAY TO HELP A COUPLE OF DIRTY VAGRANTS, OR TO FIND MOTHER?

139

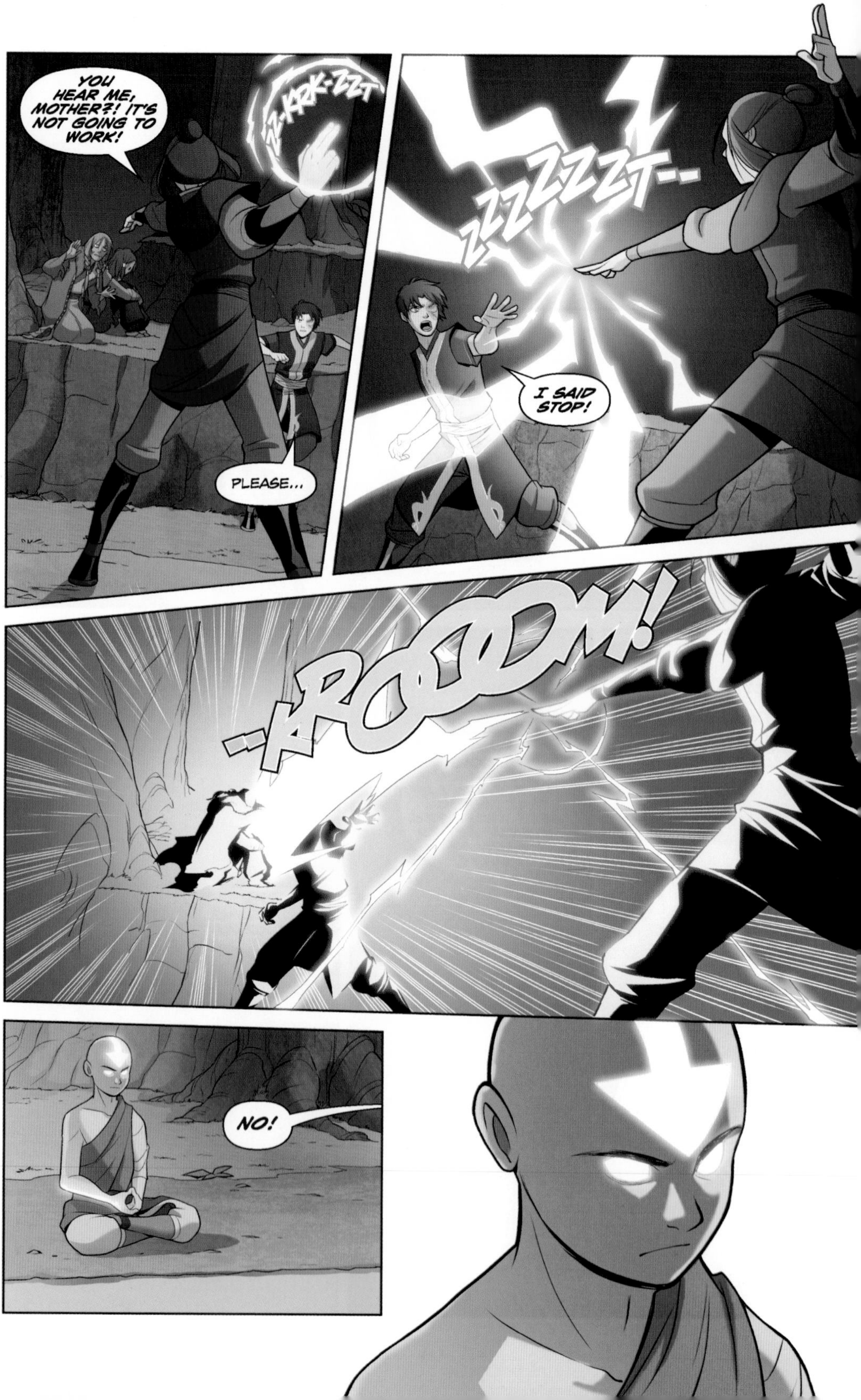
YOU HEAR ME, MOTHER?! IT'S NOT GOING TO WORK!
ZZ-KRK-ZZ-T
PLEASE...
ZZZZZZZT--
I SAID STOP!
--KROOOOM!
NO!

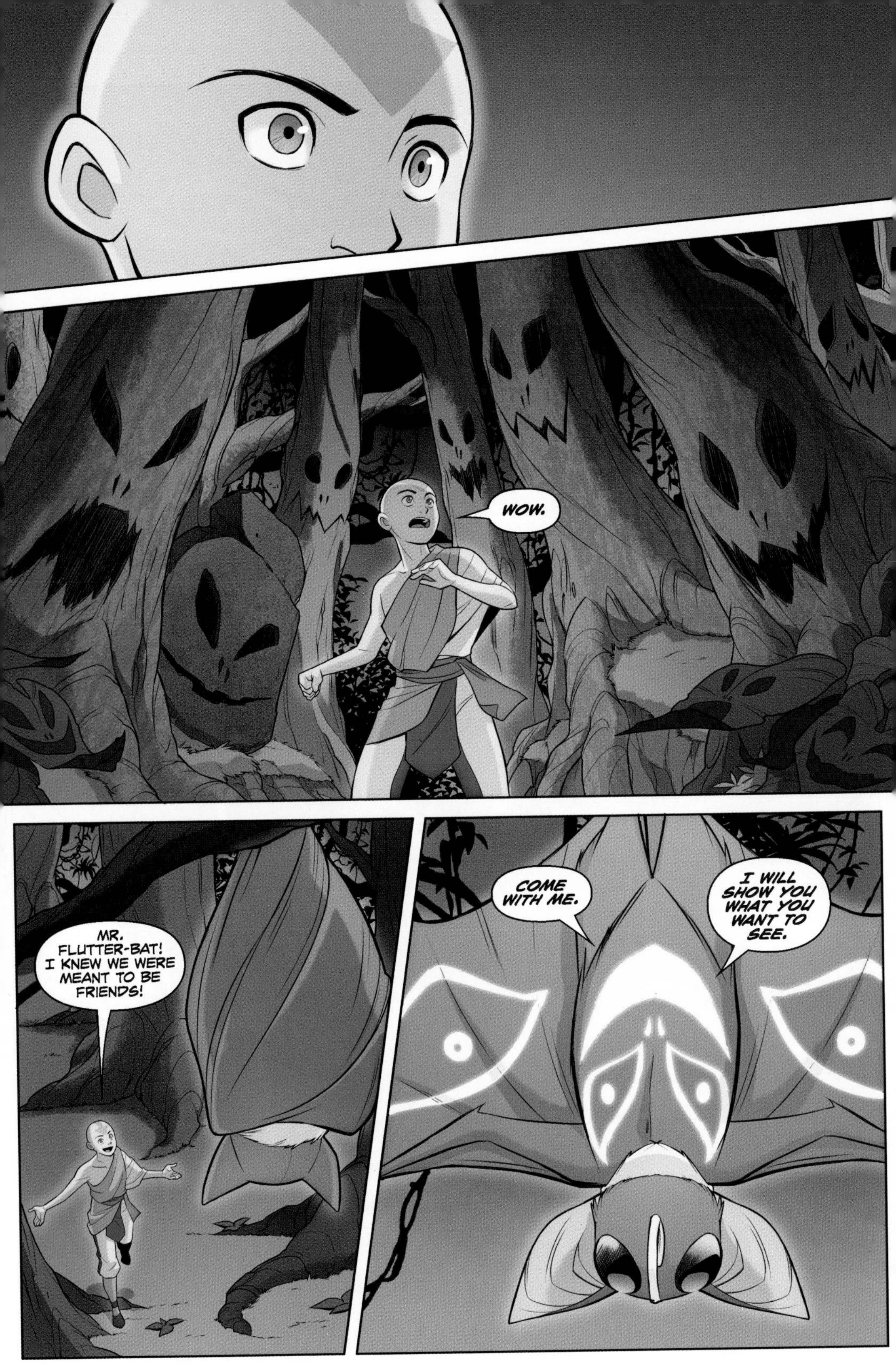
WOW.
MR. FLUTTER-BAT! I KNEW WE WERE MEANT TO BE FRIENDS!
COME WITH ME.
I WILL SHOW YOU WHAT YOU WANT TO SEE.

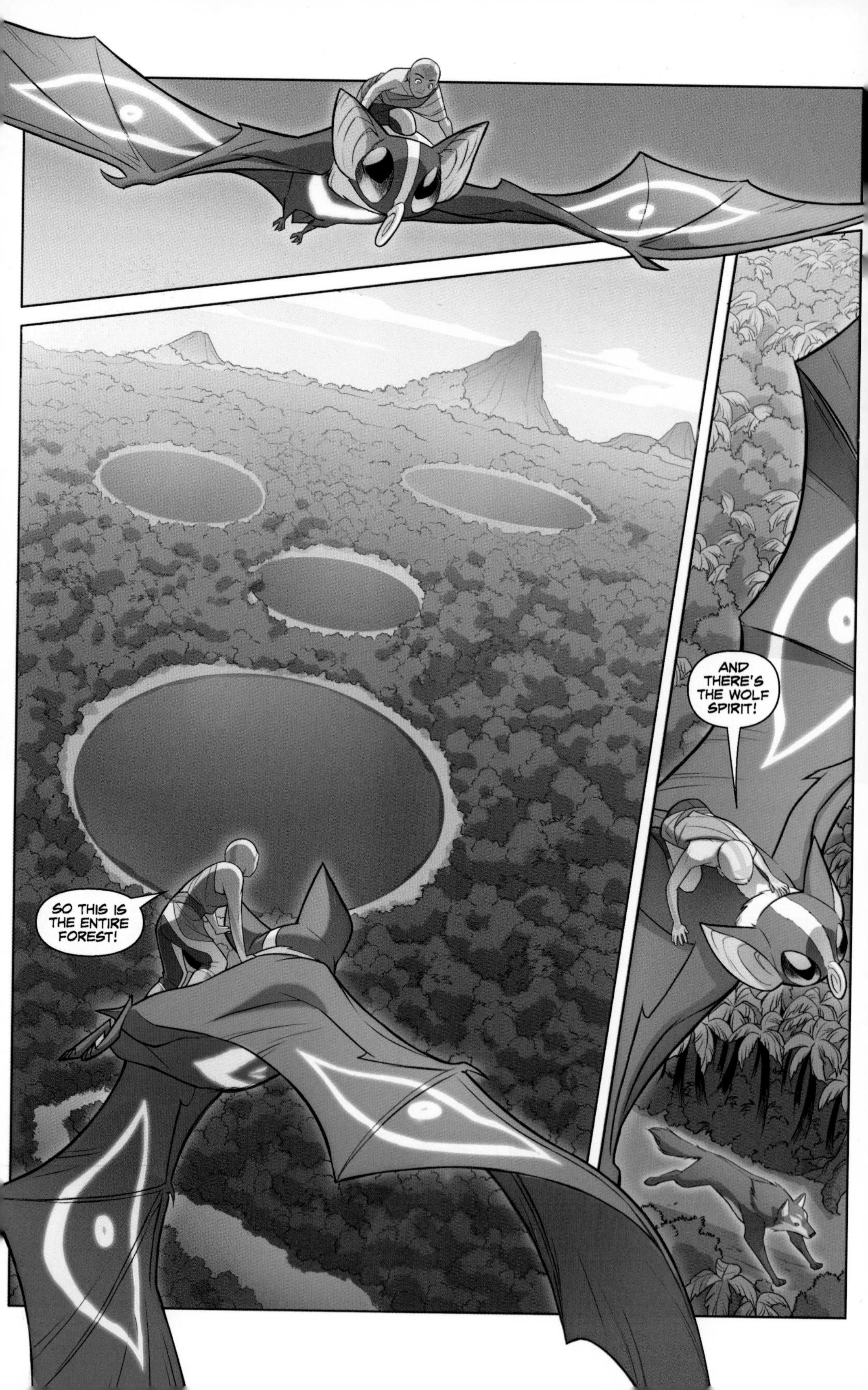
SO THIS IS THE ENTIRE FOREST!
AND THERE'S THE WOLF SPIRIT!

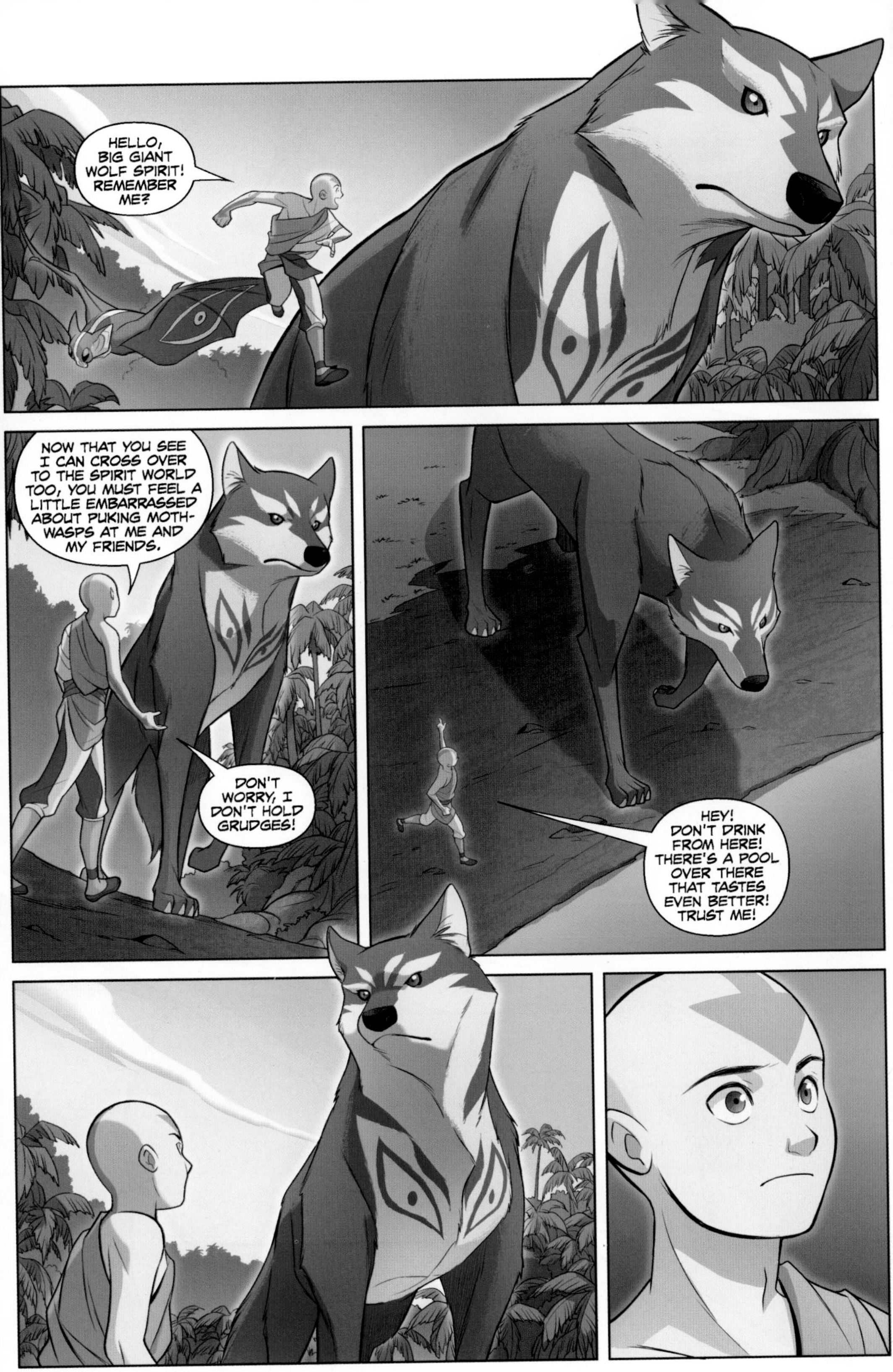
HELLO, BIG GIANT WOLF SPIRIT! REMEMBER ME?
NOW THAT YOU SEE I CAN CROSS OVER TO THE SPIRIT WORLD TOO, YOU MUST FEEL A LITTLE EMBARRASSED ABOUT PUKING MOTH-WASPS AT ME AND MY FRIENDS.
DON'T WORRY, I DON'T HOLD GRUDGES!
HEY! DON'T DRINK FROM HERE! THERE'S A POOL OVER THERE THAT TASTES EVEN BETTER! TRUST ME!

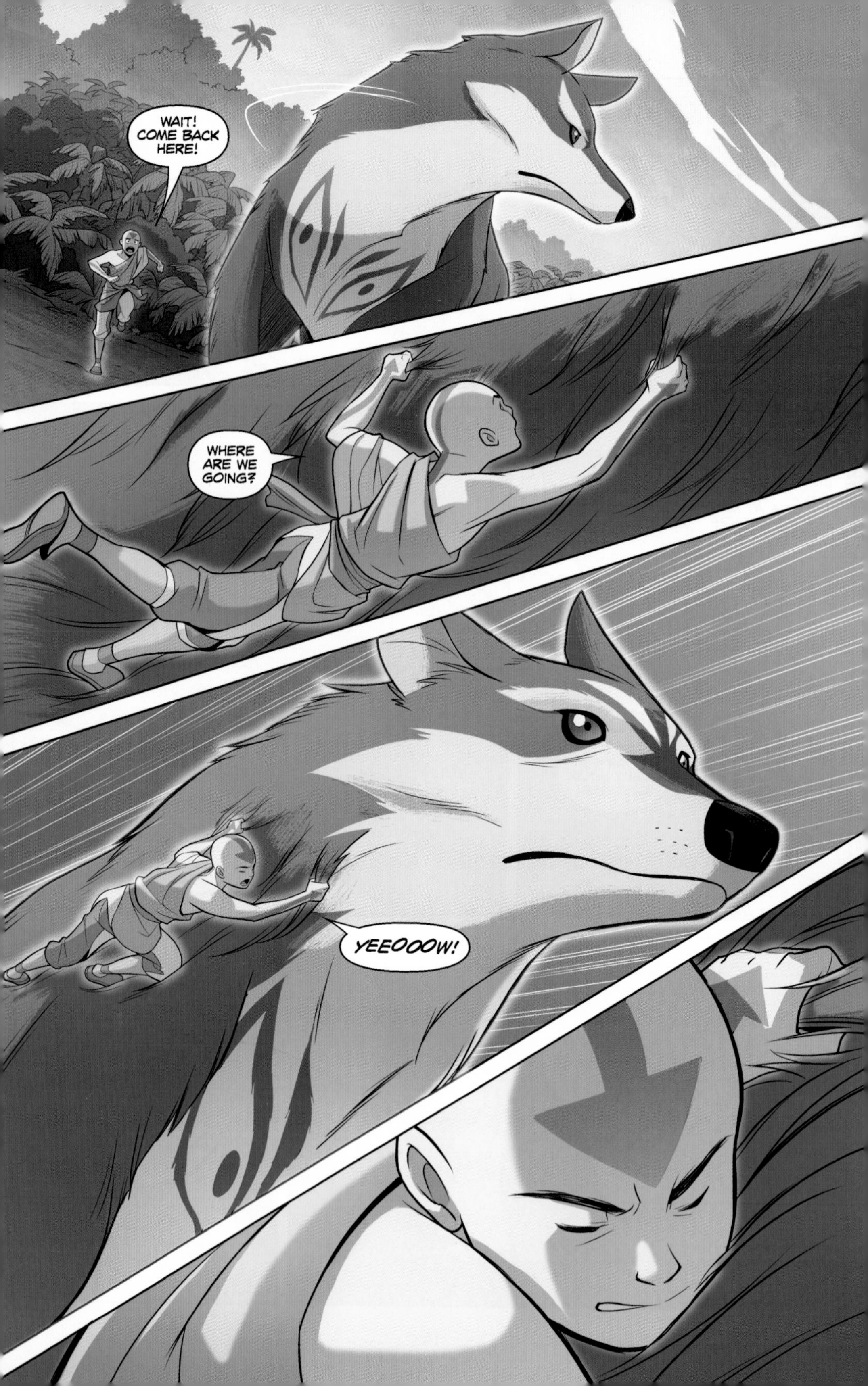
WAIT! COME BACK HERE!
WHERE ARE WE GOING?
YEEOOOW!

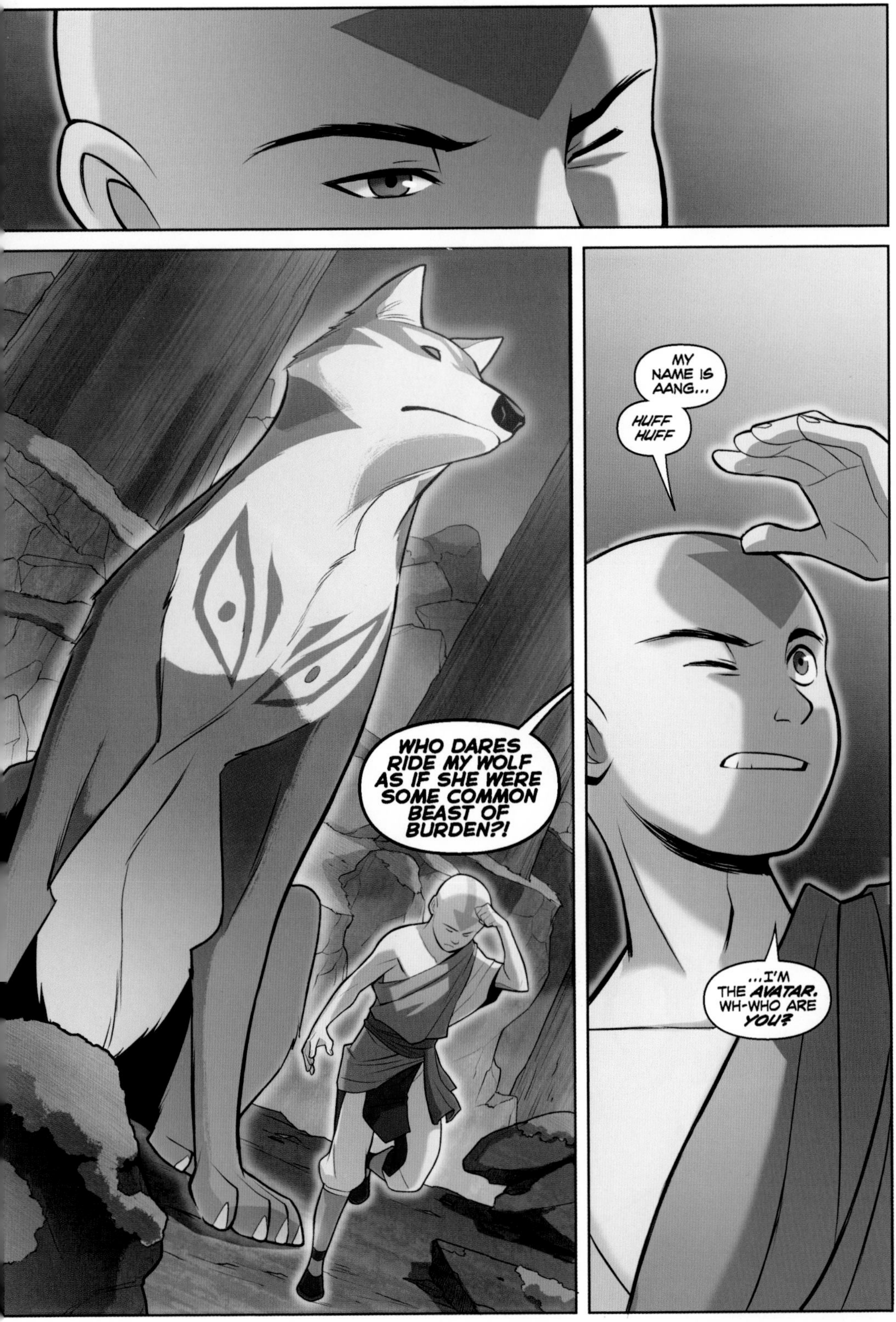
WHO DARES RIDE MY WOLF AS IF SHE WERE SOME COMMON BEAST OF BURDEN?!
MY NAME IS AANG...
HUFF HUFF
...I'M THE AVATAR. WH-WHO ARE YOU?

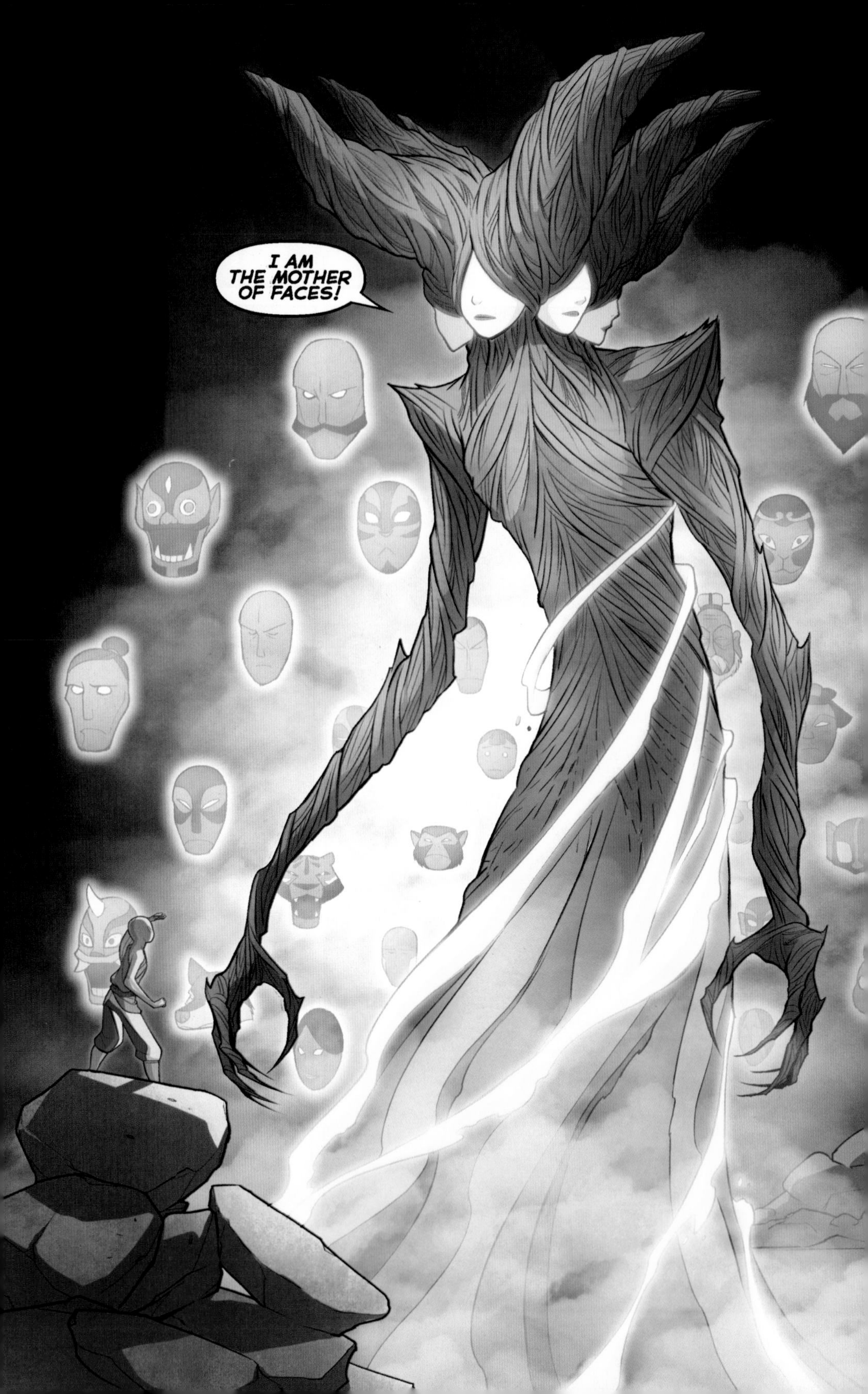
I AM THE MOTHER OF FACES!

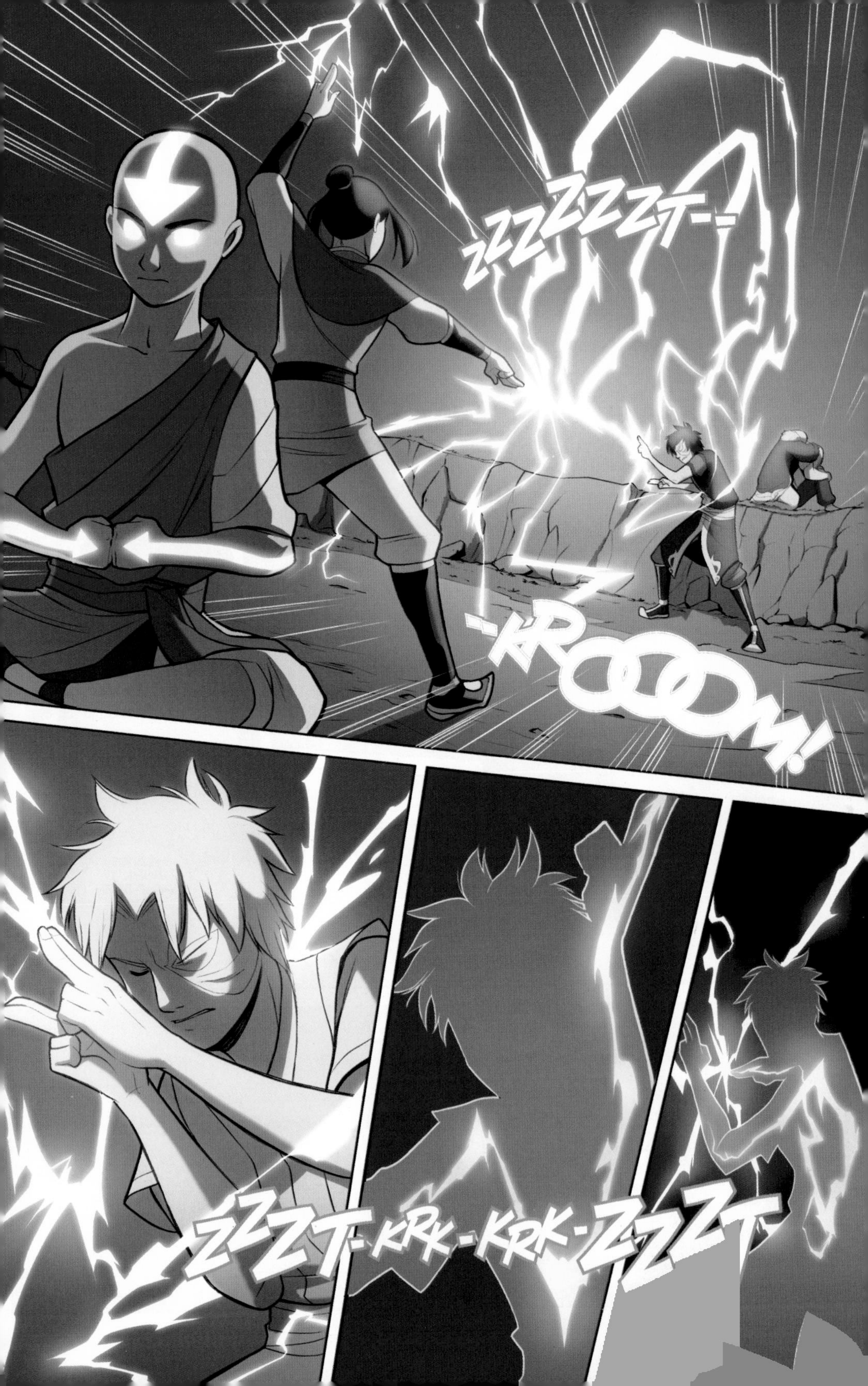
ZZZZZZT--
-KROOOOM!
ZZZT-KRK-KRK-ZZZT

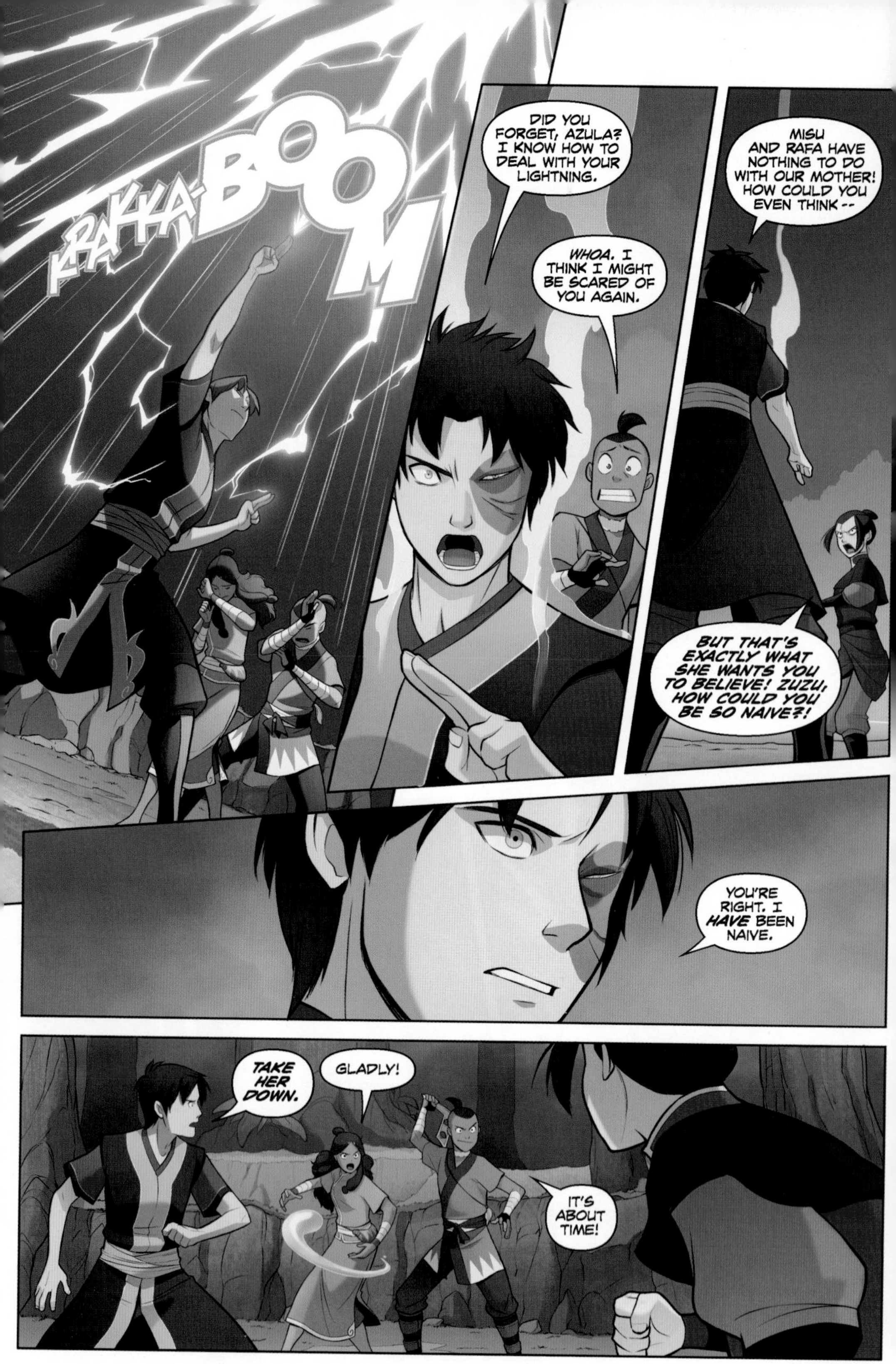
KRAKKA-BOOM
DID YOU FORGET, AZULA? I KNOW HOW TO DEAL WITH YOUR LIGHTNING.
WHOA. I THINK I MIGHT BE SCARED OF YOU AGAIN.
MISU AND RAFA HAVE NOTHING TO DO WITH OUR MOTHER! HOW COULD YOU EVEN THINK --
BUT THAT'S EXACTLY WHAT SHE WANTS YOU TO BELIEVE! ZUZU, HOW COULD YOU BE SO NAIVE?!
YOU'RE RIGHT. I HAVE BEEN NAIVE.
TAKE HER DOWN.
GLADLY!
IT'S ABOUT TIME!

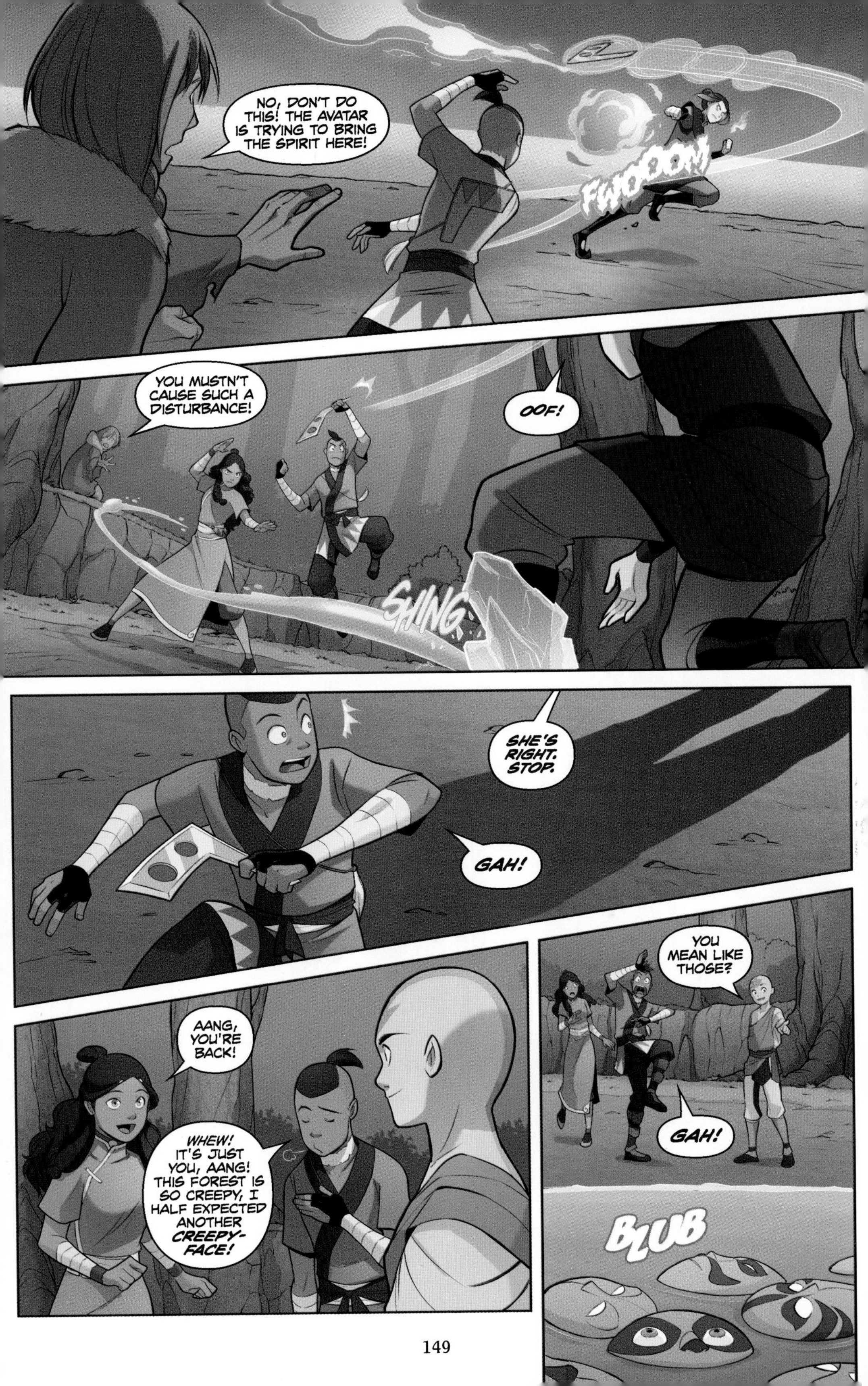

NO, DON'T DO THIS! THE AVATAR IS TRYING TO BRING THE SPIRIT HERE!
FWOOOM
YOU MUSTN'T CAUSE SUCH A DISTURBANCE!
OOF!
SHING
SHE'S RIGHT. STOP.
GAH!
AANG, YOU'RE BACK!
WHEW! IT'S JUST YOU, AANG! THIS FOREST IS SO CREEPY, I HALF EXPECTED ANOTHER CREEPY-FACE!
YOU MEAN LIKE THOSE?
GAH!
BLUB

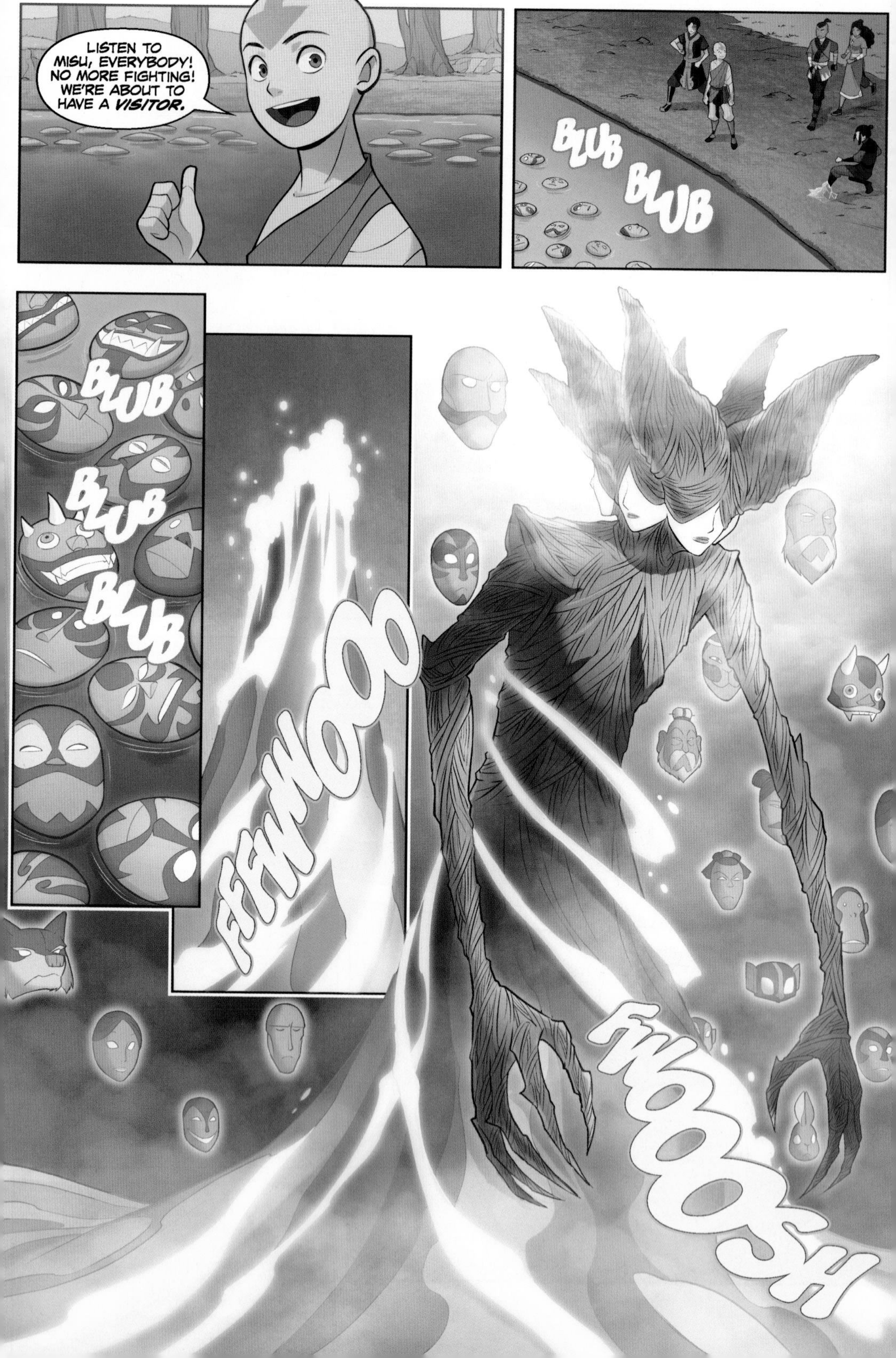

LISTEN TO MISU, EVERYBODY! NO MORE FIGHTING! WE'RE ABOUT TO HAVE A *VISITOR*.
BLUB BLUB
BLUB
BLUB
BLUB
FFFWOOOO
FWOOOSH

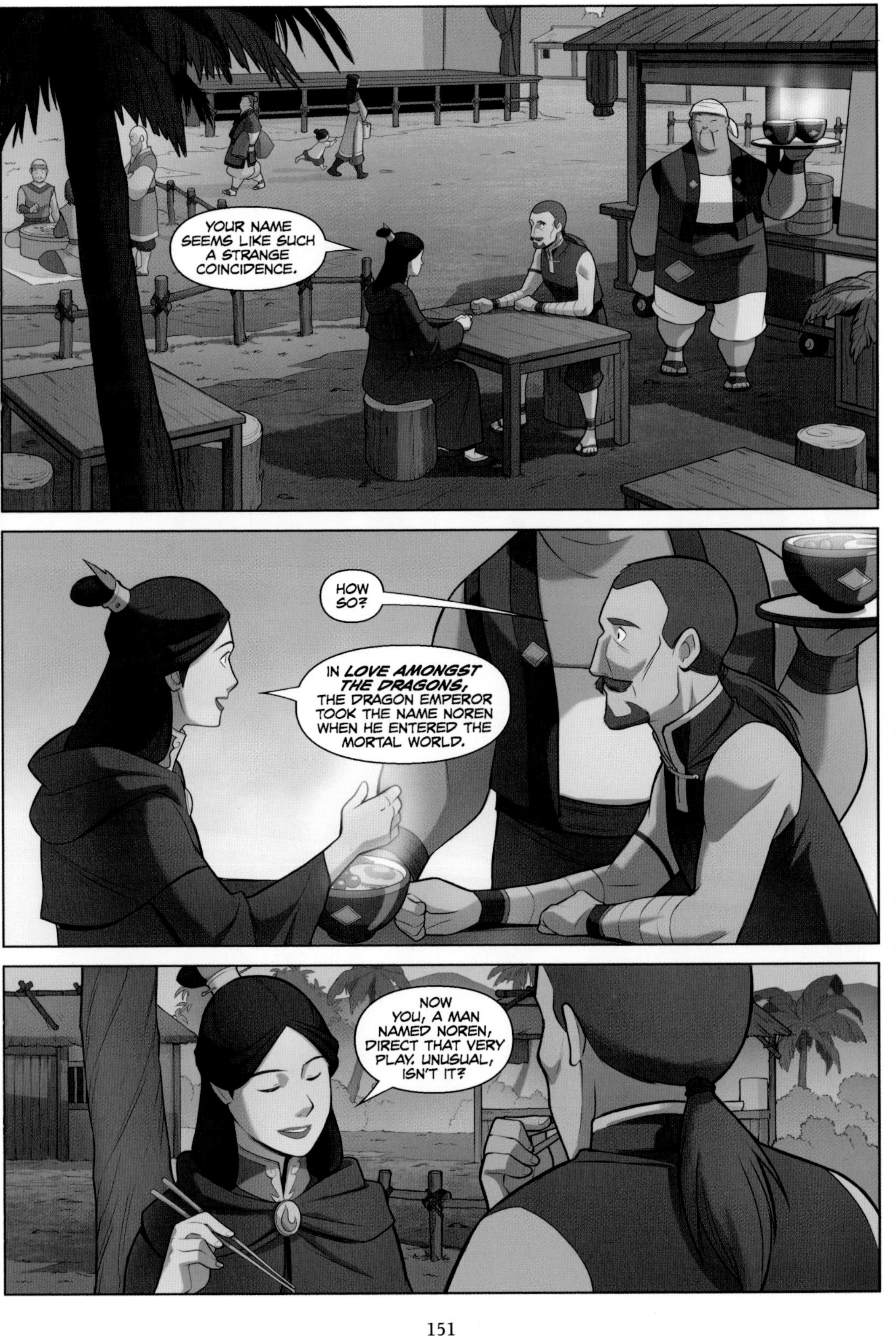
YOUR NAME SEEMS LIKE SUCH A STRANGE COINCIDENCE.
HOW SO?
IN ***LOVE AMONGST THE DRAGONS,*** THE DRAGON EMPEROR TOOK THE NAME NOREN WHEN HE ENTERED THE MORTAL WORLD.
NOW YOU, A MAN NAMED NOREN, DIRECT THAT VERY PLAY. UNUSUAL, ISN'T IT?

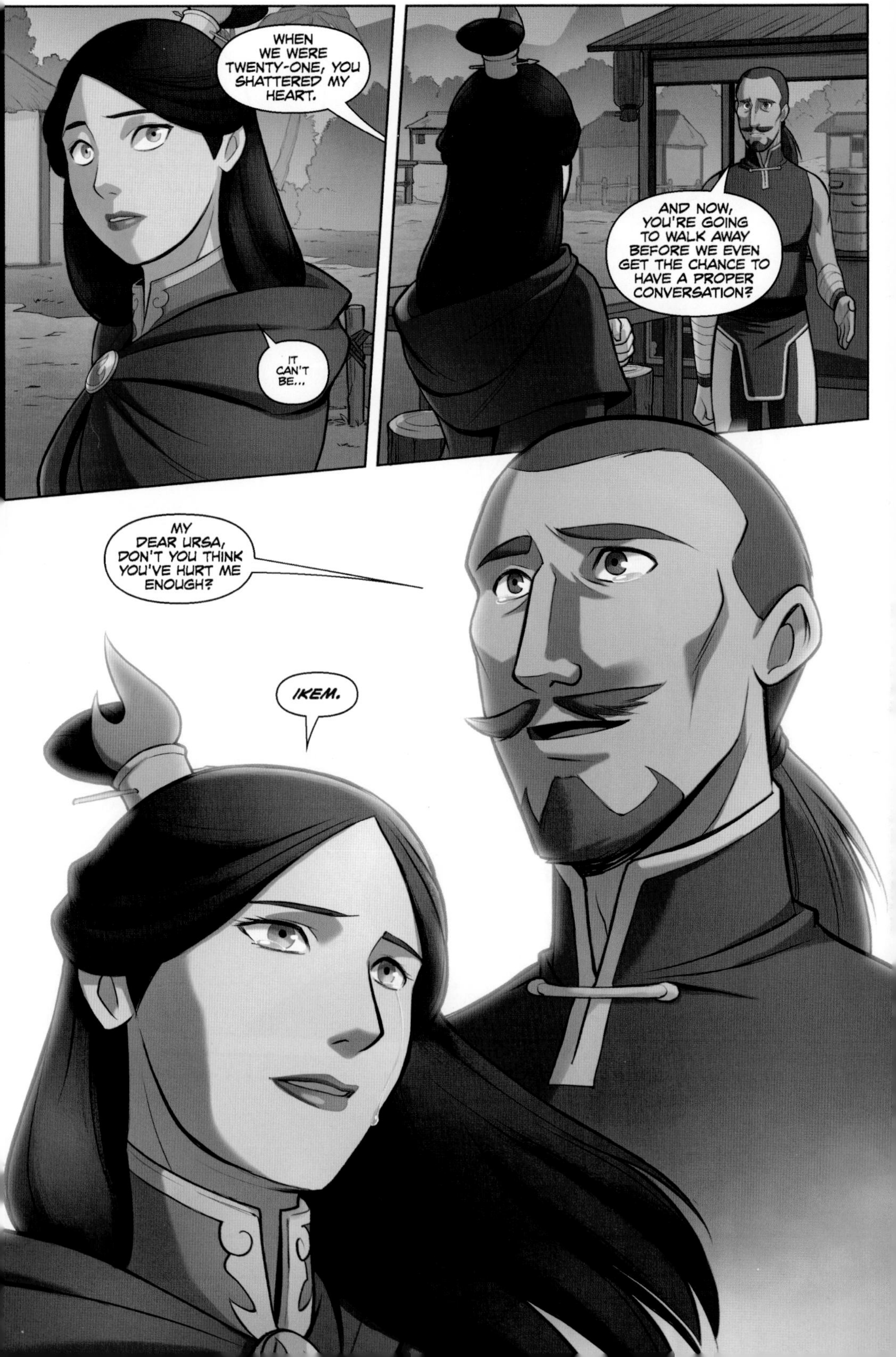
WHEN WE WERE TWENTY-ONE, YOU SHATTERED MY HEART.
IT CAN'T BE...
AND NOW, YOU'RE GOING TO WALK AWAY BEFORE WE EVEN GET THE CHANCE TO HAVE A PROPER CONVERSATION?
MY DEAR URSA, DON'T YOU THINK YOU'VE HURT ME ENOUGH?
IKEM.

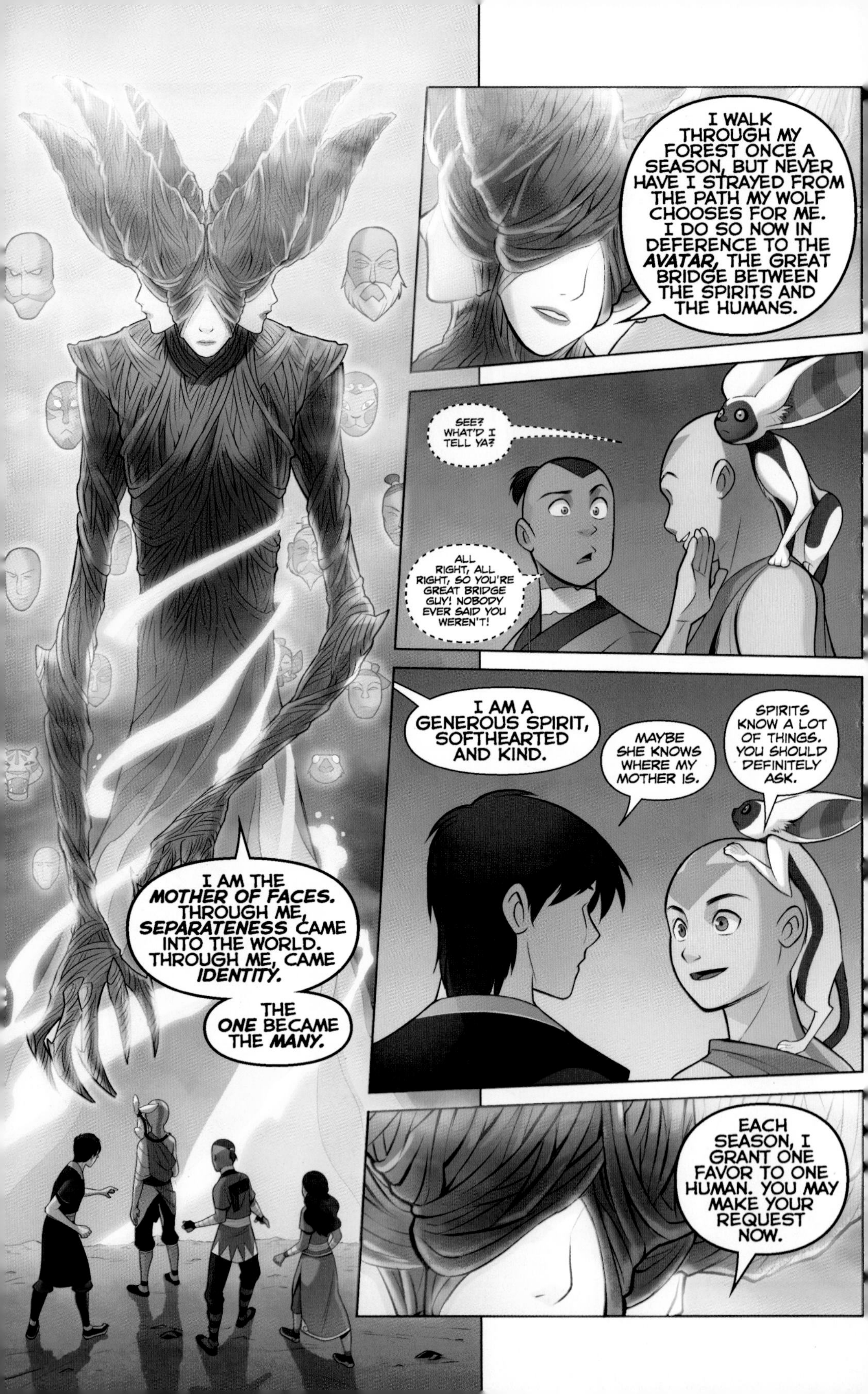
I AM THE MOTHER OF FACES. THROUGH ME, SEPARATENESS CAME INTO THE WORLD. THROUGH ME, CAME IDENTITY.
THE ONE BECAME THE MANY.
I WALK THROUGH MY FOREST ONCE A SEASON, BUT NEVER HAVE I STRAYED FROM THE PATH MY WOLF CHOOSES FOR ME. I DO SO NOW IN DEFERENCE TO THE AVATAR, THE GREAT BRIDGE BETWEEN THE SPIRITS AND THE HUMANS.
SEE? WHAT'D I TELL YA?
ALL RIGHT, ALL RIGHT, SO YOU'RE GREAT BRIDGE GUY! NOBODY EVER SAID YOU WEREN'T!
I AM A GENEROUS SPIRIT, SOFTHEARTED AND KIND.
MAYBE SHE KNOWS WHERE MY MOTHER IS.
SPIRITS KNOW A LOT OF THINGS. YOU SHOULD DEFINITELY ASK.
EACH SEASON, I GRANT ONE FAVOR TO ONE HUMAN. YOU MAY MAKE YOUR REQUEST NOW.

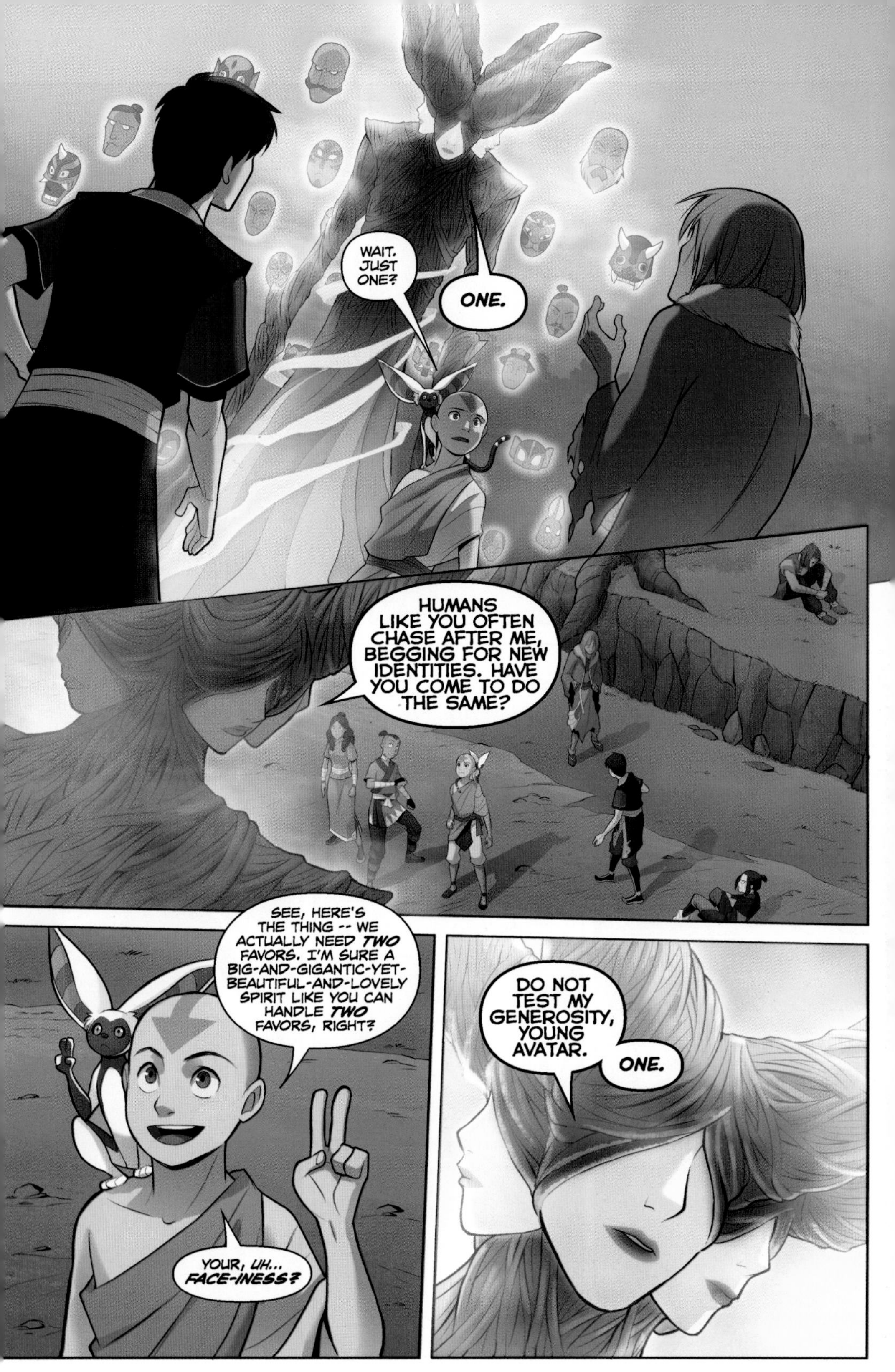
WAIT. JUST ONE?
ONE.
HUMANS LIKE YOU OFTEN CHASE AFTER ME, BEGGING FOR NEW IDENTITIES. HAVE YOU COME TO DO THE SAME?
SEE, HERE'S THE THING -- WE ACTUALLY NEED TWO FAVORS. I'M SURE A BIG-AND-GIGANTIC-YET-BEAUTIFUL-AND-LOVELY SPIRIT LIKE YOU CAN HANDLE TWO FAVORS, RIGHT?
YOUR, UH... FACE-INESS?
DO NOT TEST MY GENEROSITY, YOUNG AVATAR.
ONE.

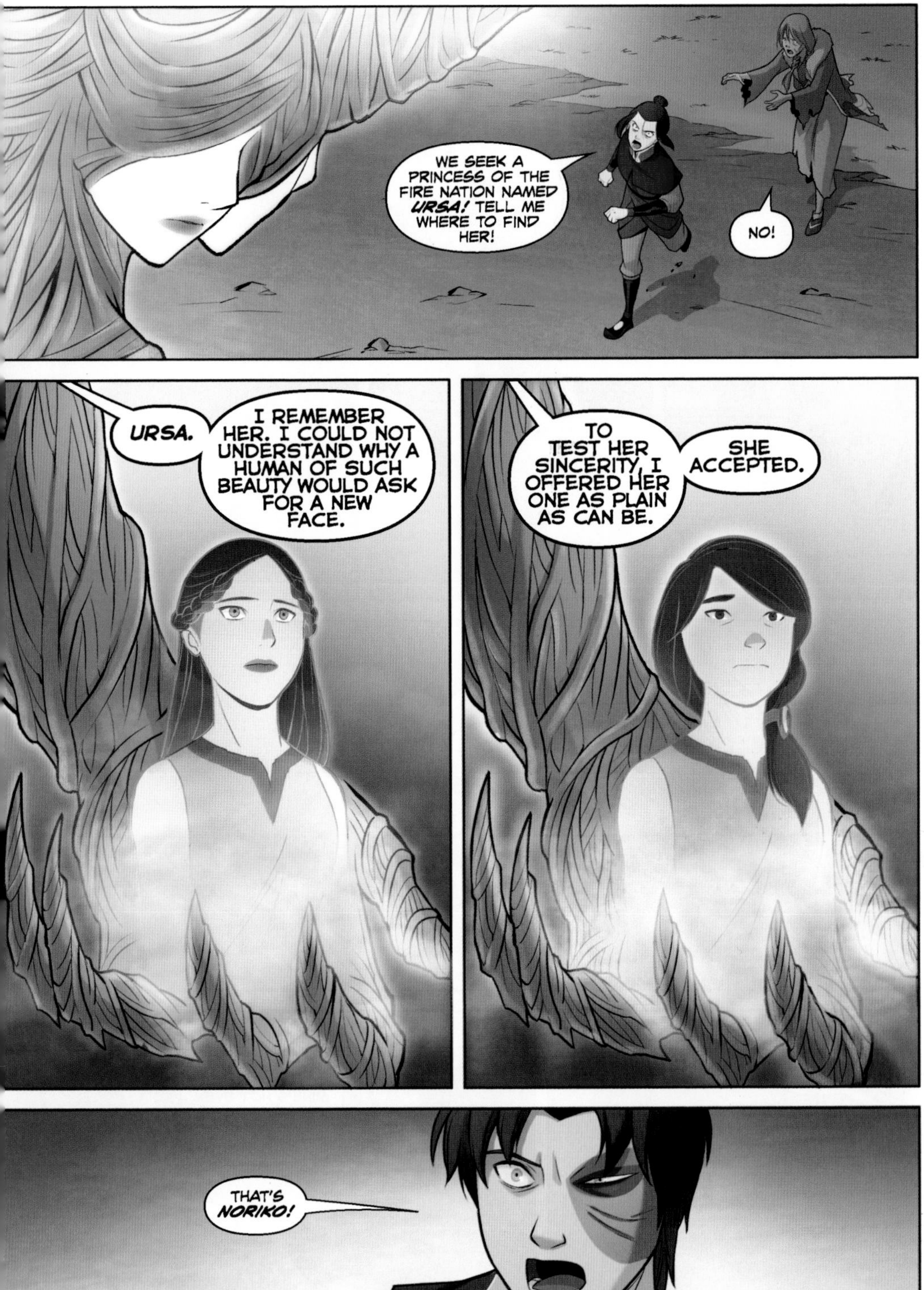
WE SEEK A PRINCESS OF THE FIRE NATION NAMED URSA! TELL ME WHERE TO FIND HER!
NO!
URSA.
I REMEMBER HER. I COULD NOT UNDERSTAND WHY A HUMAN OF SUCH BEAUTY WOULD ASK FOR A NEW FACE.
TO TEST HER SINCERITY, I OFFERED HER ONE AS PLAIN AS CAN BE.
SHE ACCEPTED.
THAT'S NORIKO!

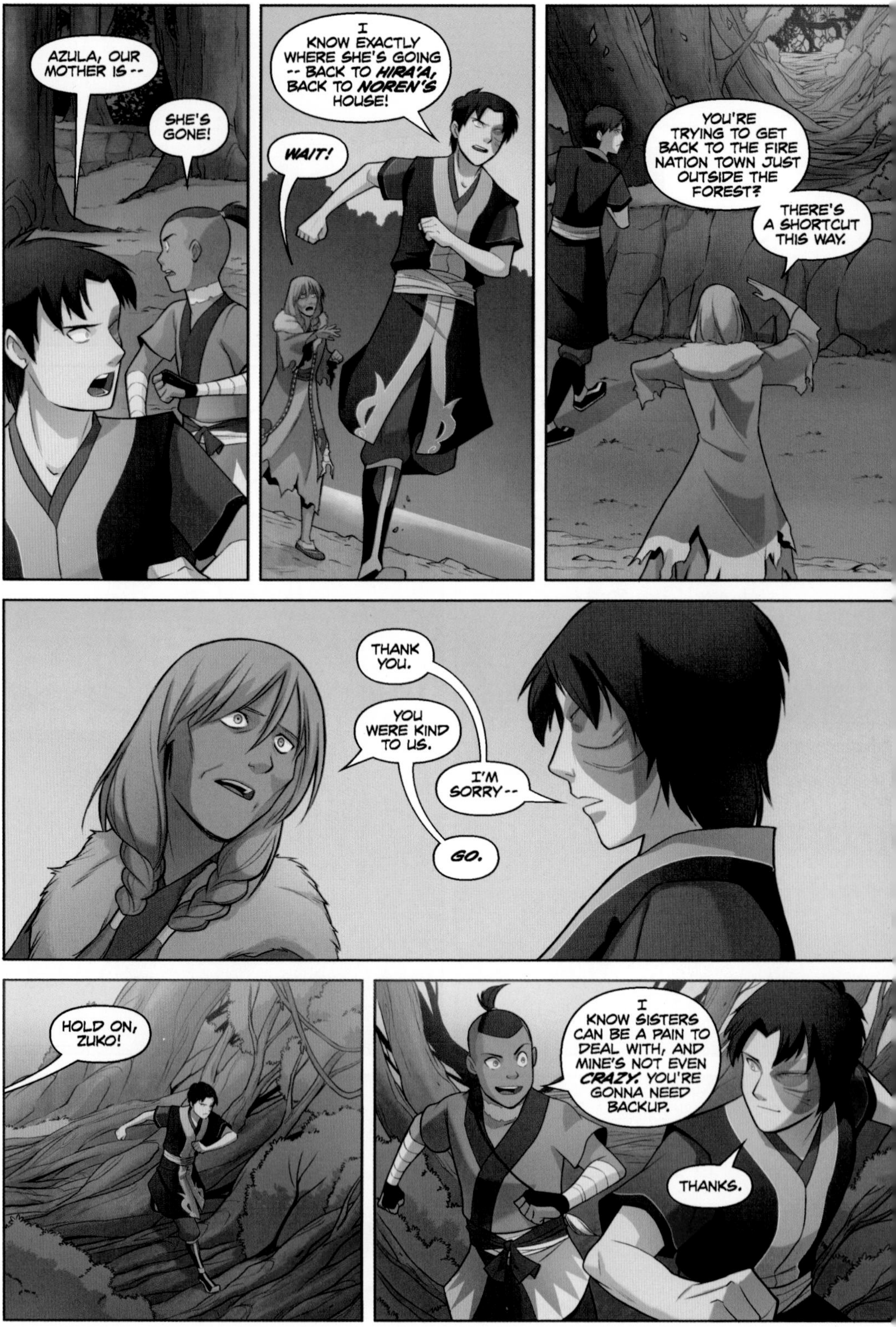
AZULA, OUR MOTHER IS --
SHE'S GONE!
I KNOW EXACTLY WHERE SHE'S GOING -- BACK TO HIRA'A, BACK TO NOREN'S HOUSE!
WAIT!
YOU'RE TRYING TO GET BACK TO THE FIRE NATION TOWN JUST OUTSIDE THE FOREST?
THERE'S A SHORTCUT THIS WAY.
THANK YOU.
YOU WERE KIND TO US.
I'M SORRY --
GO.
HOLD ON, ZUKO!
I KNOW SISTERS CAN BE A PAIN TO DEAL WITH, AND MINE'S NOT EVEN CRAZY. YOU'RE GONNA NEED BACKUP.
THANKS.

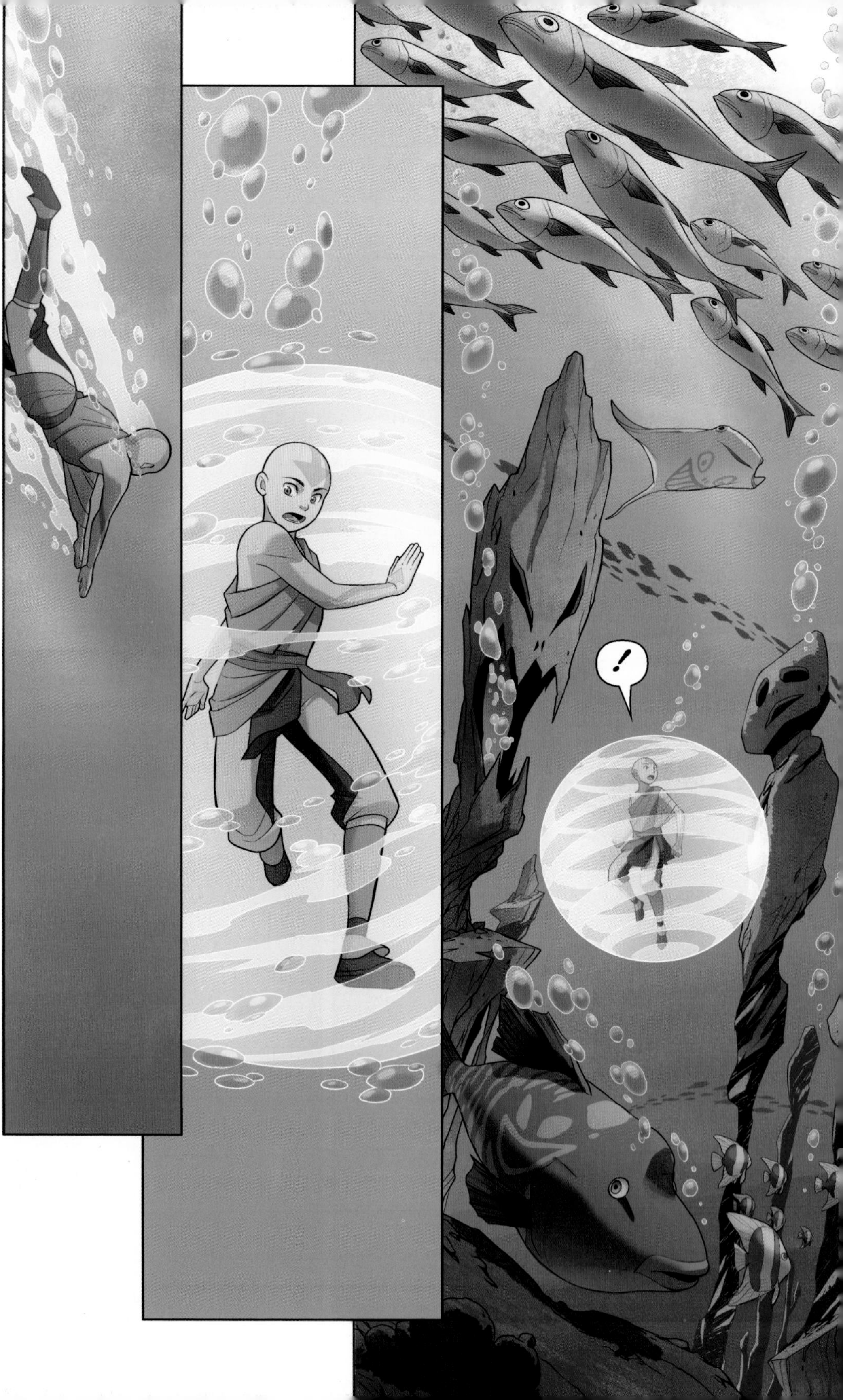
!

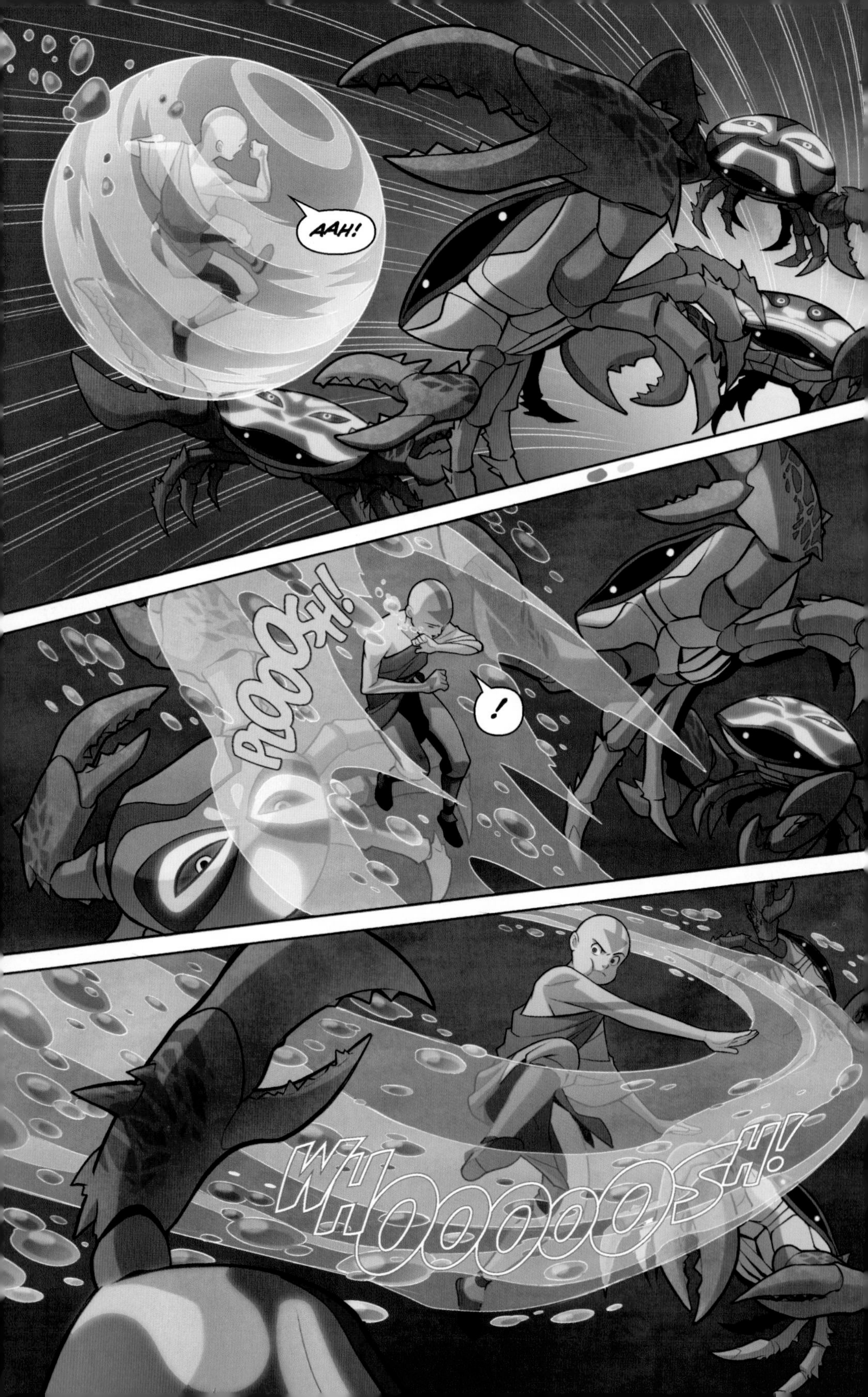
AAH!
FLOOSH!
!
WHOOOOOOSH!

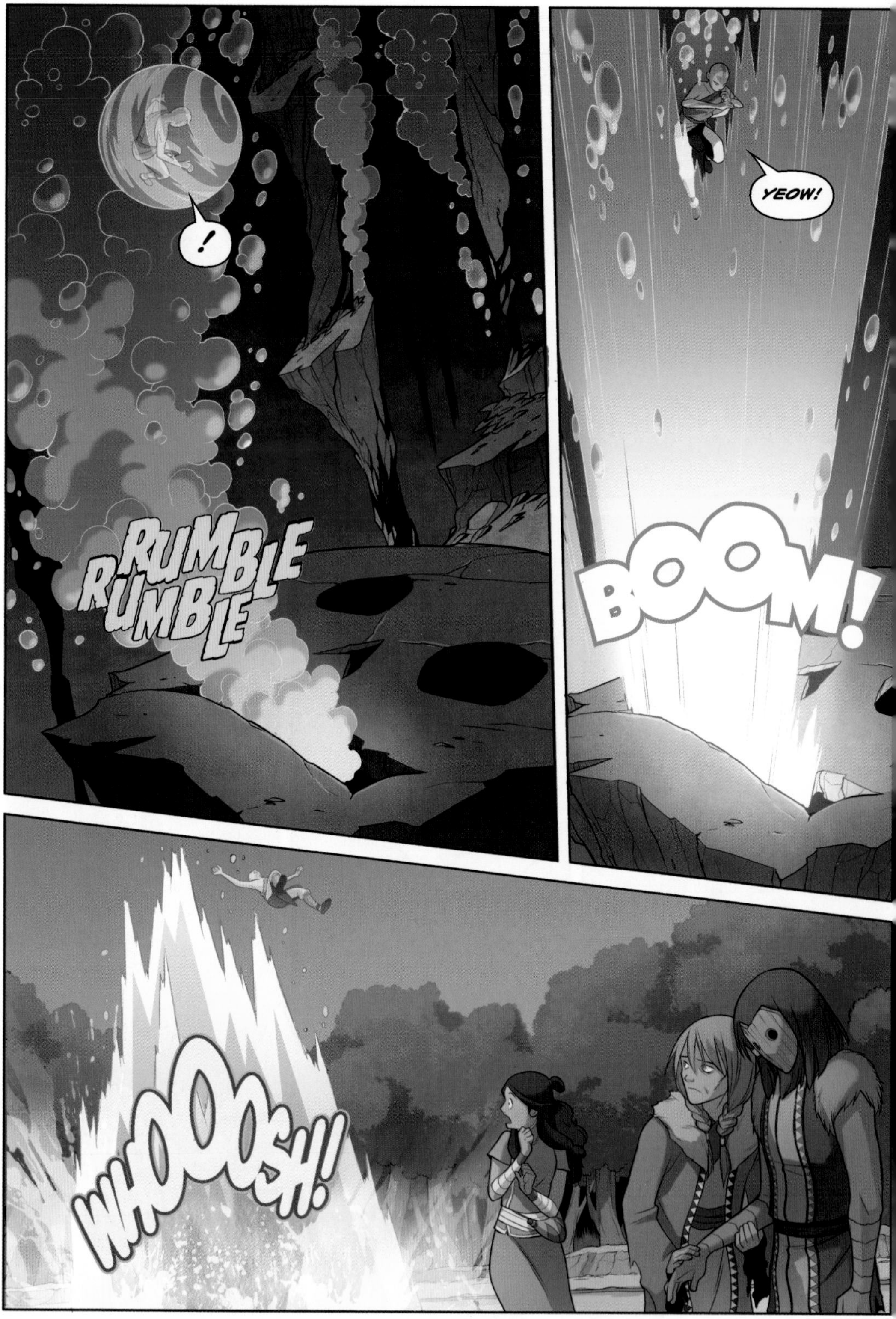
!
RUMBLE RUMBLE
YEOW!
BOOM!
WHOOOSH!

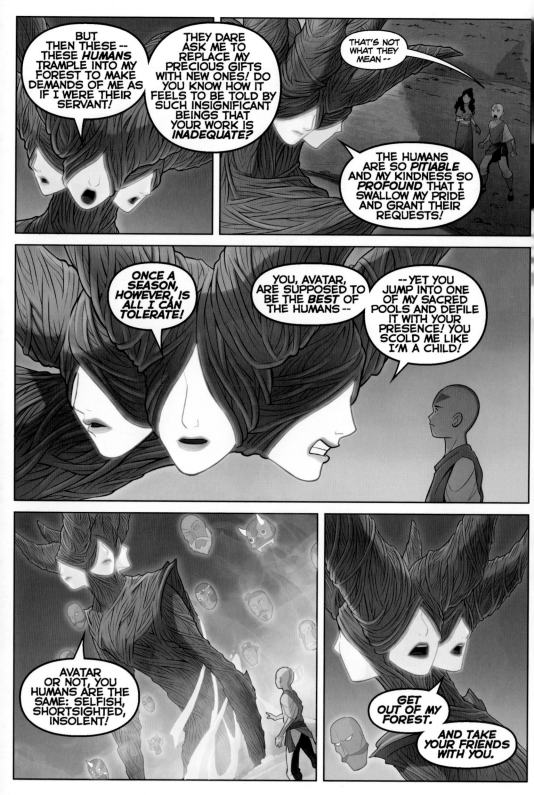

170

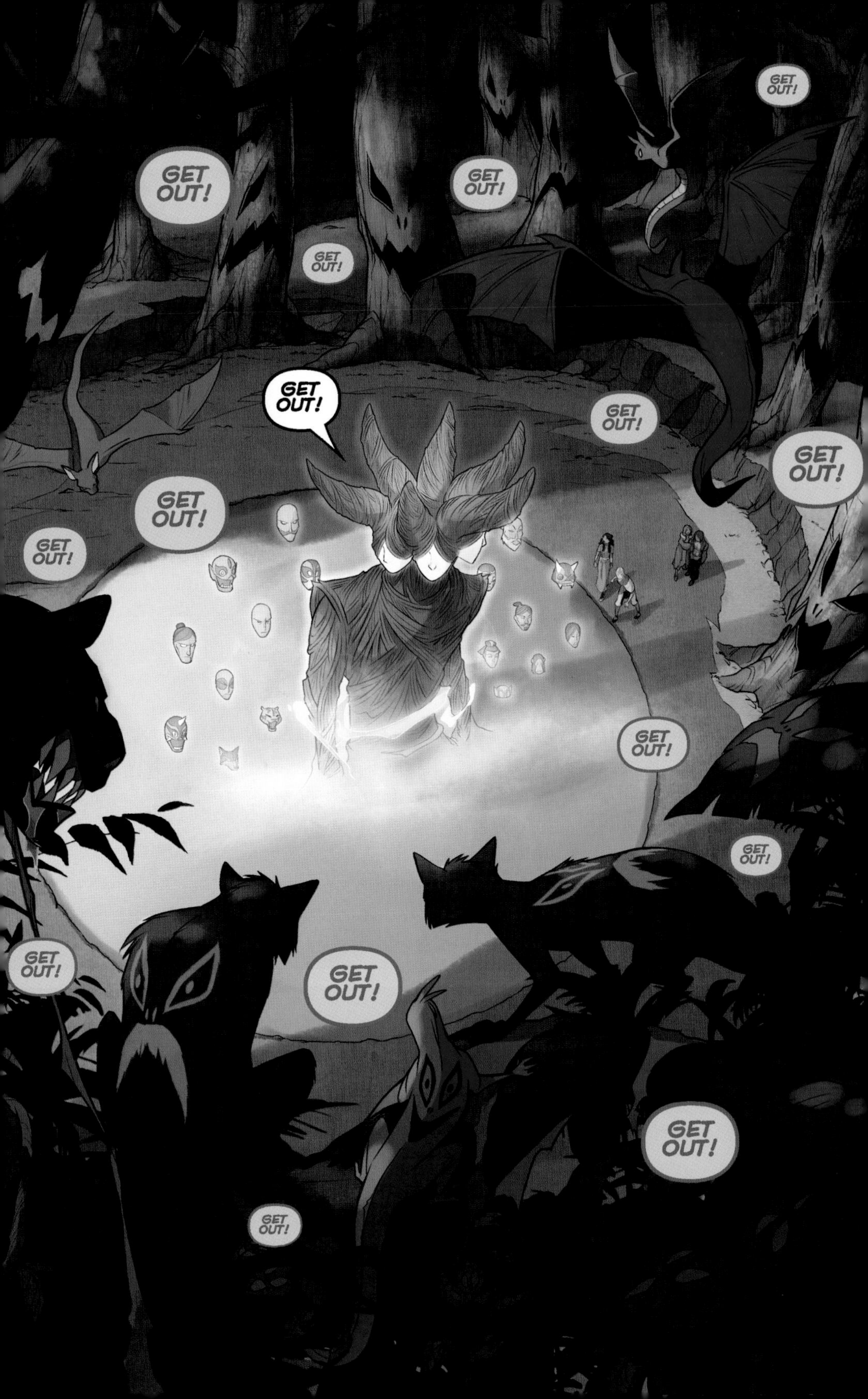
GET OUT!
GET OUT!
GET OUT!
GET OUT!
GET OUT!
GET OUT!
GET OUT!
GET OUT!
GET OUT!
GET OUT!
GET OUT!
GET OUT!
GET OUT!
GET OUT!
GET OUT!

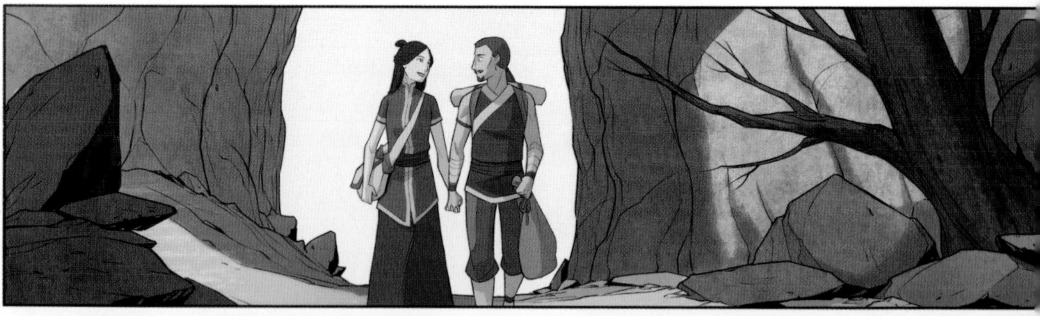
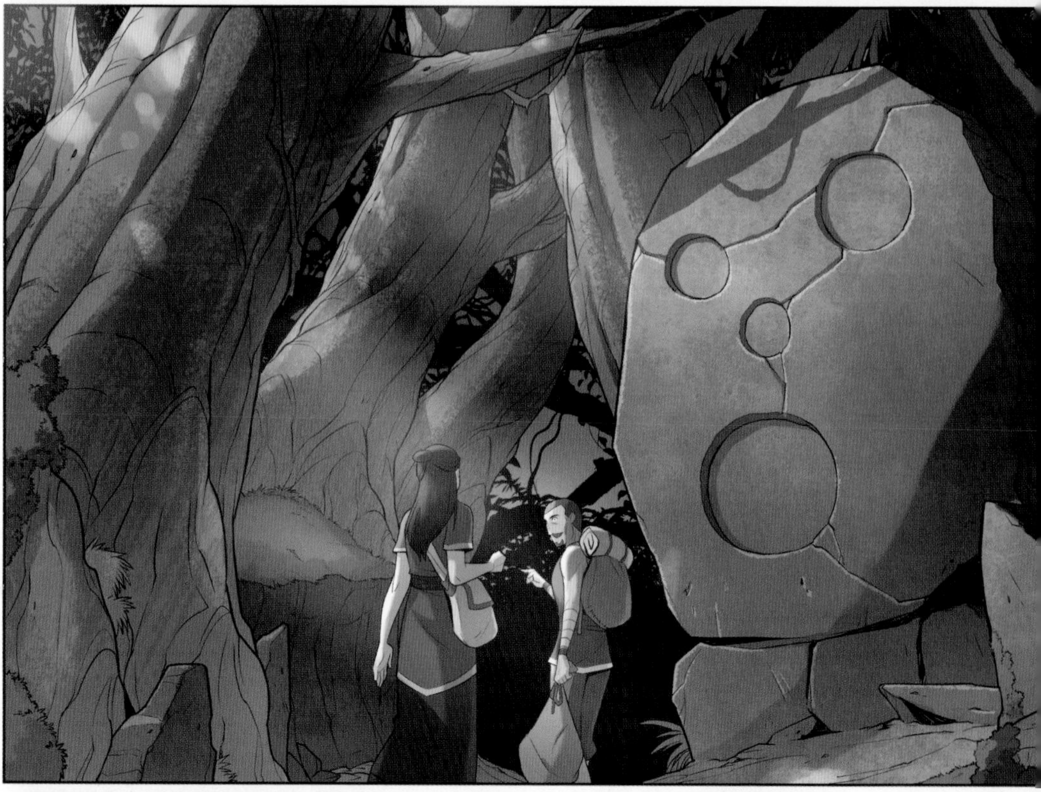
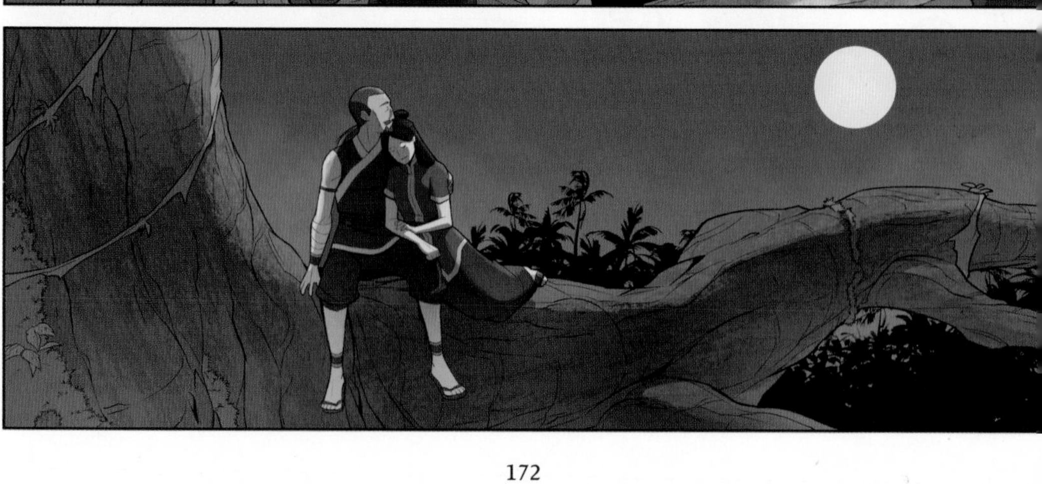

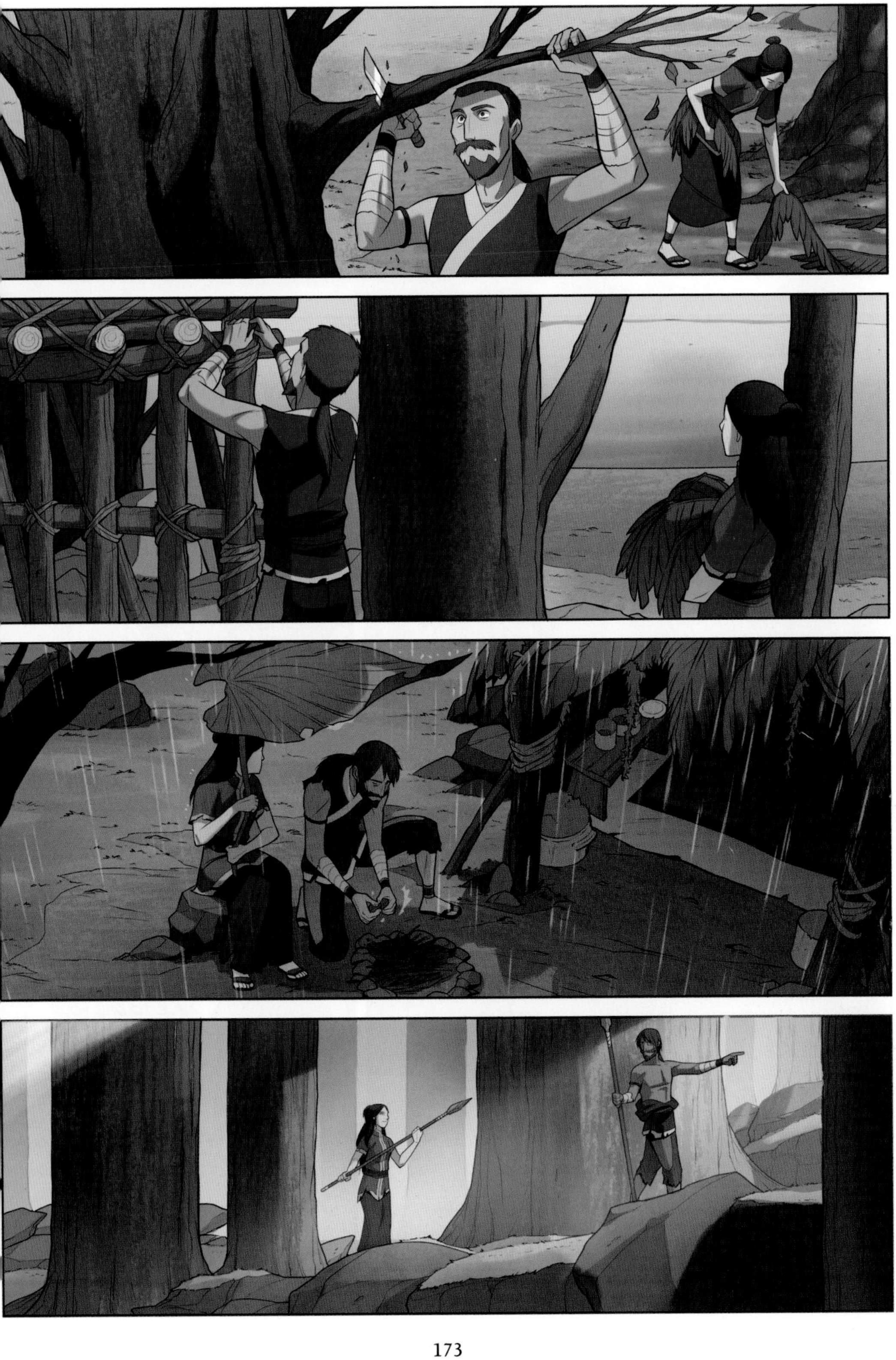

175

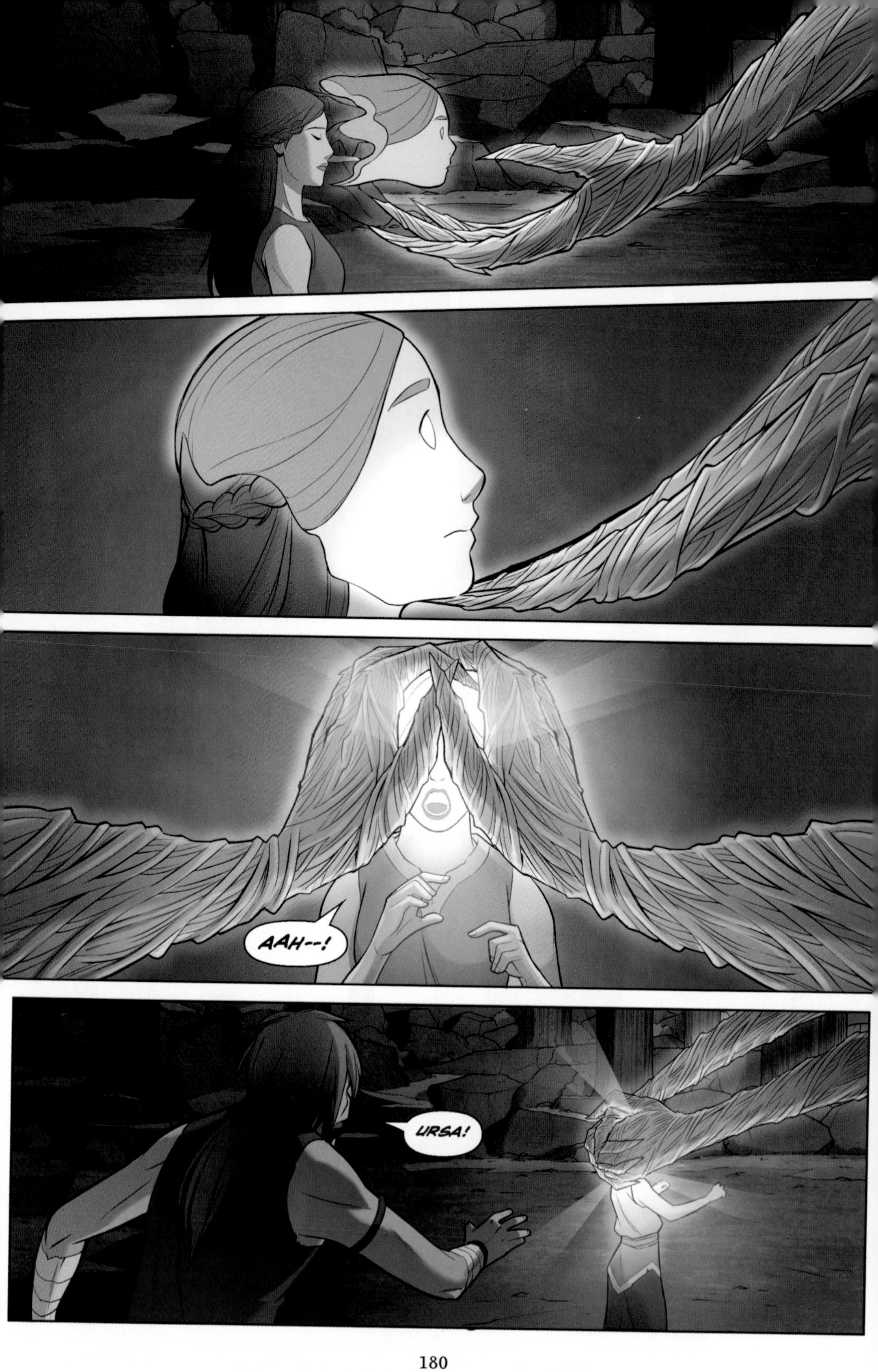
AAH--!
URSA!

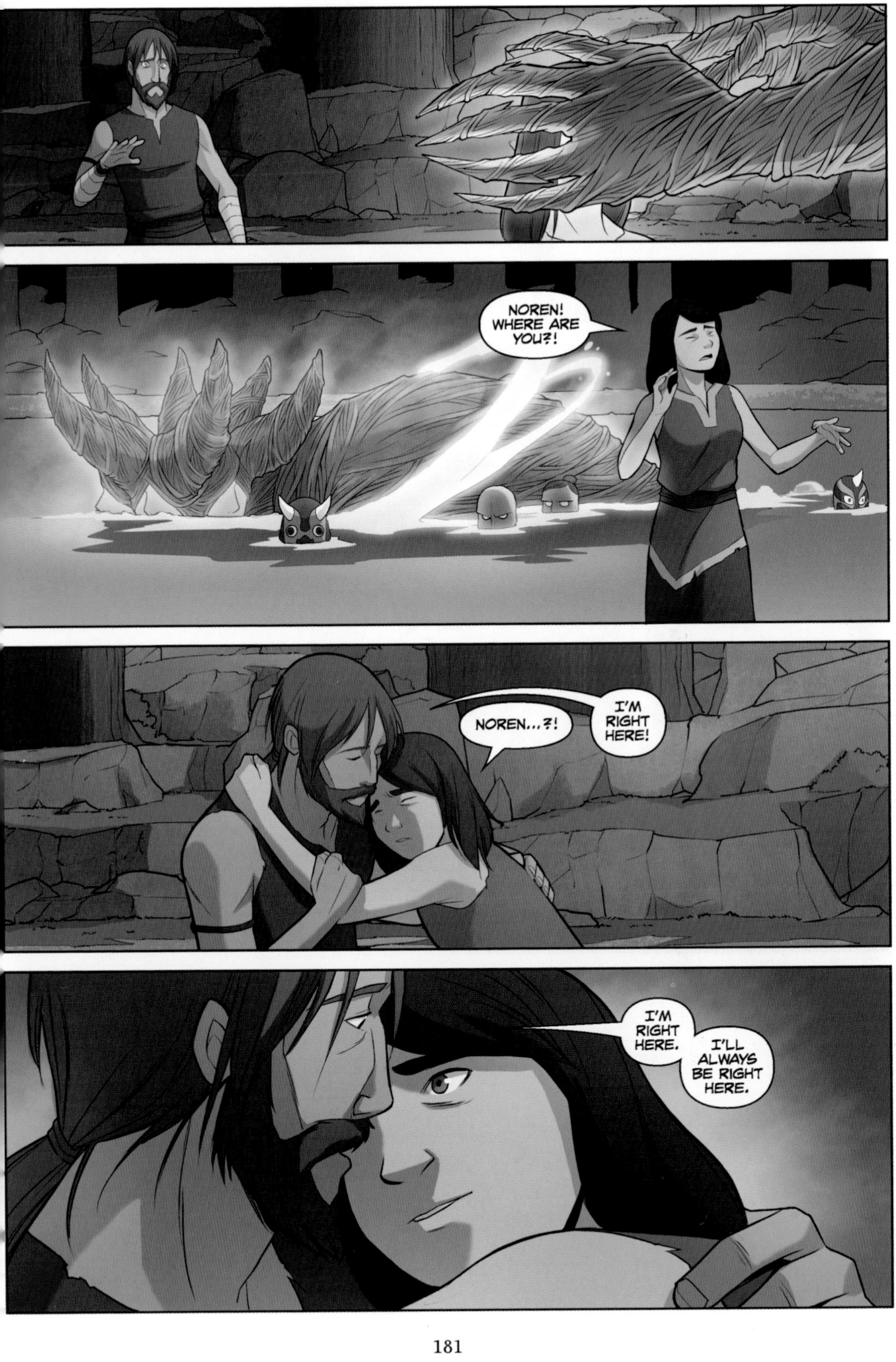
NOREN! WHERE ARE YOU?!
NOREN...?!
I'M RIGHT HERE!
I'M RIGHT HERE.
I'LL ALWAYS BE RIGHT HERE.

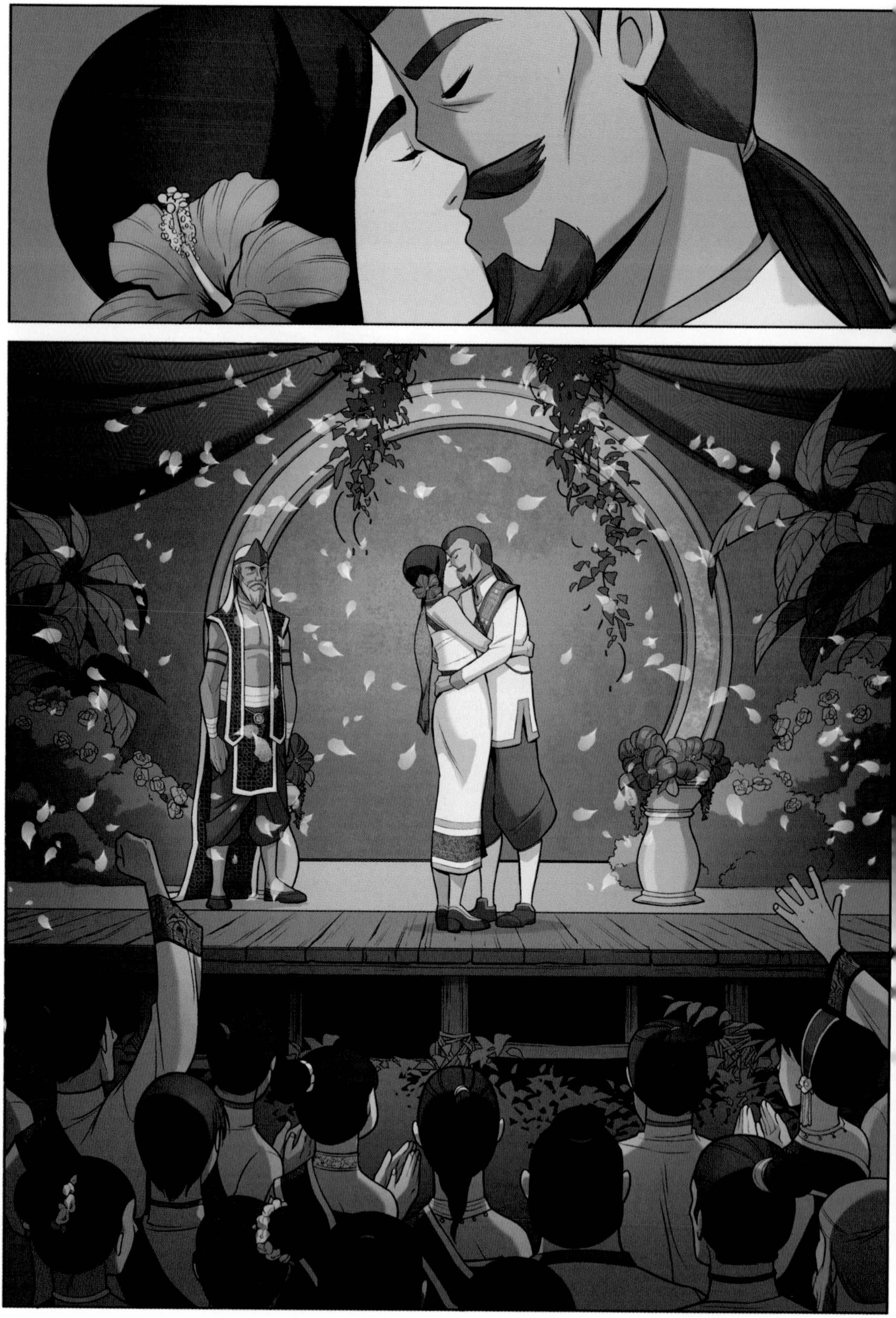

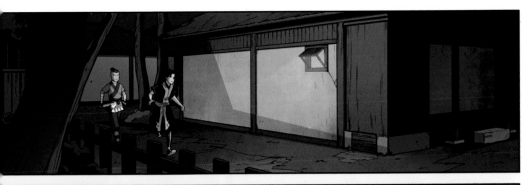

IT'S SO QUIET.

TOO QUIET.

ZUKO, WHAT'S GOING ON IN THERE? NOREN'S FAMILY... DON'T TELL ME AZULA --!

184

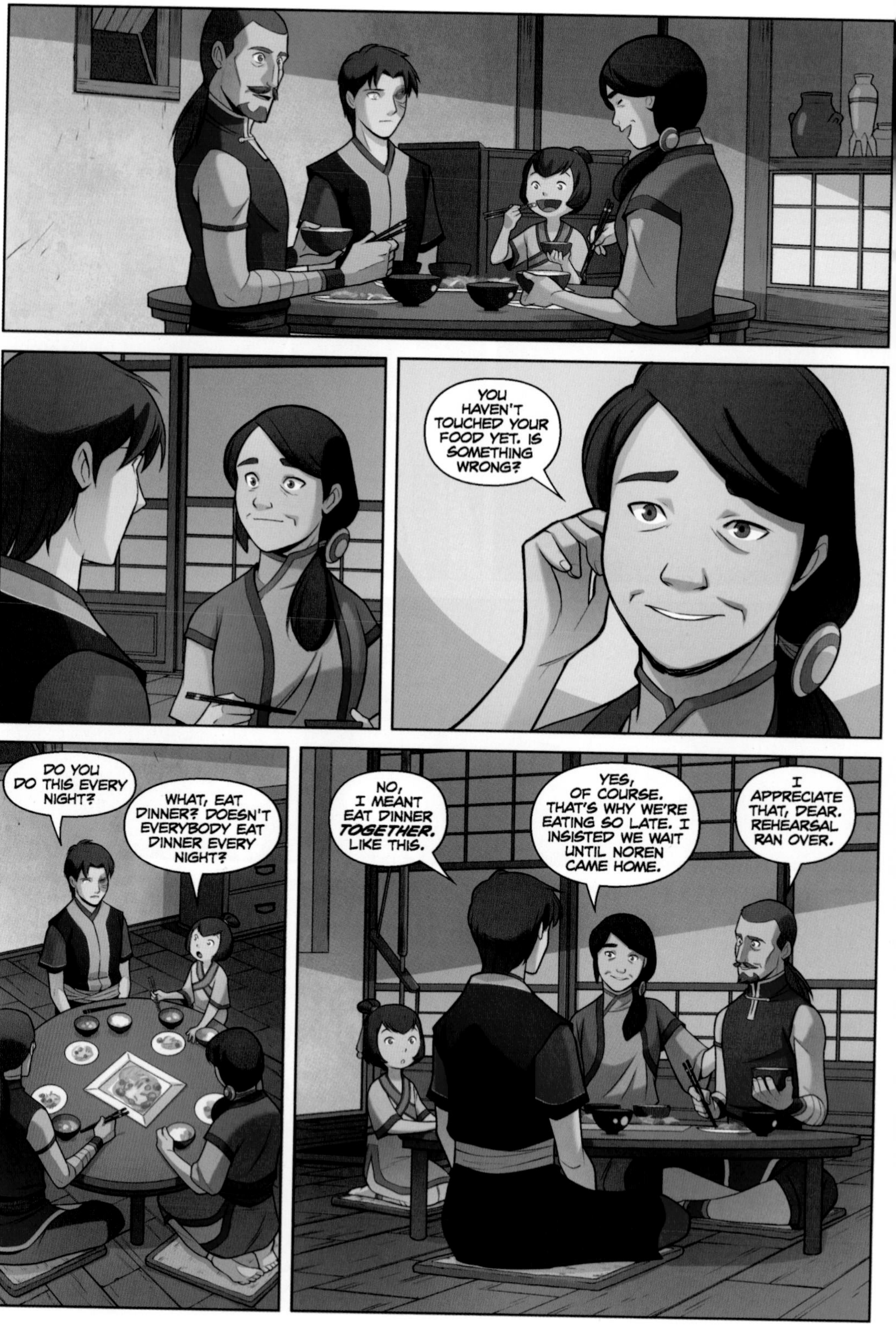
YOU HAVEN'T TOUCHED YOUR FOOD YET. IS SOMETHING WRONG?
DO YOU DO THIS EVERY NIGHT?
WHAT, EAT DINNER? DOESN'T EVERYBODY EAT DINNER EVERY NIGHT?
NO, I MEANT EAT DINNER *TOGETHER.* LIKE THIS.
YES, OF COURSE. THAT'S WHY WE'RE EATING SO LATE. I INSISTED WE WAIT UNTIL NOREN CAME HOME.
I APPRECIATE THAT, DEAR. REHEARSAL RAN OVER.

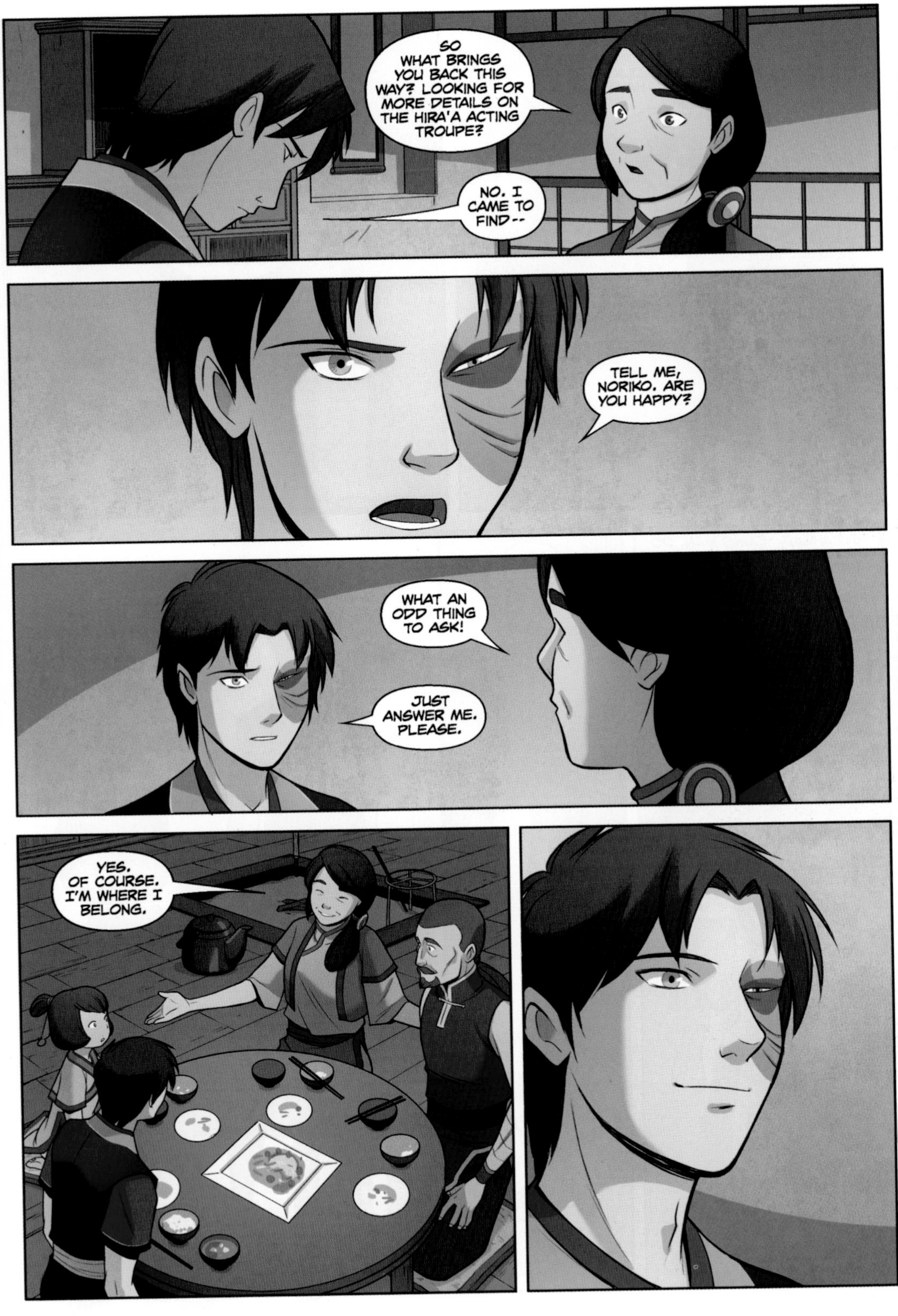
SO WHAT BRINGS YOU BACK THIS WAY? LOOKING FOR MORE DETAILS ON THE HIRA'A ACTING TROUPE?
NO. I CAME TO FIND--
TELL ME, NORIKO. ARE YOU HAPPY?
WHAT AN ODD THING TO ASK!
JUST ANSWER ME. PLEASE.
YES. OF COURSE. I'M WHERE I BELONG.

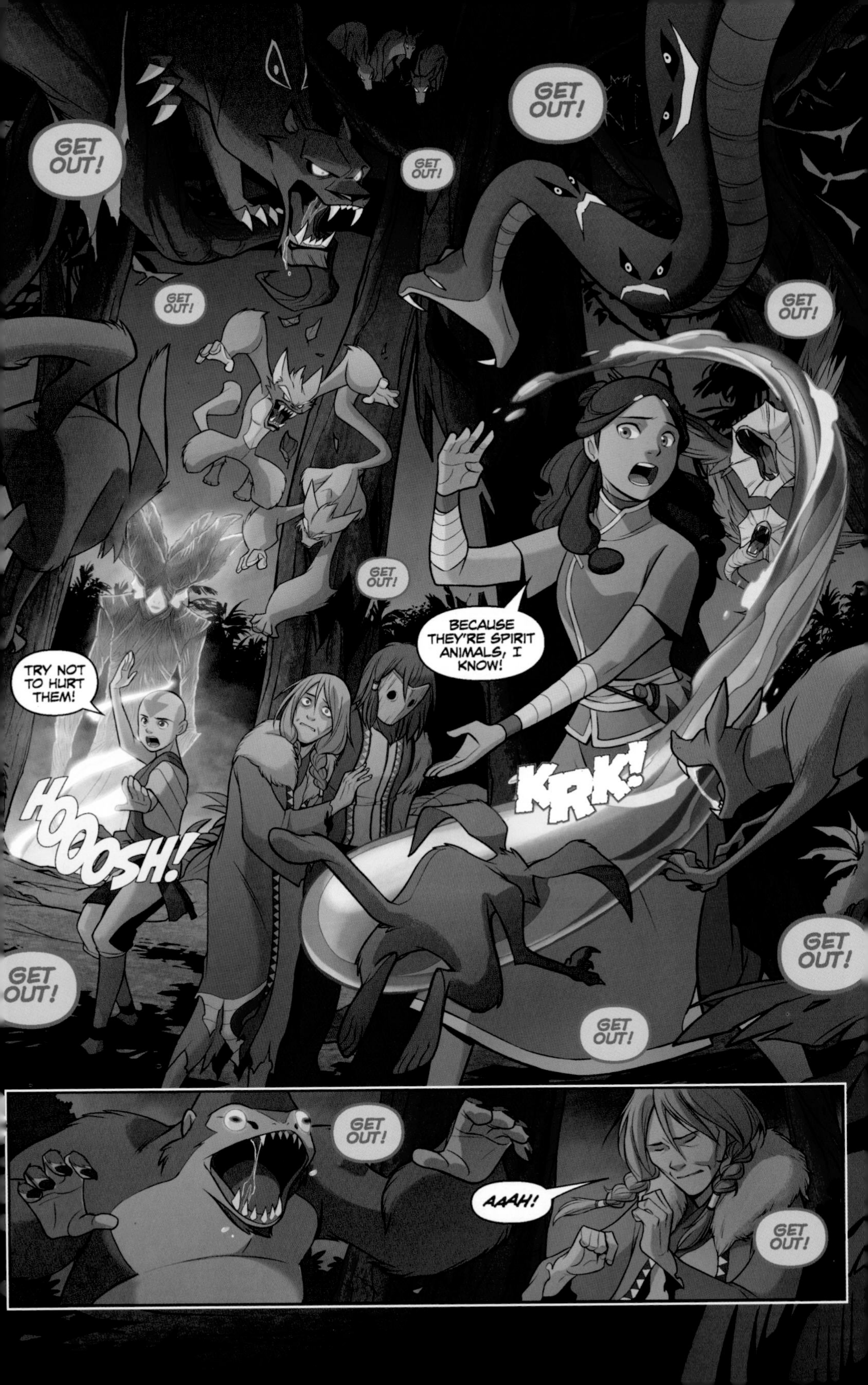
GET OUT!
GET OUT!
GET OUT!
GET OUT!
GET OUT!
GET OUT!
TRY NOT TO HURT THEM!
BECAUSE THEY'RE SPIRIT ANIMALS, I KNOW!
KRK!
HOOOOSH!
GET OUT!
GET OUT!
GET OUT!
GET OUT!
AAAH!
GET OUT!

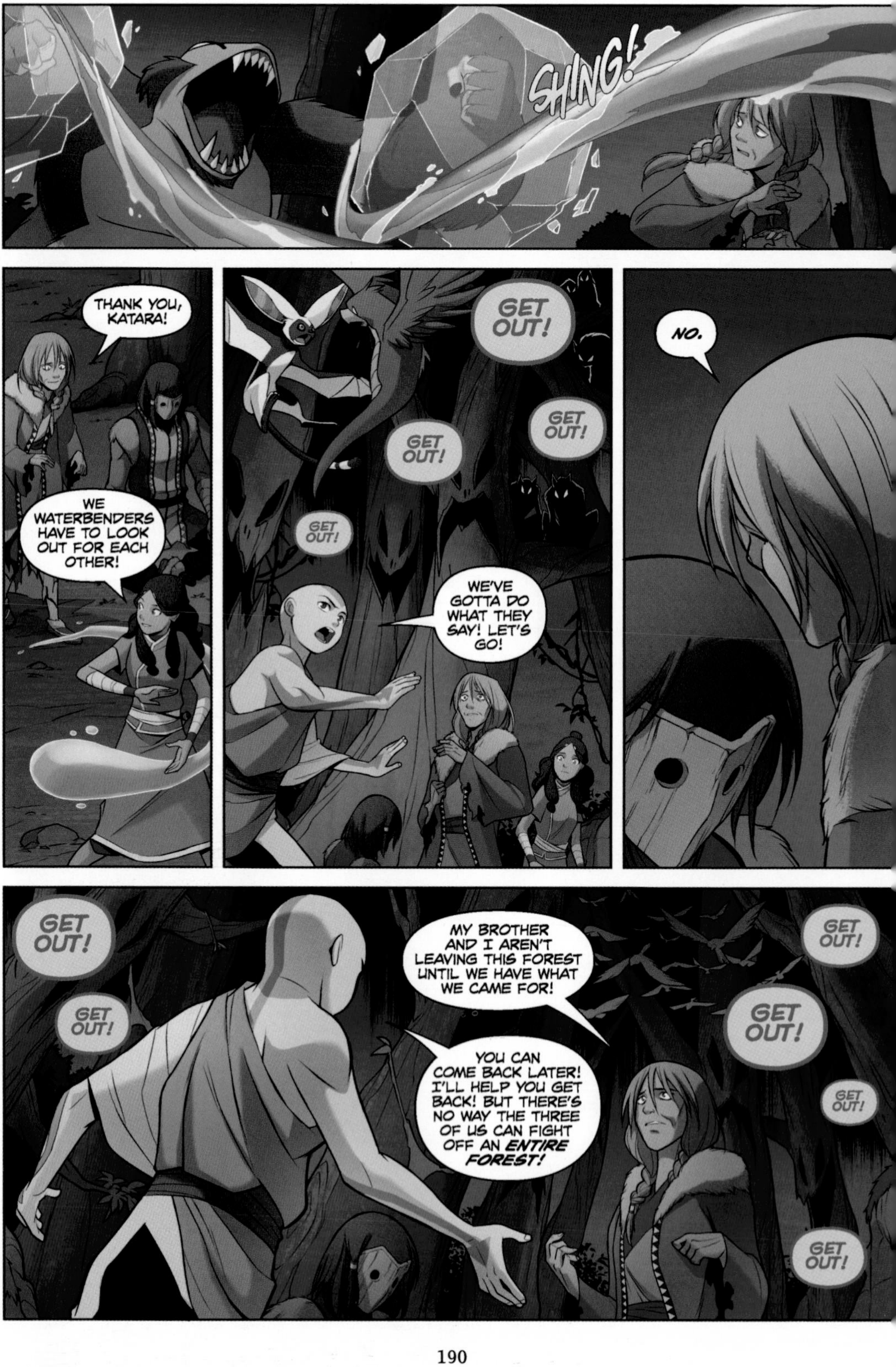
SHING!
THANK YOU, KATARA!
WE WATERBENDERS HAVE TO LOOK OUT FOR EACH OTHER!
GET OUT!
GET OUT!
GET OUT!
GET OUT!
WE'VE GOTTA DO WHAT THEY SAY! LET'S GO!
NO.
GET OUT!
GET OUT!
MY BROTHER AND I AREN'T LEAVING THIS FOREST UNTIL WE HAVE WHAT WE CAME FOR!
YOU CAN COME BACK LATER! I'LL HELP YOU GET BACK! BUT THERE'S NO WAY THE THREE OF US CAN FIGHT OFF AN *ENTIRE FOREST!*
GET OUT!
GET OUT!
GET OUT!
GET OUT!

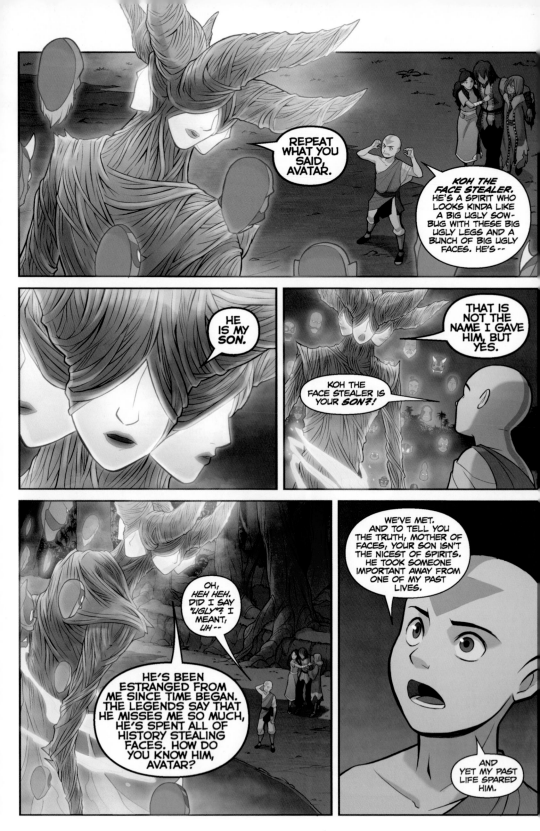

192

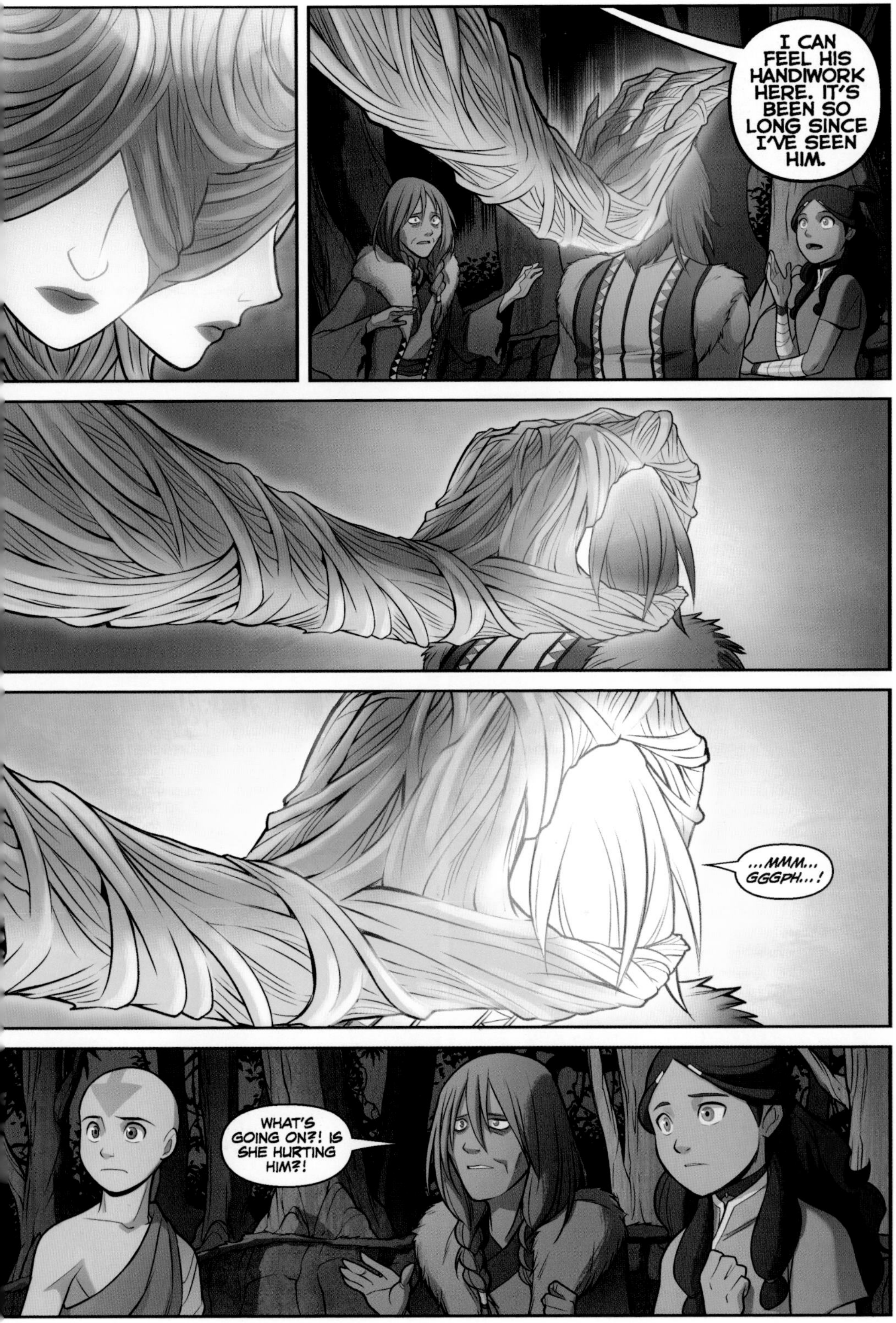
I CAN FEEL HIS HANDIWORK HERE. IT'S BEEN SO LONG SINCE I'VE SEEN HIM.
...MMM... GGGPH...!
WHAT'S GOING ON?! IS SHE HURTING HIM?!

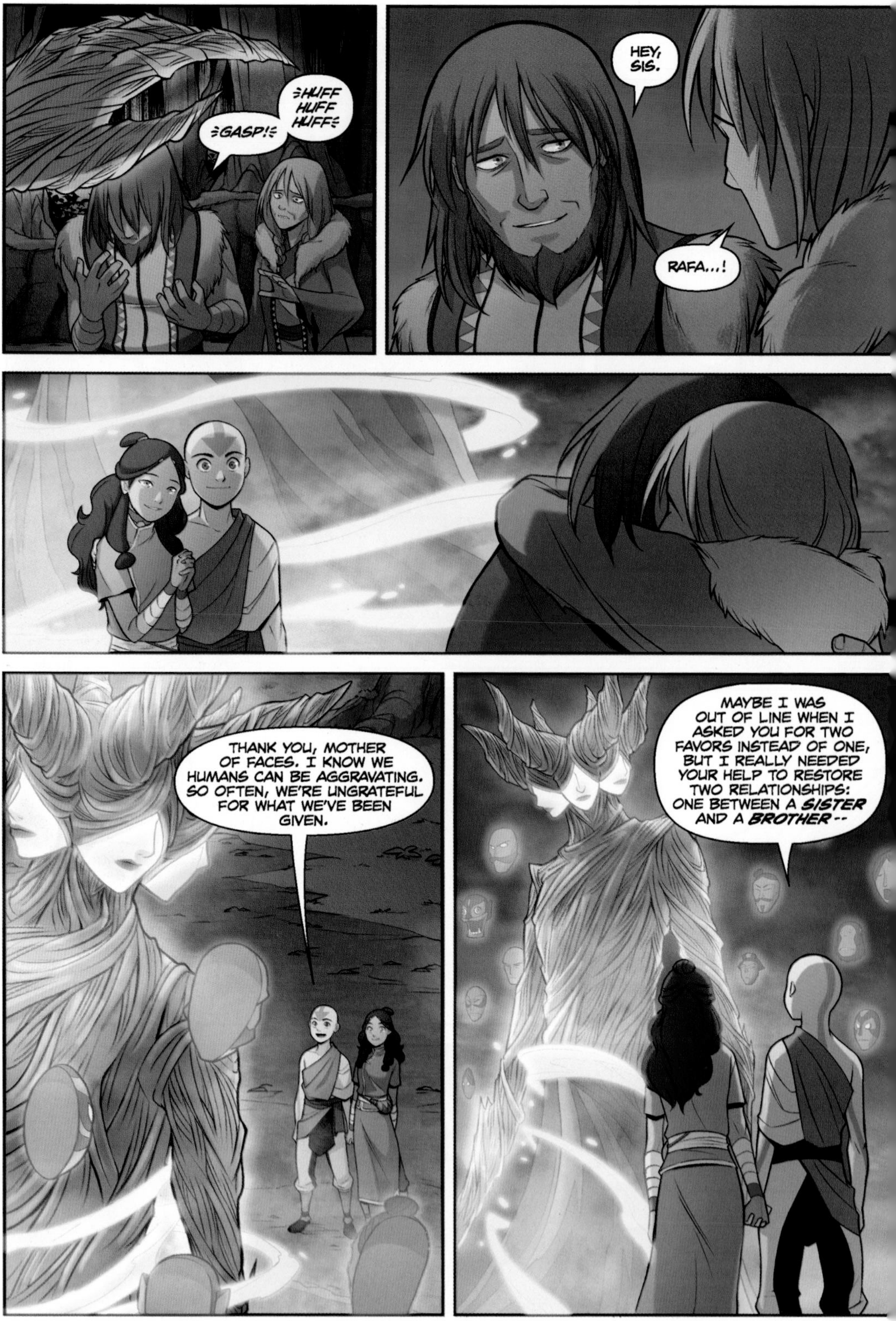
GASP!
HUFF HUFF HUFF
HEY, SIS.
RAFA...!
THANK YOU, MOTHER OF FACES. I KNOW WE HUMANS CAN BE AGGRAVATING. SO OFTEN, WE'RE UNGRATEFUL FOR WHAT WE'VE BEEN GIVEN.
MAYBE I WAS OUT OF LINE WHEN I ASKED YOU FOR TWO FAVORS INSTEAD OF ONE, BUT I REALLY NEEDED YOUR HELP TO RESTORE TWO RELATIONSHIPS: ONE BETWEEN A SISTER AND A BROTHER --

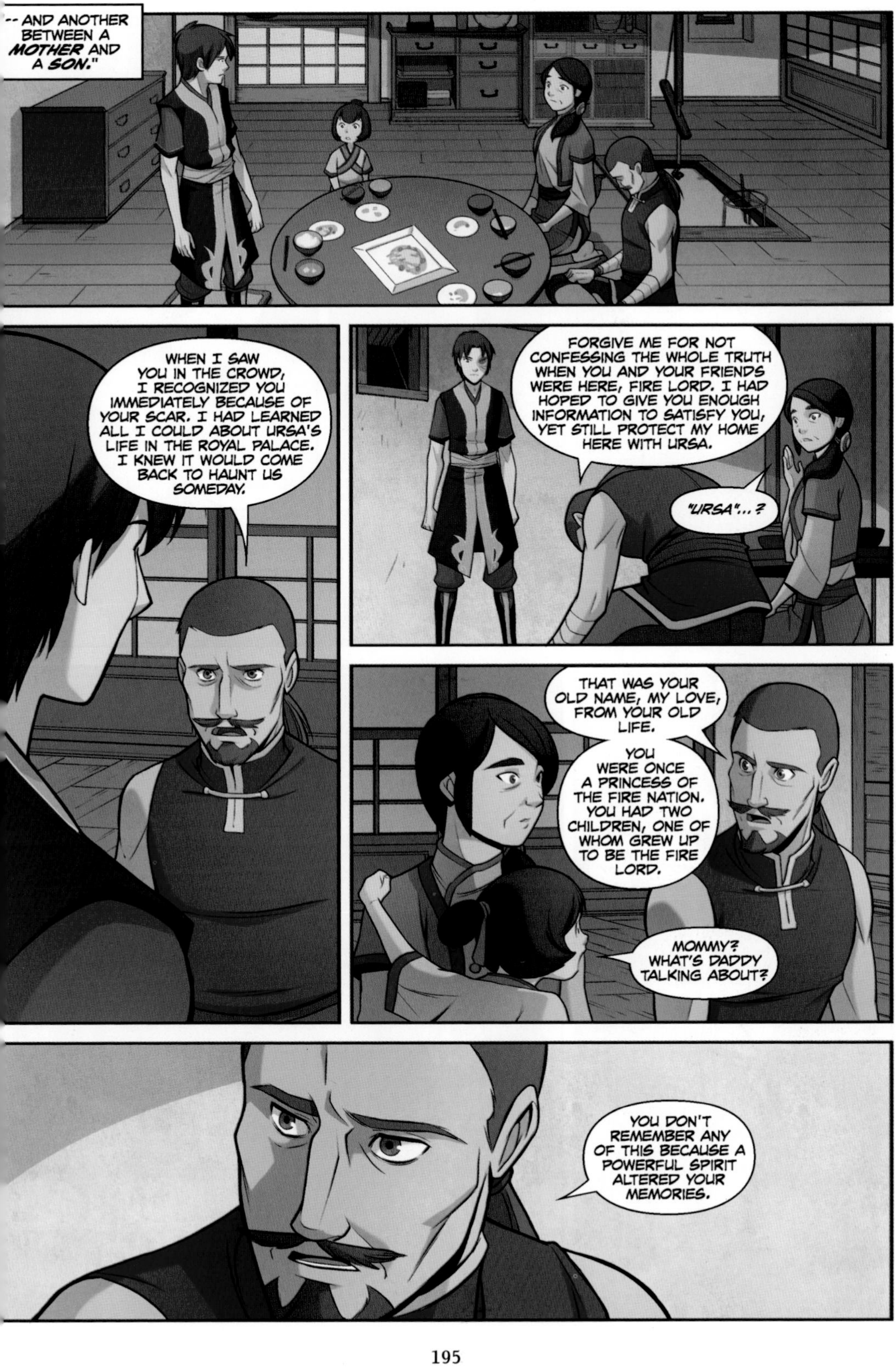
-- AND ANOTHER BETWEEN A MOTHER AND A SON."
WHEN I SAW YOU IN THE CROWD, I RECOGNIZED YOU IMMEDIATELY BECAUSE OF YOUR SCAR. I HAD LEARNED ALL I COULD ABOUT URSA'S LIFE IN THE ROYAL PALACE. I KNEW IT WOULD COME BACK TO HAUNT US SOMEDAY.
FORGIVE ME FOR NOT CONFESSING THE WHOLE TRUTH WHEN YOU AND YOUR FRIENDS WERE HERE, FIRE LORD. I HAD HOPED TO GIVE YOU ENOUGH INFORMATION TO SATISFY YOU, YET STILL PROTECT MY HOME HERE WITH URSA.
"URSA"...?
THAT WAS YOUR OLD NAME, MY LOVE, FROM YOUR OLD LIFE.
YOU WERE ONCE A PRINCESS OF THE FIRE NATION. YOU HAD TWO CHILDREN, ONE OF WHOM GREW UP TO BE THE FIRE LORD.
MOMMY? WHAT'S DADDY TALKING ABOUT?
YOU DON'T REMEMBER ANY OF THIS BECAUSE A POWERFUL SPIRIT ALTERED YOUR MEMORIES.

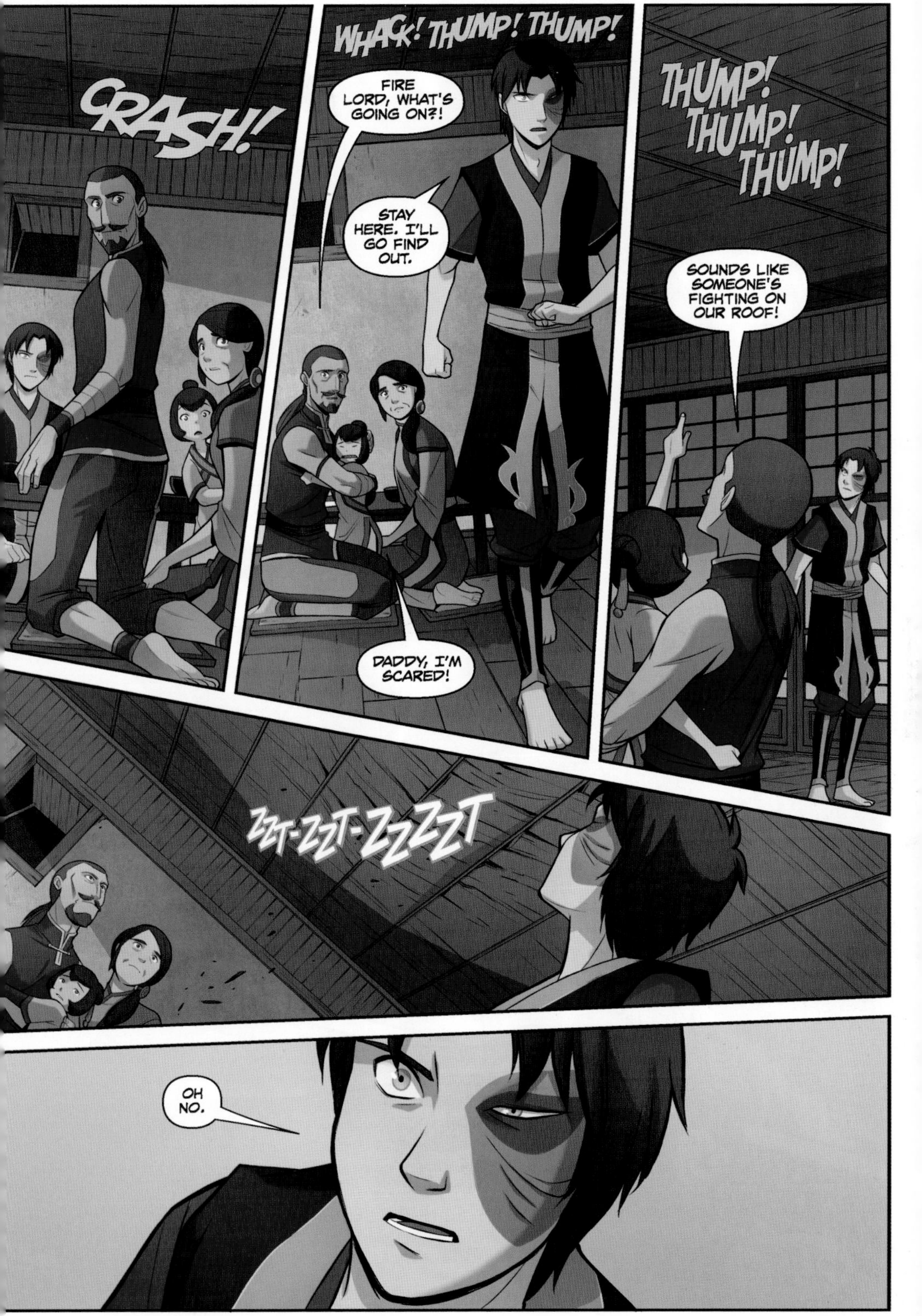
CRASH!
WHACK! THUMP! THUMP!
FIRE LORD, WHAT'S GOING ON?!
STAY HERE. I'LL GO FIND OUT.
DADDY, I'M SCARED!
THUMP! THUMP! THUMP!
SOUNDS LIKE SOMEONE'S FIGHTING ON OUR ROOF!
ZZZT-ZZZT-ZZZZZT
OH NO.

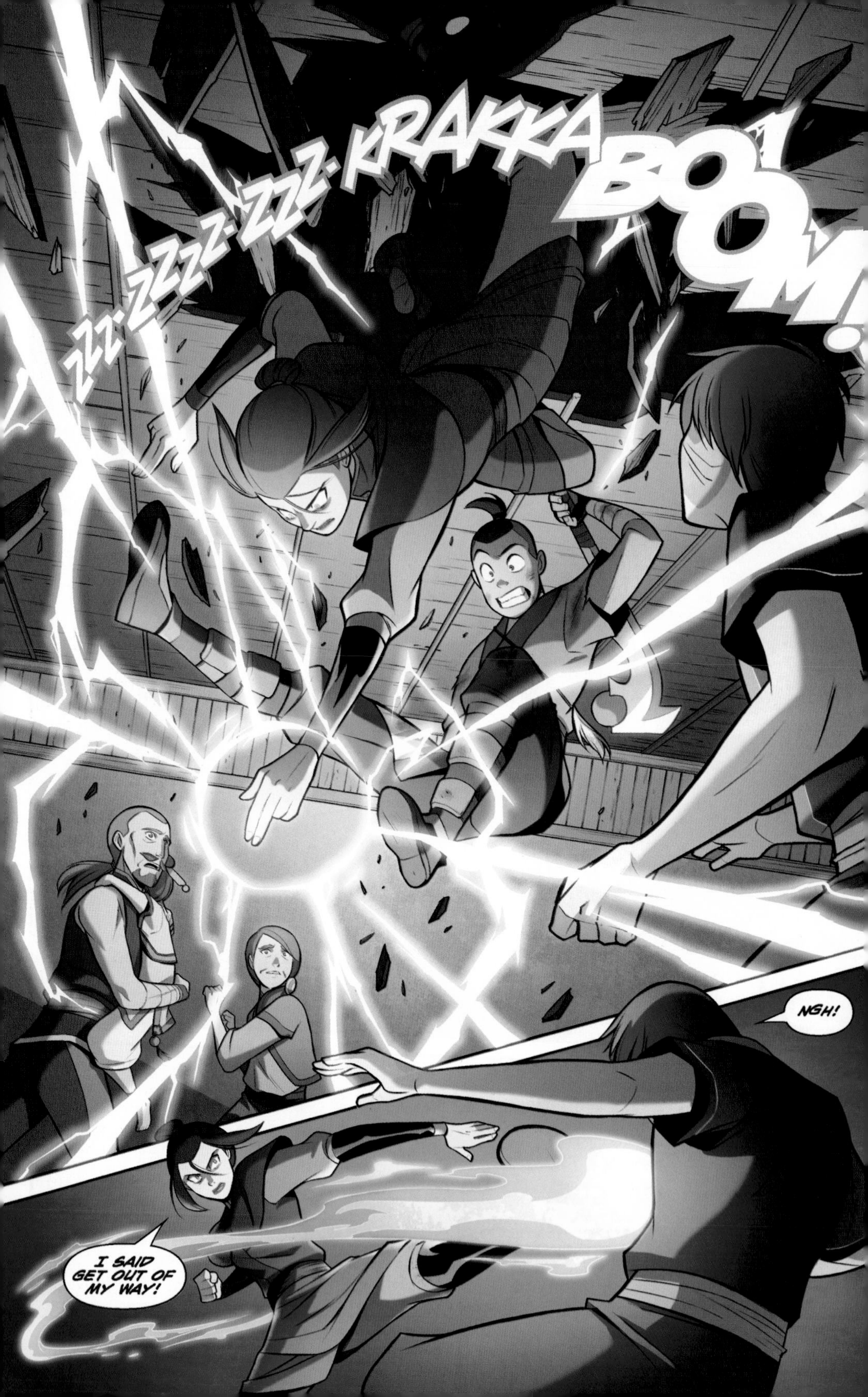
ZZZ-ZZZZZ-ZZZ-KRAKKABOOM!
NGH!
I SAID GET OUT OF MY WAY!

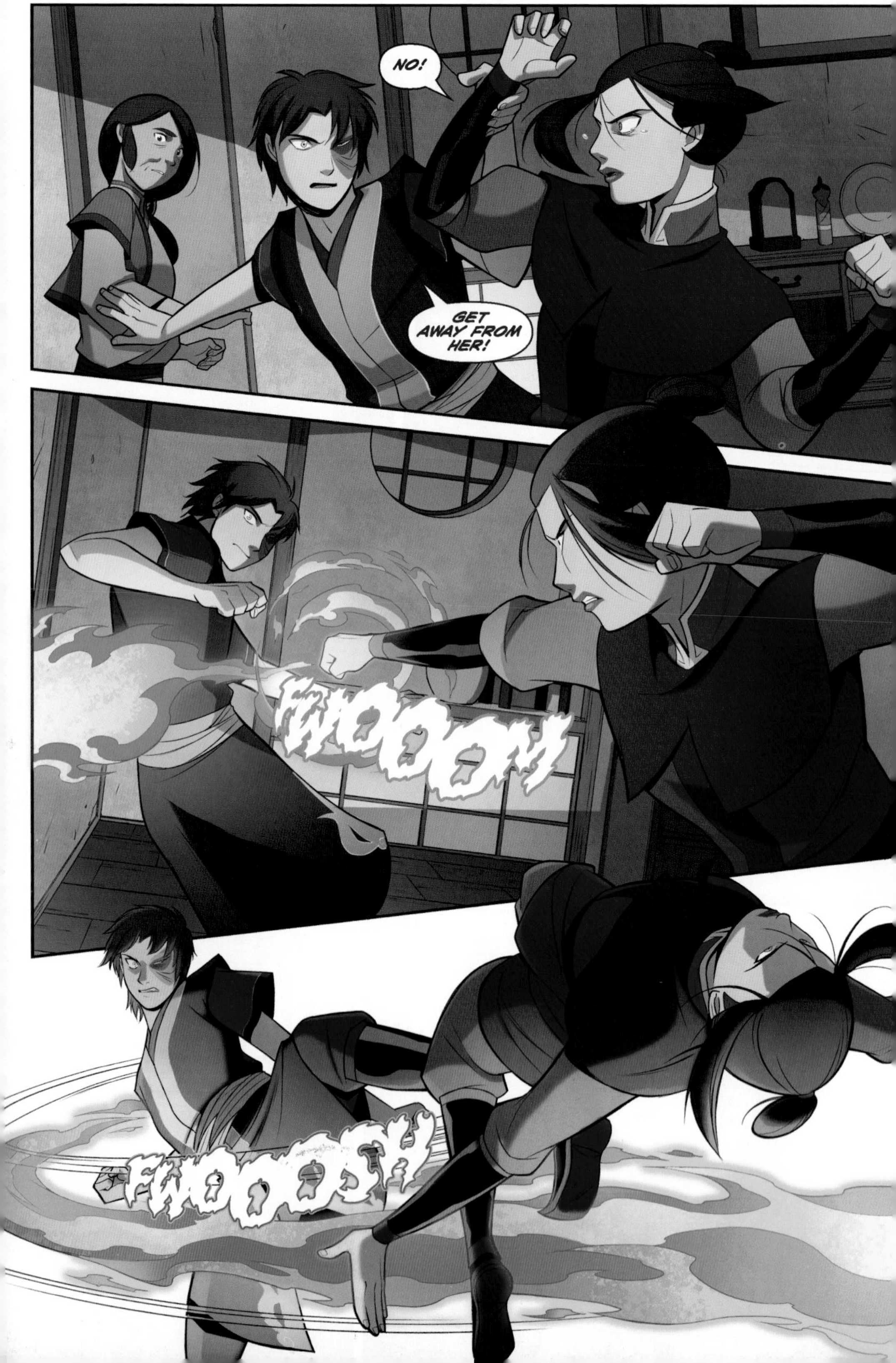
NO!
GET AWAY FROM HER!
FWOOOM
FWOOOSH

205

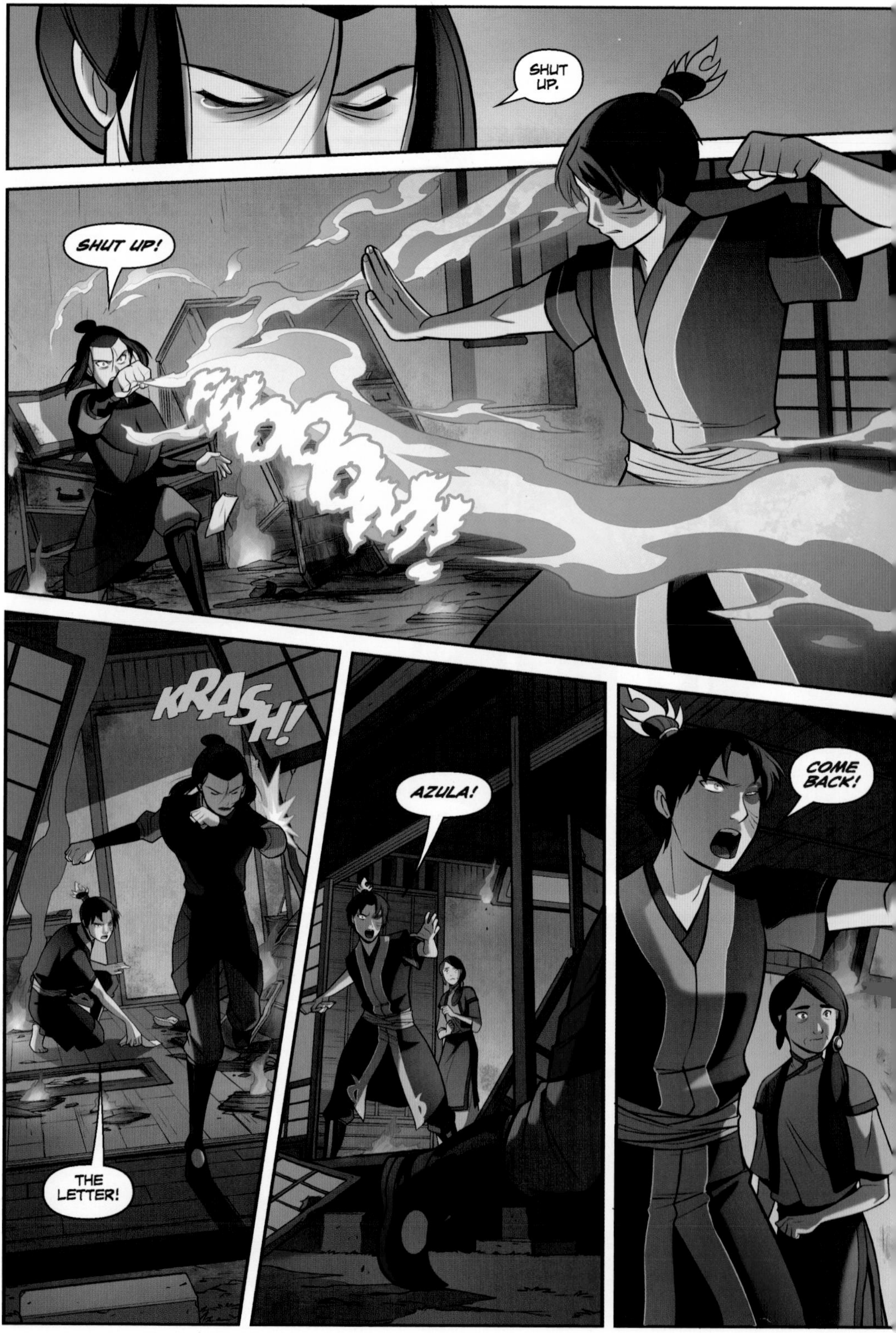
SHUT UP.
SHUT UP!
FWOOOM!
KRASH!
THE LETTER!
AZULA!
COME BACK!

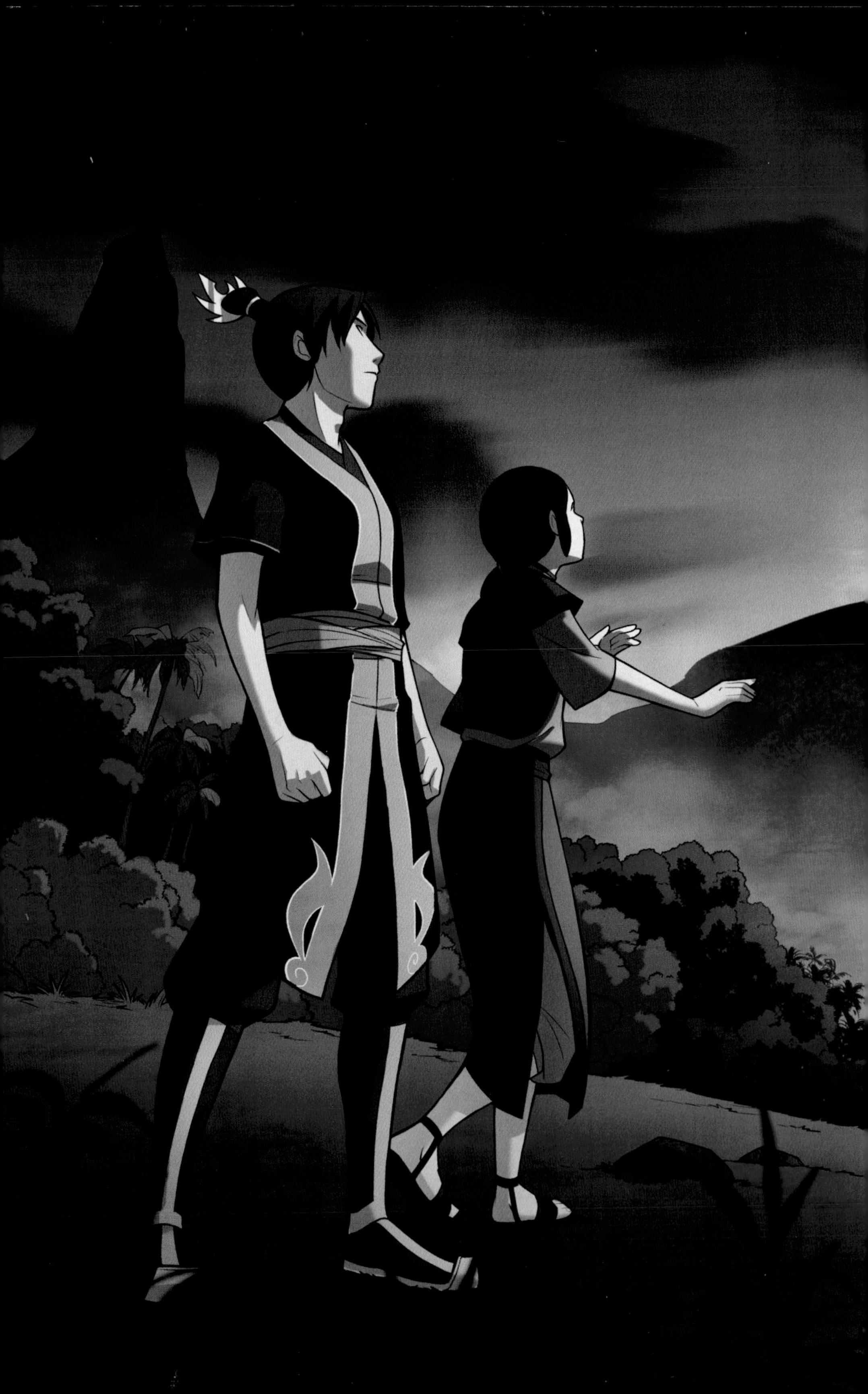

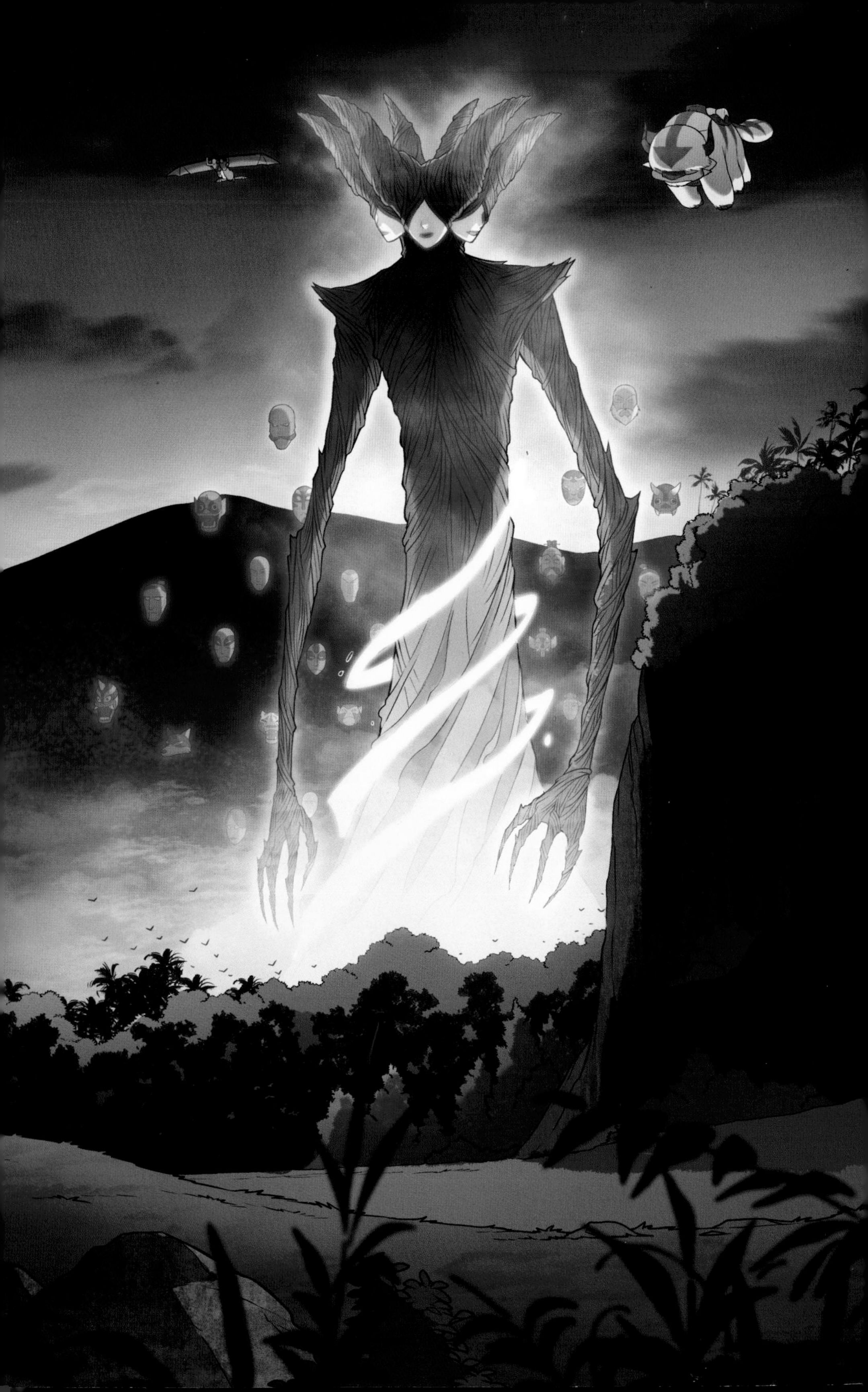

210

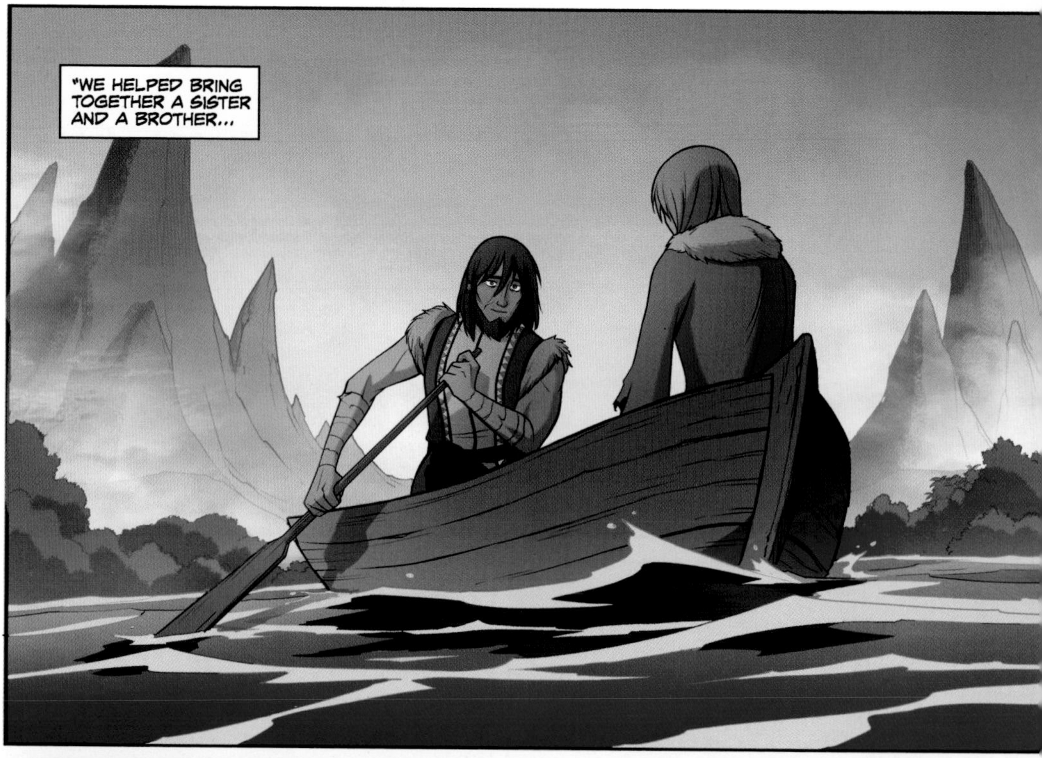
"WE HELPED BRING TOGETHER A SISTER AND A BROTHER...

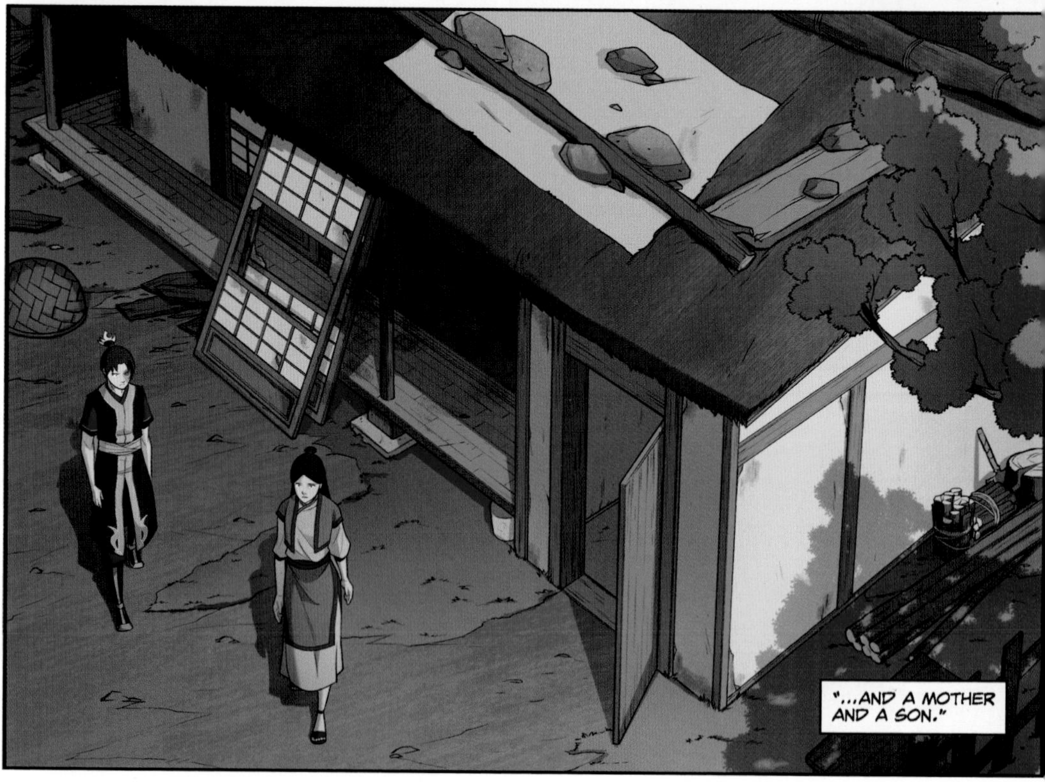
"...AND A MOTHER AND A SON."

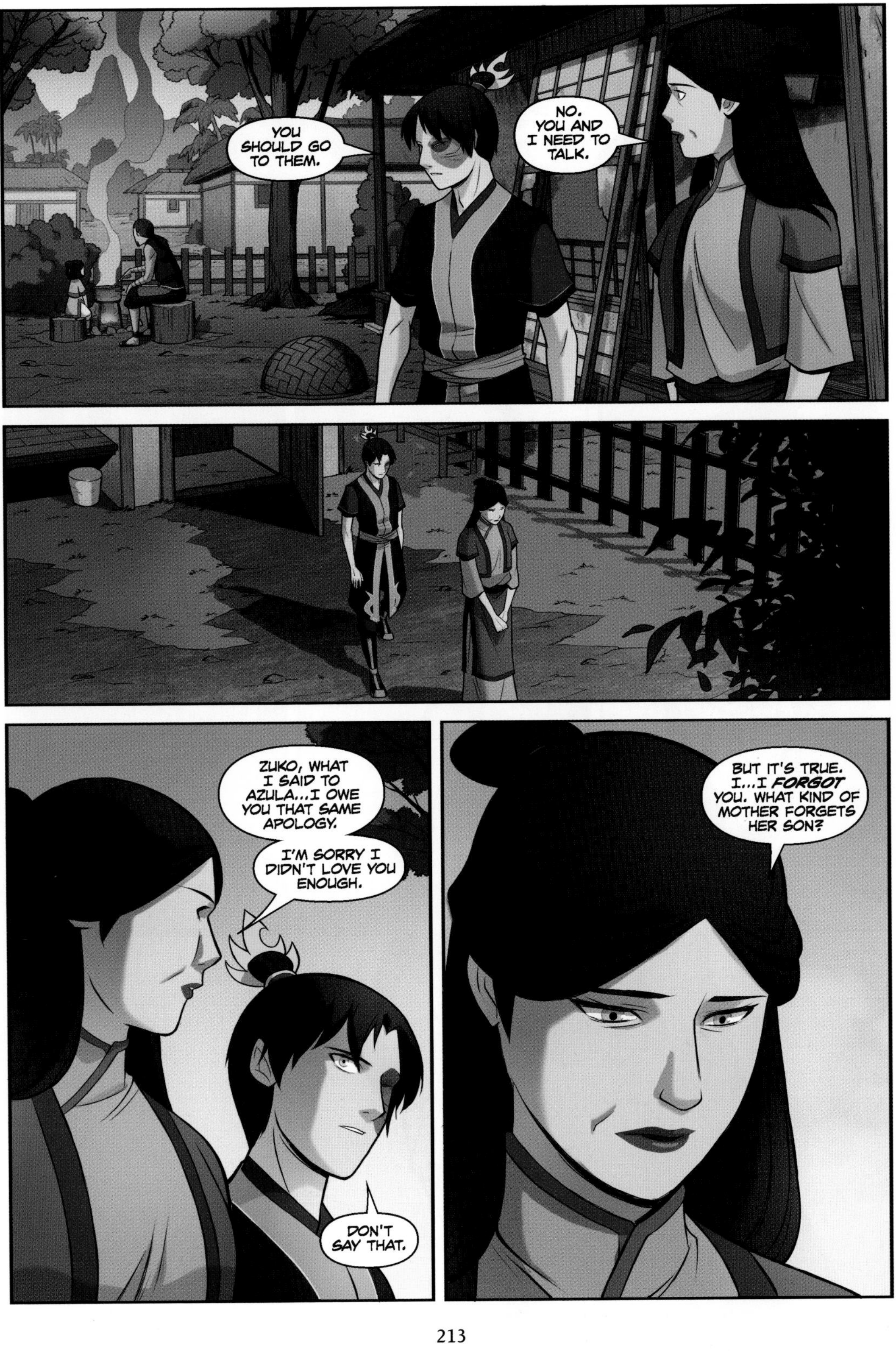
YOU SHOULD GO TO THEM.
NO. YOU AND I NEED TO TALK.
ZUKO, WHAT I SAID TO AZULA...I OWE YOU THAT SAME APOLOGY.
I'M SORRY I DIDN'T LOVE YOU ENOUGH.
DON'T SAY THAT.
BUT IT'S TRUE. I...I *FORGOT* YOU. WHAT KIND OF MOTHER FORGETS HER SON?

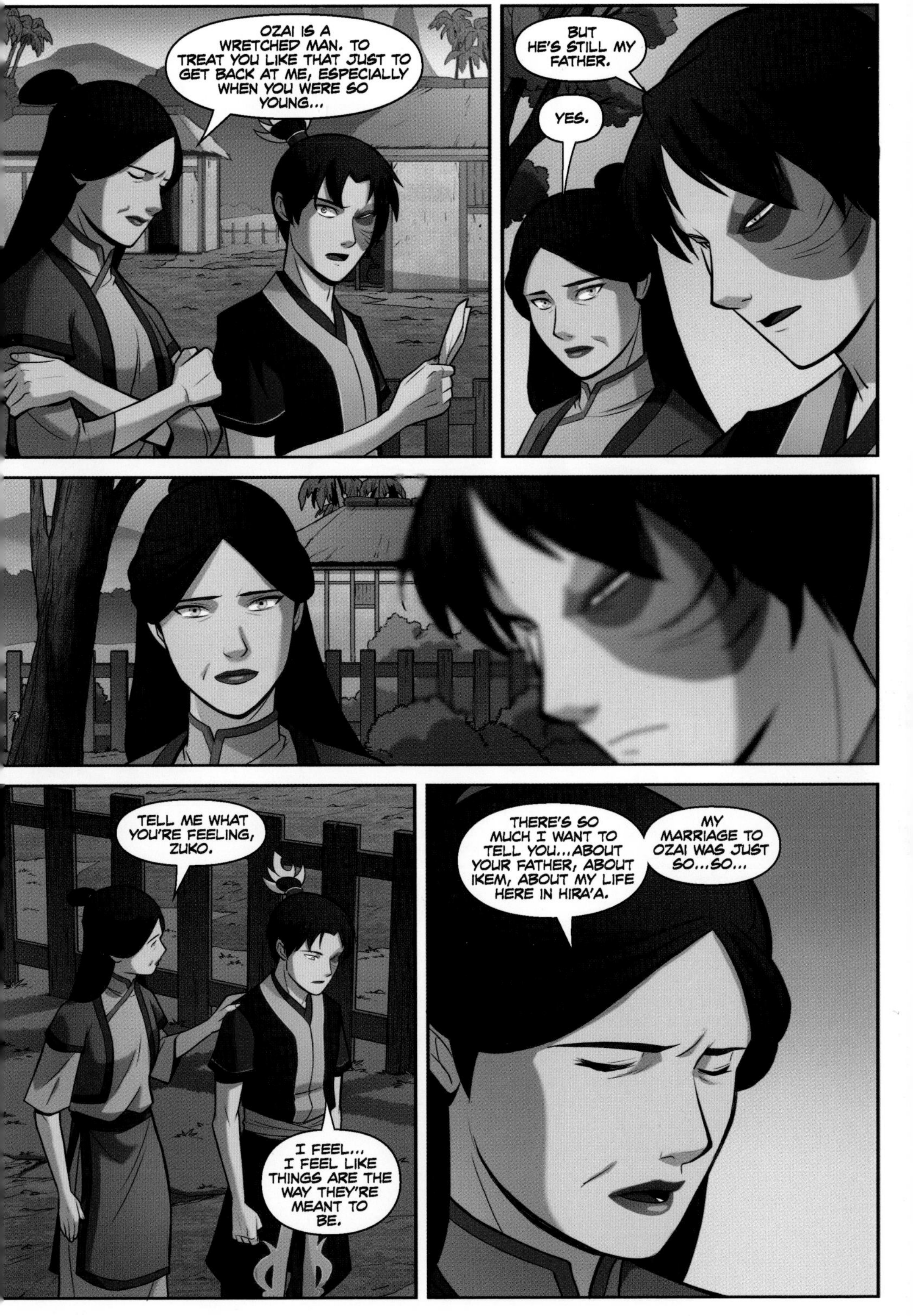
OZAI IS A WRETCHED MAN. TO TREAT YOU LIKE THAT JUST TO GET BACK AT ME, ESPECIALLY WHEN YOU WERE SO YOUNG...
BUT HE'S STILL MY FATHER.
YES.
TELL ME WHAT YOU'RE FEELING, ZUKO.
I FEEL... I FEEL LIKE THINGS ARE THE WAY THEY'RE MEANT TO BE.
THERE'S SO MUCH I WANT TO TELL YOU...ABOUT YOUR FATHER, ABOUT IKEM, ABOUT MY LIFE HERE IN HIRA'A.
MY MARRIAGE TO OZAI WAS JUST SO...SO...

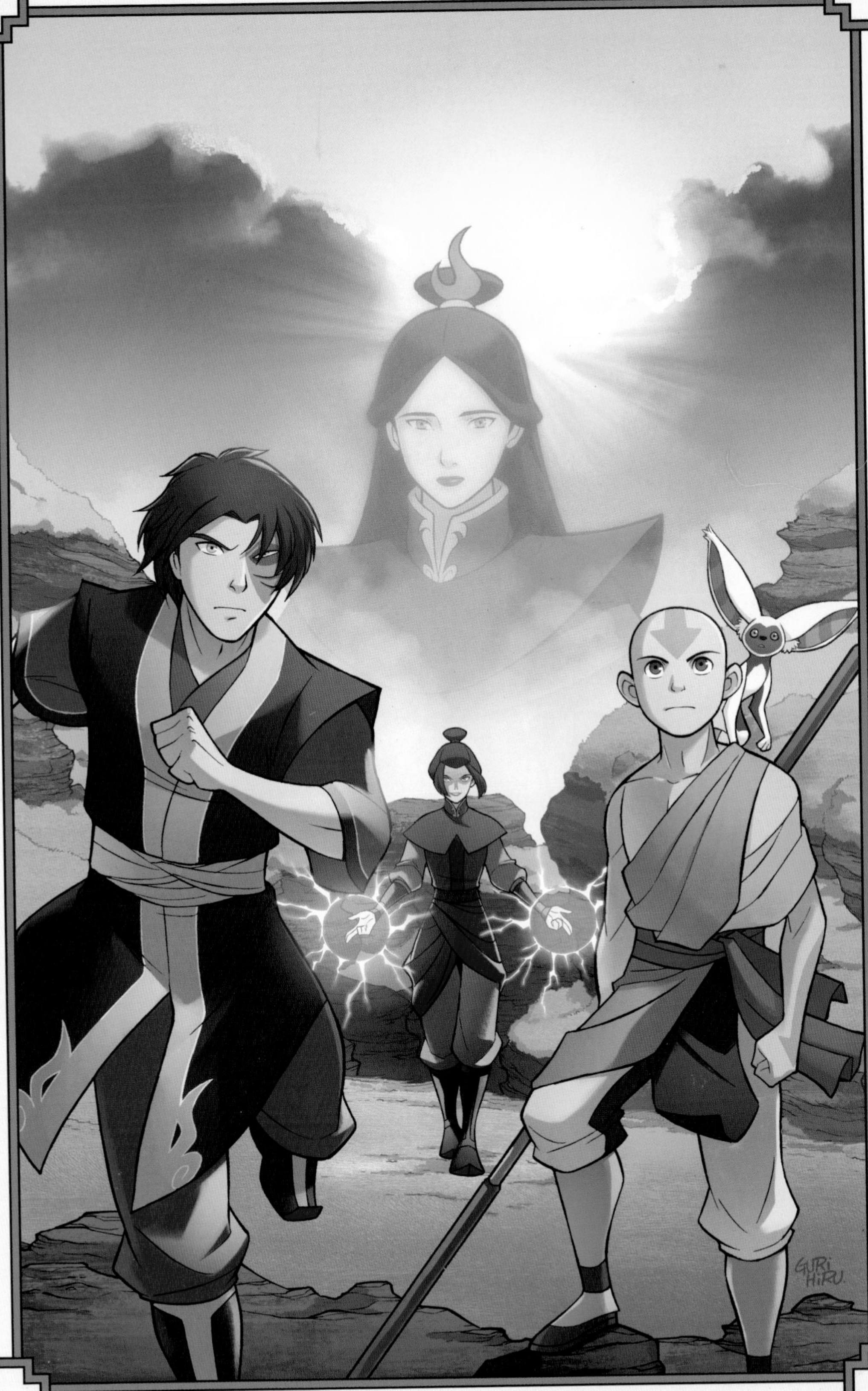
GURI HIRU.

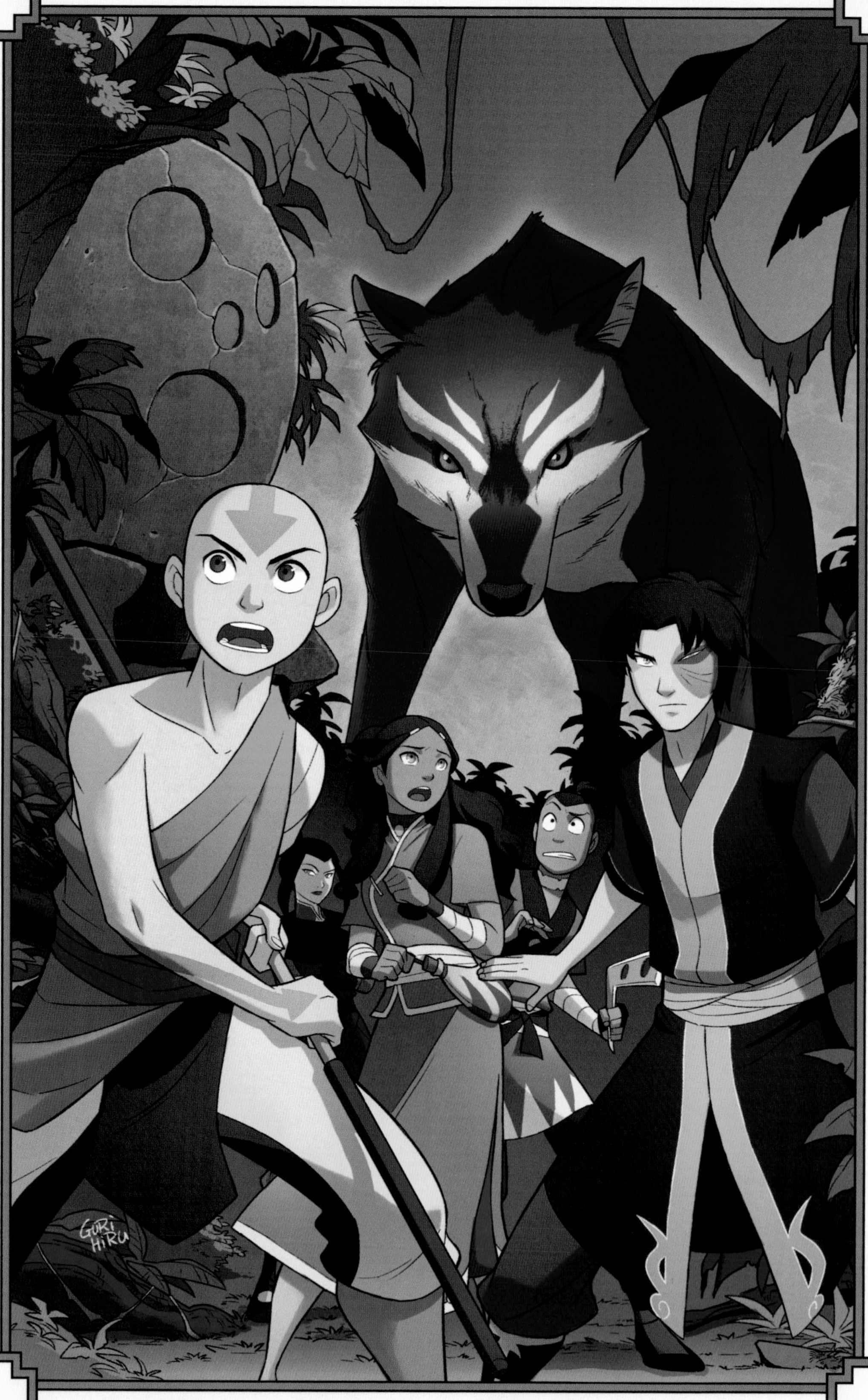
GURI
HIRU

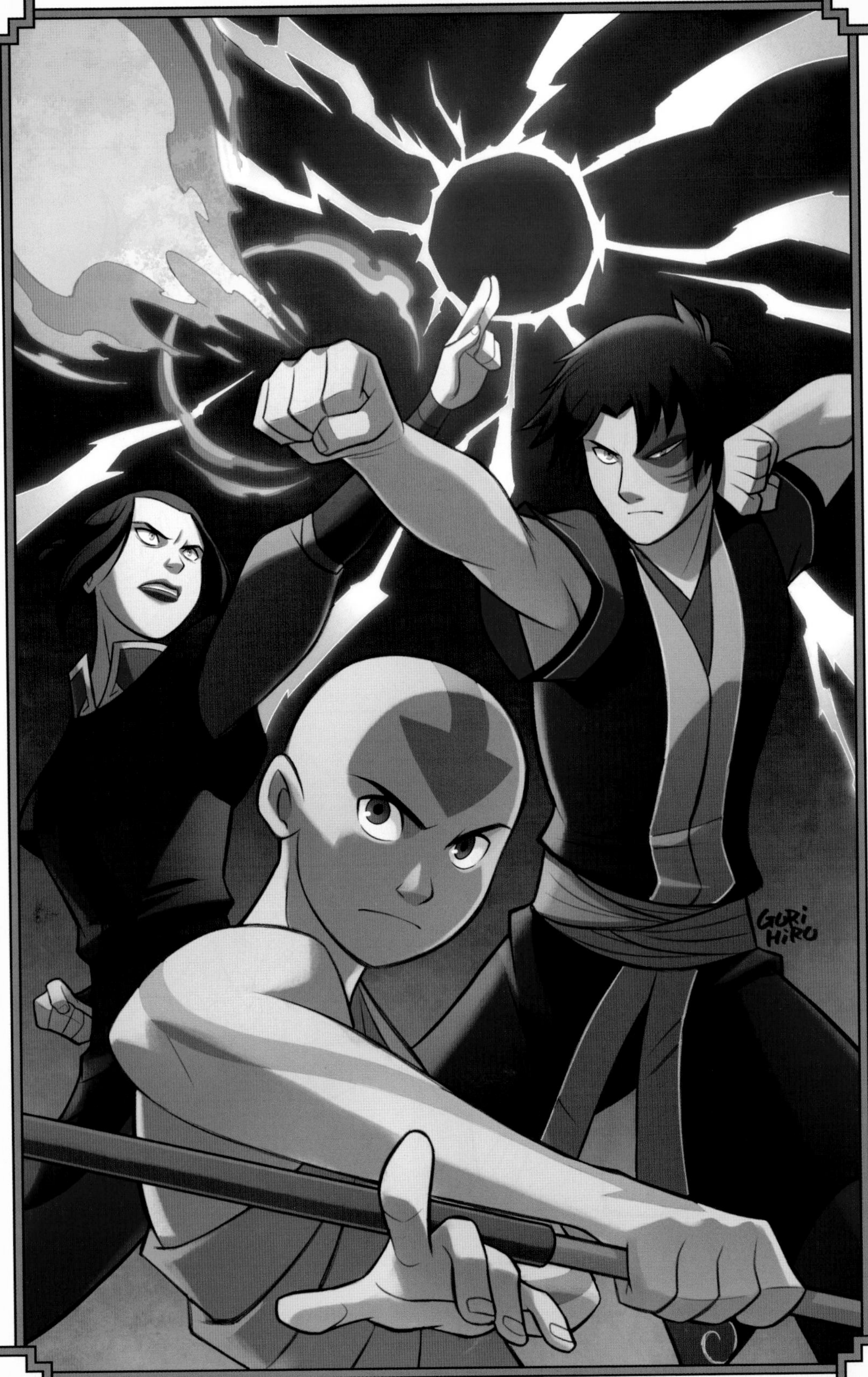
GURI
HIRU

Avatar: The Last Airbender—The Search Sketchbook

Artwork and captions by Gurihiru

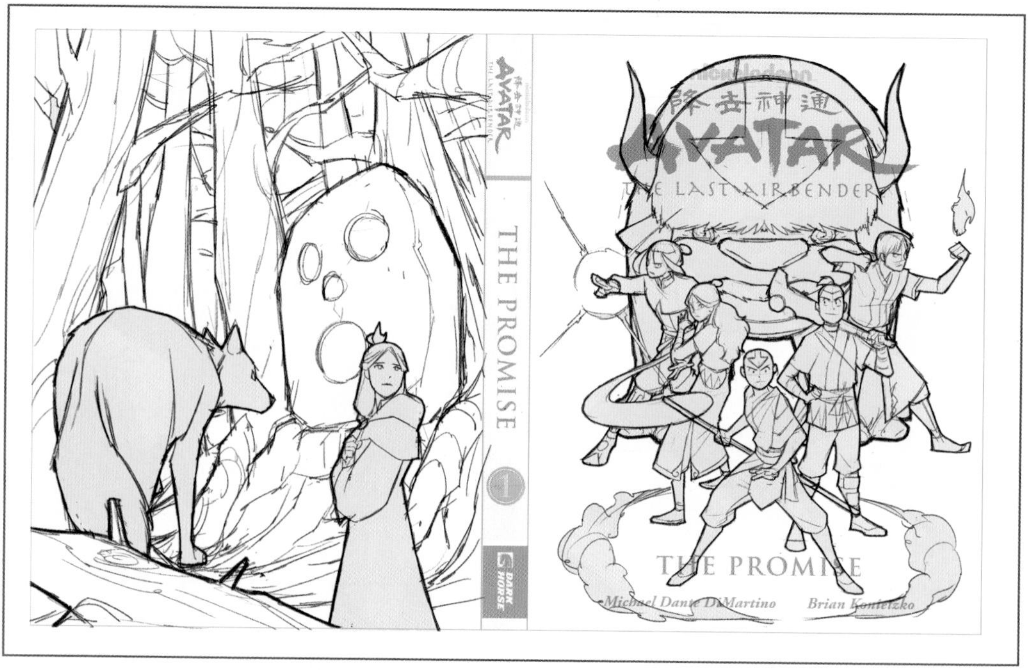
nickelodeon
降去神通
AVATAR
THE LAST AIRBENDER
THE PROMISE
Michael Dante DiMartino
Brian Konietzko
DARK HORSE

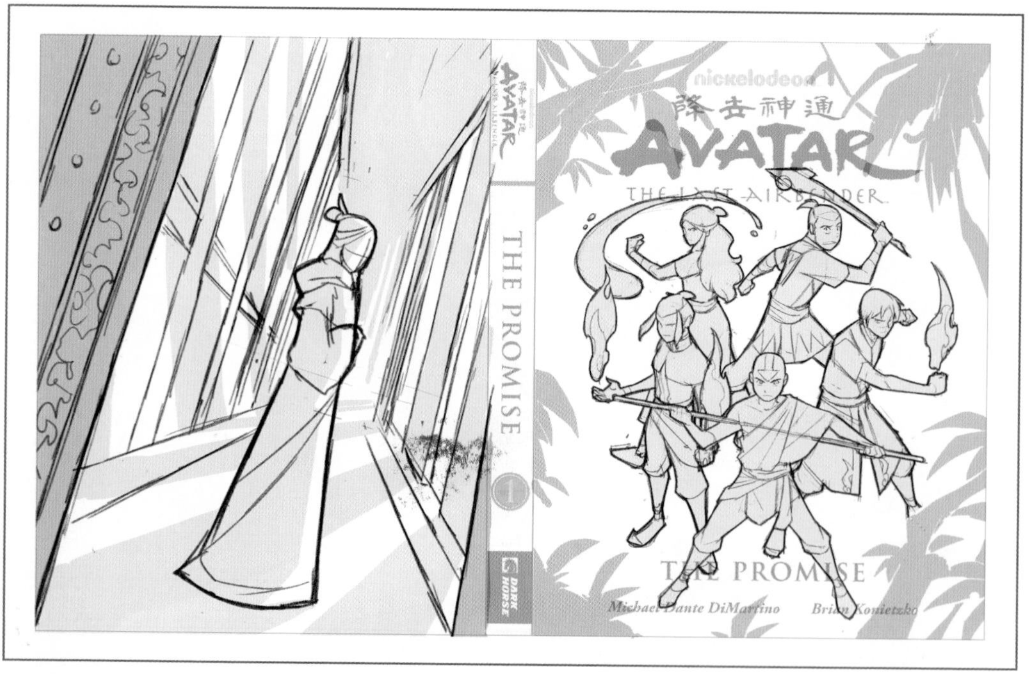
nickelodeon
降去神通
AVATAR
THE LAST AIRBENDER
THE PROMISE
Michael Dante DiMartino
Brian Konietzko
DARK HORSE

On the front cover, we show the ongoing story of Aang. The back cover depicts Ursa's history.

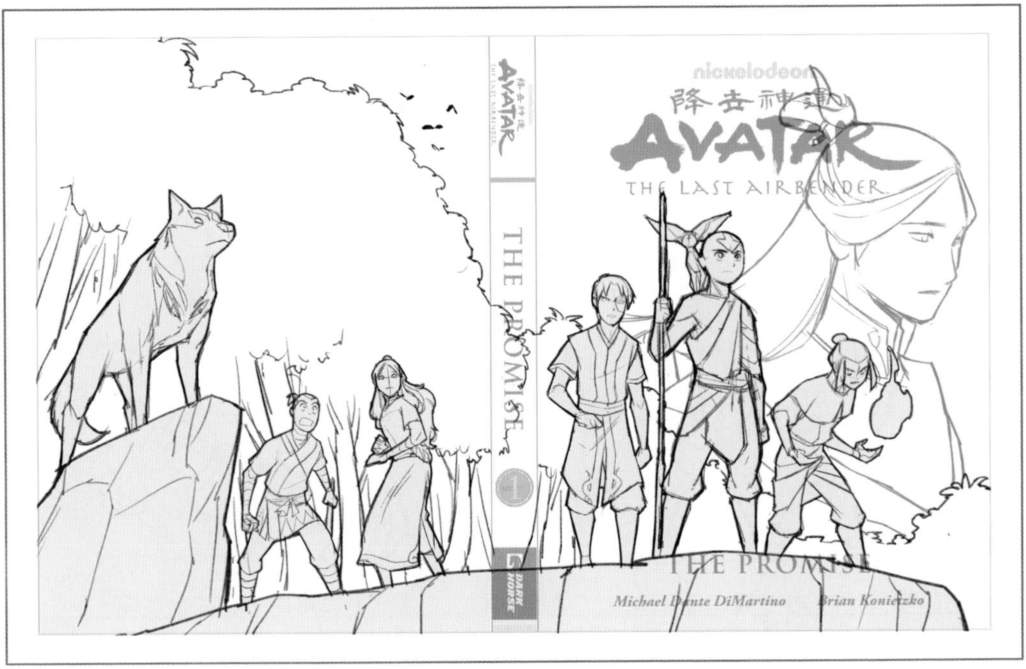
nickelodeon
降世神通
AVATAR
THE LAST AIRBENDER
THE PROMISE
1
DARK HORSE
THE PROMISE
Michael Dante DiMartino
Brian Konietzko

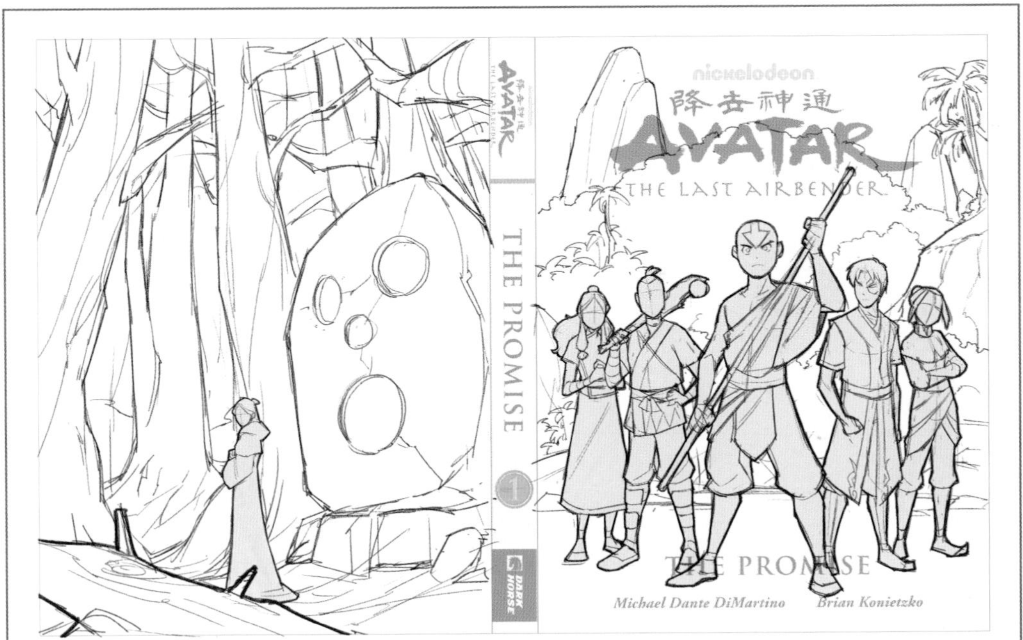
nickelodeon
降世神通
AVATAR
THE LAST AIRBENDER
THE PROMISE
1
DARK HORSE
THE PROMISE
Michael Dante DiMartino
Brian Konietzko

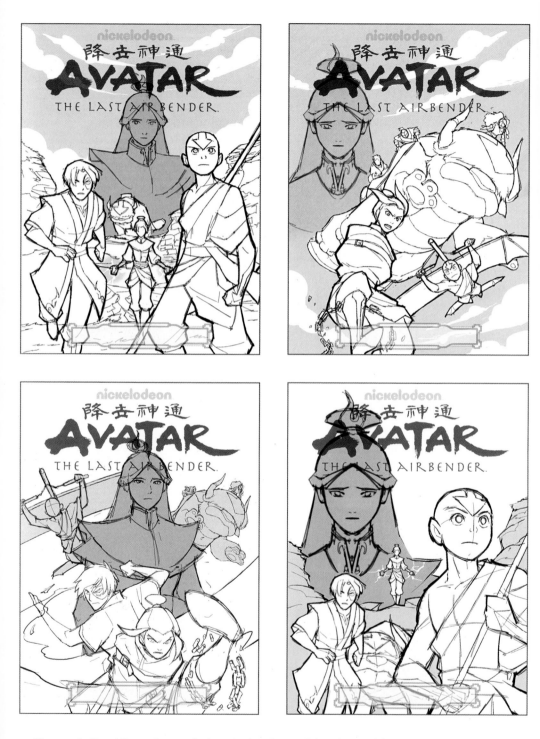

We were asked to put Ursa on the cover for these sketches. Since Azula is at the core of the story, we had her appear, too.

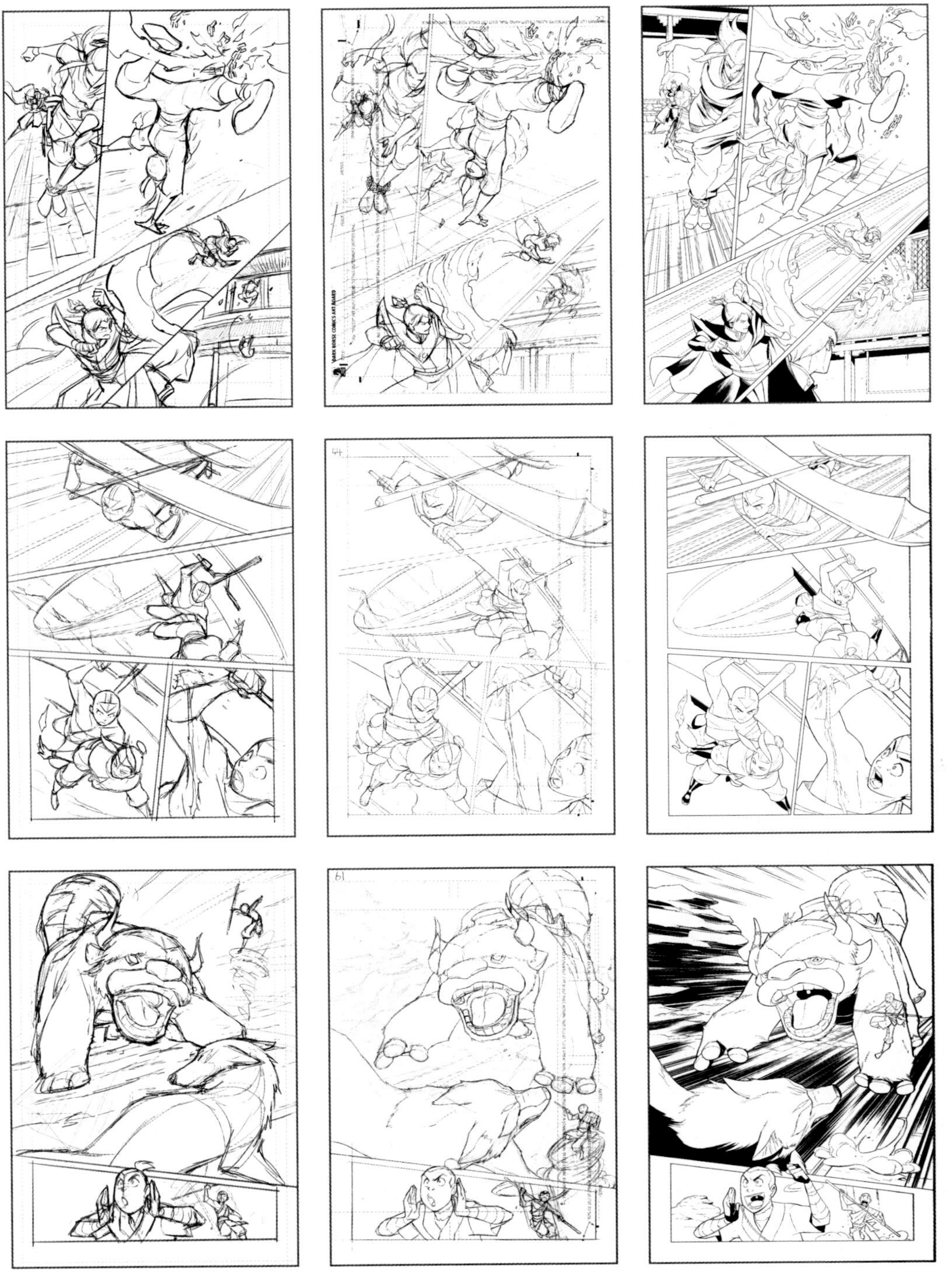

We always struggle with portraying action scenes. Unlike in animation, we have to show action in static images. We try to have the characters appear lively.

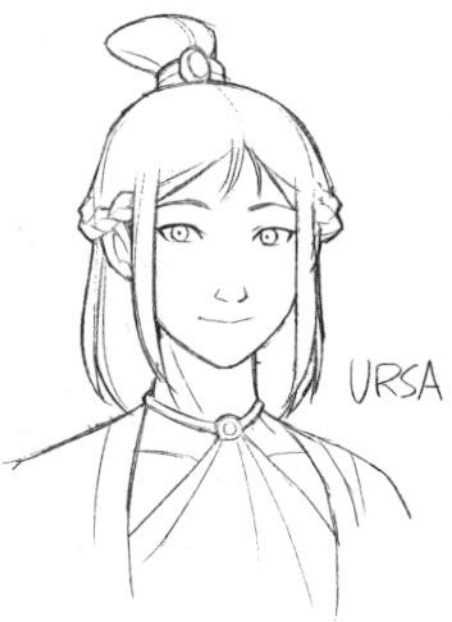
URSA

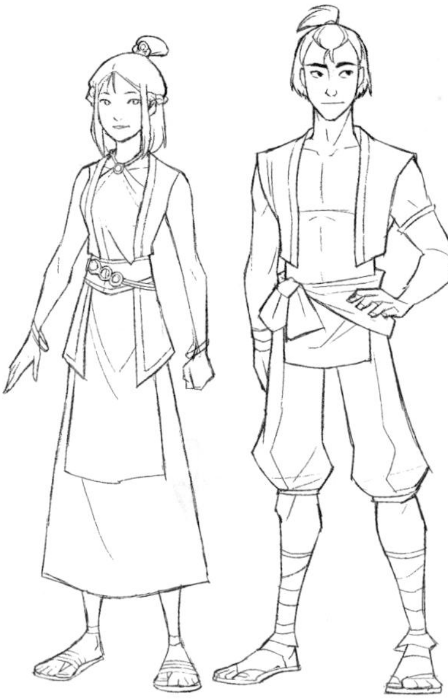

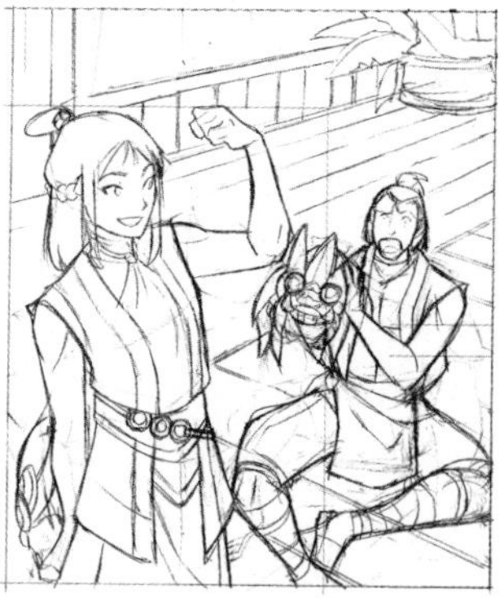

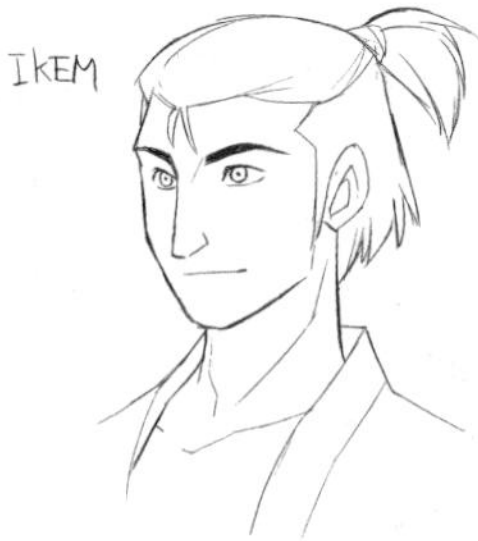
IKEM

URSA AND IKEM

In the early stages, Ursa's hairstyle looked too much like Katara's, so we changed it considerably. We drew Ikem as handsome to distinguish him from Noren. Since Ursa and Ikem live in a warm area, the fabrics they wear are more sheer and show more bare skin.

OZAI

Ozai was younger and wore his hair bound up. Since Ozai was thirty and Ursa was twenty-one when they married, they appear similar to how they are on the show. We also decided to give Ozai a beard, though it's not in the sketch.

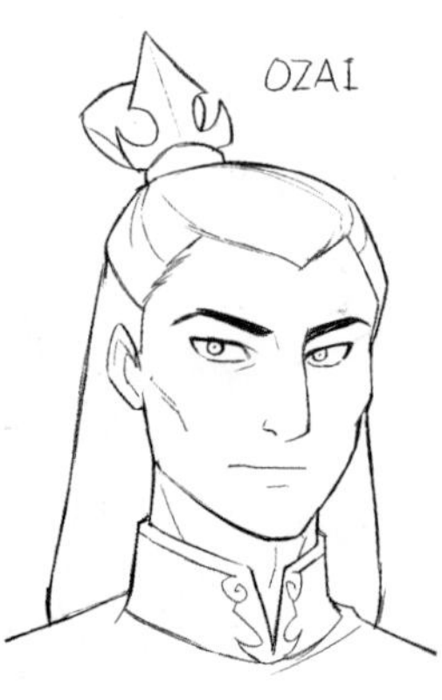
OZAI

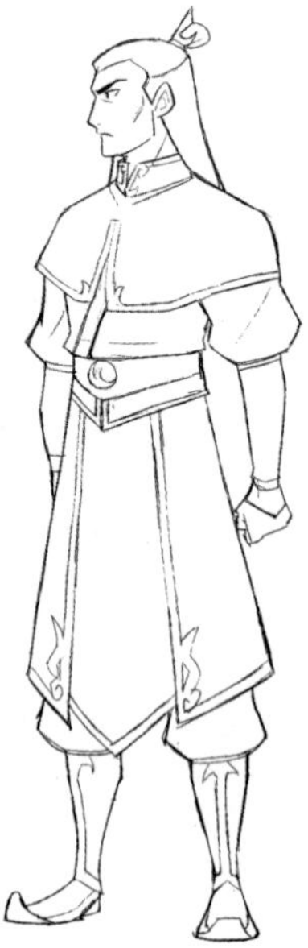

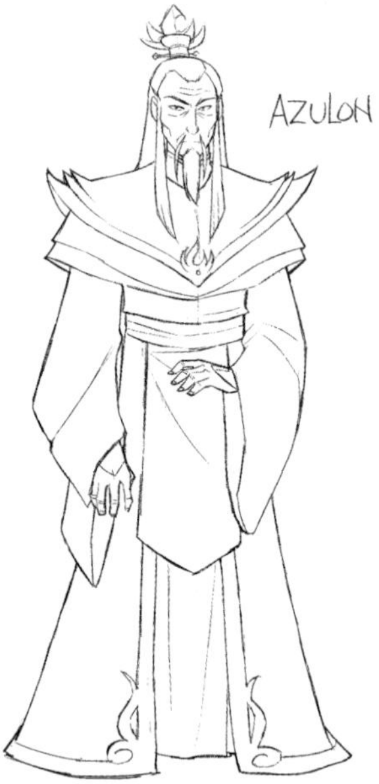
AZULON

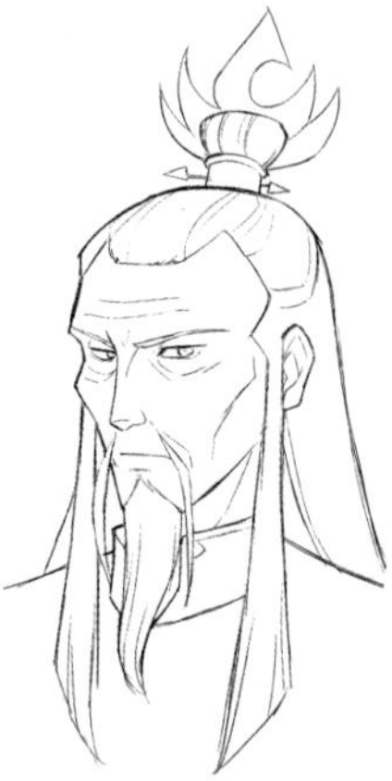

AZULON

In the early designs, Azulon was younger, with shorter facial hair. But since he is eighty-five in *The Search*, we made him look just a little younger than he is in the TV show.

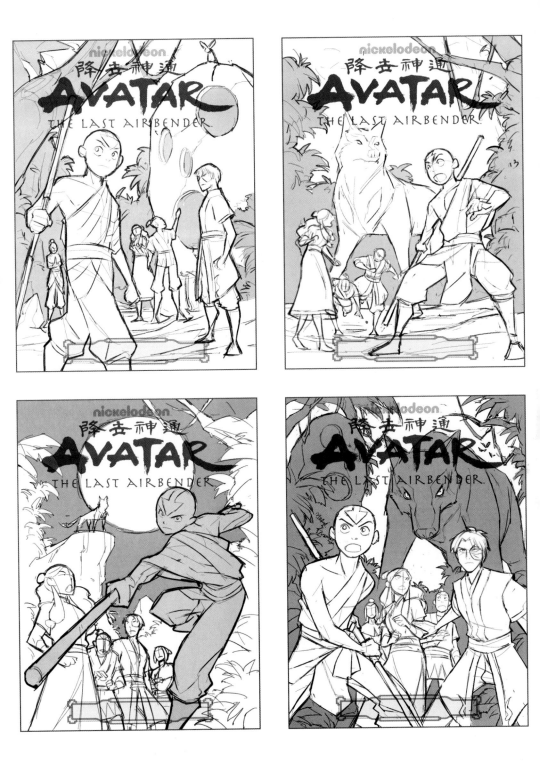

We liked the one at the bottom left, but the ones we like best aren't always the ones chosen.

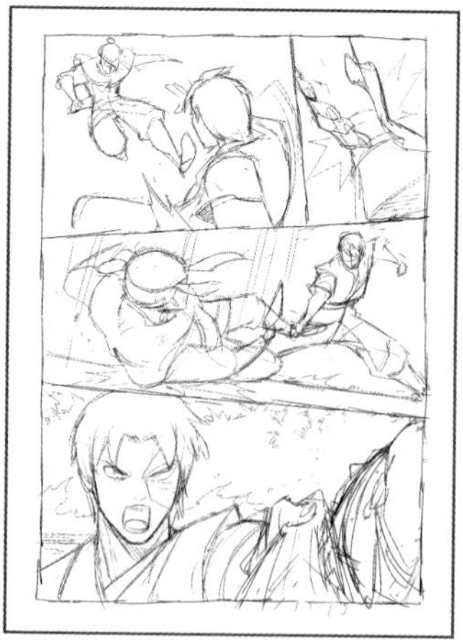
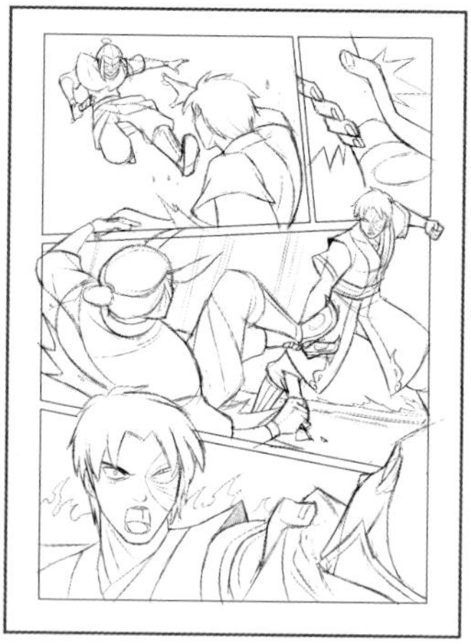
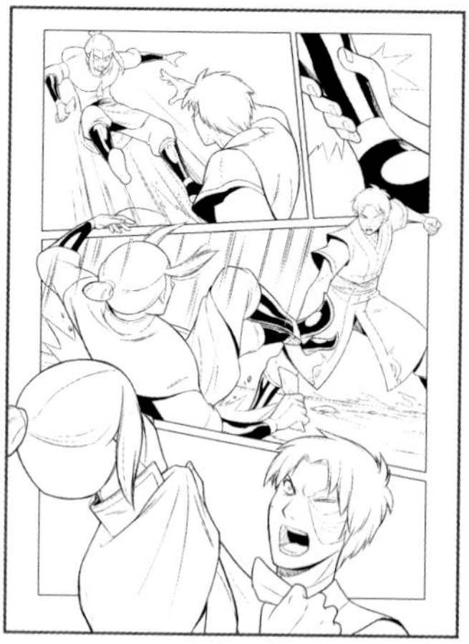
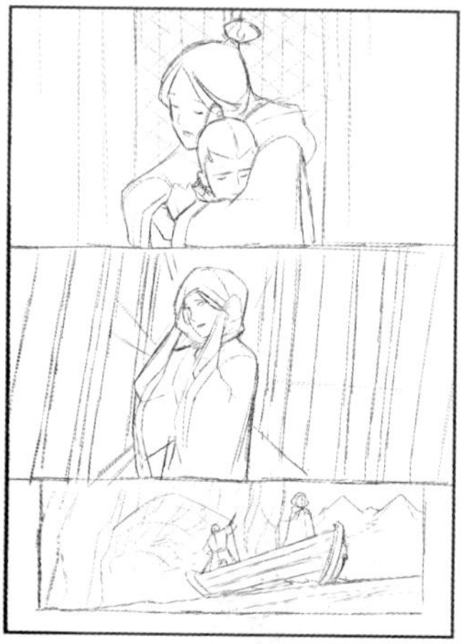
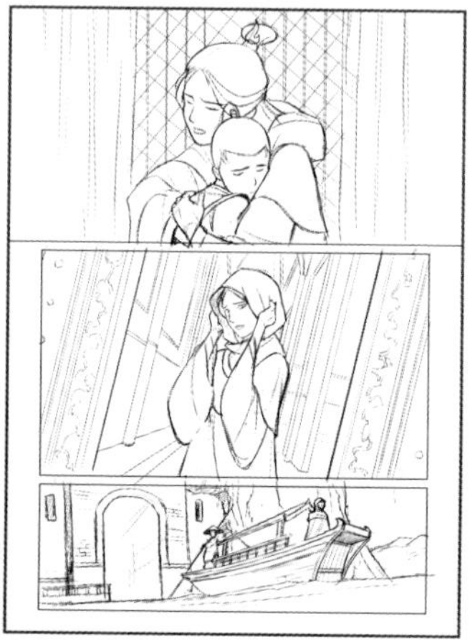
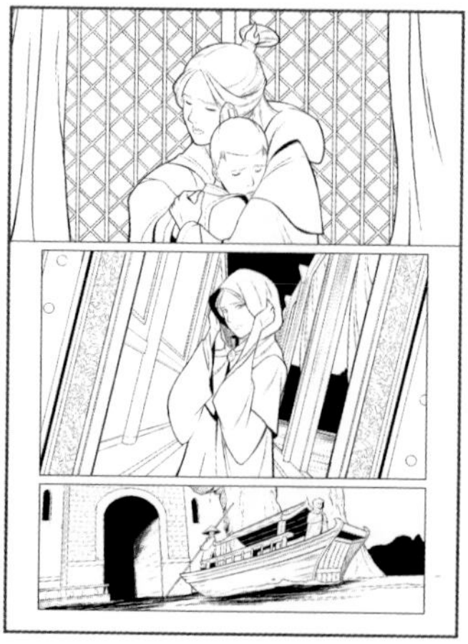
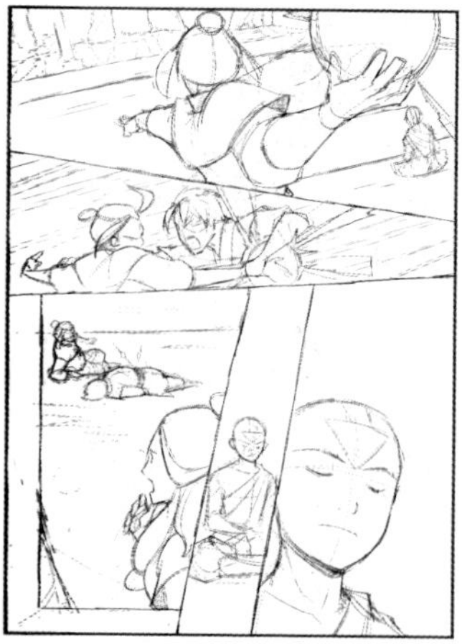
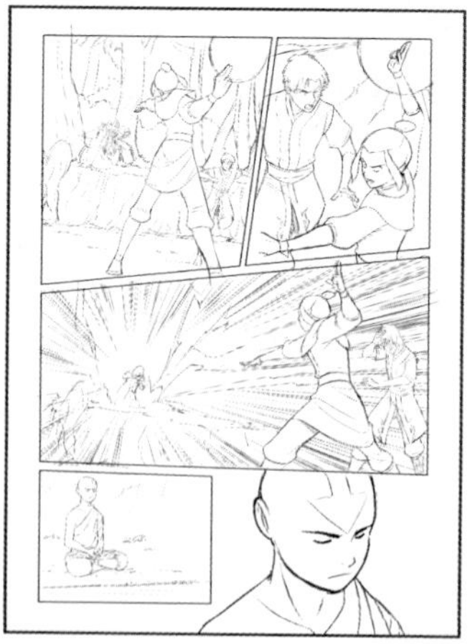
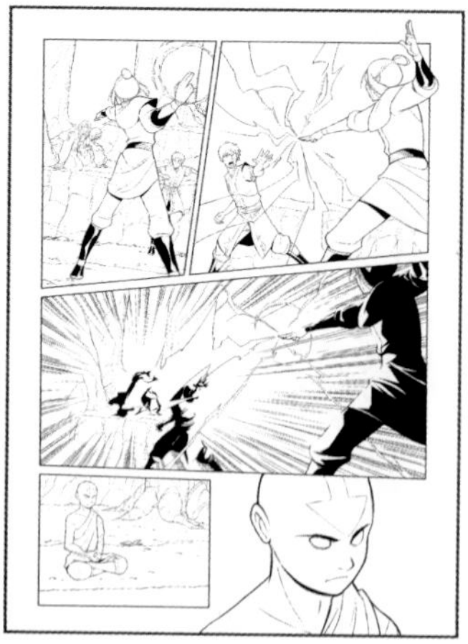

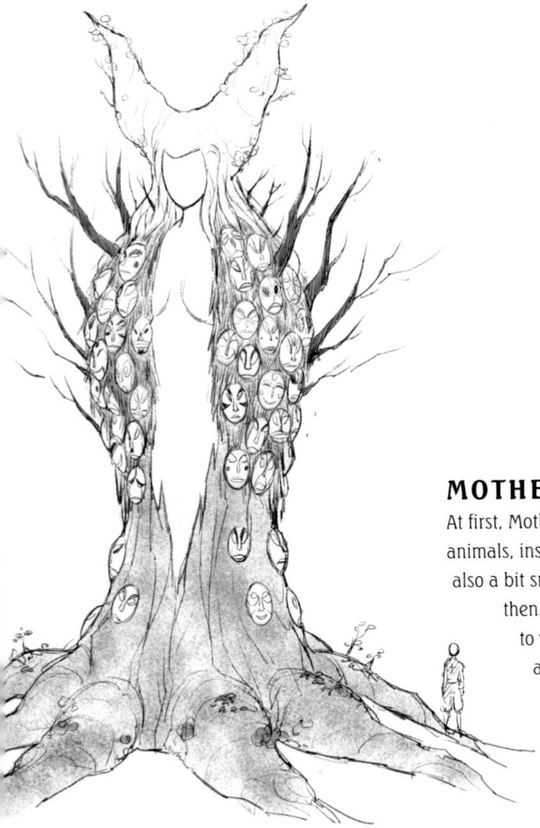

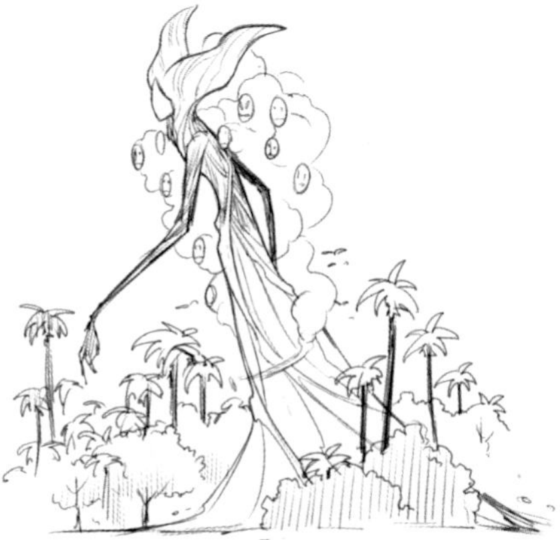

MOTHER OF FACES

At first, Mother of Faces was based on various motifs, such as animals, insects, plants, and the like. Something with four legs, but also a bit snake and spider, a little, scary-looking creature . . . And then, we settled on a type of giant tree. Since it was meant to walk around and have many faces, it eventually became a combination of plants and water. This character came from the ideas of many people.

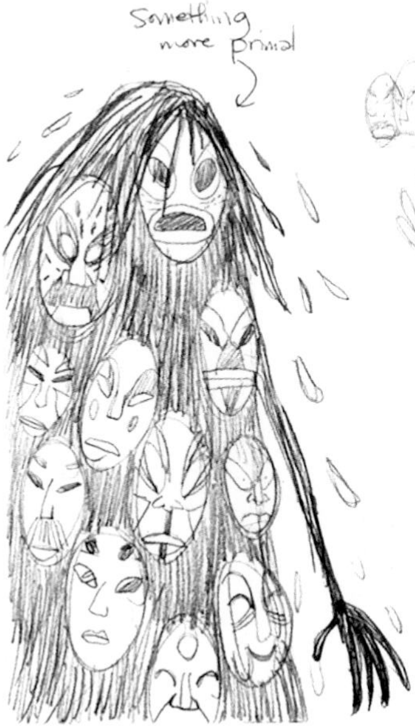
Something more primal

Sketch by Gene Luen Yang

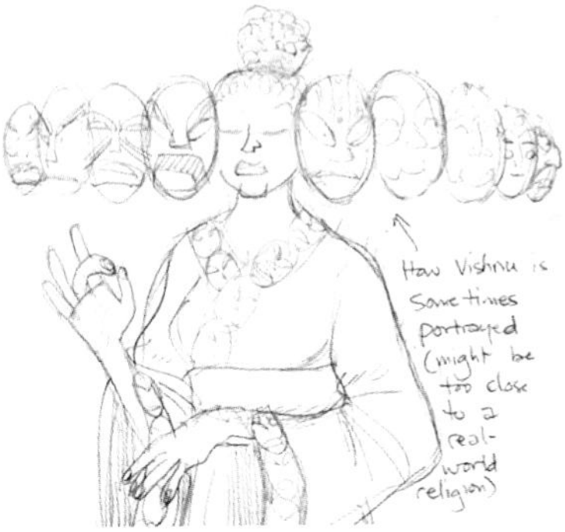
How Vishnu is sometimes portrayed (might be too close to a real-world religion)

Sketch by Gene Luen Yang

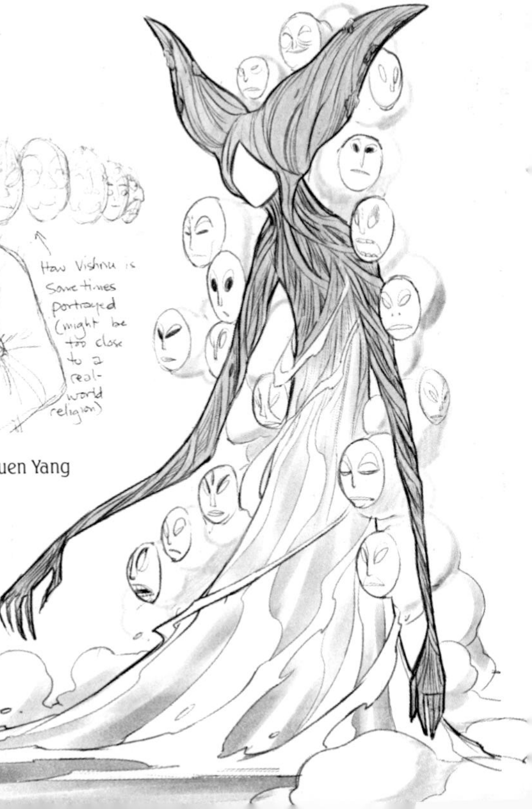

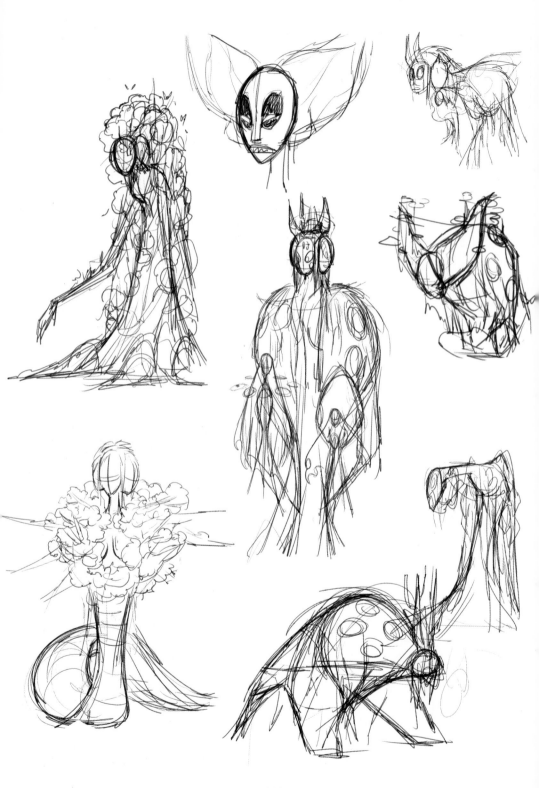

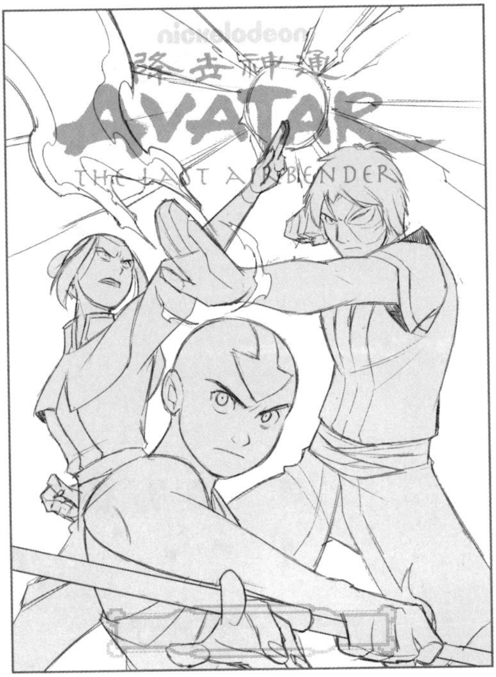
nickelodeon
AVATAR
THE LAST AIRBENDER

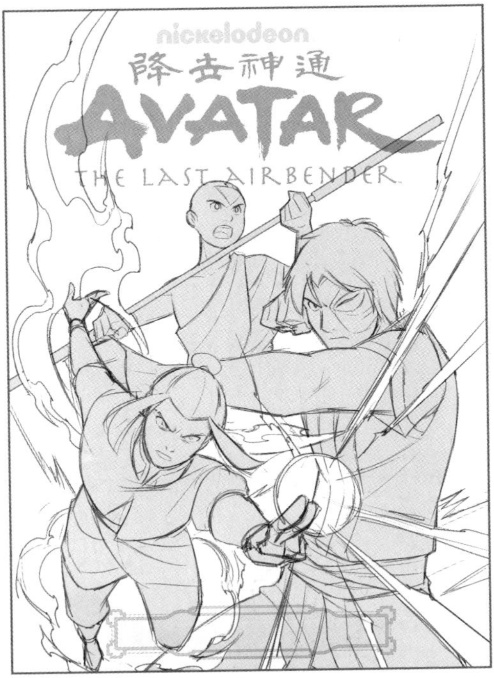
nickelodeon
AVATAR
THE LAST AIRBENDER

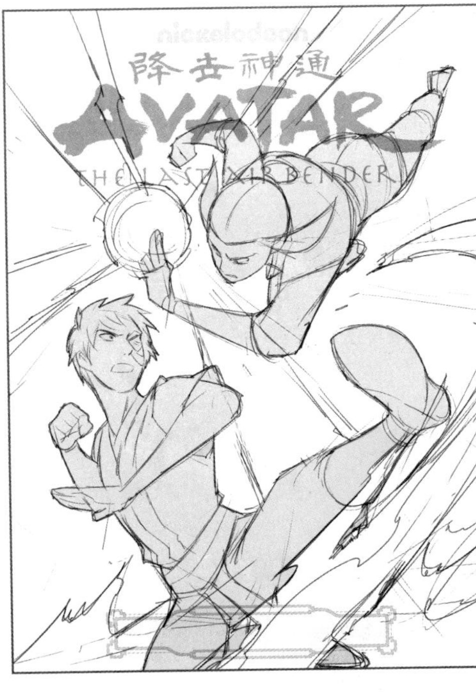
nickelodeon
AVATAR
THE LAST AIRBENDER

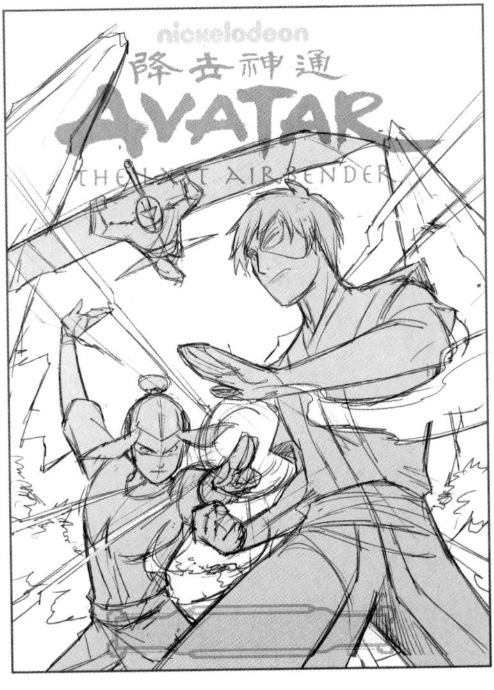
nickelodeon
AVATAR
THE LAST AIRBENDER

This is an image of Zuko and Azula. The one on the top left was chosen, and Bryan gave us helpful direction to get Zuko's bending pose just right.

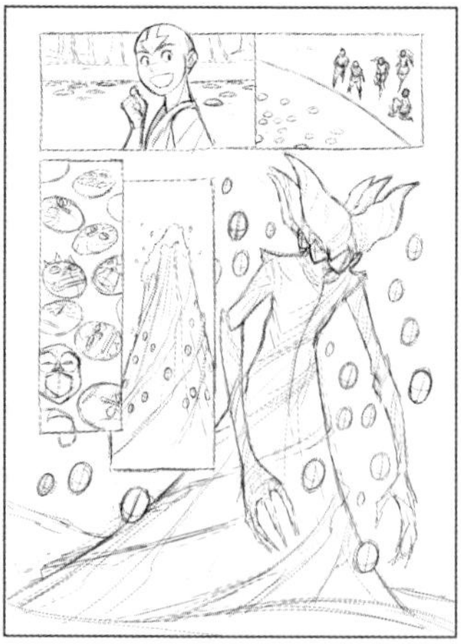
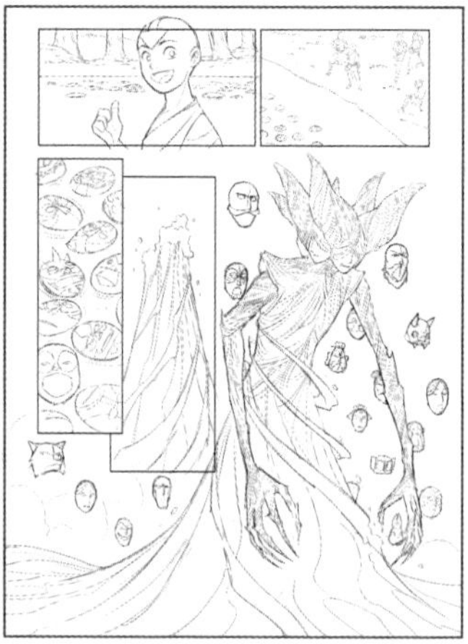
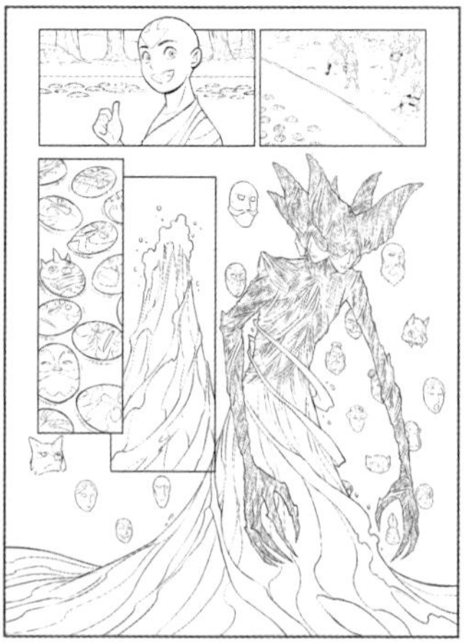
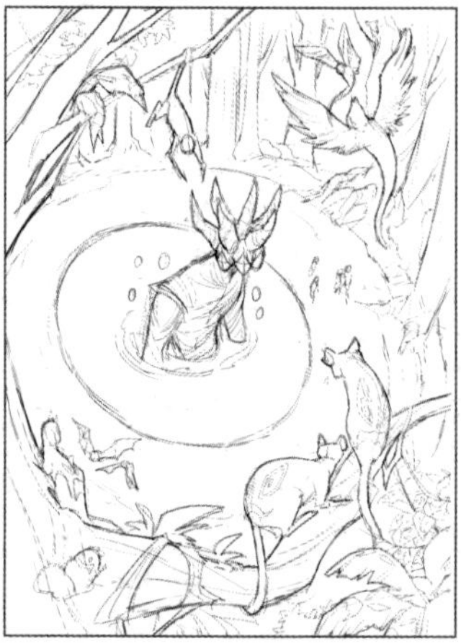
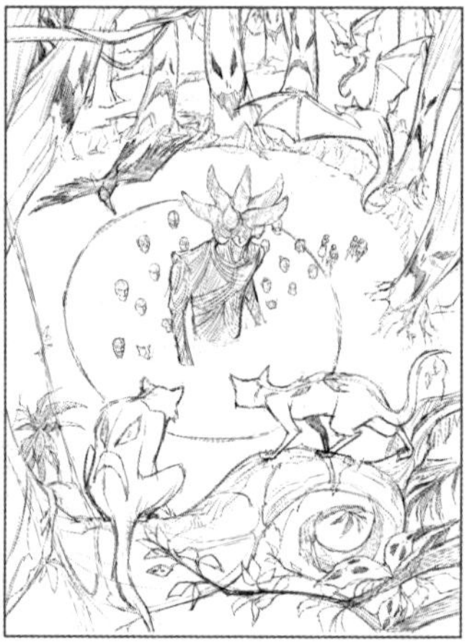
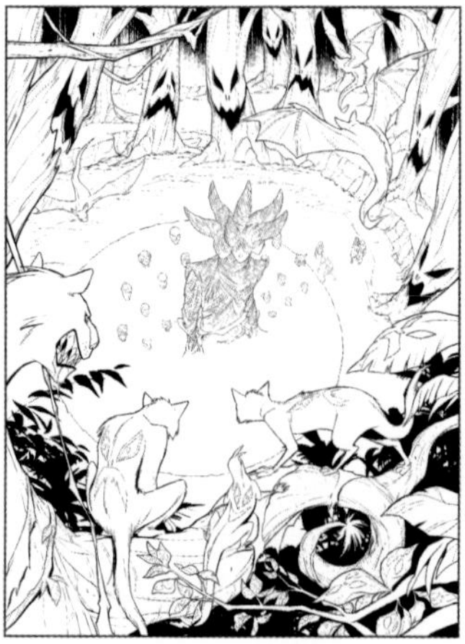
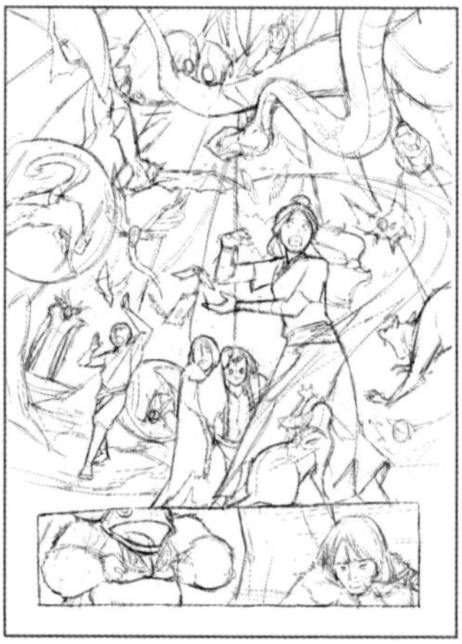
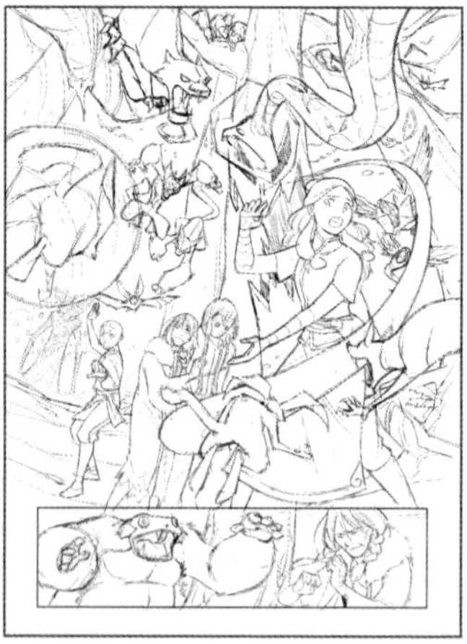
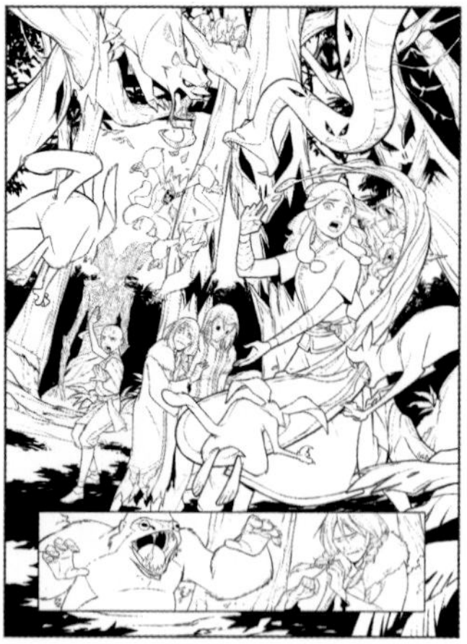